Lecture Notes in Computer Science   10525

Commenced Publication in 1973
Founding and Former Series Editors:
Gerhard Goos, Juris Hartmanis, and Jan van Leeuwen

More information about this series at http://www.springer.com/series/7409

Mitsuko Aramaki · Richard Kronland-Martinet
Sølvi Ystad (Eds.)

Bridging People and Sound

12th International Symposium, CMMR 2016
São Paulo, Brazil, July 5–8, 2016
Revised Selected Papers

 Springer

Editors

Mitsuko Aramaki
Laboratoire PRISM, CNRS-AMU
Marseille
France

Richard Kronland-Martinet
Laboratoire PRISM, CNRS-AMU
Marseille
France

Sølvi Ystad
Laboratoire PRISM, CNRS-AMU
Marseille
France

ISSN 0302-9743   ISSN 1611-3349   (electronic)
Lecture Notes in Computer Science
ISBN 978-3-319-67737-8   ISBN 978-3-319-67738-5   (eBook)
DOI 10.1007/978-3-319-67738-5

Library of Congress Control Number: 2017954606

LNCS Sublibrary: SL3 – Information Systems and Applications, incl. Internet/Web, and HCI

Printed on acid-free paper

This Springer imprint is published by Springer Nature
The registered company is Springer International Publishing AG
The registered company address is: Gewerbestrasse 11, 6330 Cham, Switzerland

Preface

The 12th International Symposium on Computer Music Multidisciplinary Research, CMMR 2016 "Bridging People and Sound" (http://cmmr2016.ime.usp.br), took place in São Paulo, Brazil on 5–8 July 2016 at the Computer Science and Music Departments located on the main campus of the University of São Paulo, the University City, which constitutes an amazing green area of the city.

This was the first time that CMMR had been organized on the American continent. CMMR 2016 was co-organized by the Computer Music Research Group (http://compmus.ime.usp.br/en), the NuSom - Research Centre on Sonology (http://www2.eca.usp.br/nusom/node/22), and the former "Audio Group" of the LMA - CNRS (Centre National de la Recherche Scientifique), Marseilles, France, which in January 2017 moved to the new laboratory PRISM (Perception, Representations, Image, Sound, Music - www.prism.cnrs.fr) - CNRS-AMU, Marseilles, France.

This year's conference theme "Bridging People and Sound" aimed at encouraging contributions from artists and listeners on the one side and audio and music technology researchers on the other. A strong interest for the conference from the artistic community was revealed through the large number of music contributions (more than 60) that were submitted to the conference.

The scientific program contained 3 keynote presentations (Pedro Rebelo, SARC/QUB, Belfast, UK; Jônatas Manzolli, NICS/UNICAMP, Campinas, Brazil; and Sølvi Ystad, LMA-CNRS, France), seven paper sessions, one poster session, four demo sessions, and a panel discussion that concluded the conference. During the first 3 days of the conference, a series of 3 concerts with the selected music contributions was organized.

The CMMR 2016 post proceedings edition is the 12th CMMR proceedings volume published by Springer in the Lecture Notes in Computer Sciences series (LNCS 2771, LNCS 3310, LNCS 3902, LNCS 4969, LNCS 5493, LNCS 5954, LNCS 6684, LNCS 7172, LNCS 7900, LNCS 8905, and LNCS 9617). This year's symposium edition contains a total of 22 peer-reviewed and revised articles. It has been divided into 7 sections containing various subjects that reveal the pluridisciplinary nature of the conference, spanning from technology-oriented questions related to music information retrieval and music structure analysis to music production systems, new musical interfaces, music composition, and multisensory inquiries.

We would like to thank all the participants of CMMR 2016, who contributed to making this 12th symposium a memorable happening. We would also like to thank the Program and Music Committee members for their indispensable selection tasks. We are very grateful to the Local Organizing Committee at the Computer Science and Music Departments of the University of São Paulo, who took care of the practical organization and insured a smooth and efficient coordination between attendees, speakers, audiences, and musicians in both the scientific and artistic program. Finally, we would like to thank Springer for accepting to publish the CMMR 2016 post proceedings edition in their LNCS series.

July 2017

Richard Kronland-Martinet
Mitsuko Aramaki
Sølvi Ystad

Organization

The 12th International Symposium on Computer Music Multidisciplinary Research, CMMR 2016 "Bridging People and Sound", was co-organized by the Computer Music Research Group, the NuSom - Research Centre on Sonology, and the former "Audio Group" of the LMA (now PRISM) - CNRS (Centre National de la Recherche Scientifique), Marseilles, France.

Symposium Chairs

Marcelo Queiroz   IME/USP, São Paulo, Brazil
Fernando Iazzetta   ECA/USP, São Paulo, Brazil

Paper, Program, and Proceedings Chairs

Richard Kronland-Martinet   CNRS-LMA Marseilles, France
Mitsuko Aramaki   CNRS-LMA Marseilles, France
Sølvi Ystad   CNRS-LMA Marseilles, France
Marcelo Queiroz   IME/USP, São Paulo, Brazil

Committees

Local Organizing Committee

Marcelo Queiroz   IME/USP, São Paulo, Brazil
Fernando Iazzetta   ECA/USP, São Paulo, Brazil
Regis Faria   FFCLRP/USP, Ribeirão Preto, Brazil

Paper Committee

Mitsuko Aramaki   CNRS-LMA, France
Federico Avanzini   University of Padua, Italy
Mathieu Barthet   Queen Mary University of London, UK
Frédéric Bevilacqua   IRCAM, France
Marta Bienkiewicz   Aix-Marseille University-ISM, France
Christophe Bourdin   Aix-Marseille University-ISM, France
Lionel Bringoux   Aix-Marseille University-ISM, France
John Ashley Burgoyne   University of Amsterdam, The Netherlands
Marcelo Caetano   INESC Porto, Portugal
Emilios Cambouroupoulos   Aristotle University of Thessaloniki, Greece
Amilcar Cardoso   University of Coimbra, Portugal
Olivier Derrien   Toulon-Var University and CNRS-LMA, France

Joel Eaton   University of Plymouth, UK
Georg Essl   University of Michigan, USA
Regis R.A. Faria   University of São Paulo, Brazil
Bruno Giordano   University of Glasgow, UK
Rolf Inge Gødoy   University of Oslo, Norway
Mick Grierson   Goldsmiths Digital Studios, London, UK
Brian Gygi   Veterans Affairs Northern California Health Care
                                   Service, USA
Kristoffer Jensen   Independent Researcher, Denmark
Luis Jure   University of Montevideo, Uruguay
Maximos   University of Thessaloniki, Greece
   Kaliakatsos-Papakostas
Timour Klouche   National Institute for Music Research, Germany
Richard Kronland-Martinet   CNRS-LMA, France
Darius Kucinskas   Kaunas University of Technology, Lithuania
Fernando Iazzetta   University of São Paulo, Brazil
Thor Magnusson   University of Sussex, UK
Jônatas Manzolli   University of Estadual Campinas, Brazil
Sylvain Marchand   University of Brest, France
Jean-Arthur   University of Bordeaux, France
   Micoulaud-Franchi
Eduardo Miranda   University of Plymouth, UK
Marcelo Queiroz   University of São Paulo, Brazil
Davide Rocchesso   Università Iuav di Venezia, Italy
Matthew Rodger   Queen's University Belfast, UK
Flavio Schiavoni   Federal University of São João Del Rey, Brazil
Diemo Schwarz   IRCAM, France
Stefania Serafin   Aalborg University Copenhagen, Denmark
Julius Smith   Stanford University, USA
Tiago Tavares   State University of Campinas (UNICAMP), Brazil
Marcelo Wanderley   CIRMMT, Canada
Ian Whalley   University of Waikato, New Zealand
Duncan Williams   University of Plymouth, UK
Sølvi Ystad   CNRS-LMA, France

Contents

Music Structure Analysis - Music Information Retrieval

deepGTTM-I&II: Local Boundary and Metrical Structure Analyzer Based on Deep Learning Technique

Masatoshi Hamanaka[1]([⊠]), Keiji Hirata[2], and Satoshi Tojo[3]

[1] Center for Advanced Integrated Intelligence Project, RIKEN,
Nihonbashi 1-chome Mitsui Building, 15F 1-4-1 Nihonbashi, Chuo-ku,
Tokyo 103-0027, Japan
masatoshi.hamanaka@riken.jp
[2] Future University Hakodate, 116-2 Kamedanakano-cho,
Hakodate, Hokkaido 041-8655, Japan
hirata@fun.ac.jp
[3] Graduate School of Information Science,
Japan Advanced Institute of Science and Technology (JAIST),
1-1 Asahidai, Nomi, Ishikawa 923-1292, Japan
tojo@jaist.ac.jp

Abstract. This paper describes an analyzer for detecting local grouping boundaries and generating metrical structures of music pieces based on a generative theory of tonal music (GTTM). Although systems for automatically detecting local grouping boundaries and generating metrical structures, such as the full automatic time-span tree analyzer, have been proposed, musicologists have to correct the boundaries or strong beat positions due to numerous errors. In light of this, we use a deep learning technique for detecting local boundaries and generating metrical structures of music pieces based on a GTTM. Because we only have 300 pieces of music with the local grouping boundaries and metrical structures analyzed by musicologist, directly learning the relationship between the scores and metrical structures is difficult due to the lack of training data. To solve this problem, we propose a multi-task learning analyzer called deepGTTM-I&II based on the above deep learning technique to learn the relationship between scores and metrical structures in the following three steps. First, we conduct unsupervised pre-training of a network using 15,000 pieces of music in a non-labeled dataset. After pre-training, the network involves supervised fine-tuning by back propagation from output to input layers using a half-labeled dataset, which consists of 15,000 pieces of music labeled with an automatic analyzer that we previously constructed. Finally, the network involves supervised fine-tuning using a labeled dataset. The experimental results indicate that deepGTTM-I&II outperformed previous analyzers for a GTTM in terms of the F-measure for generating metrical structures.

Keywords: Generative theory of tonal music (GTTM) · Local grouping boundary · Grouping structure · Metrical structure · Deep learning

© Springer International Publishing AG 2017
M. Aramaki et al. (Eds.): CMMR 2016, LNCS 10525, pp. 3–21, 2017.
DOI: 10.1007/978-3-319-67738-5_1

1   Introduction

We propose an analyzer for automatically detecting local grouping boundaries and generating metrical structures of music pieces based on a generative theory of tonal music (GTTM) [21]. A GTTM is composed of four modules, each of which assigns a separate structural description to a listener's understanding of a piece of music. These four modules output a grouping structure, metrical structure, time-span tree, and prolongational tree. Since the detection of the local grouping boundaries and generation of metrical structures is the early stage in a GTTM, an extremely accurate analyzer will make it possible to improve the performance of all later analyzers.

We previously constructed several analyzers, such as the automatic time-span tree analyzer (ATTA) [7] and fully automatic time-span tree analyzer (FATTA) [8], that enable us to detect local grouping boundaries. However, the performance of these analyzers is inadequate in that musicologists have to correct the boundaries due to numerous errors.

Our deepGTTM-I&II is based on a deep learning technique [16] to improve the performance of detecting local grouping boundaries and generating metrical structures of music pieces. Unsupervised training in the deep learning of deep-layered networks called pre-training helps in supervised training, which is called fine-tuning [5].

Our goal was to develop a GTTM analyzer that enables the output of the results obtained from analysis that were the same as those obtained by musicologists based on deep learning by learning the analysis results obtained by the musicologists. We had to consider the following three issues in constructing this analyzer.

Multi-task learning

A model or network in a simple learning task estimates the label from an input feature vector. However, local grouping boundaries can be found in many note transitions. Also, a strong beat can be found in many beat positions. Therefore, we consider a single learning task for estimating whether one note transition can be a boundary (a strong beat).

A problem in detecting local grouping boundaries or strong beats can then be solved using multi-task learning.

Subsection 4.3 explains multi-task learning by using deep learning.

Large-scale training data

Large-scale training data are needed to train a deep-layered network, and labels are not needed in pre-training the network. Therefore, we collected 15,000 pieces of music formatted in musicXML from Web pages that were introduced in the MusicXML page of MakeMusic Inc. citeMakeMusic. We needed labeled data to fine-tune the network. Although we had 300 pieces with labels in the GTTM database [12], this number was too small to enable the network to learn.

Subsection 4.1 explains how we collected the data and how we got the network to learn effectively with a small dataset.

GTTM rules

A GTTM consists of multiple rules, and a note transition that is applied to many rules tends to be a local grouping boundary in the analysis of local grouping boundaries. Similarly, a beat that is applied to many rules tends to be a strong beat in the analysis of the metrical structure. As a result of analysis by musicologists, 300 pieces of music in the GTTM database were not only labeled with local grouping boundaries and metrical structures but also labeled with applied positions of preference rules (PRs). Therefore, the applied positions of PRs were helpful clues in detecting local grouping boundaries and strong beats.

Subsection 4.3 explains how the network learned with the PRs.

Sequential vs recurrent models

There are two types of models, i.e., recurrent and sequential, that can be used for GTTM analysis. The recurrent neural network provides recurrent models, which are suitable for analyzing a metrical structure in which cyclical change results in strong and weak beats. However, the recurrent neural network is difficult to train, and training time is very long. On the other hand, sequential models, such as deep belief networks (DBNs), are not suitable for detecting the repetition of strong beats. However, the deepGTTM-I DBN of our analyzer is very simple and performs well in detecting the local grouping boundary of a GTTM.

Therefore, we chose two DBNs for GTTM analysis. Subsection 4.2 explains how these DBNs are trained for analyzing metrical structures.

Hierarchical metrical structure

A hierarchical metrical structure is generated by iterating the choice of the next-level structure. The next level structure is recursively generated using the previous structure. However, when we use learning with a single standard network of deep learning, it is difficult to lean a higher-level structure because many network representations are used for learning a lower-level structure.

Subsection 4.2 explains how to learn a higher level structure.

The results obtained from an experiment indicate that our GTTMI&II involving multi-task learning using the deep learning technique outperformed previous GTTM analyzers.

The paper is organized as follows. Section 2 describes related work and Sect. 3 explains our analyzer called deepGTTM-I&II. Section 4 explains how we evaluated the performance of deepGTTM-I&II, and Sect. 5 concludes with a summary and overview of future work.

2   Related Work

We now briefly look back through the history of cognitive music theory. The imprecation realization model (IRM) proposed by Narmour abstracts and expresses music according to symbol sequences from information from a score [27,28]. Recently, the IRM has been implemented on computers, and its chain structures can be obtained from a score [37]. The *Schenkerian* analysis analyzes deeper structures called "Urline" and "Ursatz" from the music surface [32]. Short segments of music can be analyzed through Schenkerian analysis on a computer [24]. There is another approach that constructs a music theory for adopting computer implementation [22,35].

We consider a GTTM to be the most promising of the many theories that have been proposed [2,27,28,32,35] in terms of its ability to formalize musical knowledge because a GTTM captures the aspects of musical phenomena based on the Gestalt occurring in music and is presented with relatively rigid rules. The main advantage of analysis by using a GTTM is that it can acquire tree structures called time-span and prolongation trees.

We have been constructing both analyzers and an application of a GTTM for more than a decade (Fig. 1) [14]. The horizontal axis in Fig. 1 indicates years. The analyzers we developed are above the timeline.

2.1 Analyzers for GTTM Based on Full Parameterization

We first constructed a grouping structure analyzer and metrical structure analyzer (Figs. 1a and b). We developed the ATTA (Fig. 1c) [7] by integrating a grouping structure analyzer and a metrical analyzer. We extended the GTTM by full externalization and parameterization and proposed a machine-executable extension of the GTTM, exGTTM. We implemented exGTTM on a computer that we call the ATTA. The ATTA has 46 adjusted parameters to control the strength of each rule. The ATTA we developed enables us to control the priority of rules, which enables us to obtain extremely accurate groupings and metrical structures. However, we need musical knowledge that musicologists have to properly tune the parameters.

The FATTA [8] (Fig. 1d) does not have to tune the parameters because it automatically calculates the stability of structures and optimizes the parameters so that the structures would be stable. It achieved excellent analysis results for metrical structures, but the results for grouping structures and time-span trees were unacceptable.

We constructed an interactive GTTM analyzer [11] (Fig. 1e) that enables seamless changes in the automatic analysis and manual editing processes because it was difficult to construct an analyzer that could output analysis results in the same way as musicologists. The interactive GTTM analyzer is still used to collect GTTM analysis data, and anyone can download and use it for free [15].

However, all these analyzers [7,8,11,15] have problems. Musical knowledge is required for the ATTA to tune the parameters, and the FATTA performs poorly.

2.2 Analyzers for GTTM Based on Statistical Learning

The σGTTM analyzer [25] (Fig. 1f) enables us to automatically detect local grouping boundaries by using a decision tree. Although σGTTM performed better than the FATTA, it was worse than the ATTA after the ATTA parameters had been tuned.

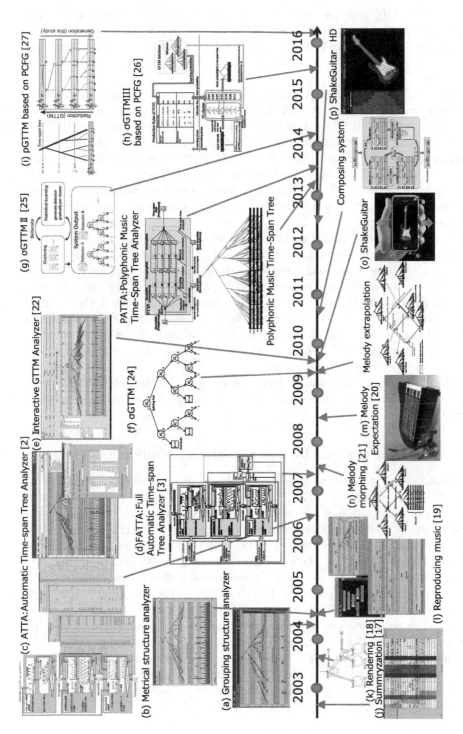

Fig. 1. Related work on analysis and application systems for GTTM

The σGTTMII analyzer [20] (Fig. 1g) involves clustering steps for learning the decision tree and outperforms the ATTA if we can manually select the best decision tree. Although σGTTMII performed the best in detecting grouping boundaries, it was difficult to select the proper decision tree without musical knowledge.

The σGTTMIII analyzer [13] (Fig. 1h) enables us to automatically analyze time-span trees by learning with a time-span tree of 300 pieces of music from the GTTM database [12] based on probabilistic context-free grammar (PCFG). The σGTTMIII analyzer performed the best in acquiring time-span trees. The pGTTM anlayzer [26] (Fig. 1i) also uses PCFG, and we used it to attempt unsupervised learning. The main advantages of σGTTMIII and pGTTM are that they can learn the contexts in difference hierarchies of the structures (e.g., beats were important in the leaves of time-span trees, or chords were important near the roots of the trees).

However, all these analyzers [13,20,25,26] have problems with regard to detecting local grouping boundaries. The σGTTM III and pGTTM analyzers are focused on acquiring time-span trees and cannot acquire local grouping boundaries. Musical knowledge is required for σGTTM II to select the decision tree. Since σGTTM and σGTTM II use rules that musicologists applied, they cannot work as standalone analyzers. For example, information on parallel phrases is needed when detecting local grouping boundaries because parallel phrases create parallel structures in a GTTM. However, σGTTM and σGTTM II do not have processes for acquiring parallel phrases.

In light of this, we introduce a deep learning analyzer for detecting the local grouping boundaries and generating hierarchical metrical structures of music pieces based on a GTTM.

2.3   Application Systems by Using Analysis Results of GTTM

We constructed applications systems, which are given under the time-line in Fig. 1, to use the results from GTTM analysis. A time-span or prolongation tree provides a summarization of a piece of music, which can be used as the representation of an abstraction, resulting in a music retrieval system [17] (Fig. 1j). It can also be used for performance rendering [18] (Fig. 1k) and reproducing music [19] (Fig. 1l). The time-span tree can also be used for melody prediction [9] (Fig. 1m) and melody morphing [10] (Fig. 1n). Figures 1o and p illustrate a demonstration system for the melody morphing method that changes the morphing level of each half bar by using the values from the accelerometer in the iPad/iPhone/iPod Touch. When the user stops moving the iPhone/iPod Touch, the unit plays the backing melody of "The Other Day, I Met a Bear (The Bear Song)". When the user shakes it vigorously, it plays heavy soloing. When the user shakes it slowly, it plays a morphed melody between the backing and heavy soloing.

These systems currently need a time-span tree analyzed by musicologists because our analyzers do not perform optimally.

2.4   Melody Segmentation

Because conventional approaches of melody segmentation, such as the Grouper of the Melisma Music Analyzer by Temperley [34] and the local boundary detection model (LBDM) by Cambouropoulos [1], require the user to make manual adjustments to the parameters, they are not completely automatic. Although Temperley [36] has also used a probabilistic model, it has not been applied to melody segmentation. The unsupervised learning model (IDyOM) proposed by Pearce et al. makes no use of the rules of music theory with regard to melodic phrases, and it has performed as well as Grouper and LBDM [30]. However, as deepGTTM-I&II statistically and collectively learn all the rules for the grouping structure analysis of a GTTM, we expect that deepGTTM-I&II will perform better than an analyzer that only uses statistical learning.

2.5   Beat Tracking

The metrical structure analysis in a GTTM is a kind of beat tracking. Current methods based on beat tracking [3,4,6,31] can only acquire the hierarchical metrical structure in a measure because they do not take into account larger metrical structures such as two and four measures.

3   GTTM and Its Implementation Problems

Figure 2 shows local grouping boundaries, a grouping structure, metrical structure, timespan tree, and prolongational tree.

The grouping structure is intended to formalize the intuitive belief that tonal music is organized into groups that are in turn composed of subgroups. These groups are presented graphically as several levels of arcs below a music staff.

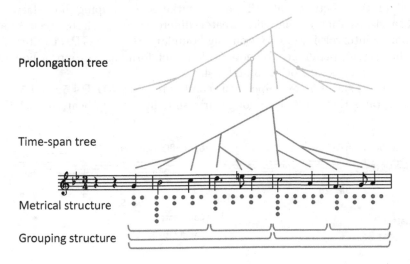

Fig. 2. Grouping structure, metrical structure, time-span tree, and prolongation tree

The metrical structure describes the rhythmical hierarchy of a piece of music by identifying the position of strong beats at the levels of a quarter note, half note, measure, two measures, four measures, and so on. Strong beats are illustrated as several levels of dots below the music staff.

3.1 Preference Rules

There are two types of rules in a GTTM, i.e., "well-formedness" and "preference". Well-formedness rules (WFRs) are necessary for the assignment of a structure and restrictions on the structure. When more than one structure satisfies the WFRs, the PRs indicate the superiority of one structure over another.

There are seven grouping PRs (GPRs) (**GPRs**): **GPR1** (alternative form), **GPR2** (proximity), **GPR3** (change), **GPR4** (intensification), **GPR5** (symmetry), **GPR6** (parallelism), and **GPR7** (time-span and prolongational stability). The **GPR2** has two cases: (a) (slur/rest) and (b) (attack-point). The **GPR3** has four cases: (a) (register), (b) (dynamics), (c) (articulation), and (d) (length).

There are ten metrical PRs (MPRs) (**MPRs**): **MPR1** (parallelism), **MPR2** (strong beat early), **MPR3** (event), **MPR4** (stress), **MPR5** (length), **MPR6** (bass), **MPR7** (cadence), **MPR8** (suspension), **MPR9** (time-span interaction), and **MPR10** (binary regularity). The **MPR5** has six cases: (a) pitch-event, (b) dynamics, (c) slur, (d) articulation, (e) repeated pitches, and (f) harmony.

3.2 Conflict Between Rules

Because there is no strict order for applying PRs, a conflict between rules often occurs when applying PRs, which results in ambiguities in analysis.

Figure 3(a) outlines a simple example of the conflict between **GPR2b** (attack-point) and **GPR3a** (register). **GPR2b** states that a relatively greater interval of time between attack points initiates a grouping boundary. The **GPR3a** states that a relatively greater difference in pitch between smaller neighboring intervals initiates a grouping boundary. Because **GPR1** (alternative form) has strong preference for note 3 alone not forming a group, a boundary cannot be perceived at both 2–3 and 3–4.

Figure 3(b) shows an example of the conflict between **MPRs 5c** and **5a**. The **MPR5c** states that a relatively long slur results in a strong beat, and **MPR5a**

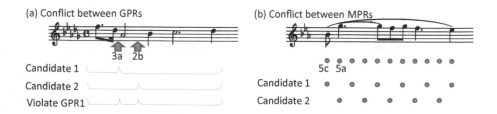

Fig. 3. Examples of conflict between PRs

states that a relatively long pitch-event results in a strong beat. Because metrical WFR 3 (**MWFR3**) states that strong beats are spaced either two or three beats apart, a strong beat cannot be perceived at both onsets of the first and second notes.

We expect to learn the rule application and priority of rules by inputting a whole song with labels of the applied rules to a deep-layered network.

3.3 Ambiguous Rule Definition

Some rules in a GTTM are expressed with ambiguous terms. The **GPR4** and **MPR5** are defined as follows as examples.

> The **GPR4 (Intensification)**, where the effects selected by GPRs 2 and 3 are relatively more pronounced, a larger-level group boundary may be placed.
> The **MPR5 (Length)** has preference for a metrical structure in which a relatively strong beat occurs at the inception of either
>
> a. a relatively long pitch-event,
> b. relatively long duration of a dynamic,
> c. relatively long slur,
> d. relatively long pattern of articulation,
> e. relatively long duration of a pitch in the relevant levels of the time-span reduction, or
> f. relatively long duration of a harmony in the relevant levels of the time-span reduction (harmonic rhythm).

The term "relatively" in this sense is ambiguous. The sentence also contains the phrase "more pronounced", but the comparison is unclear. Another example is that a GTTM has rules for selecting proper structures when discovering similar melodies (called parallelism) but does not define similarity. The **GPR6** and **MPR1** are defined as follows as examples.

> The **GPR6 (parallelism)**, when two or more segments of the music can be construed as parallel, they preferably form parallel parts of groups.
> The **MPR1 (parallelism)**, when two or more groups or parts of groups can be construed as parallel, they preferably receive a parallel metrical structure.

3.4 Context Dependency

To solve the problems discussed in Subsects. 3.2 and 3.3, we proposed the machine executable extension of GTTM (exGTTM) and ATTA [7]. Figure 4 gives an example of an application of **MPR4, 5a, 5b**, and **5c** in the exGTTM and ATTA. By configuring the threshold parameters $T^j (j = 4, 5a, 5b, and 5c)$, we can control whether each rule is applicable. However, proper values of the parameter depend on the piece of music and level of hierarchy in the metrical structure. Therefore, automatic estimation of proper values of the parameters is difficult.

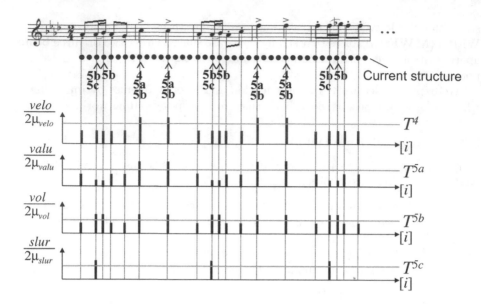

Fig. 4. Application of MPR4, 5a, 5b, and 5c in ATTA

3.5 Less Precise Explanation of Feedback Link

A GTTM has various feedback links from higher-level structures to lower-level ones. For example, **MPR9** is defined as follows.

> The **MPR9 (Time-span interaction)** has preference for a metrical analysis that minimizes conflict in the time-span reduction.

However, no detailed description and only a few examples are given. Other feedback links in the GTTM rules are not explicit. For example, analyzing the results of a time-span tree strongly affects the interpretation of chord progression, and various rules are related to chord progression, e.g., **MPR7 (Cadence)** requires a metrical structure in which cadences are metrically stable.

For complete implementation of a GTTM based on deep learning, we have to introduce the feedback link by using the recurrent neural network; however, we do not focus on the feedback link in this paper.

4   deepGTTM-I&II: Local Grouping Boundary and Metrical Strucutre Analyzer Based on Deep Learning

We introduced deep learning into deepGTTM-I&II to analyze the structure of a GTTM and solve the problems described in Subsects. 3.2, 3.3 and 3.4. There are two main advantages of introducing deep learning.

Learning rule applications

We constructed a deep-layered network that can output whether each rule is applicable on each note transition by learning the relationship between the scores and positions of applied grouping PRs with the deep learning technique.

Previous analysis systems based on GTTM were constructed by a human researcher or programmer. As described in Subsect. 3.3, some rules in a GTTM are very ambiguous and the implementations of these rules might differ depending on the person.

However, deepGTTM-I&II is a learning based analyzer, where its quality depends on the training data and trained network.

Learning priority of rules

The FATTA only determine the priority of rules from the stability of the structure. The σGTTM and σGTTMII analyzers only determine the priority of rules from applied rules. They do not work well because the priority of rules depends on the context of a piece of music.

The input of the network in deepGTTM-I&II, on the other hand, is the score and the network learns the priority of the rules as the weight and bias of the network based on the context of the score.

This section describes how we analyzed the local grouping boundaries and metrical structure by using deep learning.

4.1 Datasets for Training

Three types of datasets were used to train the network, i.e., a non-labeled dataset for pre-training, half-labeled dataset, and labeled dataset for fine-tuning (Fig. 5).

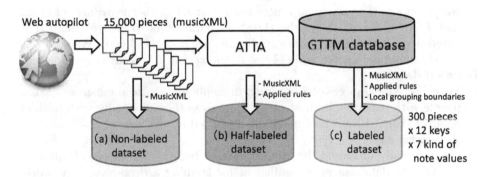

Fig. 5. Non-labeled, half-labeled, and labeled datasets

Non-labeled dataset

The network in pre-training learned the features of the music. A large-scale dataset with no labels was needed. Therefore, we collected 15,000 pieces of music formatted in musicXML from Web pages that were introduced on the musicXML page of MakeMusic Inc. [23] (Fig. 5a). The musicXMLs were downloaded in the following three steps.

    a. Web autopilot script made a list of urls that probably downloaded musicXMLs in five links from the musicXML page of MakeMusic Inc.

b. The files in the url list were downloaded after they had been omitted because they were clearly not musicXML.

c. All the downloaded files were opened using the script, and files that were not musicXML were deleted.

Half-labeled dataset

The network in fine-tuning learned with the labeled dataset. We had 300 pieces of music with a labeled dataset in the GTTM database, which included musicXML with positions of local grouping boundaries, and positions to which the GPRs were applied. However, 300 pieces are insufficient for deep learning.

Consequently, we constructed a half-labeled dataset. We automatically added the labels of thirteen applied rules of **GPR2a, 2b, 3a, 3b, 3c, 3d,** and **MPR2, 3, 4, 5a, 5b, 5c,** and **5d,** because these rules could be uniquely applied as a score. We used the ATTA to add labels to these rules (Fig. 5b). With the ATTA, the strength of the beat dependent on each MPR can be expressed as $D_i{}^j$ ($j = 2, 3, 4, 5a, 5b, 5c,$ and $5d,$ $0 \leq D_i{}^j \leq 1$). For example, **MPR4** is defined in a GTTM as follows.

The **MPR4 (Event)** has preference for a metrical structure in which beats of level L_i that are stressed are strong beats of L_i.

We formalized $D_i{}^4$ as follows.

$$D_i{}^4 = \begin{cases} 1 & velo_i > 2 \times \mu_{velo} \times T^4 \\ 0 & else, \end{cases} \tag{1}$$

where $velo_i$ is the velocity of a note from beat i, μ_{velo} is the average of $velo_i$, and T^j ($0 \leq T^j \leq 1$) are the threshold parameters to control those that determine whether the rules are applicable ($D_i{}^j = 1$) ($D_i{}^j = 0$). We used 1 as the threshold parameter value ($T^j = 1,$ $where$ $j = 2, 3, 4, 5a, 5b, 5c,$ and $5d$).

Labeled dataset

We collected 300 pieces of 8-bar-long, monophonic, classical music and asked people with expertise in musicology to analyze them manually with faithful regard to the MPRs. These manually produced results were cross-checked by three other experts.

We artificially increased the labeled dataset because 300 pieces of music in the GTTM database were insufficient for training a deep-layered network. First, we transposed the pieces for all 12 keys. We then changed the length of the note values to two times, four times, eight times, half time, quarter time, and eighth time. Thus, the total labeled dataset had 25,200 (=300 × 12 × 7) pieces of music (Fig. 5c).

4.2 Deep Belief Networks

We used deep belief networks (DBN) for detecting local grouping boundaries and generating metrical structures.

Figure 6 outlines the structure of this DBN, which we call deepGTTM-I, for detecting local grouping boundaries. The inputs of deepGTTM-I are the onset time, offset time, pitch, and velocity of note sequences from musicXML There are 11 outputs of deepGTTM-I to enable multi-tasking learning, i.e., ten GPRs (**GPR2a, 2b, 3a, 3b, 3c, 4, 5, 6,** and **7**) and a local grouping boundary.

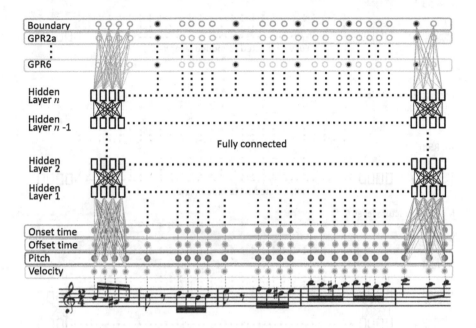

Fig. 6. DBN for detecting local grouping boundaries

Figure 7 outlines the structure of the DBN we call deepGTTM-II to generate a metrical structure. The inputs of deepGTTM-II are the onset time, offset time, pitch, and velocity, and grouping structure manually analyzed by musicologists. Each hierarchical level of the grouping structure is separately inputted by a note neighboring the grouping boundary as 1; otherwise, 0. There are eight outputs of deepGTTM-II to enable multi-tasking learning in each hierarchical level of the metrical structure, i.e., seven MPRs (**MPR2, 3, 4, 5a, 5b, 5c,** and **5d**) and one level of the metrical structure. Individual outputs have two units, e.g., rules that were not applicable (=0) and rules that were applicable (=1), or weak beats (=0) and strong beats (=1).

A metrical structure consists of hierarchical levels, and we added one hidden layer to generate the next structure level. We used logistic regression to connect the final hidden layer $(n, n+1, \ldots, n+h)$ and outputs. All outputs shared the hidden layer from 1 to the final hidden layer. The network was learned in the four steps below. The order of music pieces was changed at every epoch in all steps.

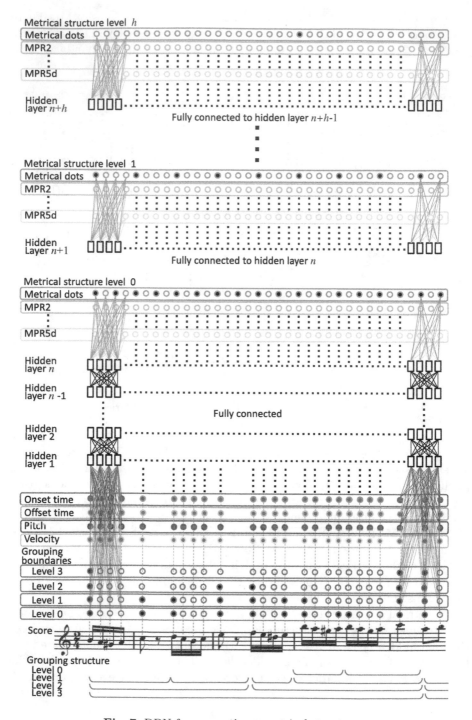

Fig. 7. DBN for generating a metrical structure

4.3 Multi-dimensional Multi-task Learning

Our deepGTTM-I&II consists of a very complex network. The fine-tuning of local grouping boundaries and one level of a metrical structure involves multi-task learning. The fine-tuning of each PR also involved multi-task learning. Therefore, the fine-tuning of PRs involves multi-dimensional multi-task learning (Fig. 8).

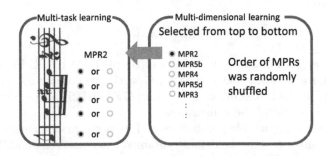

Fig. 8. Multi-dimensional multi-task learning

Multi-task Learning. The processing flow for the multi-task learning of a GPR or local grouping boundaries involves the following four steps.

Step 1: The order of the pieces of training data is randomly shuffled and a piece is selected from top to bottom.

Step 2: The note transition of the selected piece is randomly shuffled and a note transition is selected from top to bottom.

Step 3: Back propagation from output to input is carried out based on whether the note transition had a boundary or the rule was applied (=1) or not (=0).

Step 4: The next note transition or the next piece in steps 1 and 2 is repeated.

The processing flow for the multi-task learning of an MPR or metrical dots involved four steps.

Step 1: The order of the music pieces of training data is randomly shuffled and a piece is selected from top to bottom.

Step 2: The beat position of the selected piece is randomly shuffled and a beat position is selected from top to bottom.

Step 3: Back propagation from output to input is carried out based on whether the beat position had a strong beat or the rule was applied (=1) or was not (=0).

Step 4: The next beat position or the next piece in steps 2 and 3 is repeated.

Multidimensional Multi-task Learning. The processing flow for the multi-dimensional multi-task learning of PRs involves the following three steps.

Step 1: The order of PRs is randomly shuffled and a rule is selected from top to bottom.

Step 2: Multi-task learning of the selected PR is carried out.

Step 3: The next rules in step 1 are repeated.

5   Experimental Results

We evaluated the $F_{measure}$ of deepGTTM-I&II by using 100 music pieces from the GTTM database; the remaining 200 pieces were used to train the network. The $F_{measure}$ is given by the weighted harmonic mean of precision P (proportion of selected dots that are correct) and recall R (proportion of correct dots that were identified).

$$F_{measure} = 2 \times \frac{P \times R}{P+R} \qquad (2)$$

Tables 1 and 2 summarize the results of deepGTTM-I and deepGTTM-II, respectively, for a network that had 11 layers with 3000 units.

The results in the tables indicate that deepGTTM-I&II outperformed previous analyzers in terms of the F-measure.

The ATTA has adjustable parameters and its performance changes depending on the parameters. For the default parameter, we used the middle value in the parameter range [7]. The σGTTMII analyzer selected the decision tree and the performance changes on the selected tree. The performances of the ATTA and σGTTMII changed depending on the parameters or decision trees. Table 1 indicates the best performance was achieved by manual editing. However, the FATTA, σGTTM, and deepGTTM-I have no parameters for editing.

These results show that deepGTTM-I&II performed extremely robustly.

Table 1. Performances of deepGTTM-I, ATTA, σGTTM

	Precision P	Recall R	F measure
ATTA with manual editing of parameters	0.74	0.44	0.55
σGTTM	0.47	0.74	0.57
σGTTM with manual selection of decision tree	0.68	0.92	0.78
deepGTTM-I	0.78	0.81	0.80

Table 2. Performances of deepGTTM-II, ATTA, and FATTA

Melodies	deepGTTM-II	ATTA (default parameters)	ATTA (configured parameters)	FATTA
1. Grande Valse Brillante	0.94	0.88	0.93	0.88
2. Moments Musicaux	1.00	0.95	1.00	1.00
3. Trukish March	0.98	0.91	0.96	0.96
4. Anitras Tanz	0.90	0.82	0.86	0.82
5 Valse du Petit Chien	0.99	0.87	0.92	0.95
	:	:	:	:
Total (100 melodies)	0.96	0.84	0.90	0.88

6   Conclusion

We developed an analyzer for detecting local grouping boundaries and generating a metrical structure called deepGTTM-I&II that is based on deep learning. The following three points are the main results of this study.

Music analyzer based on deep learning
It has been revealed that deep learning is strong for various tasks. We demonstrated that deep leaning is also strong for music analysis. We will attempt to implement other music theories based on deep learning. Although we collected 300 pieces of music and analyzed the results of a GTTM by musicologists, the labeled dataset of these pieces was not sufficient for learning a deep-layered network. We therefore used our previous GTTM analyzer called ATTA to prepare three types of datasets, non-labeled, half-labeled, and labeled, to learn the network.

High-accuracy GTTM analyzer without manual editing
Previous GTTM analyzers, such as the ATTA and σGTTM, require manual editing; otherwise, the performance will be much worse. The F_{measure}s of GTTM analyzers without manual editing, such as the FATTA, σGTTM, σGTTMIII, and pGTTM, are too low (under 0.8). However, deepGTTM-I&II exhibited extremely high performance, which indicates the possibility of practical use in GTTM applications [9,10,17–19]. We plan to implement the entire GTTM analysis process based on deep learning.

Multi-dimensional multi-task learning
We constructed a multi-dimensional multi-task learning analyzer that efficiently learns the grouping boundaries and hierarchical level of the metrical structure and PRs by sharing the network. Multi-dimensional multi-task learning is expected to be applied to other data that have a hierarchy and time series such as film [33] and discussion [29]. After a network that had 11 layers with 3000 units had been learned, the deepGTTM-I&II outperformed the previously developed analyzers in terms of the F_{measure}.

This work was one step in implementing a GTTM based on deep learning. The remaining steps are to implement time-span reduction analysis and prologational reduction analysis of a GTTM based on deep learning. The following two problems remain. One is generating tree structures because time-span and prolongation tree structures are more complex than local grouping boundaries or a hierarchical metrical structure. The other problem is the lack of training samples because there are many combinations of tree structures, and an unlearned sample sometimes appears in test data. We will attempt to solve these problems and make it possible to construct a complete GTTM system based on deep learning.

At the current stage, we are not able to understand the details on why deep learning works extremely well for metrical analysis in a GTTM. Thus, we also plan to analyze a network after a metrical structure is learned.

Acknowledgments. This work was supported by JSPS KAKENHI Grant Number 25700036, 16H01744, 23500145.

References

1. Cambouropoulos, E.: The Local Boundary Detection Model (LBDM) and its application in the study of expressive timing. In: Proceedings of the International Computer Music Conference (ICMC 2001), pp. 290–293 (2001)
2. Cooper, G., Meyer, L.B.: The Rhythmic Structure of Music. The University of Chicago Press, Chicago (1960)
3. Davies, M., Bock, S.: Evaluating the evaluation measures for beat tracking. In: Proceedings of the International Conference on Music Information Retrieval (ISMIR 2014), pp. 637–642 (2014)
4. Dixon, S.: Automatic extraction of tempo and beat from expressive performance. J. New Music Res. **30**(1), 39–58 (2001)
5. Erhan, D., Bengio, Y., Courville, A., Manzagol, P.-A., Vincent, P., Bengio, S.: Why does unsupervised pre-training help deep learning? J. Mach. Learn. Res. **11**, 625–660 (2010)
6. Goto, M.: An audio-based real-time beat tracking system for music with or without drum-sounds. J. New Music Res. **30**(2), 159–171 (2001)
7. Hamanaka, M., Hirata, K., Tojo, S.: Implementing 'a generative theory of tonal music'. J. New Music Res. **35**(4), 249–277 (2006)
8. Hamanaka, M., Hirata, K., Tojo, S.: FATTA: full automatic time-span tree analyzer. In: Proceedings of the 2007 International Computer Music Conference (ICMC 2007), pp. 153–156 (2007)
9. Hamanaka, M., Hirata, K., Tojo, S.: Melody expectation method based on GTTM and TPS. In: Proceeding of the 2008 International Society for Music Information Retrieval Conference (ISMIR 2008), pp. 107–112 (2008)
10. Hamanaka, M., Hirata, K., Tojo, S.: Melody morphing method based on GTTM. In: Proceeding of the 2008 International Computer Music Conference (ICMC 2008), pp. 155–158 (2008)
11. Hamanaka, M., Hirata, K., Tojo, S.: Interactive GTTM Analyzer. In: Proceedings of the 10th International Conference on Music Information Retrieval Conference (ISMIR 2009), pp. 291–296 (2009)
12. Hamanaka, M., Hirata, K., Tojo, S.: Music structural analysis database based on GTTM. In: Proceedings of the 2014 International Society for Music Information Retrieval Conference (ISMIR 2014), pp. 325–330 (2014)
13. Hamanaka, M., Hirata, K., Tojo, S.: σGTTM III: learning-based time-span tree generator based on PCFG. In: Kronland-Martinet, R., Aramaki, M., Ystad, S. (eds.) CMMR 2015. LNCS, vol. 9617, pp. 387–404. Springer, Cham (2016). doi:10.1007/978-3-319-46282-0_25
14. Hamanaka, M., Hirata, K., Tojo, S.: Implementing methods for analysing music based on Lerdahl and Jackendoff's *generative theory of tonal music*. Comput. Music Anal., pp. 221–249. Springer, Cham (2016). doi:10.1007/978-3-319-25931-4_9
15. Hamanaka, M.: Interactive GTTM Analyzer/GTTM Database. http://gttm.jp. Accessed 4 Jan 2017
16. Hinton, G.E., Osindero, S., Teh, Y.-W.: A fast learning algorithm for deep belief nets. Neural Comput. **18**(7), 1527–1554 (2006)
17. Hirata, K., Matsuda, S.: Interactive music summarization based on generative theory of tonal music. J. New Music Res. **32**(2), 165–177 (2003)
18. Hirata, K., Hiraga, R.: Ha-Hi-Hun plays Chopin's Etude. In: Working Notes of IJCAI-03 Workshop on Methods for Automatic Music Performance and Their Applications in a Public Rendering Contest, pp. 72–73 (2003)

19. Hirata, K., Matsuda, S.: Annotated music for retrieval, reproduction, and sharing. In: Proceeding of International Computer Music Conference (ICMC 2004), pp. 584–587 (2004)
20. Kanamori, K., Hamanaka, M.: Method to detect GTTM local grouping boundaries based on clustering and statistical learning. In: Proceedings of the 2014 International Computer Music Conference (ICMC 2014), pp. 125–128 (2014)
21. Lerdahl, F., Jackendoff, R.: A Generative Theory of Tonal Music. MIT Press, Cambridge (1983)
22. Lerdahl, F.: Tonal Pitch Space. Oxford University Press, Oxford (2001)
23. MakeMusic Inc.: Finale. http://www.finalemusic.com/. Accessed 4 Jan 2017
24. Marsden, A.: Software for Schenkerian analysis. In: Proceeding of International Computer Music Conference (ICMC2011), pp. 673–676 (2011)
25. Miura, Y., Hamanaka, M., Hirata, K., Tojo, S.: Use of decision tree to detect GTTM group boundaries. In: Proceedings of the 2009 International Computer Music Conference (ICMC 2009), pp. 125–128 (2009)
26. Nakamura, E., Hamanaka, M., Hirata, K., Yoshii, K.: Tree-structured probabilistic model of monophonic written music based on the generative theory of tonal music. In: Proceedings of the 41st IEEE International Conference on Acoustics, Speech and Signal Processing (ICASSP 2016), pp. 276–280 (2016)
27. Narmour, E.: The Analysis and Cognition of Basic Melodic Structure. University of Chicago Press, Chicago (1990)
28. Narmour, E.: The Analysis and Cognition of Melodic Complexity. The University of Chicago Press, Chicago (1992)
29. Oshima, T., Hamanaka, M., Hirata, K., Tojo, S., Nagao, K.: Development of discussion structure editor for discussion mining based on music theory. In: IPSJ SIG DCC, 7 p. (2013). (in Japanese)
30. Pearce, M.T., Müllensiefen, D., Wiggins, G.A.: A comparison of statistical and rule-based models of melodic segmentation. In: Proceedings of the International Conference on Music Information Retrieval (ISMIR 2008), pp. 89–94 (2008)
31. Rosenthal, D.: Emulation of human rhythm perception. Comput. Music J. **16**(1), 64–76 (1992)
32. Schenker, H.: Der frei Satz. Universal Edition, Vienna (1935). Published in English as Free Composition, translated and edited by E. Oster. Longman, New York (1979)
33. Takeuchi, S., Hamanaka, M.: Structure of the film based on the music theory. In: JSAI 2014, 1K5-OS-07b-4 (2014). (in Japanese)
34. Temperley, D.: The Melisma Music Analyzer (2003). http://www.link.cs.cmu.edu/music-analysis/. Accessed 2017-1-4
35. Temperley, D.: The Congnition of Basic Musical Structures. MIT Press, Cambridge (2004)
36. Temperley, D.: Music and Probability. The MIT Press, Cambridge (2007)
37. Yazawa, S., Hamanaka, M., Utsuro, T.: Melody generation system based on a theory of melody sequences. In: Proceedings of ICAICTA 2014, pp. 347–352 (2014)

Melody and Rhythm Through Network Visualization Techniques

Guillaume Blot[✉], Pierre Saurel, and Francis Rousseaux

Paris-Sorbonne University and CNRS SND Laboratory
"Sciences, Normes, Decision" - FRE 3593, 28 Rue Serpente, 75006 Paris, France
{guillaume.blot,pierre.saurel}@paris-sorbonne.fr,
francis.rousseaux@univ-reims.fr

Abstract. Halfway between music analysis and graph visualization, we propose tonal pitch representations from the chromatic scale. On the first part of the experiment, a 12-node graph is connected as a Rhythm Network and visualized with a Circular Layout, commonly known as Pitch constellation. This particular graph topology focuses on node structure and gives strength to weak edges. At this occasion, we unveil the Singularity Threshold, giving an opportunity to isolate structure from singular parts of melodies. Where usual Pitch constellations focus on chords, we focus on successive pitch intervals. On the second part, we propose a rhythm representation using a Force-Directed layout. In addition to structural information, our second technique shows proximal and peripheral elements. This experiment features 6 melodies that we propose to visualize using Gephi.

Keywords: Rhythm Network · Graph visualization · Circular layout · Geometry of Music · Pitch interval · Key-finding · Singularity

1 My Eyes, My Ears

When music turns visual, it gives artists and listeners new senses to express themselves. Sciences and artistic movements have always bridged eyes and ears. But, more recent practices are further accelerating the relationship. Video-sharing platforms, social network posting tools, music streaming and podcast: multimedia is a ubiquitous phenomenon in the web. Hence, before it is shared, a musical composition is already altered by vision. At the first steps of their lives, more and more musical objects are manipulated with the help of computers. Artists, musicians, remixers, producers or djs rely on user interfaces to manipulate Music.

In this paper, we study a graph topology and a visualization algorithm representing pitch patterns of a Melody. As Score remains the official written musical language, visual representations of music can take other shapes. In musical tuning and harmony, graphs are interesting to represent pitch connections: bipartite network [28], Tonetz [19], pitch constellation [8], simplical complex [3], Birdcage [20] or Self-organizing maps [27]. Visualization algorithms vary depending on

© Springer International Publishing AG 2017
M. Aramaki et al. (Eds.): CMMR 2016, LNCS 10525, pp. 22–40, 2017.
DOI: 10.1007/978-3-319-67738-5_2

the graph structure and the message it is supposed to deliver. In the scope of Pitch Constellation or Krenek diagram, our experiment focuses on Pitch Intervals represented using circular layouts. Where usual implementations of pitch constellation, concern the study of harmony [12,22,26], we deliver an exploration of successive pitches.

The graph structure is explained in next Sect. 2.1. It is called Rhythm Network, but in this experiment we focus on structural aspects rather than on temporal metrics. Rhythm Network is a graph structure focusing on time interval between events. It was first designed by Guillaume Blot in the context of a digital agenda where correlations between events were identified. It was also studied in other contexts such as E-learning systems and Road Traffic Management [4,5]. Following the paradigm *strength of weak ties* [21], the network is composing with pitches, rewarding node presence before node occurrence. As a result, a pattern appearing once has the same impact on the structure, than a repeated pattern. Hence, successive occurrences of the same pitch are not considered. Moreover, as we are dealing with temporal metrics, Rhythm Network keeps no record of pitch occurrences. In this context, analyzing and representing a melody, comes along with specific computational and visual techniques, that we explain in Sect. 3. In Subscct. 3.2, we present a method to extract singularities from a composition. Singularity is to be understood as a particular behavior in a piece of music, but no attempt is made to treat the concept in the mathematical way. Then we rely on key-finding techniques to validate our representations 3.3.

2   Pitch Interval Topology

2.1   Rhythm Network: Our Melody Structure

The Rhythm Network is a single-mode directed and weighted graph. A Graph (or Network) is a mathematical structure composed by a set N of n Nodes and a set E of e Edges. In a single-mode graph, nodes belong to only one class, which in our context will be pitches from the chromatic scale. That is a set of n = 12 nodes (C, $C\#$, D, $D\#$, E, F, $F\#$, G, $G\#$, A, $A\#$, B), connected to each other by edges. An edge (e_A, e_B) means that a connection exists between the source note A and the destination note B (and no connection from B toward A, as we are in a directed graph). What makes a graph special is its topology: when and how do we connect edges? This great freedom of action allows various degree of customization.

Edge creation is simple with Rhythm Network: we connect two successive nodes and measure the resulting edge with the interval of time between the two nodes. Lets try it with a three notes melody: C-A-D. Here the Rhythm Network has 3 nodes (C, A, D) and 2 edges (e_C, e_A) and (e_A, e_D). Now lets consider that C is a half-note and A, D are quarters, all played legato. Then (e_C, e_A) = $1/2$ and (e_A, e_D) = $1/4$; or with a 60 bpm tempo: (e_C, e_A) = 1 s and (e_A, e_D) = 0.5 s. Our experiment is based on the second notation.

2.2   The Experiment Workflow

Realizing a Rhythm Network is a simple process. Nevertheless, (re)producing our experiment implies a typical data treatment starting with a MIDI file and ending with an interoperable graph format: GEXF.

MIDI file is divided in channels and for each channel events are declared. The event we are interested in is "Note on" (x9 hexa, which comes along with a x8 "Note off") associated with a key and a timestamp. Data *"Note, Time, Channel"* are all what is considered in this experiment, even though other instructions might refine the composition of the sound: Modulation Wheel, Breath Controller, Portamento Time, Channel Volume, Balance or also Pan. Metadata are also available: Sequence Name, Tempo Setting or also Key Signature. For a full understanding, MIDI files format specifications 1.1 are published [2].

A MIDI file is our input dataset, but it needs to be manipulated in order to be visualized as a Rhythm Network. In this section, we present all 4 steps of the process: *Format, Organize, Connect* and *Visualize* (Fig. 1).

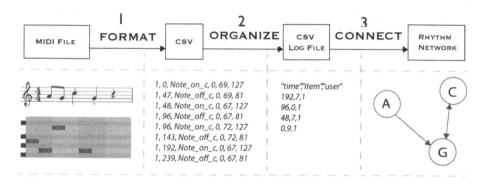

Fig. 1. Experiment workflow: format, organize and connect. We take a MIDI file as an input and produce a GEXF graph document.

– **Format:** The goal of this first step is to transform the binary MIDI file into a more readable text format. We use MIDICSV a program developed by John Walker in 2004 and revised in 2008[1]. This program takes the MIDI file as an argument and produces a CSV file with the details of the events for each channel. For example a "Note on" event looks like this: track, time, $Note_on_c$, channel, note, velocity. Using this representation a C played 30 s after the start of the song will be written as follow: 2, 30, $Note_on_c$, 0, 60, 127. Middle C is a 60 and all other notes are sequentially relatives to this point on a chromatic scale. Once we know that a C is played on channel 0 at 30 seconds, we do not use the first and the last arguments: track and velocity.

---

[1] http://www.fourmilab.ch/webtools/midicsv/.

- **Organize:** This step sorts all *"Note on"* events in a descending chronological order. Organization also comes along with a cleaning sub-task with two axes: keeping only *"Note on"* events and advancing in an octave-free mode. At the end of this sequence, the CSV file only contains lines of triples *(time, note, channel)*, where notes are numbers between 0 and 11 (0 is a C and 11 is a Cb). The PHP script that we developed has been made available with data in a public package[2]. Two scripts are used: (1) organizing a specific channel *($organize_o ne.php$)* and (2) organizing all channels *($organize_a ll.php$)*. In the second mode, we keep the chronological descending organization, then two notes played at the same time on different channels will be written one after another in the output CSV (unlike input CSV where events are still organized in channels).
- **Connect:** Now we produce a graph respecting the topology of the Rhythm Network. Guillaume Blot is currently developing a Python/Rpy2 program, which has been used to generate Rhythm Networks. The program is not yet fully featured, but a documented version is still published in the context of this experiment. The program takes the CSV log file from the previous step and connect successive pitches using a time-based metric: the interval of time between the two pitches. A G played 2 seconds after a A adds a connection between A and G. If the connection already exists, a mean interval is calculated with all intervals. Successive events of the same pitch are not considered. The result is a directed graph dealing with a set of N nodes (up to 12 nodes/pitches). For a full understanding of Rhythm Network, please refer to other experiments where the data structure has been studied following the same process [5,6].

Graph Exchange XML Format (GEXF) is an open and extensible XML document used to write network topologies. GEXF 1.2 specifications are published by GEXF Working Group [24]. The last step of our workflow is producing a GEXF file with 12 nodes and a variable number of weighted and directed connections.

3   Geometry of the Circle in Western Tonal Music

3.1   Chromatic Scale and Circular Layout

Musicians have a good command of circle representations. The most significant is the circle of fifths: a 12-tone circle where 2 successive pitches have 7 semi-tones differential. Most of occidental tonal music practitioners rely on this feature to get a partial image of a scale, ascending fifths by reading it clockwise and descending fifths reading it counterclockwise. Getting the fundamental and the fifth at a glance gives a quick and concrete idea of a chord or an entire scale. If we had to describe the circle of fifths with a graph terminology, we would say that it is a perfect cycle graph with a set N of 12 nodes and a set E of 12 edges, sometimes known as a 12-cycle. This graph has a unique Eulerian cycle, starting

---

[2] http://www.gblot.com/BLOTCMMR2016.zip.

and ending at the same node and crossing all edges exactly once. The chromatic number of the graph is 2, which is the smallest number of colors needed to draw nodes in a way that neighbors don't share the same color.

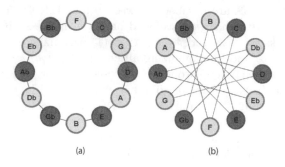

(a)   (b)

Fig. 2. Two graph representations of the circle of fifths drew using Gephi. The two graphs share same properties but node order is diverging (a) 7 semi-tones interval (b) chromatic order.

The circular layout commonly used to draw the graph of fifths employs a very specific order of nodes, with 7 semi-tones differential between 2 successive notes. That is the foundation of the concept. But, we can draw other representations of the same graph. For example, Fig. 2(b) is a chromatic representation of the graph of fifths. With the chromatic order, the circle becomes a regular dodeca-gram, but the graph keeps all its properties. The dodecagram graph (chromatic representation of the graph of fifths) is isomorphic to the cycle graph (classical representation of the graph of fifths Fig. 2(a)).

Switching from a circle to a dodecagram sends to the musician another mental projection of the circle of fifths, based on the division of the chromatic scale. As a matter of fact, the chromatic order (the order of the 12 notes of an octave on a piano) is widely spread in musician minds. Less spread is the *circlar* representation of the octave, which goes by the name of Krenck diagram, pitch constellation, pitch-class space, chromatic circle or clock diagrams. As in McCartin article, this circular representation of the octave bears the name of Ernest Krenek, after the composer has represented scales using polygons [8,15]. This major feature of the research field *Geometry of Music*, addresses issues in either music analysis and music practice: pointing out nuances between playing modes [12], appreciating distance between notes and between harmonics [17,19] or finding symmetric scales [22]. In the Fig. 3, we see the polygon shape of diatonic scales: (a) C scale or Ionian mode and (b) A# scale. (c) and (d) focus on C, A#, Cm and A#m chords. A simple look at the graphs informs that all major chords (c) are triangle with the exact same distances and angles, differing from minor chords triangle shape (d). In this configuration, pitch intervals have specific distance and orientation. With some practice, it can be very simple to retrieve particular connections between pitches, find relevant chords, operate chord inversions or walking on a scale.

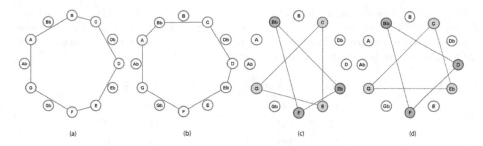

Fig. 3. Krenek diagrams, pitch constellations, pitch-class spaces, chromatic circles or clock diagrams: intervals between pitches are represented as convex polygons. (a) C scale (b) A scale (c) Major chords (d) Minor chords. Note that usual representation of Krenek diagrams start with a C as the top center node. But, we have decided to leave it the way it is realized with Gephi.

Using Gephi and Circular Layout plugin developed by Matt Groeninger[3], we propose to visualize 6 songs structured with the Rhythm network topology. For all tracks we have been through the process explained in Subsect. 2.2. But, in order to go deeper in our discovery, we have divided tracks in several subtracks. This selection is not arbitrary, but is based on MIDI channels: *Lead melody* (LM), *Arpeggio* (ARP) or *Bass* (BASS). Column Channel(s) of Table 1 informs the Midi channels that we have requested to produce each subtrack. The *Lead Melody Main Sequence* (LMS) is a sample of the Lead Melody (column Events in Table 1 presents the number of notes which composed the LMS subtrack). All samples are starting at the beginning of the song. In addition, we have aggregated all subtracks into a specific piece of music entitled *ALL* or *Song*. Each piece of track can be verified downloading the dataset published along with our experiment. Of course, final Graph GEXF is the workable outcome, but one can find the piece of data at every stage of its treatment[4].

With circular layouts, node position is fixed. Therefore distance between nodes does not depend on rhythm. That will be the case in further work 5. But here, we introduce a visual effect giving a clue about the rhythm: the more a connection is thick, the longer is the time interval between notes, and reciprocally.

3.2 Musical Singularity

The second effect we introduce is the *Singularity Threshold* (ST). In the melody pattern context, we use ST in order to bypass some accidental notes. As we mentioned in Sect. 2.2, connections are made between successive notes, occurring in the melody pattern. ST is a count of the minimum occurrence for a connection to be considered. The higher ST is, the less chance an exception to the key

---

[3] https://marketplace.gephi.org/plugin/circular-layout.
[4] http://www.linktodata.

Table 1. Six pieces of music divided in subtracks: Lead Melody (LM), Lead Melody Sample (LMS), Arpeggio (ARP), Bass (BASS) and Song (ALL). Column *Events* is the number of note occurrences. Colum *Channel* is the MIDI channel(s) requested. Last three columns are key-finding results presented in Sect. 3.3

Piece of music	ID	Events	Channel	KS	CBMS	RN
Memory	1LM	21	0	Bb	Bb	Bb
Cats	1LMS	194	0	Bb	Db	Bb
	1ARP	288	1	Dm	Db	Bb
	1ALL	482	0–1	Bb	Db	Bb
Cocaine	2LM	296	2	D	Bm	Bm, D, Em
Eric Clapton	2LMS	12	2	D	Am	D
	2BASS	376	1	Am	Bm	Em
	2ALL	672	1;2	D	Am	Em
Talkin about	3LM	348	3	C	G	D
a revolution	3LMS	16	3	G	G	G,Am
Tracy Chapman	3BASS	250	8	G	C	G
	3ALL	679	3;8	G	G	G
My band	4LM	645	1;4	F#m	A	F#m
D12	4LMS	11	1;4	A	F#m	F#m
	4BASS	238	2	F#m	Bbm	A
	4ALL	883	1;2;4	F#m	A	F#m
Forgot about Dre	5LM	696	2	Gm	Gm	Bb, Gm
Dr DRE	5LMS	6	2	Gm	Gm	Bb, Gm
	5BASS	256	1	Eb	Eb	Bb, Gm
	5ALL	952	1;2	Gm	Eb	Gm
Love is All	6LM	282	3	Bb	Bb	Bb
Roger Glover	6LMS	13	3	Gm	Eb	Cm
	6BASS	382	1	Bb	Bb	Bb
	6ALL	690	1;3	Bb	Bb	Bb

signature could be part of the structure. Figure 4 presents 4 chromatic Rhythm Networks realized from full Lead Melody *Memory* (1LM), where each graph is a sub-graph of the previous. Afterwards in this section we will discuss how to read the graph melodies, but first we wish to give a full account on ST. Obviously, amount of connections is decreasing when ST is rising. That's what we observe in Fig. 4 and Table 2, highlighting the variation of connections depending on ST.

For each subtrack, we have created 6 Rhythm Networks with ST growing from 0 to 5. That makes 6 versions of 24 subtracks, leading to 144 GEXF files. Table 3 presents the number of connections or edges for the 144 graphs. Some melodies

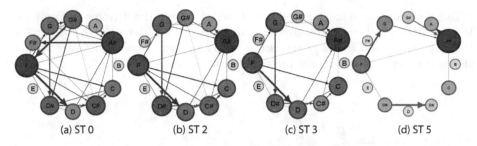

Fig. 4. Representations of the same 1LM rhythm network while Singularity Threshold (ST) is evolving. Number of connections is going down, when ST is rising. With ST = 2, a connection must be present at least twice in 1LM to be considered.

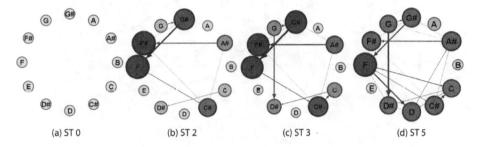

Fig. 5. Singularity networks: representations of melody 1LM, exclusively composed with connections bypassed by ST. We notice an amount of connections inversely proportional to Fig. 4.

Table 2. Evolution of the graph characteristics depending on ST.

ST	0	2	3	5
AVG. Degree	3, 583	2, 667	2, 25	0, 917
AVG path length	1, 55	1, 72	1, 86	1, 96
Density	0, 326	0, 242	0, 205	0, 083
Diameter	3	3	4	4

have much more connections than others. For example, *Memory 1ALL* has 59 connections with ST = 0 and *My Band 4ALL* has 41 connections with ST = 0, respectively density $D_{1ALL} = 0.44$ and $D_{4ALL} = 0.31$, unlike less dense melodies of the dataset: *Cocaine* $D_{2LM} = 0,038$ (ST = 0), $D_{2ALL} = 0,081$ (ST = 0), *Forgot about* Dre $D_{5ALL} = 0.098$. Using ST feature, our goal is to reveal the structure of a melody. It makes no doubt that highly connected melodies density quickly decreases when ST is iteratively incrementing; meanwhile less singular melodies are remaining stable. In Fig. 6 are displayed the 4 variations of *Memory*, with ST on horizontal axis and volume of the set E from the Rhythm Network on the vertical axis. Trend lines give relevant hints: for *1ALL* (curve (d) of Fig. 6), the slope is −7 and for *1LM* (curve (a) of Fig. 6), the slope is −7.5. Trend line slopes from every subtrack are presented in last column of Table 3.

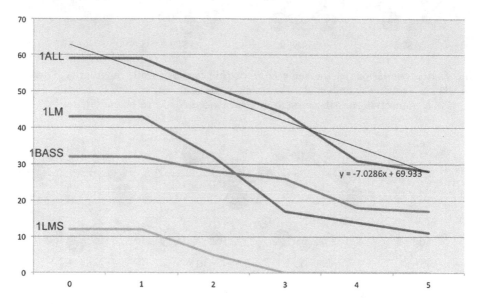

Fig. 6. Progression of the number of connections depending on ST (1LM). 1ALL curve is accompanied with its trend line. We use the slope value to analyze melody structure.

We observe heavy slopes for dense graphs. We rely on these figures to calculate the linear correlation coefficient, measuring the strength of association between density and trend. The value of a linear coefficient ranges between −1 and 1. The greater is the absolute value of a correlation coefficient, the stronger is the relationship. The association (density, trend) has a linear coefficient of −0.89. This leads us to some assertions:

– **Dense melodies have precarious connections between pitches.** In a nutshell, all musical patterns that are not repeated might create precarious connections. This can also be understood with a look to Lead Melody Sample figures: as soon as we reach ST = 2, samples lost all their connections, which means no pattern is repeated more than twice. Moreover, it is interesting to use the feature to draw Singularity Networks (Fig. 5). With an exclusion operator between 2 set E (graph) and E' (subgraph), E" is a graph keeping connections appearing only in one set and displays only singularities. This way we split structure and singularities. Figure 5 presents 4 Singularity Networks composed with the exclusion set of precarious connections. Of course, the 4 representations are inversely proportional to those from Fig. 4. The first representation (a) has no connection (ST is 0). It is very difficult to understand a clear structure for other three networks. In (b) we already notice the presence of accidental nodes with high degrees, not present in what is considered to be the scale (see 1) $A\#$ ($F\#$, $C\#$, $G\#$). In the same graph (b), we notice the very small or null degree for pitches of the $A\#$ scale: C, D, $D\#$, G, A. We also visualize in Fig. 5(d), that the melody is coming closer from Fig. 4(a): scale structure is present and accidental degrees is proportionally decreasing.

- **Withdrawing precarious connections from a melody helps to identify a more robust foundation.** Figure 4 shows evolution of connections when ST is growing. We are able to identify key of a track using a pertinent ST (see next Subsect. 3.3).
- **ST alters the melody structure.** So it is to be used wisely. The last graph from Fig. 4 presents a poorly connected graph where we had lost important information compared to the first 3 representations. We see in the last representation that D is not connected anymore to other notes, when key of the melody appears to be $A\#$, with a D as the major third (again see next Subsect. 3.3). In the same direction, the first graph might be connected far to densely to render reliable visual information. Table 2 gives identical conclusion, with a high density for ST = 0 and a clear gap between third and last column: AVG. degree falling from 2.25 to 0.917 and density falling from 0.205 to 0.0803.

3.3   A Visual Key-Finding Technique

Considering previous conclusions, we experiment key-finding techniques with ST = 2 (except for Melody samples where we kept ST = 0). In this section we give a key-finding method, visualizing circular Rhythm Networks and we compare our results with proven key-finding algorithms (KS and CBMS).

Reckoning the key of a song is a considerable feature of audio applications. Find it by ear is a musical skill sought by producers, remixers, dj, teachers or also musical students. Estimating it with *eyes* may imply interesting support for both machines and humans. Automatic key-finding methods are divided in two families: pitch profile and interval profile. Historically, Krumhansl and Schmuckler have set up a correlation formula between 2 vectors: a key-preference profile and the occurrences of pitches occurring in a piece of music [9]. David Temperley has published a similar pitch profile algorithm [13,14]. Lately, Madsen et al. focused on interval between pitches. Highlighting the importance of connections, this method makes correlation using a matrix of size 12, composed by all possible tone intervals [25]. Our method is following interval profile paradigm, focusing on connections between notes and reducing the influence of note occurrences. The major difference is that we do not use *profiles*, but visual representations.

It is important to keep in mind that we do not plan to publish a new key-finding algorithm, able to retrieve information from polyphonic audio files. We work on MIDI file and do not worry about signal processing parts. Moreover,

Table 3. Progression of the number of connections depending on ST (all pieces of music). Last column is the slope of the trend line. In this Sect. 3.2 we found a correlation between slope and density.

ST	0	1	2	3	4	5	Trend slope
1LM	43	43	32	17	14	11	−7.5
1LMS	12	12	5	0	0	0	−2.9
1ARP	32	32	28	26	18	17	−3.4
1ALL	59	59	51	44	31	28	−7
2LM	5	5	3	3	3	3	−0.5
2LMS	2	2	0	0	0	0	−0.5
2BASS	10	10	10	10	9	9	−0.2
2ALL	11	11	11	11	10	10	−0.2
3LM	21	21	19	16	14	11	−2.1
3LMS	7	7	2	0	0	0	−1.7
3BASS	8	8	6	6	6	6	−0.5
3ALL	26	26	22	20	17	16	−2.3
4LM	33	33	23	16	14	13	−4.7
4LMS	9	9	1	0	0	0	−2.1
4BASS	19	19	11	10	10	10	−2.1
4ALL	41	41	32	23	21	20	−5
5LM	6	6	6	6	6	6	0
5LMS	5	5	0	0	0	0	−1.1
5BASS	8	8	8	8	8	8	0
5ALL	13	13	13	13	13	13	0
6LM	28	28	21	15	13	12	−3.7
6LMS	8	8	1	0	0	0	−1.9
6BASS	20	20	18	14	12	11	−2.1
6ALL	32	32	30	26	25	19	−2.6

we are aware that many techniques have optimized pitch profile methods [10,11] and interval profile methods [23]. But, here we merely give a visual exercise intended to give clues about the song structure and the node connections. But, that is implying a concrete validation of our technique. In our case, key-finding get visual. For most of the melodies, it can be observed almost instantly, with 3 basic rules: (1) selecting most connected nodes, (2) finding the polygon shape and (3) Tie-breaking.

STEP 1: Selecting most connected nodes: we introduce 2 visual effects to facilitate selection, which are node size and color. Gephi can change size and color of nodes depending on the topology. Here, our objective is to show that important notes are highly connected nodes. As a consequence, we choose to

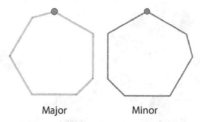

Fig. 7. Major and minor scales convex polygons: these two shapes are used in our visual key-finding technique (Color figure online).

make colors and sizes fluctuating depending on the degree of the node. Color goes from light yellow to dark blue, and size goes from small to bigger. A melody can have more or less connected nodes, while a scale is always composed with 7 distinct notes. If the set of connected nodes is greater than 7, we simply choose the 7 biggest. If lesser than 7, see next step. In some cases, there are not enough nodes to clearly retrieve a scale. Step 3, can help, but some marginal case can still be ambiguous (see step 3).

STEP 2: Among major and minor scales, finding which polygon shape is fitting the best: visualizing the 2 usual shapes major and minor (Fig. 7), and rotating it around the melody graph until it fits. At first, it might be tricky, as the 2 shapes are not perfectly printed in mind. Then starting with this, one can count intervals of major scales (TTSTTTS) and minor scales (TSTTSTT). This might help brain to print shapes. The first Rhythm Network of Fig. 8 (top left) represents the first 21 notes of *Memory* (Lead Melody sample). Juxtaposing the Major scale polygon, while crossing all connected notes must be done with $A\#$ as a starting note. But Gm, the enharmonic equivalent is fitting the graph in the same way. Then, up to this point two answers are possible: $A\#$ and Gm.

STEP 3: Breaking eventual ties: in order to discriminate $A\#$ and Gm, we choose the most connected node. Then, following our visual key-finding method, one should answer that the key of the lead melody sample Memory is $A\#$. If at step 2, the low density of the graph leads to more than 2 possibilities, this last tie-breaking step should end up with a solution. For the bass channel of *Takin about a revolution*, possible keys are G, Em, C, but we select key G. It is the same process for the full song *Cocaine*, where we had to tie-break E and Am. We have 2 examples where we were not able to decide. *Cocaine* lead melody pattern only connects 3 nodes, and each node has the same degree. Same conflict for *Forgot about Dre*, with a Lead melody in Gm or $A\#$.

We have experimented our method through the 24 graphs and then compare our results with other proven key-finding techniques. We used the Melisma Music Analyzer to run KS and CBMS algorithms[5]. Before going further, we wish to point out that the two techniques KS and CBMS do not retrieve always the same results. As a matter of fact, these algorithms have to deal with ambiguous compositions as well. KS and CBMS have retrieved the same answer with a

---

[5] http://www.link.cs.cmu.edu/melisma/.

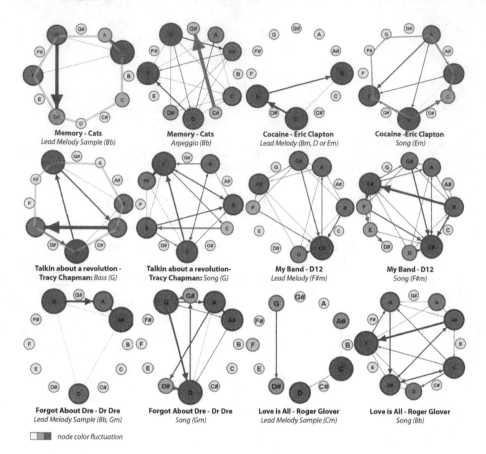

Fig. 8. A selection of circular representations of melodies rendered as Rhythm Networks. ST is 2 excepted for LMS (ST = 0). Node shape and color varies depending on its degree. Most connected nodes are big and filled with dark blue. For some cases, we juxtapose major or minor scale polygon (Color figure online).

ratio of 33%. Our method retrieves either KS or CBMS result with a ratio of 70%. This is a conclusive step of our experiment, where we highlight the fact that connections between pitches render the melody structure. Once Rhythm Network is created with the relevant configuration, a simple visual analysis of the melody agrees with one the proven key-finding techniques in more than 2 of 3 cases.

But it does not imply that the last third is flawed. We even think that these are pertinent results. Key-finding methods are tricky because it faces several level of complexity: scale could change anytime during the song, melody could be simple and present poor information to work on, musicians and composers might play out of a scale or take upon themself the fact they play or write accidental notes. However, a scale is a scale for a reason, then whatever happens, if a musician does not work on the scale or if he thinks he is working on a scale but making accidentals, the resulting melody will inevitably have a scale or will come close from an existing scale. Considering the 6 melodies where we do not agree with proven techniques, our method is the one having less accidental note (first three column of Table 4). To make last comments, we see in Table 4 that for most of the results all 3 methods have close information in terms of composition of scales. Moreover, we notice conflicts for these 6 examples, as almost all have different results for the 3 techniques. The bassline of Forgot about Dre, is the only example where KS and CBMS return same results (last column of Table 4).

Table 4. For these 6 examples, our visual key-finding technique does not share the same answer with at least one proven algorithm. In first three columns we give what is considered as accidental notes, by the given results (Table 1). The two following columns (VS) show notes present in our result scales, but not ssin the proven technique, in a sense that we can understand how close it is. Last column tells if KS and CBMS did agree.

	KS acc.	CBMS acc.	RN acc.	KS vs RN	KS vs RN	PTA
1ARP	D#, G#, C#	D, G, A	C#, G#	A#, D#	D, G, A	No
2BASS		C		F#	C#	No
2ALL	C			C#	F#	No
3LM	C, F#			F#, C#	C#	No
4BASS	A#	A#	A#		A, B, D, E	No
5BASS	A	A	G#	Eb, A or A		Yes
6LMS				Ab		No

Until this point, we have studied a *Pitch Interval-based* method to visualize melody structures. We have explored the versatility of dense melodies and experimented techniques to separate singular pieces from structural patterns. The visual key-finding technique given in last Sect. 5 validates the Rhythm Network use in melodic context.

4   Toward a New Approach of Rhythm Representation

4.1   ForceAtlas2: A Representation Between Springs and Charged Particles

Rhythm Network is an oriented and weighted graph. In the next step, we visualize melodies using Force-directed layouts. Force directed algorithms are dedicated to network spacialization. The principle is to place nodes depending on a metric, in a two-dimensional or three-dimensional space. The designation itself is giving the clue: the position of a node is directed by the force of its connections. More specifically, an Attraction-Repulsion coefficient is calculated for each connected pair of nodes. Then, it is based on the graph structure and it doesnt need contextual knowledge. Therefore, this visual analysis is popular among scientists: social [16], political [1] and computer indeed [7]. Using such an algo-rithm we visualize nodes proximity and remoteness. Similar techniques are used to identify clusters. In our context, force-directed gives rhythm clues (in addi-tion to melody structure and pitches connectivity detailed in previous section). As far as we know, no instance of Force-directed Melody representation exists in scientific literature, neither in Graph visualization or Music representation communities. That's what we are going through now; its original but useful.

We use ForceAtlas2 algorithm for the rest of the experiment. The choice of this algorithm was natural, as it is scale-free (from 10 to 10000 nodes) and it is designed for Gephi Software. The model simulate a physical system: it uses repulsion formula of electrically charged particles and the attraction formula of springs. Moreover, this feature has plenty of criterion, that we can adjust in Gephi. We will go through some (gravity, scaling, edge weight, dissuade hubs), but for an overall understanding please refer to the article of the authors [18].

4.2 Attraction - Repulsion Adjustments

ForceAtlas2 model is computing edges weight. To be more precise, weight influ-ence is an input coefficient that one can set from 0 to 1, where 0 is the absence of influence and 1 a full influence. In our experiment, if we set this value to 0, rhythm will have no impact on the representation. Sliding the value toward 1, and we will see rhythm impact increasing. Here, we set edge weight influence to 1 for the whole experiment. Which means full influence, as we focus on rhythm.

But yet, we encountered an issue related with the nature of our metric. Unlike the spring model which brings together nodes with high connections, our rhythm metric should work the opposite.

In our context, proximity means a small amount of time between nodes. Then we had to adapt the original formula.

Attraction

$$F_a(n_i, n_j) = \frac{k_l}{d(n_i, n_j)} \tag{1}$$

Repulsion

$$F_r(n_i, n_j) = \frac{k_r \times d(n_i, n_j) \times deg(n_i + 1) \times deg(n_j + 1)}{k_t} \tag{2}$$

4.3 Rhythm

In ForceAtlas2 we are still working with a circle representation, even if it does not look like a circle on the first sight. Then highly connected nodes have a cen-tral position, unlike less connected nodes which tends to appears like satellites. The model works as if a central force is pulling down all major nodes, in addi-tion to the mutual attraction-repulsion force explain earlier. With small graphs,

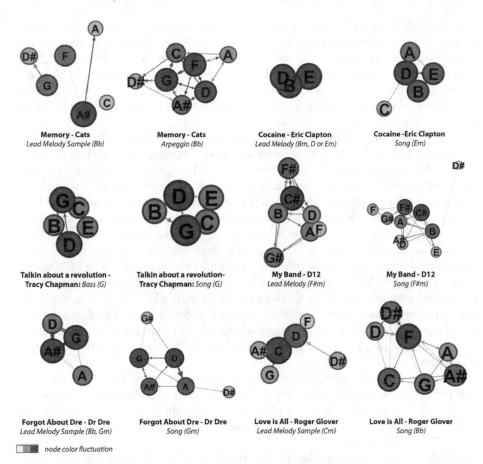

Fig. 9. Some melodies representation realized using *ForeceAtlas2* drawing technique. Gravity = 1, Weight influence = 1, Singularity threshold = 2 (excepted for samples where ST = 0).

the central point tend to be unique. Bigger graphs have several central points, corresponding to clusters centers. In this experiment, as we work on a 12-nodes graphs, where some nodes are not considered, we have only one center.

On this basis, gravity is a leading criteria which can be configured. We set it to 1. This value represent a low gravity. But it is still enough to have a relevant impact on the representation. Both absence of gravity or omnipresence of gravity are altering the visual considerations of connections and clustering. These misconfiguration will lead to either an exploded or a shrink representation. Depending of the context (metrics, number of nodes and connections), we have to find the ideal balance.

The first benefit is clearing representation, putting aside nodes that are not connected. Unlike the fixed representation of pitch constellation, ForeceAtlas2 is getting rid of unnecessary details. Unplugged nodes does not have enough forces to counteract the force of the gravity. As a consequence, these nodes are moving away very quickly toward the infinite space. For Memory we see just the sequence and of the song and of the scale. Then we have the same issues of Pitch Constellations: some melodies don't have enough nodes to understand the scale, some others have to much nodes. But, here we are not focusing on scale finding techniques, even is it is still possible to have visual information about it, as we will see.

With the same philosophy, this technique gives central position to highly connected nodes. As we have seen in the first sections, the Rhythm Network is focusing on connectivity. That gives a visual convention: important nodes are central. Following this convention, we can find the key of the melody. A quick look is enough. For some cases it is very clear, where for some we need the support of size and colors 9. In addition to key, ForceAtlas2 helps us to identified central chords. For the chord topology, it works the same as pitch constellations. In addition, it places these chords on a scale from central to peripheral, giving a hierarchical decomposition of triangles. For example, arpeggio piece of Memory shows a recurrent DFG chord, but it also shows that this central chord tends to be colored with an A, a A#, a C, and sometimes with a D#. Moreover, we see to which patterns these nodes are connected. A# is forming an A#DG chord and sometimes a A#GD#. Cocaine Lead melody has just one central chord, that we also find in the overall song, but with two additional nodes. The whole is giving 3 triangles.

The example of Cocaine overall song is interesting, because we see that the two peripheral nodes have not the same importance. A is close from its triangle ADE and it is even touching D, where C is far from it. It is the case for *My Band* Lead melody, *Forgot about Dre* Lead Melody Sample and song and *Love is All* That's Rhythm.

With a quick sight, we identify the topology of the rhythm. Even rhythms tend to look like circles. For example, *Talkin about a revolution* is a relevant example, where notes are played regularly on an eighth-note basis. Then, our representation is close from a regular circle. Cocaine has a similar behavior. The only difference is that an irregularity appends, with a C connected to the D. Other rhythms are much more irregular. Rhythm structure impacts people behaviors and emotions. An even rhythm tends to bring monotonousness, where uneven rhythms bring another energy and make people dancing or/and wondering. It is the case of *My Band*, *Forgot about Dre*, *Memory* and *Love is All*.

5   Conclusion

Visual representation of music is very important in musician every day life. Artists, musicians, remixers, producers, learners or even djs rely on visual representations of pieces of music. The score is a widespread and interoperable representation in western music. Here we give an original approach based on graph theory and graph visualization. Actually we tend to serve both fields of research: music representation and graph visualization.

On the first axis, we present a model for pieces of music. Based on the Rhythm Network it aggregates patterns and divided those structural aspects in two parts: structural patterns and singular patterns. A major feature here is the flexibility, where we can explore structure but we never lose singular characteristics, that usually make a song soul. On this basis, we propose two representations: the first one is Pitch constellation, where nodes are fixed and geometry is a proxy of musicality, the second one is ForeAtlas2, a Force-directed algorithm, where notes are placed depending on the overall rhythm of the song. Here we get a visual rhythm.

On the second axis, we give our Rhythm Network two representations, that might be used in other contexts such as E-learning, Digital collections or also Road Traffic management. We validate the efficiency of Rhythm Network at a new step: we can get rid of popularity (number of time an event occurred, here the number of time that the pitch is used in a sequence), we still have a relevant clue of the structure. In addition, we bring harmony and rhythm to other contexts. Learning, collecting and driving are actions that implies these two phenomenon: rhythm and harmony. Now, our next step is to work with our presented techniques in those contexts.

Because giving visual proof is not reliable enough, we also analyzed our work on a structural basis (average degree, density, trend). We were unable to reproduce some visual effects in the context of a written presentation. We encourage to discover all interactive features powered by Gephi, using GEXF melodies published along with our experiment: select pitch neighbors, have a walk on melodic paths or also enjoy layout personalization. Going further, Rhythm Network might be applicable to various music analysis and practices: music information retrieval, interactive learning, music recommendation tools, augmented musical instruments, auditory perception and cognition, music interface design, production and composition tools or also intelligent music tutoring systems.

References

1. Adamic, L., Glance, N.: The political blogosphere and the 2004 US election: divided they blog. In: Proceedings of the 3rd International workshop on Link discovery, pp. 36–43 (2005)
2. Association, T.I.M.: Standard midi-file format spec. $1(1)$ (2003)
3. Bigo, L., Andreatta, M., Giavitto, J.-L., Michel, O., Spicher, A.: Computation and visualization of musical structures in chord-based simplicial complexes. In: Yust, J., Wild, J., Burgoyne, J.A. (eds.) MCM 2013. LNCS (LNAI), vol. 7937, pp. 38–51. Springer, Heidelberg (2013). doi:10.1007/978-3-642-39357-0_3
4. Blot, G., Fouchal, H., Rousseaux, F., Saurel, P.: An experimentation of vanets for traffic management. In: IEEE International Conference on Communications. IEEE, Kuala Lumpur, Malaysia, May 2016
5. Blot, G., Rousseaux, F., Saurel, P.: Pattern discovery in e-learning courses: a time based approach. In: CODIT14 2nd International Conference on Control, Decision and Information Technologies. IEEE, Metz, France, November 2014

6. Blot, G., Saurel, P., Rousseaux, F.: Recommender engines under the influence of popularity. In: Benyoucef, M., Weiss, M., Mili, H. (eds.) MCETECH 2015. LNBIP, vol. 209, pp. 138–152. Springer, Cham (2015). doi:10.1007/978-3-319-17957-5_9

7. Boitmanis, K., Brandes, U., Pich, C.: Visualizing internet evolution on the autonomous systems level. In: Hong, S.-H., Nishizeki, T., Quan, W. (eds.) GD 2007. LNCS, vol. 4875, pp. 365–376. Springer, Heidelberg (2008). doi:10.1007/978-3-540-77537-9_36. http://dl.acm.org/citation.cfm?id=1784907.1784945

8. McCartin, B.J.: Prelude to musical geometry (1998)

9. Krumhansl, C.L.: A key-finding algorithm based on tonal hierarchies. Oxford University Press, New York (1990)

10. Ching-Hua, C., Chew, S.E.: Polyphonic audio key finding using the spiral array ceg algorithm. In: ICME, pp. 21–24. IEE, July 2005

11. Craig, S.: Visual hierarchical key analysis. In: Computers in Entertainment (CIE) - Theoretical and Practical Computer Applications in Entertainment, vol. 3, pp. 1–19. ACM, New York, NY, USA, October 2005

12. David, R.: Geometry and harmony. In: 8th Annual international conference of bridges: Mathematical Connections in Art, Music, and Science, pp. 67–72. Alberta, August 2005

13. David, T.: The Cognition of Basic Musical Structures. MIT Press, Cambridge (2001). p. 404

14. Temperley, D.: A Bayesian approach to key-finding. In: Anagnostopoulou, C., Ferrand, M., Smaill, A. (eds.) ICMAI 2002. LNCS (LNAI), vol. 2445, pp. 195–206. Springer, Heidelberg (2002). doi:10.1007/3-540-45722-4_18

15. Ernest, K.: Uber neue Musik (1937)

16. Fowler, J.H., Christakis, N.A.: Dynamic spread of happiness in a large social network: longitudinal analysis over 20 years in the framingham heart study (September 2008)

17. Fred, L.: Tonal Pitch Space. Oxford University Press, Oxford (2001)

18. Jacomy, M., Venturini, T., Heymann, S., Bastian, M.: Forceatlas2, a continuous graph layout algorithm for handy network visualization designed for the gephi software, June 2014

19. Burgoyne, J.A., Saul, L.K.: Visualization of low dimensional structure in tonal pitch space. In: Proceedings of the 2005 International Computer Music Conference. Barcelona, Spain (September 2005)

20. Rockwell, J.: Birdcage flights: a perspective on inter-cardinality voice leading (2009)

21. Granovetter, M.S.: The strength of weak ties (1973)

22. Masaya, Y.: Masaya Music, New York, USA, May 2006

23. Matthias, R., Thomas, R., Pierre, H.: Improvements of symbolic key finding methods. In: International Computer Music Conference (2008)

24. 1.2draft Primer, G.: Gexf working group (March 2012)

25. Soren Tjagvad, M., Gerhald, W.: Key-finding with interval profiles. In: International Computer Music Conference, August 2007

26. Toussaint, G.: Computational geometric aspects of rhythm, melody, and voice-leading. Comput. Geom. Theory Appl. **43**(1), 2–22 (2010)

27. Tzanetakis, G., Benning, M.S., Ness, S.R., Minifie, D., Livingston, N.: Assistive music browsing using self-organizing maps. In: Proceedings of the 2nd International Conference on Pervasive Technologies Related to Assistive Environments, pp. 3:1–3:7. PETRA 2009, NY, USA. ACM, New York (2009)

28. Wai Man, S., Wonga, M.H.: A graph-theoretical approach for pattern matching in post-tonal music analysis (2006)

Music Generation with Relation Join

Xiuyan Ni, Ligon Liu, and Robert Haralick[(✉)]

Computer Science Department, The Graduate Center,
City University of New York, New York, NY 10016, USA
{xni2,lliu1}@gradcenter.cuny.edu, rharalick@gc.cuny.edu
http://gc.cuny.edu/Home

Abstract. Given a data set taken over a population, the question of how can we construct possible explanatory models for the interactions and dependencies in the population is a discovery question. Projection and Relation Join is a way of addressing this question in a non-deterministic context with mathematical relations. In this paper, we apply projection and relation join to music harmonic sequences to generate new sequences in a given composer or genre style. Instead of first learning the patterns, and then making replications as early music generation work did, we introduce a completely new data driven methodology to generate music. Then we discuss exploring the difference between the original music and synthetic music sequences using information theory based techniques.

Keywords: Music generation · Projection · Relation join

1 Introduction

Could a computer compose music sequences that are indistinguishable from the work of human composers to average human listeners? Different models have been applied by researchers trying to answer this question.

Early work in music generation use a pattern matching process to identify different styles of music. The pattern matching process first designs a pattern matcher to locate the patterns inherent in the input music corpus, stores the patterns in a dictionary, and then makes replications according to the patterns [12]. Cope's Experiments in Musical Intelligence incorporates the idea of recombinancy. He breaks music pieces into small segments and then recombines them under certain music constraints to generate new music in a given style. The music constraints are learned using an augmented transition network (ATN). ATN is a type of graph theoretic structure widely used in Natural Language Processing to parse complex natural language and generate new sentences [4,20]. The pattern matching algorithm used by Cope matches intervals instead of pitch, that is, (C, E, G) can be matched to $(D, F\#, A)$, or any of the major triads [4]. Manaris et al. [10] employ genetic programming to music generation, which uses artificial music critics as fitness functions [9,13]. Schulze and Van der Merwe use Markov Chains and Hidden Markov Models (HMM) [15] to generate music. They use a certain style of music as training data, then apply the LearnPSA algorithm [14]

© Springer International Publishing AG 2017
M. Aramaki et al. (Eds.): CMMR 2016, LNCS 10525, pp. 41–64, 2017.
DOI: 10.1007/978-3-319-67738-5_3

to produce a prediction suffix tree to find all strings with a statistical significance. The relation between a hidden and an observed sequence is then modeled by an HMM. After the whole learning process, they sample from the distributions learned to generate new music sequences in the same style as the training data [15]. An HMM is also used to classify folk music from different countries [3]. These sampling methods, however, have drawbacks that they may get stuck in local optimal.

Some other music generation methods do not use music pieces as input. They generate music based on certain rules either from music theory, or principles from artificial intelligence algorithms. Ebcioglu [5] codes music rules in certain styles in a formal grammar to generate a specific style of music, which means musical knowledge related to specific style is needed to make new music. Al-Rifaie [1] applies Stochastic Diffusion Search (SDS), a swarm intelligence algorithm, to new music generation. This method generates music based on input plain text and the interaction between the algorithm and its agents. It maps each letter or pair of letters in a sentence to the MIDI number of a music note, and then calculates the pitch, the note duration and the volume of music notes based on parameters of SDS. The output music does not have any specific style.

In general, the previous music generation methods either depend on music knowledge, or use machine learning techniques that have to estimate the probability of a music sequence. In the second case, they have to learn the probability of one element given a previous number of elements in a sequence. In this paper, we use a completely different methodology to generate music specific to a certain composer or genre. We break each piece in our music corpus into overlapping small segments and use relation join to generate synthetic musical sequences. The relation join replaces the probabilities in methods like Markov Chains, and HMMs.

Consider the Markov Chain method as an example to compare a probability based method to our method. A first order Markov Chain assumes that $P(x_t|x_{t-1}, \ldots, x_1) = P(x_t|x_{t-1})$, where $<x_1, x_2, \ldots, x_t>$ is a sequence of states (a state can be a chord or a note). Changes in state are called transitions. The Markov model estimates those probabilities of transitions given a music corpus and then generates music sequences based on the probabilities by linking up the transitions. While in our method, we first break the music sequences into small segments of given length and number of overlapping notes (chords). Then we reconstruct music sequences using the set of segments.

We call each sequence or segment of musical chords a tuple (See Definition 5). For example, we have a tuple sequence $<x_1, x_2, \ldots, x_t>$, and we can set the tuple length of each segment to 4 consecutive chords, and overlapping number to 2. We first break the tuple sequence into a set of tuples $\{<x_1, x_2, x_3, x_4>, <x_2, x_3, x_4, x_5>, <x_3, x_4, x_5, x_6>, <x_5, x_6, x_7, x_8>, \ldots\}$. If we repeat the first step for all sequences, we will get a dataset that contains all possible 4-tuples with overlap of 2 for a given music corpus which contains sequences of chords. Then we generate a chord sequence by randomly selecting one 4-tuple from the set that contains all 4-tuples from the music corpus, then look at the last two chords of the selected tuple, and select another 4-tuple from the subset that contains all 4-tuples starting with the last two chords from previous 4-tuple until we reach a certain length. If the process gets stuck because there is no possible consistent selection, the process backtracks in a depth first tree search manner.

Thus, in our method, there is no need to estimate probabilities. For any 4-tuple (not the first or the last) in a generated sequence, the 4-tuple in the generated sequence is consistent with the 4-tuple that precedes it and that follows it in the generated music sequence. Our music generation method is like a solution to a constraint satisfaction problem [8]. It can therefore be posed in a rule-based mode as well.

Our method can be used without musical knowledge of different styles, and we do not need to learn music theoretic patterns or parameters from input music pieces either. We use the idea of recombination (first breaking the input music into small segments, and then recombine them to generate new music sequences), but we do not have to estimate the probabilities. The idea of this method is that the progressions inherent in music sequences carry the composer patterns themselves.

We then discuss a technique to distinguish between original music and synthetic music. We use the information based distance based on mutual information and entropy of random variables, and visualize the results the auto similarity function for both original and synthetic music sequences.

We describe our generation method in detail in Sect. 2. Section 3 will demonstrate how this method is applied to music generation. Several experiments are introduced in Sect. 4. Section 5 concludes our current work and discusses our future work which will apply an information based distance to compare original music and synthetic music.

2   Definitions

In order to introduce the procedure of applying relation join to music sequences, we formally define the concepts used in this section [6].

Definition 1. *Let* $X_1, \ldots, X_N$ *be the* N *variables associated with a relation. Let* L_n *be the set of possible values variable* X_n *can take. Let* R *be a data set or knowledge constraint relation. Then*

$$R \subseteq_{i=1}^{N} L_i$$

Example 1. When $N = 2$, and $L_1 = \{a, b\}$, and $L_2 = \{c, d, e\}$, R will be a subset of $_{i=1}^{N} L_i = \{(a, c), (a, d), (a, e), (b, c), (b, d), (b, e)\}$.

We will be working with many relations associated with different and overlapping variable sets and therefore over different domains. For this purpose we will carry an index set along with each relation. The index set indexes the variables associated with the relation. An index set is a totally ordered set.

Definition 2. $I = \{i_1, \ldots, i_K\}$ *is an index set if and only if* $i_1 < i_2 < \cdots < i_K$.

Next we need to define Cartesian product sets with respect to an index set.

Definition 3. *If* $I = \{i_1, \ldots, i_K\}$ *is an index set, we define Cartesian product:*

$$_{i \in I} L_i = {}^{K}_{k=1} L_{i_k} = L_{i_1} \times L_{i_2} \times \ldots \times L_{i_K}$$

The definition tells us that the order in which we take the Cartesian product $_{i \in I} L_i$ is precisely the order of the indexes in I.

For a natural number N, we use the convention that $[N] = \{1, \ldots, N\}$ and $|A|$ designates the number of elements in the set A.

Now we can define the indexed relation as a pair consisting of an index set of a relation and a relation.

Definition 4. *If* I *is an index set with* $|I| = N$ *and* $R \subseteq_{i \in I} L_i$, *then we say* (I, R) *is an indexed* $N - ary$ *relation on the range sets indexed by* I. *We also say that* (I, R) *has dimension* N. *We take the range sets to be fixed. So to save writing, anytime we have an indexed relation* (I, R), *we assume that* $R \subseteq_{i \in I} L_i$, *the sets* L_i, $i \in I$, *being the fixed range sets.*

Example 2. We continue the example in Example 1 to illustrate this definition. Let $I = \{7, 9\}$, the L_1 and L_2 are the same as in Example 1. We know that R is a subset of $^{N}_{i=1} L_i = \{(a, c), (a, d), (a, e), (b, c), (b, d), (b, e)\}$. Let $R = \{(a, c), (a, d), (a, e), (b, c)\}$, then (I, R) will be an indexed relation as in Table 1.

Another important concept we need before we define projection and relation join is tuple and tuple length.

Definition 5. *A tuple is a finite ordered list of elements. An n-tuple is a sequence (or ordered list) of n elements, where n is a non-negative integer. We call n the length of the n-tuple.*

Table 1. Indexed relation (I, R) where $I = \{7, 9\}$ and $R = \{(a, c), (a, d), (a, e), (b, c)\}$. The $1, 2, 3, 4$ are indexes for the row in which the tuple appears. We will make use of the row index to help illustrate how relation join works.

(I, R)
$I = \{7, 9\}$
1   (a, c)
2   (a, d)
3   (a, e)
4   (b, c)

We will be needing to define one relation in terms of another. For this purpose, we will need a function that relates the indexes associated with one relation to that of another. We call this function the index function.

Definition 6. *Let J and M be index sets with*

- $J = \{j_1, \ldots, j_{|J|}\}$
- $M = \{m_1, \ldots, m_{|M|}\}$
- $J \subset M$

The index function $f_{JM} : [|J|] \to [|M|]$ is defined by $f_{JM}(p) = q$ where $m_q = j_p$. The index function f_{JM} operates on the place p of an index from the smaller index set and specifies where – place q – in the larger index set that the index j_p can be found; thus $m_q = j_p$. To make this concrete consider the following example. Let I, J and M be index sets with $I \subseteq J \subseteq M$, where $I = \{i_1, i_2\} = \{5, 8\}$, $J = \{j_1, j_2, j_3, j_4\} = \{2, 5, 8, 9\}$ and $M = \{m_1, m_2, m_3, m_4, m_5, m_6\} = \{2, 4, 5, 6, 7, 8, 9\}$. Then, f_{IJ}, f_{JM}, and f_{IM} are defined as in Table 2. The first value in I is i_1. It has the value 5. The place where 5 occurs in the J is the second place. Therefore, $f_{IJ}(1) = 2$, and $j_{f_{IJ}(1)} = 5$. The place where 5 occurs in M is the third place. Therefore, $f_{IM}(1) = 3$ and $m_{f_{IM}(1)} = 5$.

Table 2. Shows example index sets and the index functions that relate one set to another.

p	i_p	$f_{IJ}(p)$	$j_{f_{IJ}(p)}$
1	5	2	5
2	8	3	8

p	j_p	$f_{JM}(p)$	$m_{f_{JM}(p)}$
1	2	1	2
2	5	3	5
3	8	6	8
4	9	7	9

p	i_p	$f_{IM}(p)$	$m_{f_{IM}(p)}$
1	5	3	5
2	8	6	8

Next we need the concept of projection since it is used in the definition of relation join. If (J, R) is an indexed relation and $I \subseteq J$, the projection of (J, R) onto the ranges sets indexed by I is the indexed set (I, S) where a tuple $(x_1, \ldots, x_{|I|})$ is in S whenever for some $|J|$-tuple $(a_1, \ldots, a_{|J|})$ of R, x_i is the value of that component of $(a_1, \ldots, a_{|J|})$ in place $f_{IJ}(i)$.

Definition 7. *Let I and J be index sets with $I \subseteq J$. The projection operator projecting a relation on the range sets indexed by J onto the range sets indexed by I is defined by $\pi_I(J, R) = (I, S)$ where*

$$S = \{(x_1, \ldots, x_I) \in_{i \in I} L_i \mid \exists (a_1, \ldots, a_{|J|}) \in R, a_{f_{IJ}(i)} = x_i, i \in I\}$$

That is,

$$\pi_I(J, (a_1, \ldots, a_{|J|})) = (I, (a_{f_{IJ}(1)}, \ldots, a_{f_{IJ}(|I|)}))$$

If $I \cap J^c \neq \emptyset$, then $\pi_I(J, R) = \emptyset$.
The operation of projection is overloaded, and if $R \subseteq_{n=1}^{N} L_n$ and $I \subseteq \{1, \ldots, N\}$, we define

$$\pi_I(R) = \pi_I(\{1, \ldots, N\}, R)$$

Our relation join can be thought of as the equijoin or natural join operation in the data base world.

Example 3. Use the example in Example 2, and let $I' = \{7\}, \pi_I(R)$ will be as in Table 3.

Table 3. Projection of (I, R) where $I = \{7, 9\}$ and $R = \{(a, c), (a, d), (a, e), (b, c)\}$ on $I' = \{7\}$.

$\pi_I(R)$
$I' = \{7\}$
1   a
2   b

Definition 8. *Let (I, R) and (J, S) be indexed relations, let $K = I \cup J$ and L_k be the range set for variable $k \in K$. Then the relation join of (I, R) and (J, S) is denoted by $(I, R) \otimes (J, S)$, and is defined by*

$$(I, R) \otimes (J, S) = \{t \in_{k \in K} L_k \mid \pi_I(K, t) \in (I, R) \text{ and } \pi_J(K, t) \in (J, R)\}$$

An example of relation join is given in Example 4.

Example 4. Shows an example for relation join. If we have two indexed relations, (I, R) and (J, S) as in Table 4, the relation join for the two relations will be as in Table 5.

Table 4. Values for indexed relation (I, R) and (J, S)

(I, R)	(J, S)
$I = \{1, 4, 7, 9\}$	$J - \{2, 4, 6, 7\}$
1 (a, b, e, d)	1 (e, e, a, d)
2 (b, d, e, a)	2 (d, c, b, a)
3 (e, c, a, b)	3 (a, d, b, e)
4 (c, e, d, a)	4 (b, b, c, e)

Definition 9. *Let (I, R) be an indexed relation with $R \subseteq_{i \in I} L_i$. Let $J \subseteq I$ and $a \in_{j \in J} L_j$. Then the restriction of (I, R) to (J, a) is denoted by $(I, R)|_{(J,a)}$ and is defined by*

$$(I, R)|_{(J,a)} = (I, \{r \in R \mid \pi_J(I, r) = (J, a)\})$$

Example 5. If we have an indexed relation (I, R), where $I = \{1, 2\}, R = \{(1, m), (1, n), (2, m), (3, p), (4, q), (5, p)\}, J = \{2\}$, and $a = m, (I, R)|_{(J,a)} = \{(1, m), (2, m)\}$. □

Table 5. Shows the relation join results of indexed relation (I, R) and (J, S). The first column of K indicates which row rows are joined from Table 4. The first number is the row number of the relation (I, R) and the second number is the row number of the relation (J, S). For example, $(1, 4)$ means the first row of (I, R) and the fourth row of (J, S) can be joined. However, the first row of (I, R) and the first row of (J, S) can not be joined because for index 4 of I, the component of the tuple on the first row of (I, R) has the value b. But for index 4 of J, the component on the first row of (J, S) has the value e.

	$(K, T) = (I, R) \otimes (J, S)$
	1, 2, 4, 6, 7, 9
$(1, 4)$	(a, b, b, c, e, d)
$(2, 3)$	(b, a, d, b, e, a)
$(3, 2)$	(e, d, c, b, a, b)
$(4, 1)$	(c, e, e, a, d, a)

Definition 10. *Let (K, R) be an indexed relation and $\{I, J, M\}$ a non-trivial partition of K. We say conditioned on M, I has no influence on J if and only if*

$$\sqcup_{(M,c)\in \pi_M(K,R)} \pi_I((K, R)|_{(M,c)}) \otimes (M, c) \otimes \pi_J((K, R)|_{(M,c)}) \subseteq (K, R)$$

If $\{I, J\}$ constitutes a partition of K, then we say I has no influence on J if and only if

$$\pi_I(K, R) \otimes \pi_J(K, R) \subseteq (K, R)$$

$$(I, R) \otimes (J, S) = \bigcup_{(M,c)\in \pi_M(I,R)\cap\pi_M(J,S)} \pi_{I-M}(I, R)|_{(M,c)} \otimes (M, c) \otimes \pi_{J-M}(J, S)|_{(M,c)}$$

(I, R)		(J, S)		$(I, R) \otimes (J, S)$			
1 2		**2 3**		**1 2 3**			
1 a		a α		1 a α	I	$=$	$\{1, 2\}$
1 b		a β		1 a β	J	$=$	$\{2, 3\}$
2 a		a γ		1 a γ	M	$= I \cap J =$	$\{2\}$
3 c		b α		2 a α	$I - M$	$=$	$\{1\}$
4 b		b β		2 a β	$J - M$	$=$	$\{3\}$
5 d		b δ		2 a γ	$\pi_2(I, R)$	$=$	$\{a, b, c, d\}$
		c ϵ		1 b α	$\pi_2(J, S)$	$=$	$\{a, b, c, e\}$
		c λ		1 b β	$\pi_2(I, R) \cap \pi_2(J, S) =$		$\{a, b, c\}$
		e ϵ		1 b δ			
				4 b α			
				4 b β			
				4 b δ			
				3 c ϵ			
				3 c λ			

Fig. 1. From the above table, we can see that (M, c), the value corresponding to index M in a tuple, does not give us any information about the relations between $\pi_{I-M}(I, R)$ and $\pi_{J-M}(J, S)$, since given a value corresponding to any index in M, all possible values corresponding to any index of $I - M$ pair with all possible values of any index of $J - M$. That is, $I - M$ has no influence on $J - M$ given (M, c).

The no influence concept for relations is analogous to the conditional independence concept in probability distributions. For example, in a Markov chain $<x_1, \ldots, x_N>$ of order 1, x_{i+2} is conditionally independent of x_i given x_{i+1}, $i = 2, \ldots, N - 1$. In the example of Fig. 1, 3 has no influence on 1 given 2. Here we use the index i rather than the variable x_i to simplify our writing.

Figure 1 shows an example of the no influence concept.

The relation join process also applies to the case when we have more than two relations to join. If we have N indexed relations to join, $(I_1, R_1), \ldots, (I_n, R_n)$, we write

$$(K, S) = \otimes_{n=1}^{N}(I_n, R_n).$$

3   Music Generation Through Projection and Relation Join

Section 2 introduced the definition of projection and relation join which are the core techniques we will use in the music generation. In this section, we will introduce how the techniques can be applied to music sequences (note or chord sequences). Before that, we need to introduce the mathematical definition we use for music terms.

Definition 11. *A note is a small bit of sound with a dominant fundamental to introduce the frequency and harmonics sound. For the sake of simplicity, this domain includes all the notes on a piano keyboard. We define a set of notes N as:*

$$N = \{A0, B0, C1, C\#1, D1, \ldots, B7, C8\}$$

The number after each note represents the octave the note in. The frequency of one note is the frequency of the previous note multiplied to $\sqrt[12]{2}$. Figure 2 shows the note name versus the frequency of the twelve notes in the octave Middle C in.

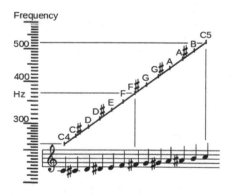

Fig. 2. Each note shown has a frequency of the previous note multiplied by $\sqrt[12]{2}$. Image from https://en.wikipedia.org/wiki/Musical_note.

In music, a chord is a set of notes that is heard sounding simultaneously.

Definition 12. *A chord is a set of notes. That is, for any chord $c, c \subseteq N$.*

Now we can define a music sequence such as an harmonic sequence.

Definition 13. *Let C be a collection of all chords, the harmonic sequence of a musical piece of length L is then a tuple $h \in C^L$, where $C^L = \underbrace{C \times C \times \ldots \times C}_{L \ times}$*

A music corpus can be represented as a set H of Z Harmonic Sequences. $H = \{h_z \in C^{L_z}\}_{z=1}^{Z}$, where L_z is the length of the tuple h_z.

An example of an harmonic sequence with 8 chords is as in Fig. 3.

<{'A4', 'E4', 'C4', 'A3'}, {'B4', 'E4', 'B3', 'G#3'}, {'C5', 'E4', 'A3'}, {'C5', 'E4', 'A3', 'A2'}, {'C5', 'E4', 'A3'}, {'D5', 'G4', 'B3', 'G3'}, {'E5', 'G4', 'C4'}, {'E5', 'G4', 'C4', 'C3'} >

(a) *The harmonic sequence written as in tuple form*

(b) *The harmonic sequence written in a sheet music*

Fig. 3. A harmonic sequence with 8 chords

We know that there exist certain dependencies in chord progressions to make a harmonic sequences sound consistent. To take advantages of those dependencies, we need to design index sets for the sequences to project on.

Definition 14. *A collection $\mathcal{I}(m, n)$ of K length m sets with uniform overlap of n $(0 < n < m)$ is represented as:*

$$\mathcal{I}(m, n) = \bigcup_{i \in \{1, \ldots, n-1\}} \mathcal{I}^i(m, n),$$

where

$$\mathcal{I}^i(m, n) = \{I_k^i \mid I_k^i = \{(m-n) \cdot k + 1 - i, \ldots, (m-n) \cdot k + m - i\}\}_{k=i}^{K-1}, i = \{0, \ldots, n-1\}$$

If $m = 4$ and $n = 2$, and $i = 0$, the tuple sets are shown in Fig. 4. When m and n are calculated, we suppress the (m, n), and write $\mathcal{I}$: $\mathcal{I} = \mathcal{I}(m, n)$.

We can now collect data sets from music sequences based on the tuple sets. Take Bach Chorales bmw26.6 as an example, Fig. 5 shows part of the original music piece from Bach Chorales bmw26.6. If we set $m = 4$, and $n = 2$, we can get tuples as shown in Fig. 6, and we will get tuples as in Fig. 7 if we set $m = 5$, and $n = 3$.

$$I_0^0 = \{1, 2, 3, 4\}$$
$$I_1^0 = \{3, 4, 5, 6\}$$
$$I_2^0 = \{5, 6, 7, 8\}$$
$$\vdots$$
$$I_{K-1}^0 = 2 \cdot (K-1) + 1, 2 \cdot (K-1) + 2, 2 \cdot (K-1) + 3, 2 \cdot (K-1) + 4$$

(a) *The tuple sets when $i = 0$*

$$I_0^1 = \{2, 3, 4, 5\}$$
$$I_1^1 = \{4, 5, 6, 7\}$$
$$I_2^1 = \{6, 7, 8, 9\}$$
$$\vdots$$
$$I_{K-1}^1 = 2 \cdot (K-1) + 1 - 1, 2 \cdot (K-1) + 2 - 1, 2 \cdot (K-1) + 3 - 1, 2 \cdot (K-1) + 4 - 1$$

(b) *The tuple sets with $i = 1$*

Fig. 4. Shows the sample tuple sets when $m = 4$, and $n = 2$. All tuple sets are as in $\mathcal{I}(4, 2) = \{I_0^0, I_1^0, \ldots, I_{K-1}^0, \ldots, I_0^{K-1}, I_1^{K-1}, \ldots, I_{K-1}^{K-1}\}$.

Fig. 5. The first line of Bach Chorales bwm26.6

Definition 15. *Let $\mathcal{I} = \mathcal{I}(m, n)$ be a collection of K length m sets with uniform overlap of n, let h be a harmonic sequence, the set R_h of all m-tuples with overlap n from h is defined by*

$$\bigcup_{I \in \mathcal{I}} \pi_I(h)$$

If H is set of harmonic sequences, the indexed set $(\mathcal{I}, R)$ is then

$$(\mathcal{I}, R) = \bigcup_{h \in H} \bigcup_{I \in \mathcal{I}} \pi_I(h).$$

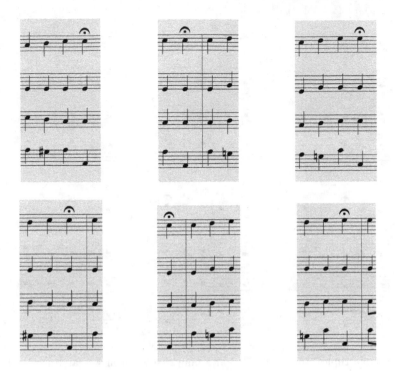

Fig. 6. Sample tuples from Bach Chorales bmw26.6 when $m = 4$, and $n = 2$. The top three sample tuples are generated when $i = 0$, the bottom three tuples are generated when $i = 1$.

The following Fig. 8 shows two short sequences, each one contains 8 chords. Figure 9 shows the results of joining the 4-tuples extracted from the two short sequences from Fig. 8.

Now we can define the relation join for harmonic sequences.

Definition 16. *If R is a set of m-tuples produced from all projections with index set $\mathcal{I} = \mathcal{I}(m, n)$, and if $I \in \mathcal{I}$ is an index set, (I, R) becomes an indexed relation with tuples of length m. Let $J = \cup_{I \in \mathcal{I}} I$, we then can get a set of new harmonic sequences by computing*

$$(J, S) = \otimes_{I \in \mathcal{I}}(I, R)$$

where $\otimes_{I \in \mathcal{I}}(I, R)$ is a set of $|J| - tuples$.

The above procedure can be applied to harmonic sequences with and without corresponding time duration. But there is no intentional control of key of harmonic sequences in this procedure.

Definition 17. *Let K be the set of all possible keys in music, then*

$$K = \{C, Db; D; Eb; E; F; Gb; G; Ab; A; Bb, B\}$$

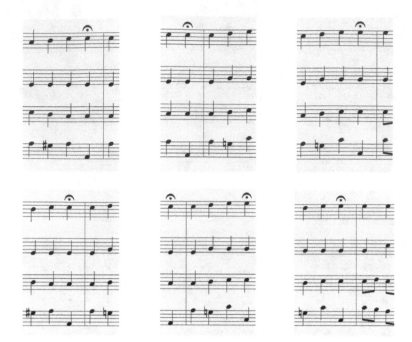

Fig. 7. Sample tuples from Bach Chorales bmw26.6 when m = 5, and n = 3. The top three sample tuples are generated when i = 0, the bottom three tuples are generated when i = 1.

Enharmonic keys are counted as one key, that is, $C\# = Db$; $D\# = Eb$; $F\# = Gb$; $G\# = Ab$; $A\# = Bb$; $Cb = B$.

When we say a piece is in a certain 'key', it means the piece is formed around the notes in a certain scale which, in music, is a set of notes ordered by certain frequency or pitch. For example, the C Major Scale contains C, D, E, F, G, A, B, and C. A piece based on the key of C will (generally) use C, D, E, F, G, A, B, and C.

Now we could do **key constraint relation join**.

Definition 18. *Let C_k be a set of chords who are in the key of k, and C^m be the set of m-tuples of chords. $R_k^b \subseteq R$ contains all m-tuples of chords in which the first chord is in the key of k,' b' means begin. Similarly, $R_k^e \subseteq R$ contains all m-tuples of chords in which the last chord is in the key of k,' e' means end. That is,*

$$R_k^b = \{(c_1, c_2, \ldots, c_m) \in C^m \mid c_1 \in C_k\}$$

$$R_k^e = \{(c_1, c_2, \ldots, c_m) \in C^m \mid c_m \in C_k\}$$

Then key constraint relation join means computing

$$(J, S) = \left(I_0, R_k^b\right) \otimes_{i=1}^{K-2} (I_i, R) \otimes (I_{K-1}, R_k^e)$$

(J, S) is the results of relation join constrained by using chords in the key of k that begin and end the piece.

<{'B4', 'E4', 'D4', 'G3'}, {'A4', 'E4', 'C#4', 'E3', 'A3'}, {'G4', 'E4', 'C#4', 'E3',
'A3'}, {'A5', 'F#4', 'E4', 'C#4', 'A3', 'A2'}, {'G5', 'E4', 'C#4', 'A3', 'A2'}, {'F#5',
'F#4', 'D4', 'A3', 'D3'}, {'E5', 'F#4', 'D4', 'A3', 'D3'}, {'D5', 'F#4', 'D4', 'A3', 'D3',
'F#3'} >

(a) *First short sequence written in tuple form*

(b) *First short sequence written in musical notation*

<{'D5', 'E4', 'D4', 'B3', 'G3', 'G2'}, {'C#5', 'E4', 'D4', 'G3'}, {'B4', 'E4', 'D4', 'G3'},
{'A4', 'E4', 'C#4', 'E3', 'A3'}, {'G4', 'E4', 'C#4', 'E3', 'A3'}, {'A5', 'F#4', 'E4',
'C#4', 'A3', 'A2'}, {'G5', 'E4', 'C#4', 'A3', 'A2'}, {'F#5', 'F#4', 'D4', 'A3', 'D3'} >

(c) *Second short sequence written in tuple form*

(d) *Second short sequence written in music notation*

Fig. 8. Shows two short sequences from Bach chorales.

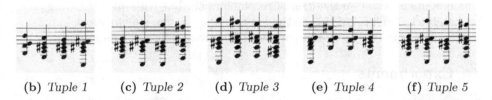

(b) *Tuple 1*   (c) *Tuple 2*   (d) *Tuple 3*   (e) *Tuple 4*   (f) *Tuple 5*

Fig. 9. Shows the 5 4-tuples generated from the two short sequences in Fig. 8 when
$m = 4, n = 2$, and $i = 0$. Given $m = 4, n = 2$, and $i = 0$, sequence (b) of Fig. 8 has
3 4-tuples, sequence (d) of Fig. 8 has 3 4-tuples. The indexed relation formed by the
corpus of sequences (b) and (d) could have 6 4-tuples, but in this case, two of them
are identical. So there are only 5 4-tuples in the indexed relation produced by the two
short sequences of Fig. 8.

We could also do **scale constraint relation join**.

Definition 19. *A scale, in music, is a set of notes ordered by certain frequency
or pitch. For example, the C Major Scale contains C, D, E, F, G, A, B, and C.*
*Let $R_S \subseteq R$ be a set of tuples of chords in which all chords are in scale S.
Then we can get new harmonic sequences in which all chords are in scale S by
computing*

$$(J, S) = \otimes_{I \in \mathcal{I}} (I, R_S)$$

Previous music generation methods try to generate music sequences $(x_1, x_2, \ldots, x_N)$ such that the probability that $(x_1, x_2, \ldots, x_N)$ is generated is equal to $P(x_1, x_2, \ldots, x_N)$. That is,

$$\{(x_1, x_2, \ldots, x_N) | P(x_1, x_2, \ldots, x_N) > 0\}.$$

They use machine learning techniques to estimate a product decomposition of the joint probability. The joint product produced by a Markov Chain is $P(x_1, x_2, \ldots, x_N) = P(x_1) \prod_{n=2}^{N} P(x_n | x_{n-1})$. This is a special case of the more general form:

$$P(x_1, x_2, \ldots, x_N) = \prod_{k=1}^{K} f_k(x_i : i \in A_k)$$

for all $x_1, \ldots x_N \in_{i=1}^{N} L_i$, where L_i are the space of music elements (such as chords), N is the length of each sequence, A_k is a set of index tuples.

Only those music sequences with $P(x_1, x_2, \ldots, x_N) > 0$ will be generated. So they have to estimate $f_k(x_i : i \in A_k)$.

In this paper, we use a completely different methodology to generate music specific to certain composers called projection and relation join. Instead of estimating the probabilities, we calculate the relation join of (A_k, R_k) for all k, in which

$$(A_k, R_k) = (A_k, \{(x_i, i \in A_k) | f_k(x_i, i \in A_k) > 0\})$$

Thus, in our method, $f_k(x_i : i \in A_k) > 0$ is ensured for any k, but we do not need to estimate the function f_k. Our method requires neither expert level domain knowledge nor learning patterns and parameters from input music pieces. The method is based on the idea of recombination, but without estimating any probabilities. The idea of this method is that the progressions inherent in music sequences themselves carry the patterns of music of different composers.

4   Experiments

In this section, we apply the techniques introduced in Sects. 2 and 3 to a music corpus from Music21[1].

4.1   Experiment 1: Harmonic Sequence

There are five steps in this experiment.

Firstly, extract chords. We extract chords from 202 music sequences of Bach Chorales from the database of Music21. Every sequence is a list including several tuples. Every tuple represents a chord, which contains all the notes in the chord. As an example,

$$<\{'F4', 'C4', 'A3', 'F3'\}, \{'G4', 'C5', 'C4', 'G3', 'E3'\}, \{'C4', 'C5', 'G3', 'E3'\}, \ldots>$$

is an harmonic chord sequence.

---

[1] Music 21 is a toolkit for computer-aided musicology. See http://web.mit.edu/music21/.

Secondly, we transform chords into integer indexes. We make a dictionary(mapping) for all the chords, the key of the dictionary is each chord itself, the value is the integer index from index set $\{0, 1, 2, \ldots, D-1\}$, where D is the number of distinct chords. Then, we transform the chords in each sample into the integer indexes according to the dictionary.

Thirdly, we compute all tuples of chord from music pieces in the corpus. In this experiment, we set $\mathcal{I} = \mathcal{I}(4, 2)$, that is, $m = 4, n = 2, K = 14$, K is set to 14 to ensure the length of each output sample is 32, which is a reasonable length of a harmonic sequence. We only use the tuple sets when $i = 0$ in this experiment. Then we compute

$$\bigcup_{h \in H} \bigcup_{I \in \mathcal{I}} \pi_I(h)$$

There are 8731 4-tuples extracted from the music sequences in this experiment.

Fourthly, we compute the relation join on the projected index relations, that is, we compute

$$(J, S) = \otimes_{I \in \mathcal{I}} (I, R)$$

Finally, we create mp3 files from the sequences generated.

The relation join procedure with $m = 4$ and $n = 2$, if done completely, generates over 24.12 million harmonic sequences in this experiment. We generate harmonic sequences using a random tree search method. We randomly pick one tuple from R, and then pick the next tuple that can join onto it. If there are no tuples can join onto it, then the procedure backtracks in a tree search manner. In this way, we can get certain number of synthetically generated sequences.

The following example shows how we generate a harmonic sequence of length 16 using tree search.

Example 6. The first three steps are the same as in the above experiments. The results after the three steps are all tuples of chords from the given music pieces. For the fourth step, instead of doing relation join as in experiment 1, we randomly pick a tuple from $\pi_{\{1,2,3,4\}}(I, R)$. The (I, R) we use in the following are extracted from Bach chorales. For example, we picked $(\{F\#4, D4, B3\}, \{G4, D4, B3\}, \{A4, D4, A3, F\#3\}, \{B4, D4, G3\})$. This tuple contains the first four chords of our synthetic sequence. Then we search over $\pi_{\{3,4,5,6\}}(I, R)$ to find a tuple that starts with the last two chords of the first tuple, that is chord $\{A4, D4, A3, F\#3\}$, and chord $\{B4, D4, G3\}$. If we find a tuple that matches like $(\{A4, D4, A3, F\#3\}, \{B4, D4, G3\}, \{A4, D4, F\#3, D3\}, \{A4, D4, G3, E3\})$, we join the two tuples we found into a 6-tuple $(\{F\#4, D4, B3\}, \{G4, D4, B3\}, \{A4, D4, A3, F\#3\}, \{B4, D4, G3\}, \{A4, D4, F\#3, D3\}, \{A4, D4, G3, E3\})$, then we search over $\pi_{\{5,6,7,8\}}(I, R)$ and find the next matched tuple, until we have 16 chords in the synthetic sequence. A sample synthetic sequence is as in Fig. 10.

Another way to pick the sample is to randomly select from the results of a full relation join. This can be very time consuming, because we need to generate all the results before sampling. After we have some samples, we can make them into $mp3$ files that can be listened to.

Fig. 10. A sample synthetic music sequence generate using tree search, the duration is set to be quarter length as default.

4.2 Experiment 2: Harmonic Sequence with Rhythm

In this experiment, instead of only extracting information of the chords, we include the information of rhythm for each chord. Thus, each chord comes with its time duration. There are 8773 4-tuples with overlap of 2 extracted in the third step in this experiment. Similarly to Experiment 1, we only use the tuple sets when $i = 0$ in this experiment.

In the first step, we extract harmonic sequence samples from given Bach chorales. A sample sequence is as following: $<\{'F4','C4','A3','F3', 0.5\}, \{'G4', 'C5','C4','G3','E3', 0.5\}, \{'C4','C5','G3','E3', 1.0\}, \ldots >$. The number at the end of each chord is the time duration in quarter length, 1.0 represents a quarter, 0.5 represents a eighth, and so on.

The other four steps are almost the same as in experiment 1 except that we need to match the rhythm of the chords when doing relation join, while in experiment 1, we only need to match the chords. The relation join generates more than 1.67 million sequences in this experiment.

4.3 Experiment 3: Harmonic Sequence in Specific Key and Scale

In the above experiments, there is no intentional control of the key of harmonic sequences and the scale the chords in. We want to see if the harmonic sequences sound better when we specify the key and scale. So we do two constraint relation join experiments based on each of the above two experiments, which will generate four combinations of experiments. The number of harmonic sequences each experiment generated are summarized in Table 6.

Table 6. The number of sequences generated with key and scale constraint while $m = 4$ and $n = 2$

Type	With key constraint	With scale constraint
Chord	65648	577602
Chord with rhythm	4958	867977

Since relation join generates new sequences using existing harmonic sequences, it relies on the transitions of chords of existing sequences. In addition, machine generated sequences will have the same length, while the human generated sequences have more sequential features of longer length.

4.4   Experiment 4: Redo the Experiments with m = 5, n = 3

We also do another set of experiments with $m = 5, n = 3$. We extract 8797 and 8813 5-tuples from the 202 Music21 sequences respectively for tuples with only chord and tuples including both chord and rhythm. The results are summarized in Table 7.

Table 7. Shows the number of sequences generated with key and scale constraint while $m = 5$ and $n = 3$

Type	No constraints	With key constraint	With scale constraint
Chord	63262	266	365
Chord with rhythm	571	119	1

Some samples from these experiments are also posted to the website: http://haralick.org/music/music.html. We also include some sample synthetic pieces in the Appendix A.2 that could be played with.

5   Conclusion and Future Work

In this paper, we introduced a new music generation method based on relation join. We first break the input music into small segments, and then recombine them to generate new music sequences using relation join. Therefore, we do not have to estimate any probabilities or parameters from input music pieces. The idea behind our method is that the patterns of music sequences are carried in the progressions of them. Compared to other music generation methods, our method does not require any knowledge about music styles. Readers who are interested in hearing some of the generated sequences in midi format can find them on http://haralick.org/music/music.html.

In the future, we will try to generate music sequences of different composers and genres. We can also try to generate music sequences of mix-genres or mix-composers. For example, we can generate music sequences using the segments from Bach chorales and Beethoven's sonatas. With the information distance and similarity introduced, we are even able to generate music sequences with a certain level of similarities. For example, we can generate music that is very much like Bach chorales, which means the similarity is close to the original Bach chorales. It will also be interesting to see the most unlikely sequences that can be generated in a Bach style.

In order to do something like this, we will need to compute auto-similarity function for any harmonic sequences. In the following subsections, we describe how to do this voice by voice. One of the dimensions of similarity between harmonic sequences will be the cross similarity function, which we can define as the similarity between their respective auto-similarity functions.

5.1   Entropy

Under information theory context, entropy measures the information embedded within a random variable. Consider a categorical random variable X with probability distribution $p(x)$, the entropy can be calculated using the formula:

$$H(X) = - \sum_{x \in \mathcal{X}} p(x) \log_b p(x)$$

where $\mathcal{X}$ is the set of possible values of X, and b is the base of logarithm. This formula is proposed by Shannon [16]. As a measure of uncertainty of a given event, it can also be extended to continuous random variable [2].

The joint entropy H(X, Y) of a pair of discrete random variables with a joint distribution p(x, y) is defined as:

$$H(X,Y) = - \sum_{x \in \mathcal{X}} \sum_{y \in \mathcal{Y}} p(x,y) \log_b p(x,y)$$

where $\mathcal{Y}$ is the set of possible values for random variable Y.

The conditional entropy $H(Y|X)$ quantifies the information required for describing Y given X, that is, the average entropy of Y conditional on the value of X, averaged over all possible values of X. Let $H(Y|X = x)$ be the entropy when $X = x$,

$$H(Y|X) = - \sum_{x \in \mathcal{X}} p(x) H(Y|X = x) = - \sum_{x \in \mathcal{X}} p(x) \sum_{y in \mathcal{Y}} p(y|x) \log_b p(y|x)$$

$$= - \sum_{x \in \mathcal{X}} \sum_{y \in \mathcal{Y}} p(x,y) \log_b \frac{p(x,y)}{p(x)}.$$

.

5.2   Mutual Information

In information theory, mutual information (MI) is a measure of mutual dependence of two given random variables, that is, MI quantifies the information revealed by one random variable through the other variable. If the two random variables are independent, MI is equal to 0. MI is closely related to the entropy of random variables. The MI of random variables X and Y is can be viewed as the information reduced if one random variable is given, that is,

$$I(X;Y) = H(X) - H(X|Y) = H(Y) - H(Y|X).$$

The formal definition for MI is as following:

$$I(X;Y) = \sum_{x \in \mathcal{X}} \sum_{y \in \mathcal{Y}} p(x,y) \log \frac{p(x,y)}{p(x)p(y)}$$

5.3   Information Based Distance and Similarity

With the definition of mutual information and entropy, we can define the distance between two random variables. A distance function $d : X \times Y \to \mathcal{R}^+$ is a metric if it satisfies the metric the following three conditions [11,19,21]:

(A) Identity. $d(X,Y) = 0$ if and only if $X = Y$
(B) Symmetry. $d(X,Y) = d(Y,X)$
(C) Triangle inequality. $d(X,Z) + d(Z,Y) \geq d(X,Y)$

Several information based distance measures have been proposed [7,11,17,18].

$$d_1(X,Y) = H(X,Y) - I(X;Y) \tag{1}$$

$$d_1'(X,Y) = 1 - \frac{I(X;Y)}{max\{H(X), H(Y)\}} \tag{2}$$

$$d_2(X,Y) = H(X,Y) - min\{H(X), H(Y)\} \tag{3}$$

$$d_3(X,Y) = \frac{H(X,Y) - min\{H(X), H(Y)\}}{max\{H(X), H(Y)\}} \tag{4}$$

It can be proved that these each of four distance metric satisfy the three conditions. The proofs are in Appendix A.1.

The similarity $s(X,Y)$ can then be defined as:

$$s(X,Y) = 1 - d(X,Y) \tag{5}$$

5.4   Difference Between Original Music and Synthetic Music

A note under music context is a small bit of sound with a dominant fundamental to introduce the frequency and harmonics sound, and can also be used to represent pitch class. A set of notes without scale is as following:

$$\mathcal{N} = \{C, C\#, D, D\#, E, F, F\#, G, G\#, A, A\#, B\}$$

From Sect. 3, we know that a music piece can then be represented by a tuple: $M = <N_1, N_2, \ldots, N_\tau, \ldots, N_T>$, $N_\tau \subseteq \mathcal{N}, i = 1, 2, \ldots, T$. Each element in the tuple is a chord, which is a subset of $\mathcal{N}$. Each chord has voices. We denote by N_t^v voice v of chord N_t.

The random variables in music are possible notes in the music piece. The joint probability can be written as:

$$p_\tau^v(x,y) = \frac{\#\{t | x \in N_t^v, y \in N_{t+\tau}^v\}}{T - \tau},$$

where $t \in \{1, \ldots, T\}$. The marginal of each random variable:

$$p_\tau^v(x) = \frac{\#\{t | x \in N_t^v\}}{T - \tau}$$

The mutual information can be calculated as:

$$I_\tau(X; Y) = \sum_{x \in \mathcal{X}} \sum_{y \in \mathcal{Y}} p_\tau^v(x, y) \log \frac{p_\tau^v(x, y)}{p_\tau^v(x) p_\tau^v(y)}$$

Then we can calculate the distance using Eqs. 1, 2, 3, or 4. For each τ, we can calculate similarity using Eq. 5. So we can calculate a sequence of similarities from each piece. We call the sequence of similarities an auto similarity function.

Appendix A.1: Proofs of Distance Metrics

The proofs show that the four distance metrics we use in this paper satisfies the conditions:

(A) Identity. $d(X, Y) = 0$ if and only if $X = Y$
(B) Symmetry. $d(X, Y) = d(Y, X)$
(C) Triangle inequality. $d(X, Z) + d(Z, Y) \geq d(X, Y)$

Proof. (A) and (B) are straightforward for all the four metrics give the properties of the entropy and mutual information. To prove the triangle inequality (C), we can first assume $H(X) \geq H(Y)$. Since $d(X, Y)$ is symmetric, the reverse case can be proved easily if we can prove one of the two cases ($H(X) \geq H(Y)$ or $H(Y) \geq H(X)$).

So we have only three cases left to consider: $H(X) \geq H(Y) \geq H(Z)$, $H(X) \geq H(Z) \geq H(Y)$, and $H(Z) \geq H(X) \geq H(Y)$.

- Case $H(X) \geq H(Y) \geq H(Z)$:
  - For $d_1(X, Y)$, first, we know that

$$\begin{aligned} d(X, Y)_1 &= H(X, Y) - I(X; Y) \\ &= H(X) + H(Y) - 2I(X; Y) \\ &= H(X|Y) + H(Y|X). \end{aligned}$$

then

$$H(X|Z) + H(Z|Y) \geq H(X|Y, Z) + H(Z|Y) = H(X, Z|Y) \geq H(X|Y),$$

so

$$\begin{aligned} d_1(X, Z) + d_1(Z, Y) &= H(X|Z) + H(Z|X) + H(Y|Z) + H(Z|Y) \\ &\geq H(X|Y) + H(Z|X) + H(Y|Z) \\ &\geq H(X|Y) + H(Y|X) = d_1(X, Y). \end{aligned}$$

- For $d_1'(X,Y) = 1 - \frac{I(X;Y)}{max\{H(X),H(Y)\}}$,

$$d_1'(X,Y) = 1 - \frac{I(X;Y)}{max\{H(X),H(Y)\}}$$
$$= 1 + \frac{H(X,Y) - H(X) - H(Y)}{max\{H(X),H(Y)\}}.$$
$$= 1 + \frac{H(X,Y) - H(X) - H(Y)}{H(X)}.$$
$$= \frac{H(X,Y) - H(Y)}{H(X)} = \frac{H(X|Y)}{H(X)}.$$

$$d_1'(X,Z) + d_1'(Z,Y) = 1 + \frac{H(X,Z) - H(X) - H(Z)}{max\{H(X),H(Z)\}} + 1 + \frac{H(Z,Y) - H(Z) - H(Y)}{max\{H(Z),H(Y)\}}$$
$$= 1 + \frac{H(X,Z) - H(X) - H(Z)}{H(X)} + 1 + \frac{H(Z,Y) - H(Z) - H(Y)}{H(Y)}$$
$$\geq 1 + \frac{H(X,Z) - H(X) - H(Z)}{H(X)} + 1 + \frac{H(Z,Y) - H(Z) - H(Y)}{H(X)}$$
$$\geq 1 + \frac{H(X|Z) - H(X)}{H(X)} + 1 + \frac{H(Z|Y) - H(Z)}{H(X)}$$
$$\geq 1 + 1 + \frac{H(X|Y) - H(X) - H(Z)}{H(X)}$$
$$\geq 1 + 1 + \frac{H(X|Y) - H(X) - H(X)}{H(X)}$$
$$\geq 1 + \frac{H(X|Y) - H(X)}{H(X)} = \frac{H(X|Y)}{H(X)} = d_1'(X,Y).$$

- For $d_2(X,Y)$, we first have $I(X;Y) = H(X) - H(X|Y) = H(Y) - H(Y|X)$, which means $H(X|Y) - H(Y|X) = H(X) - H(Y) > 0$, so
$$d_2(X,Z) + d_2(Z,Y) = H(X,Z) - min\{H(X),H(Z)\} + H(Z,Y) - min\{H(Z),H(Y)\}$$
$$= H(X,Z) - H(Z) + H(Z,Y) - H(Z)$$
$$= H(X|Z) + H(Y|Z)$$
$$\geq H(X|Z) + H(Z|Y)$$
$$\geq H(X|Y)$$
$$= H(X,Y) - H(Y)$$
$$= H(X,Y) - min\{H(X),H(Y) = d_2(X,Y).$$

- For $d_3(X,Y)$,
$$d_3(X,Z) + d_3(Z,Y) = \frac{H(X,Z) - min\{H(X),H(Z)\}}{max\{H(X),H(Z)\}} + \frac{H(Z,Y) - min\{H(Z),H(Y)\}}{max\{H(Z),H(Y)\}}$$
$$= \frac{H(X,Z) - H(Z)}{H(X)} + \frac{H(Z,Y) - H(Z)}{H(Y)}$$
$$= \frac{H(X|Z)}{H(X)} + \frac{H(Y|Z)}{H(Y)}$$
$$\geq \frac{H(X|Z)}{H(X)} + \frac{H(Z|Y)}{H(Y)}$$
$$\geq \frac{H(X|Z)}{H(X)} + \frac{H(Z|Y)}{H(X)}$$
$$\geq \frac{H(X|Y)}{H(X)} = d_3(X,Y).$$

– Case $H(X) \geq H(Z) \geq H(Y)$: Similarly to the case $H(X) \geq H(Y) \geq H(Z)$.
– Case $H(Z) \geq H(X) \geq H(Y)$: Similarly to the case $H(X) \geq H(Y) \geq H(Z)$.

$\square$

Appendix A.2: Harmonic Sequences in Scale C with 80 in Quarterlength Time Duration

(See Figs. 11 and 12).

Fig. 11. Synthetic harmonic sequence based on Bach Chorales with the scales fixed at C sample 1

Fig. 12. Synthetic harmonic sequence based on Bach Chorales with the scales fixed at C sample 2

References

1. Al-Rifaie, A.M., Al-Rifaie, M.M.: Generative music with stochastic diffusion search. In: Johnson, C., Carballal, A., Correia, J. (eds.) EvoMUSART 2015. LNCS, vol. 9027, pp. 1–14. Springer, Cham (2015). doi:10.1007/978-3-319-16498-4_1
2. Cahill, N.D.: Normalized measures of mutual information with general definitions of entropy for multimodal image registration. In: Fischer, B., Dawant, B.M., Lorenz, C. (eds.) WBIR 2010. LNCS, vol. 6204, pp. 258–268. Springer, Heidelberg (2010). doi:10.1007/978-3-642-14366-3_23
3. Chai, W., Vercoe, B.: Folk music classification using hidden Markov models. In: Proceedings of International Conference on Artificial Intelligence, vol. 6. Citeseer (2001)

4. Cope, D.: Computer modeling of musical intelligence in EMI. Comput. Music J. **16**(2), 69–83 (1992)
5. Ebcioglu, K.: An expert system for harmonization of chorales in the style of J.S. Bach. Ph.D. thesis, Buffalo, NY, USA (1986)
6. Haralick, R.M., Liu, L., Misshula, E.: Relation decomposition: the theory. In: Perner, P. (ed.) MLDM 2013. LNCS, vol. 7988, pp. 311–324. Springer, Heidelberg (2013). doi:10.1007/978-3-642-39712-7_24
7. Horibe, Y.: Entropy and correlation. IEEE Trans. Syst. Man Cybern. **5**, 641–642 (1985)
8. Mackworth, A.K.: Constraint satisfaction problems. In: Encyclopedia of AI, pp. 285–293 (1992)
9. Machado, P., Romero, J., Manaris, B.: Experiments in computational aesthetics. In: Romero, J., Machado, P. (eds.) The Art of Artificial Evolution, pp. 381–415. Springer, Heidelberg (2008). doi:10.1007/978-3-540-72877-1_18
10. Manaris, B., Roos, P., Machado, P., Krehbiel, D., Pellicoro, L., Romero, J.: A corpus-based hybrid approach to music analysis and composition. In: Proceedings of the National Conference on Artificial Intelligence, vol. 22, no. 1, p. 839. AAAI Press/MIT Press, Menlo Park/Cambridge/London 1999 (2007)
11. Meila, M.: Comparing clusterings an information based distance. J. Multivar. Anal. **98**(5), 873–895 (2007)
12. Papadopoulos, G., Wiggins, G.: AI methods for algorithmic composition: a survey, a critical view and future prospects. In: AISB Symposium on Musical Creativity, Edinburgh, UK, pp. 110–117 (1999)
13. Romero, J., Machado, P., Santos, A., Cardoso, A.: On the development of critics in evolutionary computation artists. In: Cagnoni, S. (ed.) EvoWorkshops 2003. LNCS, vol. 2611, pp. 559–569. Springer, Heidelberg (2003). doi:10.1007/3-540-36605-9_51
14. Ron, D., Singer, Y., Tishby, N.: The power of amnesia: learning probabilistic automata with variable memory length. Mach. Learn. **25**(2–3), 117–149 (1996)
15. Schulze, W., Van der Merwe, B.: Music generation with Markov models. IEEE Multimed. **3**, 78–85 (2010)
16. Shannon, C.E.: A mathematical theory of communication. Bell Syst. Tech. J. **27**, 379–423, 623–656 (1948). Math. Rev. (MathSciNet): MR10, 133e
17. Vinh, N.X., Epps, J., Bailey, J.: Information theoretic measures for clusterings comparison: variants, properties, normalization and correction for chance. J. Mach. Learn. Res. **11**(Oct), 2837–2854 (2010)
18. Wikipedia.org/wiki/Mutual_Information
19. Vitanyi, P.M., et al.: Normalized information distance. In: Emmert-Streib, F., Dehmer, M. (eds.) Information Theory and Statistical Learning, pp. 45–82. Springer, Boston (2009). doi:10.1007/978-0-387-84816-7_3
20. Winograd, T.: Language As a Cognitive Process: Syntax, vol. 1 (1983)
21. Xu, Z.: Distance, similarity, correlation, entropy measures and clustering algorithms for hesitant fuzzy information. Hesitant Fuzzy Sets Theory. SFSC, vol. 314, pp. 165–279. Springer, Cham (2014). doi:10.1007/978-3-319-04711-9_2

The Framework of Copista: An OMR System for Historical Music Collection Recovery

Marcos Laia, Flávio Schiavoni$^{(\boxtimes)}$, Daniel Madeira, Dárlinton Carvalho, João Pedro Moreira, Júlio Resende, and Rodrigo Ferreira

Computer Science Department, Federal University of São João del-Rei, São João Del Rei, MG, Brazil
marcoslaia@gmail.com, {fls,dmadeira,darlinton}@ufsj.edu.br, joaopmoferreira@gmail.com, julio.cmdr@gmail.com, rodrigoferreira001@hotmail.com

Abstract. Optical Music Recognition (OMR) is a process that employs computer science techniques to musical scores recognition. This paper presents the development framework of "Copista", an OMR system proposed to recognize handwritten scores especially regarding a historical music collection. "Copista" is the Brazilian word for Scribe, someone who writes music scores. The proposed system is useful to music collection preservation and supporting further research and development of OMR systems.

Keywords: Optical Music Recognition · Historical musical collection recovery · Copista · Development framework

1 Introduction

Some of the most important music collections in Brazil, dated from the beginning of 18th century, are located in São João Del Rei, Tiradentes and Prados. These collections include several musical genre and are the work of hundred composers from this historical Brazilian region.

The Music Department of Federal University of São João Del Rei started a program to describe and catalog these collections, called "Memória Viva" (Living Memory), trying to provide these collections to public audience. The main aspect regarding these collections is that the old sheets have several marks of degradation like folding, candle wax, tears and even bookworm holes, as depicted in Fig. 1.

In order to help the processing of these music papers, a partnership of Music Department with the Computer Science Department in the same University arose. This partnership involved several researchers on the creation of an application called Copista, a software to help musicians to rewrite music scores collections based on a digital copy of them. The project Copista comprises the digital image acquisition from the original files, digitally recovery of the files and transcript the music files to a symbolic music representation.

© Springer International Publishing AG 2017
M. Aramaki et al. (Eds.): CMMR 2016, LNCS 10525, pp. 65–87, 2017.
DOI: 10.1007/978-3-319-67738-5_4

Fig. 1. Example of music score present in the collections

Each step on this process would return partial results that are important to preserve these historical collections. The scanned original files are valuable to musicology since they keep historical features of each sheet. The digital recovered files are also important since it can be easier to read and distributed them. The symbolic music representation is another important artifact since it is easier to work with these files to check and correct some transcription problem.

After some research, development and experiments, initial results of the project was presented at the 12th International Symposium on Computer Music Multidisciplinary Research (CMMR) [18]. An extension version of this paper is presented here, stating the development framework and recent results. These results are the initial steps of the software development and include a better understand of the problem of recognize historical handwritten documents.

The remainder of this paper is organized as follows: Sect. 2 presents the framework of the Copista system, Sect. 3 presents some initial results on the system development and Sect. 4 concludes this.

2   The Framework of Copista

The purpose of the Copista system is to be a tool that is able to convert handwriting scores into a digital music representation. It belongs to a class of applications capable to interpret music scores, called Optical Music Recognition (OMR) [5,23]. These applications are similar to Optical Character Recognition (OCR) tools but they should be able to convert handwriting scores into symbolic music. In spite of existing tools that converts handwriting scores into editable scores, most of these tools (a) do not work with manuscript scores [5], (b) are very expensive and (c) are not open source, being impossible to adapt them to this project. All these reasons helped us to decide to build a brand new tool on the OMR field.

To develop such tool, we divided the OMR process into some distinct parts: the Image Acquisition, Image Preprocessing and digital image recovery, the recognition of musical Symbols with Computer Vision, the Music Notation Reconstruction and the symbolic music output. The development framework of Copista relays on this process, as depicted in Fig. 2.

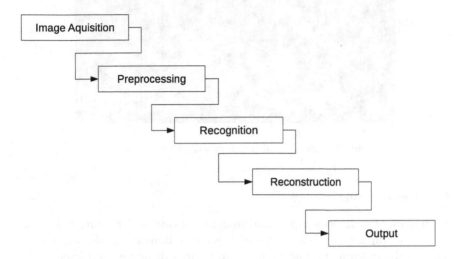

Fig. 2. The process employed in the development framework of Copista

2.1 Image Acquisition

The process starts with the image acquisition part. This part is responsible to turn a handwriting score into a digital image, useful to other parts of the system.

In the context of this development project, the input is a handwriting score from regional historical collections. In these collections, it is common for the scores, which many of them are centuries old and have been used in Masses and processions, have folds, candle wax marks, dents, tears and other damage. Figure 3 illustrates this situation.

Since these defects can mess the recognition system, a physical restoration of the sheets are being performed on the collections. Once this restoration is complete, the score should be digitized to be processed by Copista. This step should take care of providing score with the best quality as possible.

During the image acquisition, a high-resolution camera is being used. This setup has a twofold purpose. The first is due the lack of a table scanner capable to process sheet sizes as the music score from the historical collection. The second is to work with input format as common as the popular digital cameras largely available. We used a green chroma key under the original score to facilitate the identification of the sheet damage, performed by the following parts of the processing framework.

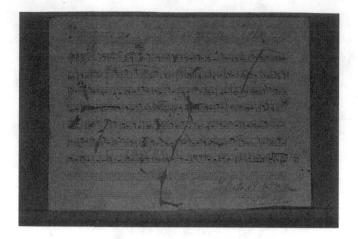

Fig. 3. Example of a damaged historical score

2.2   Preprocessing

It is common that ancient papers and manuscripts suffer degradation over time. Constant handling can rub the ink out, creating differences in shades or various marks. In the example of music score, candle wax drippings and sweaty hands creates marks in each document in several cases. In addition, improper storage caused folds, wrinkles, tears and holes caused by bookworms in the sheets. All these marks are not relevant and need to be removed to make the recognition process more adequate.

There is no universal technique suitable to preprocessing, as for each document, a specific treatment set may be required. Nonetheless, two steps can be highlighted as the basic preprocessing process for the Copista:

1. artifacts removal
2. color thresholding.

The first step involves removing all artifacts (i.e. marks) non-important to the recognition process. These artifacts, which become noise in the acquired image, cover the stains, rips, holes and all marks that are not part of the score. The paper sheet itself can be considered noise, because it is not part of the score itself. Holes and rips on the paper are the hardest artifacts presented, because they alter the paper format, while erasing the data on the score.

A set of algorithms are useful in order to accomplish this step. Image filtering [9,26] and hole filling [3] are necessary. The chroma key used in acquisition step helps to make holes easier to spot. Consequently, the hole-filling algorithm needs it in order to remove all of them efficiently. At the end of this step, the brightness and contrast are enhanced in order to clarify the acquired image, passing it along to the next step.

After the first step of noise removing, the image needs a conversion to black and white format. This is accomplished by a two-level thresholding processing (binarization). The objective of this processing is to simplify the score representation, cutting off color and grey variations. The thresholding process can be classified into two categories: global or local thresholding.

Global methods use only one value to classify all pixels on the image, regardless of whether the area it belongs has more or less noise. Values higher than the threshold become white, while lower values become black. By using only one threshold, global methods tend to be easier to implement and computationally cheaper. However, noises that occur in only one part of the image will influence the decision-making algorithm, which can lead to undesirable results.

To work around this problem, local thresholding methods work with input image subsets, calculating the optimal threshold by region. Higher adaptivity are achieved by local methods by allowing the decision-making in a region depend only in it, regardless of it neighborhood. Better results are expected on cases where different noises appear on different areas of the input image, but at a higher computational cost.

As the project's target scores have artifacts like sweat marks and candle drippings, which does not occur throughout the area, local methods tend to be more suitable for the Copista system. Therefore, a set of filtering techniques must be employed in this step to remove different noises. The techniques should be evaluated and adapt to different inputs.

2.3   Recognition of Musical Symbols

The part of Recognition of Musical Symbols employs computer vision techniques in certain specific steps in order to:

1. Identify meaningful areas as staves
2. Retrieve symbols from the staves
3. Describe each symbol.

The first step concerns about the segmentation of the music score [12], separating elements such as lines and special symbols (i.e. notations) to further recognition. Lines are particularly useful to define the location and meaning of other symbols. For instance, the height of the notes according to their relative position to the lines, separating different overlapping symbols [4] and of different sizes or rotated positions [20].

Each notation can be described by a set of features [16]. Each feature may represent something of the image to be recognized as edges, curvatures, blisters, ridges and points of interest. The features extracted are then used in a pattern recognition process [10,24], after being qualified and quantified to a statistical analysis by a filter to reduce uncertainty between the heights of notes or artifacts present in input images.

This step can use a Kalman filter [17] that will allow the correction of data generated by the features extraction. By combining computer vision techniques in OMR, there is a higher gain for generating such data, ensuring the integrity and fidelity to that which is present in the document.

In addition, computer vision techniques used for other applications such as character recognition [8], handwriting recognition [28], augmented reality with low resolution markers [11] can also be used to complete this process step.

2.4   Music Notation Reconstruction

Going on in the Copista process, the reconstruction stage of symbolic representation gets the recognized symbols and map them into an alphabet of musical symbols. This mapping may include the validation of a given symbol or a set of symbols to aid the recognition step as to the correctness of a given graphical element with an analysis from the notational model [13] or based on a musical context [19]. The validation may occur by creating a set of lexical, syntax and/or semantics rules, that define the symbolic representation format.

A major issue of defining a symbolic musical representation is to find a sufficient generic representation, which is very flexible but at the same time restricted in relation to its rules to allow a validation of the musical structure as a whole [25].

Most of the existing models is part of a hierarchical musical structure [6] where there is an overview of the music divided into several staves (i.e. lines), which are divided into bars, and these bars into time, and time into notes. For this project, it will be added to the model an even deeper hierarchy which will include information on the scores and the page of the score. A computational possibility to achieve such representation is to use an object-oriented model [27] to define the representation of a set of objects with attributes valued.

Such valued attributes should store the musical notation of a symbol as well as register symbol information within the image. For this reason, we split the musical symbolic representation for OMR into two parts, one that represents the music information and another that represents the image information.

The valued data of the original image that was found a musical symbol are necessary to allow a reassessment of erroneously recognized data. This would request the computer vision to remade a given symbol validation conference automatically.

Other original image data may be stored relate to the initial processing made in the image. Information such as brightness, contrast, color, rotation, translation, histogram and what steps were performed to remove the artifacts becomes necessary for preprocessing can be adjusted by changing these parameters in an attempt to improve the quality of page reading.

2.5   Output

The last part of the process is responsible for the generation of a file that represents the original score using a symbolic representation. The definition of the symbolic representation format is a critical task in the development of this tool.

This setting will influence the tool development since the validation of recognized symbols in the representation model can assist the learning algorithm of computer vision stage and thus reduce the need for human intervention in the process of transcription of digitized music.

The output of the tool should be as interoperable as possible in order to allow any possibility of editing and human intervention to correct a generated score, if this is necessary. Human correction performed in a score with identification problems can serve as a new entry in the system as it would enable a new learning step for the proposed algorithms.

The evaluation of adaptation takes into account: (a) the symbols used in the scores, (b) the hierarchical computational representation of this set of symbols, (c) the lexical, syntactic and semantic rules to allow scores correction in the symbolic format and (d) converting this set of symbols to commonly used formats in musical applications.

3 Development Results

This section presents initial results regarding the development of the proposed system. The recognition process of musical scores is achieved following the process presented before. The implementation is conducted as a chain of processes that may be changed individually based on successes and errors. Based on this chain, our first implementation separated each step of processing independently allowing each part to use a different programming language and exchanging data through file exchange.

3.1 Image Acquisition

Considering that the historical sheet are available in the best condition as possible, the first computational issue faced during the Image Acquisition step regards the sheet size. The music sheets are bigger than A4 sheet, so they do not fit on a regular table scanner. Moreover, considering the popularization of smartphones with high-resolution cameras, we decided to establish a camera-based setup for image acquisition. Consequently, the generated dataset was built taking into the account the use of the proposed approach in a more dynamic environment, leveraging from commonly available new technologies.

Nevertheless, it is also important to identify accurately the page borders and contours in order to verify how consistent the dataset is. Therefore, the image acquisition step uses a set of predefined rules to scan like keep image proportion, scan all files with the same distance, use the same chroma key under music files, and scan both side of paper independently if there are information on both side. Figure 4 illustrates the built setup to accomplish the image acquisition.

The Acquisition phase generates image files to the Preprocessing phase. These file libraries are also considered a first outcome of the project because we keep original data as it is.

The generated dataset is available at http://copista.dcomp.ufsj.edu.br. Table 1 presents a description of the dataset.

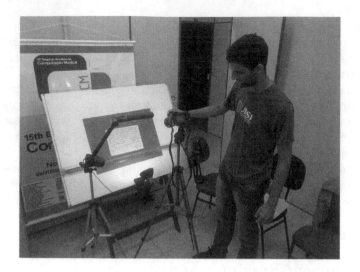

Fig. 4. Image acquisition setup

Table 1. Description of the generated dataset of historical music sheet

Dataset title	Historical music sheet pictures
Creation	2016-12-12
Description	Historical music sheet of several musical genre, created by composers from São João Del-Rei area (Brazil), dated starting from the beginning of 18th century. Some music sheets are damaged by time and bugs. The pictures were taken using a Sony NEX-7 with a 50 mm lens on a tripod. There are 150 different music sheet available in two file formats
Number of files	300
File format	ARW (Sony RAW image file) and JPG for each music sheet
Size	10 GB
License	CC-3.0-BY (https://creativecommons.org/licenses/by/3.0/)
URL	http://copista.dcomp.ufsj.edu.br

3.2   Preprocessing

The input of the preprocessing phase is the acquired digital image. This step prepares the image for computer vision process. For this step, initially the input file pass through a crop algorithm, to eliminate the area outside the score. For the crop algorithm, we used a simple strategy: the bottom part of the image is always the paper support. Simply cropping the bottom area eliminates this support. For the other three sides (left, right and top), the process envolves the same steps: from each side, pick a point in the side of the image. This point will travel to the center of it's line or column while it didn't touch the paper (while the color is still green). Six points are measured from each side to create three line segments used to create the final line segment that cuts the entire green area. This is done to erase the chroma key area outside the paper. Figure 5 shows the results of crop operation.

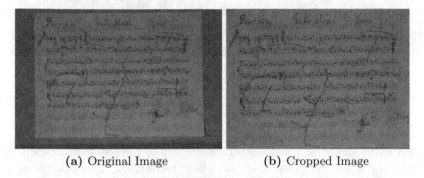

(a) Original Image   (b) Cropped Image

Fig. 5. Results of the crop operation. The chroma key border area is eliminated

After that, next step involves detecting holes inside score and classify the images according to the size of their most visible defects. Handling efficiently the holes are the hardest challenge on preprocessing. Since all images were scanned using a chroma key, the process of finding the defects is reduced to finding the points where the chroma key is visible. To do this, each image is converted to the HSV color standard. Here, it has to be that each color depends only on its hue value, regardless of saturation and brightness, allowing the green color to be easily detected. Thus, for each pixel whose hue is green (100 to 140°) its saturation and brightness are converted to the maximum value 255, giving the highest saturation possible, while the other pixels are black.

After this step, an opening morphological processing is performed to eliminate small points that can be seen as processing noises. Figure 6 shows the result of this step. For easy viewing, all pixels detected as part of the chroma key are white, while the rest are black.

So, after the crop and the chroma key saturation, two measures can be made: the first is to determine how many pixels are holes, by counting the non black pixels, and the second is to determine how many holes and how big they are. This last step is done by using a connected components detection algorithm, using the easily spotted chrome key color to find the components.

With all holes measured, one can classify the scores according to the degree of degradation suffered. Scores with higher count of holes or with bigger holes are classified as *highly damaged*. Smaller holes classifies the input score as *mild damaged*. Finally, if the scores has minimum holes or no holes, it is classified as *no damaged*. Thus, it is possible to analyze if the score has to pass through all preprocessing steps or if it can skip some. In this initial stage, only the scores

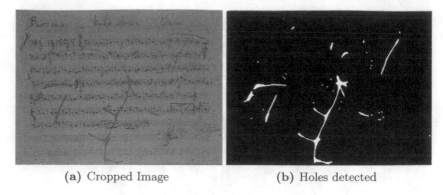

(a) Cropped Image   (b) Holes detected

Fig. 6. Results of the chroma key saturation. The holes are marked as white, while all the rest are marked as black.

classified as *no damaged* are being processed, while the team investigates how to handle the holes with context-aware filling techniques. This classification is also a partial outcome and can help to evaluate how damage is a collection.

After classification, the scores are converted to grayscale and after that, the image contrast is increased using histogram equalization. The high contrast increases the difference between the shades in each region and help the binarization to better decide if each pixel is background or object. Figure 7 show the results of same method, with and without histogram equalization. Using histogram equalization allowed to erase less information from the image, keeping almost all the lines.

(a) Niblack without histogram equal-(b) Niblack after histogram equaliza-
ization   tion

Fig. 7. Difference between binarization without and with histogram equalization

Using histogram equalized inputs, three binarization algorithms have already been tested: Niblack, Savuola and Wolf. All three methods works locally and the results are shown in Fig. 8. These are the final images in this stage of the Copista flow, and will be the inputs for the next step.

(a) Niblack   (b) Savuola   (c) Wolf

Fig. 8. Tested methods with same score

3.3 Recognition of Musical Symbols

This is a critical and hard step in the Copista process. At first, the training of models to identify musical symbols in the scores are being carried on digital images created by digital music sheet generators (Fig. 9). These images present few distortions between elements of the same type, as well as having a default identification for each symbol. Besides that, this kind of image do not require preprocessing such as brightness, color correction or guideline orientation. The use of digital scores contributes to the fact that the images have good contours and predictable forms that can guarantee a more accurate description for comparison of algorithms. When using handwritten scores in the future, algorithms can be adapted to work with this kind of document.

The first task of the proposed implementation for this part of the process is the identification of the staves within the image. The identification of the staves location allows knowing the delimitation of the notes and markings within each stave. In order to find each stave, we use the projection of the image in one dimension, as can be seen in Fig. 10.

The staves are defined as pentagrams, which are the five peaks in the picture presented in Fig. 10. They represent the five rows of each guideline [29]. Since there is the possibility of having notes and other elements close to the guidelines, it is considered that the work area is a vertical extension of the staves, as can be seen in Fig. 11.

After the identification of the staves, the five lines used to define the staves are removed from the images so that no symbol changes. Once the lines have been removed, the symbols on the banners lose their continuous connection as shown in Fig. 12. Without this link, each isolated symbol is detected separately to be independently described, as shown in Fig. 13.

Each symbol is labeled with a value that starts from 1, while the background is displayed as 0. Figure 14 shows how the array would look for two objects.

In the separation of identified symbols, each symbol is cut from the input image and binarized, as can be seen in Fig. 15a. In addition to this image, a border filter [12] is applied, which highlights the contours, as can be seen in the Fig. 15b. A skeletonization filter was also applied, as can be seen in Fig. 15c.

Fig. 9. Example of digital music score generated by software

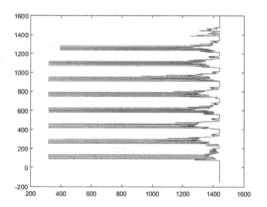

Fig. 10. Projections of the staves

Fig. 11. Found stave with its respective notes and markings

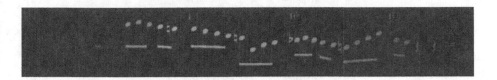

Fig. 12. Staves without lines

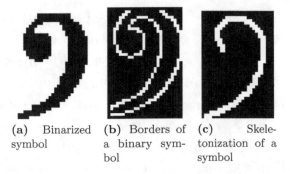

Fig. 13. Labeled symbols

```
0 0 0 0 0 0 0 0 0 0 0 0 0 0 0 0 0 0
0 0 0 1 1 1 0 0 0 2 2 2 2 0 0 0 0 0
0 0 0 1 1 1 0 0 0 0 0 2 2 2 0 0 0 0
0 0 0 1 1 1 0 0 0 0 0 0 2 2 2 2 0 0
0 0 0 1 1 1 0 0 0 0 0 0 0 2 2 2 2 0
0 0 0 1 1 1 0 0 0 0 0 0 0 0 2 2 2 2 0
0 0 0 0 0 0 0 0 0 0 0 0 0 0 0 0 0 0
```

Fig. 14. Example of a matrix with two identified symbols

(a) Binarized symbol   **(b)** Borders of a binary symbol   **(c)** Skeletonization of a symbol

Fig. 15. Example of the processing of a note

For the recognition of symbols we employ the technique of Hu Moments [32], which are invariant moments, that is, mathematical calculations with the center of mass of the image to determine that an object is independent of scale, rotation and/or translation. Several other methods can be applied to obtain more attributes of the image like the ones found in [28] (Table 2).

The calculation of the Hu moments begins with determining the two-dimensional moment of order $(p + q)$ which is given by Eq. 1:

$$m_{pq} = \sum_{x,y} x^p y^q f(x, y) \tag{1}$$

The total mass of the function $f(x, y)$ is determined by the moment m_{00}, according to the Eq. 2:

$$m_{pq} = \sum_{x,y} f(x, y), p, q \tag{2}$$

The central moments are obtained by moving the image around the centroid shown in the Eq. 2:

$$\mu_{pq} = \sum_{x,y} (x - x_c)^p (y - y_c)^q f(x, y) \tag{3}$$

Apply the results obtained in the Eq. 4 to obtain the normalized central moments that will be applied in the equations of the invariant moments:

$$\gamma = 1 + \frac{p + q}{2} \tag{4a}$$

$$\eta_{pq} = \frac{\mu_{pq}}{\mu_{00}^{\gamma}} \tag{4b}$$

With these equations are established the 8 moments of Hu, which are those invariants to the rotation, scaling and translation. Equation 5 shows 7 moments and the barycentre of the image:

$$\varphi_1 = \eta_{20} + \eta_{02} \tag{5a}$$

$$\varphi_2 = (\eta_{20} - \eta_{02})^2 + 4\eta_{11}^2 \tag{5b}$$

$$\varphi_3 = (\eta_{30} - 3\eta_{12})^2 + (3\eta_{21} - \eta_{03})^2 \tag{5c}$$

$$\varphi_4 = (\eta_{30} + \eta_{12})^2 + (3\eta_{21} + \eta_{03})^2 \tag{5d}$$

$$\varphi_5 = (\eta_{30} - 3\eta_{12})(\eta_{30} + \eta_{12}) \left[(\eta_{30} + \eta_{12})^2 - 3(\eta_{21} + \eta_{03})^2\right]$$
$$+ (3\eta_{21} - \eta_{03})(\eta_{21} + \eta_{03}) \left[3(\eta_{30} + \eta_{12})^2 - (\eta_{21} + \eta_{03})^2\right] \tag{5e}$$

$$\varphi_6 = (\eta_{20} - \eta_{02}) \left[(\eta_{30} + \eta_{12})^2 - (\eta_{21} + \eta_{03})^2\right]$$
$$+ 4\eta_{11}(\eta_{30} - \eta_{12})(\eta_{21} + \eta_{03}) \tag{5f}$$

$$\varphi_7 = (3\eta_{21} - \eta_{30})(\eta_{30} + \eta_{12}) \left[(\eta_{30} + \eta_{12})^2 - 3(\eta_{21} + \eta_{03})^2\right]$$
$$+ (3\eta_{12} - \eta_{03})(\eta_{21} + \eta_{03}) \left[3(\eta_{30} + \eta_{12})^2 - (\eta_{21} + \eta_{03})^2\right] \tag{5g}$$

All the combined equations result in the vector defining the object [31] that are the invariant moments of Hu.

Another form descriptor used is the Fourier descriptors [30] whose discrete transform of s is defined as:

$$a(u) = \frac{1}{N} \sum_{k=0}^{N-1} s(k) \exp[-j2\pi uk/N] \tag{6}$$

With u ranging from 0 to $N-1$, the complex coefficients $a(u)$ are called Fourier descriptors of the boundary and are invariant to scale and rotation.

The inverse Fourier transform of $a(u)$ reconstruct $s(k)$, as presented in Eq. 7.

$$s(k) = \sum_{u=0}^{N-1} a(u) \exp[j2\pi uk/N] \tag{7}$$

Assuming that in place of all values of $a(u)$ only the first M coefficients are used, this is equivalent to making $a(u) = 0$ for $u > M - 1$ in the Eq. 8. The result is the following approximation of $s(k)$:

$$\hat{s}(k) = \sum_{u=0}^{M-1} a(u) \exp[j2\pi uk/N] \tag{8}$$

Table 2. Hu moments of the Fa key

Figure	First	Second	Third	Fourth	Fifth	Sixth	Seventh	Eighth
15a	0.3838	−0.0380	0.0126	0.0054	0.0000	0.0005	−0.0000	−0.0014
15b	1.1101	−0.0975	0.2515	0.0486	0.0025	0.0096	0.0009	−0.0129
15c	1.2737	0.0228	0.5529	0.1513	0.0237	0.0322	0.0261	−0.0334

After this step, the presence of circles is checked. This technique is used to identify notes. All objects that have at least one circle are classified as notes. Since the parameters are only to identify if it is a note or markup, some objects with three notes may have only one circle detected, but it is already enough to identify as a note. The detection of circles can be seen in the Fig. 16.

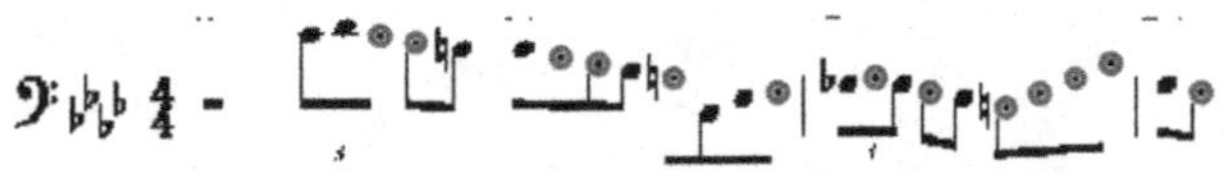

Fig. 16. Stave with circle detection

After this step, the structure of each idenfited object differs from note and markings, as you can see in Fig. 17.

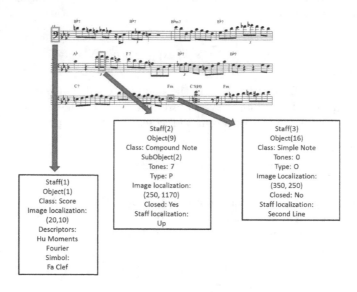

Fig. 17. Different structures to represent symbols

The description for symbols is made using the Hu moments and the Fourier descriptors. Each symbol is compared with a dictionary of known symbols. Through the correlations of the vectors, in which the correlation is a statistical function that indicates how linearly related two variables are, the data that are most correlated are accepted and the object is preclassified. The Fig. 18 shows two Hu moment vectors of the Fa key skeleton and the Fig. 19 a correlation graph.

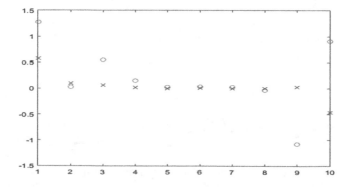

Fig. 18. Vectors of Hu moments for the Fa key skeleton

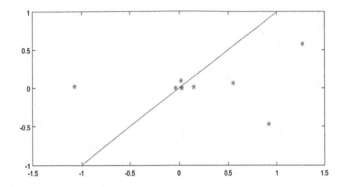

Fig. 19. Correlation graph for the Fa key skeleton

Now the notes go through another process: once again the circles within each note are identified, with new detection parameters (Fig. 20). If a note has more than one circle, it is classified as composite and each part is separated, as shown in Fig. 21a. It is classified according to its type (p, d or o). If it is inside the pentagram, its location is passed in relation to the pentagram line. If it is above or below, it counts the lines that cut it and it is defined the tone that it in relation to the pentagram, as can be seen in Fig. 21d.

The entire process of separating notes and counting up to the result shown in Fig. 21d is done through morphological operations [12].

Fig. 20. Detected circles in the symbol

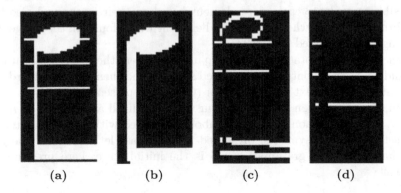

    (a)   **(b)**   **(c)**   **(d)**

Fig. 21. Recognizing lines in a note

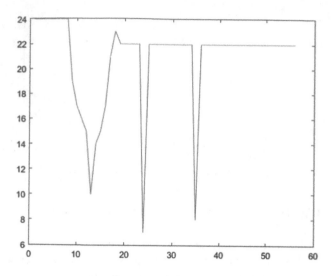

Fig. 22. Row count on each element

The count of lines is done by projecting again [29] as exemplified in Fig. 22.

All of this description data can still undergo another pattern recognition process so that elements not recognized or erroneously recognized can be described again.

3.4   Reconstruction and Validation

The input data of our reconstruction process is a textual file containing information about every recognized element of the original sheet, as depicted on Fig. 17. This textual file brings information about all recognized elements and their order. To easily manage these elements, we created an object-oriented model to represent the recognized elements. It includes the musical data and the image information about the recognized elements on the original document. Thus, it will be possible to evaluate each score element based on their image and also keep the information about where the musical element where found in the image. Our class diagram is depicted in Fig. 23.

These class representation would help us to represent the recognized data and also validate it. To validate the recognized symbols and their processing order we defined an initial Context-Free Grammar (CFG) to represent our symbolic music notation, as presented on Listing 1.1. Our CFG is defined as $G =< V, \Sigma, R, S >$ where V is the set of non terminal symbols, presented with Capital Letters, Σ is the set of terminal symbols, presented in lower case letters, R are the rules or productions of the grammar and S is the initial state, here presented by Document.

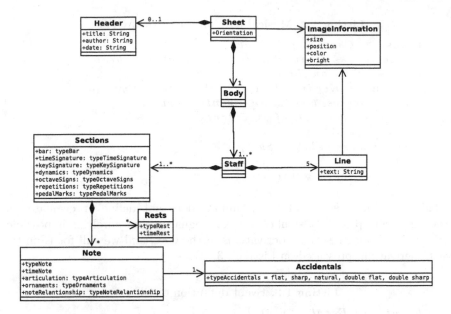

Fig. 23. Object-oriented representation of a symbolic music

Listing 1.1. Document and textual production of CFG

$$Document \rightarrow Header\ Body$$
$$Header \rightarrow Title\ Author\ Date$$
$$Title \rightarrow text\ |\ \epsilon$$
$$Author \rightarrow text\ |\ \epsilon$$
$$Date \rightarrow text\ |\ \epsilon$$

$$Body \rightarrow Chords\ Lines\ Lyrics$$
$$Chords \rightarrow text\ |\ \epsilon$$
$$Lyrics \rightarrow text\ |\ \epsilon$$

Our first set of rules identifies text elements. It is important to identify all text elements because it can be necessary to use an OCR (Optical Character Recognition) tool to identify these text elements. Despite the chords being a special set of text elements, we are classifying they as text just for the sake of simplicity. Certainly it is possible to define a better grammar to verify if chords are valid (correctly recognized) or not even as it is also possible to define grammatical rules to validate lyrics, Author, Date and Title.

The musical part main abstraction are Lines, that can be a single staff or a collection of staves connected by a Bracket or a Brace. A Bracket is used to connect staves of separated instruments of an ensemble. Brace connect multiple parts of a single instrument, like left and right hand on a piano. A part of this CFG is presented on Listing 1.2.

Listing 1.2. Musical part productions of CFG

```
Lines  →  Connector | Line
Connector  →  Connector Line | bracket | brace
Line  →  Section Line | ε
Section  →  KeySignature TimeSignature Dynamics
        Octave PedalMark Events BarLine
KeySignature  →  Clef Accidents
Cleff  →  g | c | f | ε
Accidents  →  Flat | Sharp
Flat  →  Flat b | ε
Sharp  →  Sharp # | ε
```

This simplified version of our grammar does not define or evaluate the sequence of Sharp or Flat symbols on Key signature but surely it is possible. Again, we will not present all derivations of the CFG and we will focus on the Events derivation, presented on Listing 1.3.

Listing 1.3. Event definition of CFG

```
Events  →  Events Event | ε
Event  →  Rest | Notes
Rest  →  timeRest
Notes  →  Notes Note
Note  →  Accident timeNote Articulation Ornament Dynamic
```

An Event can be a Rest or a chord (set of notes) and a note can has several attributes like Accidents, Articulations and Ornaments.

The defined grammar can help the data validation using some compilers techniques like a Syntax Analyzer to verify several features like: (a) an accident or a dynamic symbol is not used before a rest, (b) the sum of note times in a section should not be bigger than it could, (c) it is not normal to have a clef or a time signature in the middle of a section, (d) a natural symbol is not used in a line or space that is not changed with sharp or flat, (e) a del segno symbol must be used with a segno symbol, (f) a left repeat sign without a right repeat sign, (g) volta brackets (1st and 2nd endings) without repeat sign. All these validation are not a rigid rule but a clue that maybe something is wrongly recognized.

These rules are not rigid rules for some reasons like the composition has more than one sheet and the identified incoherence is not an error because it presents only a part of the music. Also it is possible that the original document has a mistake and if we intend to reflect the original music, it has to be transcripted as is.

Some of these rules can be implemented directly from our defined CFG, like the position of a clef in the section, and some must use an attribute grammar, like the sum of note times in a section.

Also, the defined CFG can help to define our lexical set. Every terminal present in Σ will be a valid graphic representation of a musical symbol. These symbols are the presented here as sets, like the Accidents (flat, sharp, natural, double flat, double sharp), Articulations, Ornaments, Dynamics or defined as terminal like timeNotes, timeRest, bracket and brace.

More than validate the identified data, it is possible to convert the Object model presented here into a common Symbolic Music format file. Next section will present a list of researched formats that can be used to this task.

3.5   Output

Our object model can easily represents a music score and validate it but to grant interoperability with legacy tools it is important to our tool output to be compatible with some existent tool to allow score editions and corrections. For this reason, we listed several Symbolic Music Notation file formats that could aim a good output choice.

The researched file formats that can be used as an output format are:

- ABC [22]
- MusicXML [13]
- Lilypond [21]
- Music21 [1,7]
- GUIDO [15].

All these formats are ASCii and are input file format for several Score Editors. Also, there are several tools to convert one format to other and they are a kind of interchangeable music formats. We also researched other formats like MIDI [2] and NIFF (Notation Interchange File Format) [14] that were discarded since they use a binary file format.

4   Conclusion

This paper presents the development framework of Copista, an Optical Music Recognition (OMR) system created to support recovery and preservation of historical musical collection. The framework is defined by process composed of many parts with specific purpose. Each part is described and the development results so far of them are detailed.

This project triggered the joint research collaboration from different areas of Computer Science like Computer Vision, Image Processing, Computer Music, Artificial Intelligence and Compilers. The union of these areas should help the development of the desired tool in the project and bringing gains for interdisciplinary research in the area of Computer Science. In addition to collaborating as interdisciplinary research in science, the project will also assist in the area of music creating an open-source tool for recognition and rewriting scores.

The first steps of this project involved the research of techniques and computational tools to be used in each step of Copista flow. The survey of these algorithms allowed preliminary tests in every planned activity with good initial results. The next steps of the project should merge the raised techniques and codes through individual steps of this research in a first functional proto-type. Possibly, this first prototype will still work with digital music and non-handwritten for training recognition of a neural network to be used for decision-making in relation to the correctness of an identified symbol.

Another step that should be taken soon is to integrate the data representation with the Computer Vision step and to verify all elements identified by a symbolic music compiler. This step should also assist in the training tool, being another step in seeking a more suitable result for the proposed objective.

References

1. Ariza, C., Cuthbert, M.: The music21 Stream: A New Object Model for Representing, Filtering, and Transforming Symbolic Musical Structures. MPublishing, University of Michigan Library, Ann Arbor (2011)
2. MIDI Manufacturers Association: The complete MIDI 1.0 detailed specification: incorporating all recommended practices. MIDI Manufacturers Association (1996)
3. Avidan, S., Shamir, A.: Seam carving for content-aware image resizing. In: ACM Transactions on Graphics (TOG), vol. 26, p. 10. ACM (2007)
4. Bainbridge, D., Bell, T.: Dealing with superimposed objects in optical music recognition (1997)
5. Bainbridge, D., Bell, T.: The challenge of optical music recognition. Comput. Hum. **35**(2), 95–121 (2001)
6. Buxton, W., Reeves, W., Baecker, R., Mezei, L.: The use of hierarchy and instance in a data structure for computer music. Comput. Music J. 10–20 (1978)
7. Cuthbert, M.S., Ariza, C.: Music21: a toolkit for computer-aided musicology and symbolic music data (2010)
8. Dori, D., Doerman, D., Shin, C., Haralick, R., Phillips, I., Buchman, M., Ross, D.: Handbook on optical character recognition and document image analysis, chapter the representation of document structure: a generic object-process analysis (1996)
9. Fujinaga, I.: Staff detection and removal. In: Visual Perception of Music Notation: On-line and Off-line Recognition, pp. 1–39 (2004)
10. Fukunaga, K.: Introduction to Statistical Pattern Recognition. Academic Press, Cambridge (2013)
11. Furht, B.: Handbook of Augmented Reality. Springer, Heidelberg (2011)
12. Gonzalez, R.C., Woods, R.E., Eddins, S.L.: Digital Image Processing Using MAT-LAB. Pearson Education India, London (2004)
13. Good, M.: Musicxml for notation and analysis. Virtual Score: Represent. Retr. Restor. **12**, 113–124 (2001)
14. Grande, C.: The notation interchange file format: a windows-compliant approach. In: Beyond MIDI, pp. 491–512. MIT Press (1997)
15. Hoos, H.H., Hamel, K.A., Renz, K., Kilian, J.: The guido notation format - a novel approach for adequately representing score-level music (1998)
16. Koendrik, J.J.: Computational vision (book). Ecol. Psychol. **4**(2), 121–128 (1992)
17. Laia, M.A.d.M.: Filtragem de Kalman não linear com redes neurais embarcada em uma arquitetura reconfigurável para uso na tomografia de Raios-X para amostras da física de solos. Ph.D. thesis, Universidade de São Paulo (2013)

18. Laia, M., Schiavoni, F., Madeira, D., Carvalho, D., Moreira, J.P., Paulo, A., Ferreira, R.: Copista – OMR system for historical musical collection recovery. In: Proceedings of the 12th International Symposium on Computer Music Multidisciplinary Research, p. 51, Marseille Cedex 13 – France: The Laboratory of Mechanics and Acoustics (2016)
19. Medina, R.A., Smith, L.A., Wagner, D.R.: Content-based indexing of musical scores. In: Proceedings of the 3rd ACM/IEEE-CS Joint Conference on Digital Libraries, JCDL 2003, pp. 18–26. IEEE Computer Society, Washington, DC, USA (2003)
20. Mundy, J.L., Zisserman, A., et al.: Geometric Invariance in Computer Vision, vol. 92. MIT Press, Cambridge (1992)
21. Nienhuys, H.-W., Nieuwenhuizen, J.: Lilypond, a system for automated music engraving. In: Proceedings of the XIV Colloquium on Musical Informatics (XIV CIM 2003), vol. 1. Citeseer (2003)
22. Oppenheim, I., Walshaw, C., Atchley, J.: The ABC standard 2.0 (2010)
23. Rebelo, A., Fujinaga, I., Paszkiewicz, F., Marcal, A., Guedes, C., Cardoso, J.: Optical music recognition: state-of-the-art and open issues. Int. J. Multimed. Inf. Retr. 1(3), 173–190 (2012)
24. Ripley, B.D.: Pattern Recognition and Neural Networks. Cambridge University Press, Cambridge (1996)
25. Selfridge-Field, E.: Beyond codes: issues in musical representation. In: Beyond MIDI, pp. 565–572. MIT Press (1997)
26. Szwoch, M.: A musical score recognition system. In: ICDAR, pp. 809–813 (2007)
27. Travis Pope, S.: Object-oriented music representation. Org. Sound 1(01), 56–68 (1996)
28. Xu, L., Krzyzak, A., Suen, C.: Methods of combining multiple classifiers and their applications to handwriting recognition. IEEE Trans. Syst. Man Cybern. 22(3), 418–435 (1992)
29. e Thiago Margarida, A.G.S.: Reconhecimento automático de símbolos em partituras musicais
30. Erpen, L.R.C.: Reconhecimento de padrões em imagens por descritores de forma. Universidade Federal do Rio Grande do Sul, Brazil (2004)
31. Souza, K.P., Pistori, H.: Implementção de um Extrator de Caracterısticas baseado em Momentos da Imagem
32. Hu, M.-K.: Visual pattern recognition by moment invariants. IRE Trans. Inf. Theory 8(2), 179–187 (1962)

Sound, Motion and Gesture

Recent Findings on Sound and Posture:
A Position Paper

Lennie Gandemer[1,2]([✉]), Gaëtan Parseihian[1], Christophe Bourdin[2],
and Richard Kronland-Martinet[1]

[1] Aix Marseille Univ, CNRS, PRISM (Perception, Représentations, Image, Sound,
Music), 31 Chemin J. Aiguier, 13402 Marseille Cedex 20, France
{gandemer,parseihian,kronland}@prism.cnrs.fr
[2] Aix Marseille Univ, CNRS, ISM, 13288 Marseille, France
christophe.bourdin@univ-amu.fr

Abstract. Although neglected for a long time, the field of sound and
posture seems to have aroused increasing interest over the last few years.
In the present position paper, we present an overview of our recent findings in this field and we put them in perspective with the literature. We
bring evidence to support the view that spatial cues provided by auditory information can be integrated by humans to improve their postural
control. Then, two complementary trails are proposed to explain these
postural effects: on the one hand, sound can be used to build a spatial
mental map of the surrounding space, helping subjects to better stabilize. On the other hand, our findings suggest that some multisensory
interactions occur, in which sound can facilitate the integration of the
other modalities involved in the postural control.

Keywords: Posture · Sound spatialization · Auditory perception ·
Acoustic cues · Acoustic space · Multisensory integration

1 Introduction

It is well known that human upright stance control relies on the integration
of various sensory cues by the central nervous system [29]. The role of visual,
vestibular and proprioceptive inputs has been well documented, leading to complex multisensory models of postural control (e.g., the Disturbance Estimation
and Compensation model, [4]). The role of audition in postural control received
less interest, in spite of a couple of earlier studies on this issue tending to show
that the lack of auditory input can be detrimental for postural control [10,19].
However, this topic seems from now on to arouse an increasing interest, as a couple of studies have emerged in the last years [13,14,28,40,41,48,49]. All these
studies, which were conducted in different contexts, tended to show that sound
can influence posture, and more particularly that integration of auditory information by human subjects helps them reduce their postural sway.

In the framework of a project involving two laboratories, one specialized in
acoustics and the other in movement sciences, we conducted several studies on

© Springer International Publishing AG 2017
M. Aramaki et al. (Eds.): CMMR 2016, LNCS 10525, pp. 91–108, 2017.
DOI: 10.1007/978-3-319-67738-5_5

the role of auditory perception in postural control. In the present paper, we propose to present these studies and to put them in perspective with the existing literature, in order to better understand how sound is integrated in the postural control process[1]. Our goal is not to describe in details all the studies we conducted, as they are already described in pending publications, but rather to give an overview of the emerging field of sound and posture, exploring various hypotheses concerning the attributes of sound which are useful for postural purposes. In particular, we will bring evidence to support the view that **humans can use spatial content of auditory information for postural control.**

Before the presentation of our contributions, we will start by a state of the art of the emerging domain of sound and posture. Then, we will present the results of our investigations on the influence of moving sound sources (Sects. 3, 4, and 5) and static sound environment (Sect. 6) on human posture. The first study we will describe investigated the role of auditory stimuli rotating around subjects (Sect. 3). In a second study involving the same rotating sound stimuli, we investigated the influence of subjects' attentional focus on their postural responses. Then, in a third study using moving sound, we manipulated the various attributes of sound source movement (Sect. 5). Finally, we built different kinds of static sound environments to better understand the role of auditory spatial information (Sect. 6).

2   State of the Art

In this section, we propose a quick overview of the sound and posture literature. This literature is not large and may at first glance appear contradictory. Here, we will show that the differences between the various studies are due to the different approaches used.

Loss of Hearing

To our knowledge, the first studies concerning the role of audition in the postural control addressed the influence of auditory loss on postural sway. In 1985, Era and Heikkinen [10] showed that the postural sway in young adults who had been exposed to noise in their work was more pronounced than in those who had not been exposed. This result was confirmed two years later, in a study by Jununten et al. [19] investigating the influence of auditory loss in soldiers on their postural control. The soldiers, who had been exposed to high-energy intermittent noise from firearms, showed significantly more body sway than the control group; moreover, subjects with more severe hearing loss exhibited more sway than those with less severe hearing loss.

Similar results were obtained later, with workers [21] and congenitally deaf children [44] or adults [28]. But the most numerous studies concerned hearing

---

[1] Note that in this paper, we will focus on studies using comfortable level of auditory stimulation. We will neither deal with studies using high intensity noise to activate the vestibular system, as in [27] or [3], nor mention studies using sounds that convey emotion (e.g., threatening sounds, or music [12,39]).

loss in the elderly and its association with an increased risk of falling (e.g. [47] and [26]). Some authors suggested that this association might be explained by a global age-related loss of vestibular function, in which auditory loss is simply a marker for vestibular losses leading to imbalance. However, a recent study by Rumalla et al. [41] compared the postural sway in hearing-aid users, in aided (aid switched on) or unaided (aid switched off) conditions. Postural performance of subjects was significantly better in the aided than the unaided condition which proves the benefits of having the auditory input fully available.

Finally, a study conducted by Kanegaonkar et al. [20] compared the postural sway in subjects in various auditory environments: normal room *vs* soundproof room, wearing ear defenders or not, eyes closed *vs* eyes open. With their eyes open, subjects exhibited a greater sway when there were set in the soundproof room *vs* in a normal room, or wearing ear defenders *vs* without ear defenders.

All these studies tend to show that the **lack of auditory input results in subjects exhibiting a poorer postural control**. This suggests that humans integrate sound in their postural control process, opening the way to the study of the sound and posture interactions. However, we will see in the following that the influence of sound on posture has been little studied to date.

The Sound Helps to Stabilize...

Firstly, a couple of studies involving static sound stimulations exhibited a decrease in sway in the presence of sound stimuli. In a study conducted by Easton et al. [9], subjects were set in a tandem Romberg stance (heel-to-toe position) with two sound sources on both sides of their head, eyes open *vs* eyes closed. Authors reported a 10% decrease of sway for subjects in the presence of auditory cues vs 60% in the presence of visual cues. This study highlighted the slightness of the effect of sound when compared with the effect of vision. In a more recent study also involving subjects in tandem Romberg stance, authors showed a 9% decrease in sway for subjects exposed to a pink noise sound source facing them [49].

Then, other studies focused on the role of moving sound sources. In a study conducted by Deviterne et al. [8], authors used sound stimuli rotating around elderly subjects. They compared two types of rotating stimulations: a "non-meaningful auditory message" (440 Hz continuous tone) and a "meaningful auditory message" (a short recorded story). In the "meaningful auditory message" condition, subjects were asked to carefully listen to the story, and they were questioned afterwards about details in the story. The results showed a stabilization of the subject only in this meaningful condition: authors concluded that the attention paid to the sound forced the subject to take into consideration the regularity and the rotation of the stimulation, which provided them with an 'auditory anchorage' and so facilitated their postural regulation. Another study conducted by Agaeva and Altman [2] used moving sounds played by an arc of loudspeakers in the sagittal plane. With sound moving back and forth, subjects exhibited a slight reduction in their postural sway, and tended to lean slightly forward in the presence of the sound.

In all these studies, sound stimuli were presented through loudspeakers. Thus, the auditory stimulations could provide spatial information on the space surrounding subjects through the auditory localization cues [6]; authors generally explained their results in terms of **auditory anchorage effect: the sound sources provide landmarks through the spatial information they convey**, which enables subjects to decrease their body sway.

Other studies were conducted using headphones: when presented through headphones, the auditory stimulation is not independent of the subject's movement. Thus, in that case, sound does not provide spatial cues on the environment surrounding the subject: this could explain why a study by Palm et al. [32] did not highlight any postural sway differences between a condition without headphones and a condition with headphones playing background noise. However, a more recent study by Ross and Balasubramaniam [40] exhibited a significant reduction in the body sway of subjects exposed to auditory stimuli through headphones. In this study, postural sway in subjects wearing noise reduction headphones was compared in two conditions: a pink noise *vs* no sound played by headphone. Here, the reduction in sway could not be considered as the result of the integration of spatial auditory cues. Authors hypothesized that their results could be due to the "stochastic resonance" phenomenon. Stochastic resonance is a phenomenon that occurs when a sensory signal containing information is subthreshold, that is, too weak to be detected and integrated by the central nervous system. In that case, adding noise (a signal which does not contain information) to the initial sensory input amplifies the whole signal which can pass the threshold and then be integrated. This phenomenon is well known for proprioception: subsensory vibrations applied to the soles of the feet have been shown to reduce postural sway [36]. Ross and Balasubramaniam hypothesized that this phenomenon could also occur in audition. Even though this lead is interesting, we can object that in their experiment, there was no initial auditory information to be enhanced by adding noise. Indeed, subjects wore headphones "designed to reduce noise from any other external source": thus, in both silent and noise conditions, there was no auditory information from the environment reaching subjects' ears. However, these results suggest that **more complex multisensory phenomena** could be involved in the interactions between posture and auditory perception. We will discuss this second hypothesis in Sect. 6 of this paper.

... But Sound Can Also Destabilize

Then, a few studies in literature missed highlighting a reduction in sway when the subject was exposed to sound stimuli. In a study conducted on young and elderly subjects exposed to rotating stimuli rendered using the binaural spatialization technique, authors showed that the lateral body sway for the elderly group was more influenced by the lateral moving auditory stimulation than that for the young group [45]. But they did not compare postural regulation for subjects in the presence and in the absence of sound, which makes the comparison with the studies previously described difficult. Another study conducted by Ha Park et al. addressed the influence of various frequencies and amplitudes of sound on postural stability [33]. They highlighted a significant increase in sway when sound frequency increased. But here again, there was no reference condition without sound allowing this study to be compared with the studies referred to in the previous section.

In two more studies, involving respectively static sounds and moving sounds rendered with four loudspeakers, Raper and Soames exhibited a disturbing effect of sound on subjects posture [37,42]. Sound stimuli were pure tone and background conversation. Similarly, a recent study conducted by Gago et al. [13] exhibited a disturbing effect of background noise on postural regulation for standing subjects. In that study, authors compared, among other conditions, the postural regulation in subjects wearing or not wearing ear defenders. Subjects were tested in a quiet laboratory, with a normal level of background noise. Authors concluded that the background noise was not informative, and thus may have created more distraction than a total lack of auditory information.

Thus, the **nature of the sound source** might be a determinant factor explaining the differences in the literature on sound and posture. It seems that when the sound does not appear to be informative, it is not integrated in the postural control process.

Our Framework

The exploration of the sound and posture literature shows that the results are highly dependent on the experimental conditions. In all the following, the studies we will present were conducted with almost the same paradigm, schematically represented in Fig. 1. From a general point of view, we investigated the **static upright stance** in **young and healthy subjects**, **blindfolded** and standing with their **feet well joined**. The deprivation of visual cues as well as the joined feet stance made it possible to put subjects in a slightly uncomfortable postural situation, inducing increased postural sways and the need to actively control the posture. This also makes it possible to better observe the expected effects

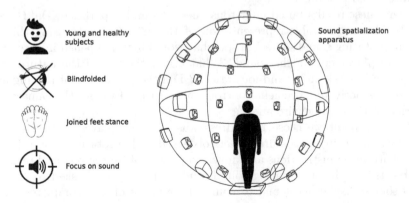

Fig. 1. Spatialization apparatus and experimental paradigm of the various studies presented in this paper

of auditory stimulus exposure. Subject postural sway was measured using a **force platform**, and sound stimuli were produced using **sound spatialization techniques** in an **auditory CAVE** (a spherical loudspeaker array surrounding the subjects - for further details, this system is presented in [34]). Subjects were asked to **stand still**, and their task was to **focus on sound stimuli**.

3   First Experiment: When a Moving Sound Stabilizes

In a first experiment described in [14], we addressed the role of a rotating sound source on the postural sway in standing subjects. Twenty young subjects, standing in the dark on a force platform, were exposed to a pink noise sound source rotating around them at various speeds. Subjects were asked to stay still while focusing on the moving sound (counting the number of laps completed by the sound source).

Our first hypotheses were based on studies manipulating visual information for postural control. Moving visual stimuli are known to induce postural responses [25]. Similarly, we thought that a moving auditory stimulus could induce postural sway. Moreover, a rotating sound can possibly induce circular vection (illusory self-motion) [24]. We wanted to explore the postural response of subjects exposed to circular vection, as it is known that vection comes with postural responses [18].

However, subjects did not experience any vection. On the contrary, our results demonstrated that they rather **decreased their postural sway when confronted to rotating auditory stimuli**. Indeed, subjects' amplitude of sway and mean sway velocity both decreased in the presence of rotating sound, when compared with the reference conditions (without sound or with a static sound source facing subjects). The decrease in sway reached 30% with the quickest rotating sound. These counter-intuitive results suggest that auditory information, which is by nature very different from visual information, may be processed and integrated in a different way.

Then, these results raised numerous questions and hypotheses: Did the subjects build a more stable representation of the acoustic space using this surrounding rotating sound source? If so, what would have happened in case of less regular displacements of the sound? What about the role of the nature of the task (counting task and sound-focus task)? Did the perception of moving auditory sources activate movement control centers? Could we get the same results in a rich static sound environment?

The first point we chose to address was the part played by the subjects attentional focus in the postural effects observed with a rotating sound. Indeed, focus of attention instructions are known to play a role in the postural responses of subjects [31]. In our rotating sound study, subjects were asked to focus on sound source displacement and to count the number of laps completed by the sound source. Thus, the reduction in postural sway could be due to this task implying an external focus of attention and a slight cognitive load.

4 Focus on Sound: A Tree Among the Trees

In a second study, we addressed the role of attentional focus in the integration of dynamic sound information for postural purposes. To this end, we followed a procedure very similar to the one used in the first rotating sound study described Sect. 3: we produced the same rotating auditory stimuli around blindfolded subjects (n = 17) in the same stance, and the same reference auditory conditions (without sound and with one static sound source facing subjects). We then compared their postural regulations when completing three different tasks:

- a **postural-focus** task: staying still, focusing on their postural control (a single reference postural task)
- a **sound-focus** task: staying still, focusing on sound (dual-task: the same as in Sect. 3)
- a **mental arithmetic** task: staying still while counting backward by 7 (purely cognitive dual-task)

Unsurprisingly, the effect of sound condition on postural sway described in the previous experiment was observed again in the sound-focus task, which is exactly the same task as in the first experiment (see the gray bars Fig. 2a). However, in the two other tasks (postural-focus task and mental arithmetic task), results showed that sound conditions no longer have a significant effect on postural control. This could be explained in two ways: 1- subjects had to allocate attention to sound to be able to integrate auditory information or 2- subjects did not integrate sound and their decrease in sway in the sound-focus task is only due to the cognitive load of the counting task, not present in the two reference conditions without sound and with a static sound. The results obtained in the two other tasks support the first explanation. Indeed, during the mental arithmetic task (which is purely cognitive) the subjects exhibited a significantly higher sway velocity than during the two other tasks (see the white bars Fig. 2b), associated with a small amplitude of sway, whatever the sound condition. This "freezing" behavior, different from subject behavior in the two other tasks, is consistent with what has been observed in the literature when subjects are exposed to cognitive loads [43]. This behavior is not observed during the sound focus task, proving that the slight cognitive load included in the sound focus task (the counting task) did not drive the postural effects observed. Moreover, subjects exhibited a significantly smaller velocity of sway in the sound-focus task than in the reference postural-focus task, which suggests that they integrated the auditory information in the former and not in the latter.

Thus, with this second experiment, we showed that the **subject stabilization** observed in our first rotating study (Sect. 3) was **not due to them being involved in the counting task**, but rather to the integration of auditory information. We also showed that **focusing on sound enables subjects to integrate this auditory information**. The results of our two first rotating sound studies could be related to the results of the previously mentioned study by Deviterne et al. [8] in which authors compared the effect of two types of rotating stimulations around subjects: a "non-meaningful auditory message" (440 Hz

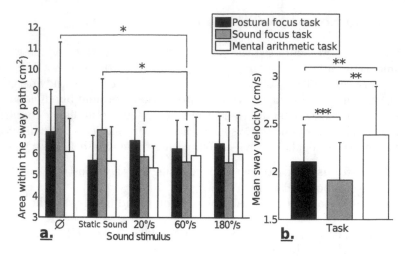

Fig. 2. Results of the rotating sound study with various focuses of attention of subjects. Mean on 17 subjects. **a.** Area within the sway path across the five sound conditions and the three tasks. **b.** Mean sway velocity across the three tasks. Bars represent the 95% confidence interval. Stars represent significant differences between conditions.

continuous tone) and a "meaningful auditory message" (a short recorded story). In the "meaningful auditory message" condition, subjects had a similar sound-focus task: they were asked to carefully listen to the story. Similarly to our study, their results showed a stabilization of the subjects only in this sound-focus task. Authors concluded that the attention paid to the rotating sound forced the subjects to take into consideration the regularity and rotation of the stimulation, which provided them with an auditory anchorage, allowing them to improve their posture regulation. Similarly, we postulate that **allocating more attention to the sound favors the integration of auditory information** in the postural control process. Thus, in all the following studies, to stimulate the potential effects of sound on posture, we went on giving subjects a sound-focus task.

Of course, this very interesting and new effect of sound stimulation on postural control remains of small amplitude, mainly when compared to the possible effects of vision on posture. For example, in the study by Easton et al. [9] conducted with subjects standing in between two static sound sources, eyes closed versus eyes open, authors showed a 10% decrease in sway in the presence of auditory cues vs 60% in the presence of visual cues. In comparison, our results suggesting a decrease in sway amplitude of about 30% with sound seems to be the only study with such results. The explanation may lead to the typology of the sounds used and to the way we produced the auditory stimulation. It is now clear that the quality of our innovating experimental device could be part of the explanation. The following experiments will address these points, exploring the various attributes of sound possibly involved in the stabilization.

5   Dissecting Movement: Space Vs Morphology

A sound source which is moving in space provokes variations of the acoustic cues (interaural time difference, interaural level difference and head related transfer function) that humans use to localize it [6]. Such variations represent what is traditionally labeled as the **spatial attributes** of a moving sound. But a moving sound source also intrinsically contains information on its own movement: its spectral content will be modified by the Doppler effect, filtering due to the air absorption, or changes in the ratio between direct sound and reverberated sound [30]. This information is what we will call here the **morphological features** of a moving sound source.

In the real world, the dynamic features of a moving sound source are mixed together with its morphological features. A sound source moving in space induces simultaneous modifications of its spatial and morphological attributes. Experimentally, we can separately synthesize both these attributes. We can then apply various attributes to a static source to evoke movement. On the one hand, there are various sound spatialization techniques allowing control of the spatial displacement of virtual sound sources. In our rotating sound studies for instance, we used a sound spatialization technique called High Order Ambisonics (see [34]). On the other hand, it is possible to implement separately each morphological feature linked to one movement. For example, by applying the equivalent Doppler effect of a moving sound source to a static sound rendered on a single loudspeaker (in mono), we can easily create a strong source movement impression [23].

In our first rotating sound study, we showed that a rotating sound source around subjects induced a decrease in their body sway. To explain this stabilization, we can formulate two hypotheses:

- the stabilization provoked by the rotating sound could be due to **changes in the spatial cues**, which are integrated by our auditory system and give spatial landmarks which can be used to stabilize. In this case, we can wonder to what extend the regularity and predictability of the trajectory is important in allowing stabilization.
- postural responses to the rotating sound could solely be due to the **motion perception** in general. As our postural control is managed by motor control areas, the perception of a moving sound could possibly activate the brain areas linked to the movement. In this latter case, evoking movement simply by morphological treatments of sound could be sufficient to induce postural changes.

To explore these two hypotheses concomitantly, we decided to dissect the rotating sound scenario which produced the better stabilization in our first studies, separating the spatial features of sound from its morphological features. For that purpose, we compared postural regulation in subjects exposed to 1 - a dynamic rotating sound, synthesized using a sound spatialization technique and adding morphological features: "**morphologico-spatial**" condition or 2 - a "morphology-evoked" movement rendered on a single loudspeaker: "**morphological**" condition. In this latter condition, the Doppler effect equivalent to the one produced for the "morphologico-spatial" condition was applied

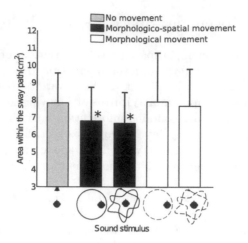

Fig. 3. Results of the spatial VS morphology study: area within the sway path across the various sound stimuli. Mean on 21 subjects. Bars represent the 95% confidence interval. The stars (*) represent a significant difference from the reference condition without movement.

to a static sound source rendered on a single loudspeaker, to give the impression that the sound source was traveling on the same trajectory.

Two different trajectories were implemented in each sound-feature condition. The first trajectory, regular and **predictable**, was a circle on the horizontal plane (at ear level) shifted to the right. The second was a **pseudo random trajectory**, rotating around the subject at the same average speed but following a more chaotic and random path (cf Fig. 3).

The results, partly presented in Fig. 3, showed that the morphology-evoked movement did not lead to a decrease in sway, but to an amplitude of sway comparable to that for the static sound reference condition. By contrast, the two trajectories with spatial displacement induced a decrease in sway to reach an amplitude of sway significantly different from the reference. Moreover, there was no differences between the two morphologico-spatial trajectories, which seems to show that the predictability and regularity of trajectories was not a determinant factor in the integration of sound by the subjects. This third experiment allowed us to validate the first hypothesis on sound movement we formulated: stabilization provoked by the rotating sound is due to the **variation of spatial cues**. Thus, it seems to confirm that the spatial attributes of sound are the main features involved in subject stabilization. We will explore this hypothesis in more detail in the next section.

6 Static Sound Environment for Postural Stabilization

In the previous sections, we showed that a sound source moving around a listener can help him to stabilize, but that the precise movement of the trajectory is of no interest. We can hypothesize that subjects use the spatial cues they can get from the moving source. Therefore, we wonder to what extent the moving sound could be replaced by several static sources surrounding subjects. Indeed, a rotating sound can be seen as an infinity of alternate static sources. Some techniques of sound motion simulation use this principle to create an apparent auditory movement (see, for example, [15]). Moreover, static sources also provide spatial cues, and we can imagine that it would be at least as easy for subjects to use the landmarks provided by static spatial cues as those provided by changing cues.

In this section, we will present two studies we conducted with static sound stimuli. The main idea behind these two studies was to investigate whether subjects were able to construct a putative "spatial hearing map" [20,48] using spatial cues from static sound sources, and then reach the same stabilization effects as those observed for rotating sounds.

Construction of an Auditory Environment

In our first studies, we showed that one static sound source facing subjects was not sufficient to make an important decrease in sway of subjects possible. Thus, we built a richer auditory environment from three recordings of ecological sources[2]: a motor, a fountain and a cicada. These 3 sources were positioned around subjects, and we compared postural sway of subjects (n = 35) exposed to 1, 2 or 3 sources, and in the absence of sound. Subjects were asked to focus on sound, counting the number of sources surrounding them. This study was conducted in a normal room and in an anechoic soundproof room. Indeed, in an soundproof environment, there is no background noise: the reference condition was perfectly silent. Moreover, each sound source provides more spatial information in a normal room, thanks to sound reflection in the space. Sound reflection has been shown to improve some localization features [38], as well as the estimation of sound source distance [22]. We wanted to know whether removing these reflections (in the anechoic environment), which reduced information provided by sound, could result in subjects exhibiting greater postural sway than in a normal room.

Subjects exhibited a decrease in their postural sway in the presence of static sound sources, when compared with the reference condition without sound (Fig. 4a). Moreover, adding sources seemed to reinforce the decrease in sway, although this tendency was not found to be significant. The decrease in sway reached 10% with 3 static sources. This result is consistent with the results of other studies involving static sound stimuli. As mentioned before, Easton et al. [9] reported a decrease in sway of 10% for subjects in tandem Romberg stance (heel-to-toe position) with two sound sources on both sides of subject head. In a more recent study also involving subjects in tandem Romberg stance, authors showed a decrease in sway of 9% of subjects exposed to a pink noise sound source facing them [49].

---

[2] The sources are labeled "ecological" because they represent sounds which exist in nature, in contrast to a more abstract sound source such as pink noise. This is a reference to the ecological approach to perception developed by Gibson [16].

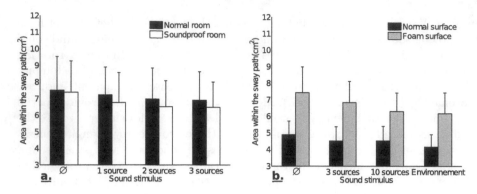

Fig. 4. Results for the amplitude of sway in the two static source studies. **a.** First study: No sound, 1, 2 or 3 static sources; soundproof room vs normal room. Mean on 35 subjects. **b.** Second study: No sound, 3 sources, 10 sources or an immersive environment; firm surface vs foam surface. Mean on 30 subjects. Bars represent the 95% confidence interval.

In contrast, the results of our study showed no differences in postural behavior between the normal room and the anechoic room. This result suggests that the information brought by the sound reflections is not usable in a postural task. But this absence of difference can also be interpreted in a multisensory way. In a study conducted by Kanegaonkar et al. [20], authors also compared the postural sway of subjects in a normal room *vs* an anechoic room, eyes open *vs* eyes closed. They demonstrated that with eyes open, subjects exhibited a significantly greater postural sway in an anechoic room than in a normal room. Similarly to our study, they found no difference between the two rooms when subjects' eyes were closed. We can hypothesize that when subjects are deprived of both visual and auditory information, as their postural situation is more challenging, a sensory reweighting may occur [5]: their sensory information needs may be reported on the other available modalities, probably considered as more reliable (plantar touch, proprioception and vestibular system).

This first static sound study confirms that the spatial cues provided by static sound sources can be integrated by subjects to decrease their postural sway. However, subjects reached a decrease of sway of 10% with 3 static sources, which is far less than the 30% in our first rotating sound study. The auditory environment built in this static sound study was quite simple. It only consisted of 3 sound sources spatially limited, which we could label "isolated": indeed, the sources were 3 recorded sounds played independently by 3 different loudspeakers. We can hypothesize that if we enrich the auditory environment, we will bring more information to subjects and thus allow them to better stabilize.

Toward a More Immersive Environment

For that purpose, in a last experiment, we decided to create richer auditory environments by means of two different approaches: firstly, adding other isolated sources, using more samples played by other loudspeakers. Secondly, by recording a real sound environment and then by re-synthesizing it in our auditory CAVE using ambisonic spatialization techniques. These techniques aim to recreate an auditory stimulation closer to natural listening. Thus, the auditory environment recreated in the spatialization apparatus was much more realistic and immersive than what we could create adding isolated sources on separate loudspeakers.

Thus, in this study, we used four different auditory conditions:

- a reference condition without sound
- 3 isolated ecological sources (same condition as the previous static sound experiment)
- 10 isolated ecological sources
- an immersive environment consisted of the same kind of ecological sources as in the previous experiment (fountain, motor sound and cicadas) recorded and re-synthesized using ambisonics.

Moreover, in this study, we decided to compare the body sway of subjects standing either on a firm surface (as in the previous static sound experiment), or on foam. The foam is classically used in postural studies to reduce proprioceptive feedback from the plantar touch [35]. We were interested here in determining whether less plantar touch feedback could result in a sensory reweighting in favor of sound. In this case, sound would then have more influence on posture.

Unsurprisingly, the amplitude of sway of subjects was found to be far greater on the foam surface than on the normal firm surface [35]. Then, the results showed a decrease in sway in all the sound conditions when compared with the no sound reference condition. More interestingly, the decrease in sway was significantly greater in the presence of the immersive environment than of 3 or 10 isolated sources (Fig. 4b). In the immersive environment condition, the decrease in sway reached 15%. This result shows that the richer the auditory environment, the more subjects can integrate sound information to decrease their postural sway, which is in accordance with our hypothesis. Finally, these tendencies were similar on both firm and foam surfaces, which suggests that auditory and plantar touch inputs are integrated independently.

Thus, the results of these two studies as well as those of other static sound studies in literature [9,49] showed that the **spatial cues embedded in the sound environment can be integrated by subjects, and help them to better stabilize.**

To explain how humans use this auditory information, the emergent hypothesis is that auditory cues allow listeners to build a cognitive representation of the surrounding environment, the so called 'spatial hearing map' [20,48]. In a study addressing the potential role of auditory information in spatial memory, conducted by Viaud Delmon et al. [46], authors built a realistic auditory soundscape rendered over headphones. The soundscape was updated in real time according to subject movements and displacements in 3D space, thanks to subject tracking and advanced binaural technologies. Subjects were blindfolded and their task was to explore a delimitated area in order to find a hidden auditory target. In that study, authors showed that the listeners were able to build a representation of space thanks to sensorimotor and auditory cues only, and then navigate and find their way in this environment in an allocentric manner. In our studies, subjects did not navigate in the space, but we can state that they nevertheless built a spatial representation of auditory environment and used it as an auditory landmark that provided them with cues to stabilize. Indeed, the mental representation of the surrounding space, also called "spatial image" can be made from the sole sensory inputs (vision, audition and/or touch) [17]. Most of the studies on the spatial cognitive map built by sound were conducted on blind people. They showed that the auditory information could be sufficient to build a precise and metrically accurate spatial map of the environment [1].

Moreover, the richer the environment, the better the stabilization. We assume that the sound source rotating around subjects provides them with numerous spatial cues, and thus could be seen as a rich sound environment too. This could explain the greater decrease in sway reached by subjects in these studies (around 30%). But it is also possible that other phenomena occur during multisensory integration of the various inputs in the postural control system.

Multisensory Approach

Indeed, even if the 'spatial landmarks provided by sound' theory we just developed makes it possible to explain a great number of results of the sound and posture studies (especially the static sound studies), there remain some results that we cannot explain based on this theory: firstly, those from studies conducted using headphones and then, some results of our moving sound studies.

The recent study conducted by Ross and Balasubramaniam [40] highlighted a subject stabilization in the presence of a pink noise delivered by headphones. When the sound is delivered by headphones, the auditory stimulation is not independent of the listener movement, and thus cannot provide him with acoustic landmark. Moreover, in our third moving sound study (see Sect. 5), we found no difference between the two moving sound conditions in which sound was following either predictable or pseudo-random trajectory. Following our acoustic landmark hypothesis, we expected to observe a stabilization in the predictable trajectory condition only. But our results showed that subjects reached the same stabilization with the pseudo-random trajectory, even though this trajectory did not provide them with a stable spatial reference.

Thus, for these two situations (moving sound source and sound delivered by headphones), we propose a multisensory approach that could explain (at least in part) the observed stabilization. During multisensory integration of the various sensory inputs involved in postural control, some intersensory interaction mechanisms can occur [11], and the presence of a sensory input can influence the integration of other inputs in various ways. Sound could thus influence the way the other modalities are integrated by the system. In many different paradigms, sound has for instance been proved to facilitate the processing of the visual input, as for example in visual search tasks in which sound was not directly useful for the visual task but nevertheless improved the performances of this task [7]. This phenomenon is called intersensory facilitation. In our experiments, there was no visual input but sound could facilitate the processing of the other modalities involved in the postural control (proprioception, vestibular input, plantar touch).

This second theory is compatible with the spatial hearing map theory. It is possible that, according to the situation, the subjects use spatial auditory landmarks and/or experience intersensory facilitation.

7   Conclusion and Perspectives

In this paper, we have presented an overview of the recent studies conducted on the emerging topic of the influence of sound on posture.

The exploration of the sparse literature about sound and posture (Sect. 2) showed that sound can play a role in the postural regulation. The results of some studies are somehow contradictory, which proves that there is a need for further investigation in the field. First, numerous studies showed that the lack of auditory information (partial or total loss of hearing) results in a poorer postural regulation. Then, a couple of studies investigated the specific role of auditory stimulation on human posture. Some studies highlighted a stabilization effect of sound: the main hypothesis which emerged from these studies is that sound can provide an auditory landmark helping people to stabilize. Other studies demonstrated that sound can also induce destabilization, which suggests that the nature of the auditory stimuli plays a role in the sound and posture interaction.

Through the five postural studies we have conducted, we could confirm that subjects are able to use auditory information to better stabilize, when there are deprived of visual information. We explored the various attributes of sound that could possibly contribute to subject stabilization. We showed that forcing subjects to **allocate attention to the auditory stimulation favors the effects** of sound on posture (Sect. 4). Then, we brought forward evidence to support the view that the **spatial cues provided by auditory stimulation are the main attribute of sound responsible for subject stabilization**, either with a sound source moving around subjects (Sects. 3 and 5) or within a static sound environment (Sect. 6). The richer the sound environment, the better the subjects stabilize.

To explain our results, we propose two complementary trails. One the one hand, the spatial hearing map hypothesis: the spatial auditory cues provided by sound allow subjects to build their own representation of their surrounding environment, and to use it as a spatial landmark to improve their stability. On the other hand, depending on the situation, some intersensory facilitation mechanisms may occur, in which the presence of sound improves the processing of the other modalities implied in the postural control process.

Our studies are still raising numerous questions. Firstly, research is lacking on the perception of 3D sound when using sound spatialization techniques (such as ambisonics we used in our studies). We are convinced that a better understanding of how humans perceive 3D sound would help to understand how sound interacts with posture. That is why we are currently investigating the perception of sound trajectories in space. Then, now that we better understand how subjects rely on auditory information, it would be interesting to use a reverse approach and try to induce postural perturbations by perturbing spatial sound environment. Then, we did not address the question of the nature of the sound source. The couple of studies in the literature that exhibit a destabilizing effect of non-informative stimuli (pure tones, background noise or conversation, or pure tones) suggest that subjects can use auditory information only if it provides spatial cues. In our studies, we used either static ecological sound sources, which provided spatial reference cues, or a moving abstract sound (pink noise) which provided spatial information thanks to its movement (variation of the spatial cues). Moreover, we forced subjects to pay attention to these auditory stimuli and thus probably to extract spatial information from the sound stimulation.

All the results we presented here and all related questions associated show that interaction between sound and posture is a promising area of research. Following the present overview, we are now convinced that auditory cues are a significant source of information for the postural control. Thus, auditory perception may be helpful for improvement of postural control in various fields, including sport, rehabilitation or sensory substitution for instance.

Acknowledgments. This work was funded by the French National Research Agency (ANR) under the SoniMove: Inform, Guide and Learn Actions by Sounds project (ANR-14-CE24-0018- 01).

References

1. Afonso, A., Blum, A., Katz, B.F., Tarroux, P., Borst, G., Denis, M.: Structural properties of spatial representations in blind people: scanning images constructed from haptic exploration or from locomotion in a 3-D audio virtual environment. Memory Cogn. **38**(5), 591–604 (2010)
2. Agaeva, M.Y., Altman, Y.A.: Effect of a sound stimulus on postural reactions. Hum. Physiol. **31**(5), 511–514 (2005)
3. Alessandrini, M., Lanciani, R., Bruno, E., Napolitano, B., Di Girolamo, S.: Posturography frequency analysis of sound-evoked body sway in normal subjects. Eur. Arch. Otorhinolaryngol. Head Neck **263**(3), 248–252 (2006)
4. Assländer, L., Hettich, G., Mergner, T.: Visual contribution to human standing balance during support surface tilts. Hum. Mov. Sci. **41**, 147–164 (2015)
5. Assländer, L., Peterka, R.J.: Sensory reweighting dynamics in human postural control. J. Neurophysiol. **111**(9), 1852–1864 (2014)
6. Blauert, J.: Spatial Hearing: The Psychophysics of Human Sound Localization. The MIT Press, Cambridge (1997)
7. Van der Burg, E., Olivers, C.N., Bronkhorst, A.W., Theeuwes, J.: Pip and pop: nonspatial auditory signals improve spatial visual search. J. Exp. Psychol. Hum. Percept. Perform. **34**(5), 1053 (2008)
8. Deviterne, D., Gauchard, G.C., Jamet, M., Vançon, G., Perrin, P.P.: Added cognitive load through rotary auditory stimulation can improve the quality of postural control in the elderly. Brain Res. Bull. **64**(6), 487–492 (2005)
9. Easton, R., Greene, A.J., DiZio, P., Lackner, J.R.: Auditory cues for orientation and postural control in sighted and congenitally blind people. Exp. Brain Res. **118**(4), 541–550 (1998)
10. Era, P., Heikkinen, E.: Postural sway during standing and unexpected disturbance of balance in random samples of men of different ages. J. Gerontol. **40**(3), 287–295 (1985)

11. Ernst, M.O., Bülthoff, H.H.: Merging the senses into a robust percept. Trends Cogn. Sci. **8**(4), 162–169 (2004)
12. Forti, S., Filipponi, E., Di Berardino, F., Barozzi, S., Cesarani, A.: The influence of music on static posturography. J. Vestib. Res. **20**(5), 351–356 (2010)
13. Gago, M.F., Fernandes, V., Ferreira, J., Yelshyna, D., Silva, H.D., Rodrigues, M.L., Rocha, L., Bicho, E., Sousa, N.: Role of the visual and auditory systems in postural stability in Alzheimers disease. J. Alzheimers Dis. **46**(2), 441–449 (2015)
14. Gandemer, L., Parseihian, G., Kronland-Martinet, R., Bourdin, C.: The influence of horizontally rotating sound on standing balance. Experimental Brain Research, pp. 1–8 (2014). http://dx.doi.org/10.1007/s00221-014-4066-y
15. Getzmann, S., Lewald, J.: Localization of moving sound. Percept. Psychophysics **69**(6), 1022–1034 (2007)
16. Gibson, J.J.: The Ecological Approach to Visual Perception, Classic edn. Psychology Press, Hove (2014)
17. Giudice, N.A., Klatzky, R.L., Bennett, C.R., Loomis, J.M.: Combining locations from working memory and long-term memory into a common spatial image. Spatial Cogn. Comput. **13**(2), 103–128 (2013)
18. Guerraz, M., Bronstein, A.M.: Mechanisms underlying visually induced body sway. Neurosci. Lett. **443**(1), 12–16 (2008)
19. Juntunen, J., Ylikoski, J., Ojala, M., Matikainen, E., Ylikoski, M., Vaheri, E.: Postural body sway and exposure to high-energy impulse noise. Lancet **330**(8553), 261–264 (1987)
20. Kanegaonkar, R., Amin, K., Clarke, M.: The contribution of hearing to normal balance. J. Laryngol. Otol. **126**(10), 984 (2012)
21. Kilburn, K.H., Warshaw, R.H., Hanscom, B.: Are hearing loss and balance dysfunction linked in construction iron workers? Br. J. Ind. Med. **49**(2), 138–141 (1992)
22. Kolarik, A.J., Moore, B.C., Zahorik, P., Cirstea, S., Pardhan, S.: Auditory distance perception in humans: a review of cues, development, neuronal bases, and effects of sensory loss. Attention Percept. Psychophys. **78**, 1–23 (2015)
23. Kronland-Martinet, R., Voinier, T.: Real-time perceptual simulation of moving sources: application to the leslie cabinet and 3D sound immersion. EURASIP J. Audio Speech Music Process. **2008**, 7 (2008)
24. Lackner, J.R.: Induction of illusory self-rotation and nystagmus by a rotating sound-field. In: Aviation, Space, and Environmental Medicine (1977)
25. Laurens, J., Awai, L., Bockisch, C., Hegemann, S., van Hedel, H., Dietz, V., Straumann, D.: Visual contribution to postural stability: Interaction between target fixation or tracking and static or dynamic large-field stimulus. Gait Posture **31**(1), 37–41 (2010)
26. Lin, F.R., Ferrucci, L.: Hearing loss and falls among older adults in the United States. Arch. Intern. Med. **172**(4), 369–371 (2012)
27. Mainenti, M.R.M., De Oliveira, L.F., De Lima, M.A.D.M.T., Nadal, J., et al.: Stabilometric signal analysis in tests with sound stimuli. Exp. Brain Res. **181**(2), 229–236 (2007)
28. Mangiore, R.J.: The effect of an external auditory stimulus on postural stability of participants with cochlear implants (2012)
29. Maurer, C., Mergner, T., Peterka, R.: Multisensory control of human upright stance. Exp. Brain Res. **171**(2), 231–250 (2006)
30. Merer, A., Ystad, S., Kronland-Martinet, R., Aramaki, M.: Semiotics of sounds evoking motions: categorization and acoustic features. In: Kronland-Martinet, R., Ystad, S., Jensen, K. (eds.) CMMR 2007. LNCS, vol. 4969, pp. 139–158. Springer, Heidelberg (2008). doi:10.1007/978-3-540-85035-9_9

31. Mitra, S., Fraizer, E.: Effects of explicit sway-minimization on postural-suprapostural dual-task performance. Hum. Mov. Sci. **23**(1), 1–20 (2004)
32. Palm, H.G., Strobel, J., Achatz, G., von Luebken, F., Friemert, B.: The role and interaction of visual and auditory afferents in postural stability. Gait Posture **30**(3), 328–333 (2009)
33. Park, S.H., Lee, K., Lockhart, T., Kim, S., et al.: Effects of sound on postural stability during quiet standing. J. Neuroeng. Rehabil. **8**(1), 1–5 (2011)
34. Parseihian, G., Gandemer, L., Bourdin, C., Kronland-Martinet, R.: Design and perceptual evaluation of a fully immersive three-dimensional sound spatialization system. In: International Conference on Spatial Audio (ICSA): 3rd International Conference (2015)
35. Patel, M., Fransson, P., Lush, D., Gomez, S.: The effect of foam surface properties on postural stability assessment while standing. Gait Posture **28**(4), 649–656 (2008)
36. Priplata, A., Niemi, J., Salen, M., Harry, J., Lipsitz, L.A., Collins, J.: Noise-enhanced human balance control. Phys. Rev. Lett. **89**(23), 238101 (2002)
37. Raper, S., Soames, R.: The influence of stationary auditory fields on postural sway behaviour in man. Eur. J. Appl. Physiol. **63**(5), 363–367 (1991)
38. Ribeiro, F., Zhang, C., Florêncio, D.A., Ba, D.E.: Using reverberation to improve range and elevation discrimination for small array sound source localization. IEEE Trans. Audio Speech Lang. Process. **18**(7), 1781–1792 (2010)
39. Ross, J.M., Warlaumont, A.S., Abney, D.H., Rigoli, L.M., Balasubramaniam, R.: Influence of musical groove on postural sway. J. Exp. Psychol. Hum. Percept. Perform. **42**, 308 (2016)
40. Ross, J.M., Balasubramaniam, R.: Auditory white noise reduces postural fluctuations even in the absence of vision. Exp. Brain Res. **233**(8), 2357–2363 (2015)
41. Rumalla, K., Karim, A.M., Hullar, T.E.: The effect of hearing aids on postural stability. Laryngoscope **125**(3), 720–723 (2015)
42. Soames, R., Raper, S.: The influence of moving auditory fields on postural sway behaviour in man. Eur. J. Appl. Physiol. **65**(3), 241–245 (1992)
43. Stins, J.F., Roerdink, M., Beek, P.J.: To freeze or not to freeze? affective and cognitive perturbations have markedly different effects on postural control. Hum. Mov. Sci. **30**(2), 190–202 (2011)
44. Suarez, H., Angeli, S., Suarez, A., Rosales, B., Carrera, X., Alonso, R.: Balance sensory organization in children with profound hearing loss and cochlear implants. Int. J. Pediatr. Otorhinolaryngol. **71**(4), 629–637 (2007)
45. Tanaka, T., Kojima, S., Takeda, H., Ino, S., Ifukube, T.: The influence of moving auditory stimuli on standing balance in healthy young adults and the elderly. Ergonomics **44**(15), 1403–1412 (2001)
46. Viaud-Delmon, I., Warusfel, O.: From ear to body: the auditory-motor loop in spatial cognition. Front. Neurosci. **8**, 283 (2014)
47. Viljanen, A., Kaprio, J., Pyykkö, I., Sorri, M., Pajala, S., Kauppinen, M., Koskenvuo, M., Rantanen, T.: Hearing as a predictor of falls and postural balance in older female twins. J. Gerontol. Ser. A: Biol. Sci. Med. Sci. **64**(2), 312–317 (2009)
48. Vitkovic, J., Le, C., Lee, S.L., Clark, R.A.: The contribution of hearing and hearing loss to balance control. Audiol. Neurotol. **21**(4), 195–202 (2016)
49. Zhong, X., Yost, W.A.: Relationship between postural stability and spatial hearing. J. Am. Acad. Audiol. **24**(9), 782–788 (2013)

Eluding the Influence of Postural Constraints on Cellists' Bowing Movements and Timbral Quality

Jocelyn Rozé[1]([⊠]), Richard Kronland-Martinet[1], Mitsuko Aramaki[1], Christophe Bourdin[2], and Sølvi Ystad[1]

[1] Aix Marseille Univ, CNRS, PRISM (Perception, Représentation, Image, Sound, Music), 31 Chemin J. Aiguier, 13402 Marseille Cedex 20, France
{roze,kronland,aramaki,ystad}@prism.cnrs.fr
[2] ISM (Institut des Sciences du Mouvement), CNRS, UMR 7287, Aix-Marseille Université, 13288 Marseille, France
christophe.bourdin@univ-amu.fr

Abstract. While playing expressively, cellists tend to produce postural movements, which seem to be part of their musical discourse. This article describes how their instrumental bowing gestures and timbral features of the produced sounds may be affected when constraining these postural (or ancillary) movements. We focus here on a specific acoustic timbre alteration qualified as *harshness* in the constrained condition. A method based on Canonical Correlation Analysis (CCA) is used to extract the correlations between the bowing displacement and the sound rendition with and without postural constraint among several cellists. Then a detailed investigation of the covariation between gestural and sound data for the duration of the note is carried out, using Functional Data Analysis (FDA) techniques. Results reveal interesting effects of the postural constraint on the coupling patterns between the bowing movement and the spectro-temporal acoustical features.

Keywords: Cellist · Ancillary/postural gestures · Gesture-sound relationship · Acoustical features · Musical expressivity · Functional Data Analysis

1 Introduction

Musical expressiveness of instrumentalists is the result of interactions within a multimodal context, in which the perceived acoustic features turn out to be embedded into continuous gesture processes [10]. By gestures, we refer to those directly responsible of the sound production, but also to so-called ancillary gestures, in particular the performers' postural movements, which may form an integral part of their subtle expressive variations [18]. In the present study, we investigate expressivity related to cello playing and focus on the influence of the musicians' bowing gesture on the timbre quality in normal playing, and in posturally constrained situations.

© Springer International Publishing AG 2017
M. Aramaki et al. (Eds.): CMMR 2016, LNCS 10525, pp. 109–124, 2017.
DOI: 10.1007/978-3-319-67738-5_6

This study falls within a more global experimental context of sound-gesture relationship for the cello players in musical performance situations [14]. Related works explored the instrumentalists' postural movements for the clarinet [6], the piano [16], the harp [3], or the violin [17]. It was shown that these ancillary displacements turn out to be part of the musician's motor program, and in the case of the cellist, their limitation seemed to induce an impoverishment of the expressiveness in terms of rhythmic deviations and timbre color variations. In this paper, we assess the timbral degradations which may occur on certain notes while constraining the cellist's posture.

The postural constraint should also give rise to some alterations in the bowing gesture execution, and our aim here consists in highlighting them by assessing the covarying effects with the sound characteristics. Acoustical studies carried out on the physics of the violin [15] and the cello [7] revealed the bowing pressure and velocity as the main parameters of timbral control. Furthermore, the correlations with the spectral energy distribution (referred as the spectral centroid) and its variations over time, allowed to better understand the role played by these physical parameters with respect to the perceived *brightness* [5] and musical tense [4].

After presenting the experimental methodology, we describe the sound-gesture descriptors used in the study. Analysis of type Canonical Correlation (CCA) [2] and Functional Principal Component (FPCA) [1,13] are then carried out to investigate how these sound and gesture descriptors mutually covary, while applying a postural constraint.

2 Methodology

2.1 Experimental Conditions

Seven cellists participated in the study and were asked to play a specifically designed score in the most expressive way, while being subjected to two kinds of postural conditions. Figure 1 illustrates these two conditions. The first one was a natural condition, in which cellists were asked to play naturally as in a performance context. The second one was a physically fully constrained situation, in which the torso was attached to the back of the chair by a 5-point safety race harness and a neck collar adjusted to limit the head movements. We are aware that these kinds of physical constraints raise an epistemological issue, since bowing or acoustic alterations may result from other factors than the only limitation of postural movements, such as physical, psychological discomfort, estrangement from the concert situation... All the selected cellists were professional or very experimented, to ensure that no kind of technical weaknesses would potentially result in a lack of expressivity. These two experimental conditions are part of a larger experiment thoroughly described in [14].

2.2 Data Acquisition and Pre-analysis

Cellists' corporeal movements were recorded by a VICON motion capture system, composed of 8 infrared cameras acquiring data at a frame rate of 125 Hz.

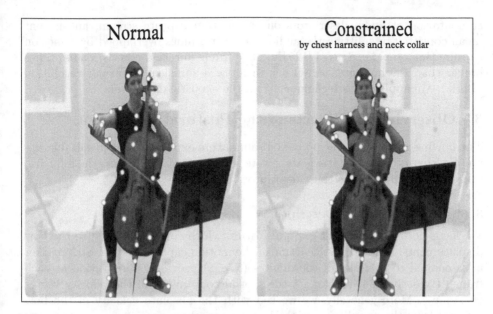

Fig. 1. The 2 types of experimental postural condition *Normal* and *Constrained*

The system tracked the 3D kinematical displacements of a set of sensors placed on the performer body, the cello and the bow. In this paper, we are interested in the bow displacements, and therefore focus on a bow marker located at the bow frog (close to the musician's right hand). Audio data were recorded at a 44.1 kHz sampling rate by a DPA 4096 microphone placed under the cello bridge and connected to a MOTU interface. The gestural and audio streams were manually synchronized by a clap at the beginning of each recording.

When analyzing acoustic data collected from the constrained condition, a specific note of the score which sounded poor, shrill and quaver as a beginners sound frequently emerged for all the cellists. Following the terminology used by one of the performers, we qualified this as a *harshness* phenomenon produced by acoustic timbre alterations. When this *harsh* feature was perceived, we extracted the note, as well as its nice (or *round*) counterpart produced in the normal condition for the same cellist. This extraction process was carefully carried out by a pitch-tracking algorithm adapted from the MIR toolbox [9]. A corpus of 8 pairs of *round/harsh* notes were hereby extracted among all the participating cellists. The corresponding sequences of bowing displacements were segmented from the motion capture stream, by using the temporal landmarks of the note in the audio stream.

To further investigate potential functional correlations between sound and bowing gesture (in particular for analysis presented in Sect. 5), the computation of acoustic descriptors were adapted to the bowing gesture data. In practice, the frame rate of acquisition within the audio device (44.1 KHz) was much higher than that of the motion capture system (125 Hz). To synchronize the computation of audio descriptors on the motion capture stream, an efficient mean consisted in splitting the audio stream in frames overlapped by a motion capture time step, i.e. 8 ms (1/125 Hz). The frame duration was chosen ten times higher than the hop size, i.e. 80 ms, to allow a sufficient frequency resolution (12 Hz). We applied this technique for all the acoustic descriptors.

3   Observing the Effects of the Postural Constraint

The bowing gesture and the perceived sound were explored through suitable signal descriptors. Simple statistic tests were then performed to assess the influence of the cellists' posture on these descriptors.

3.1   Bowing Gesture Descriptor

We focus here on a compact gestural feature which could be related to the bow displacements. In the reference frame of the motion capture system, each marker is associated to a triplet of coordinates (x, y, z) providing its position at each frame. By derivation, we can get the spatial coordinates of the velocity vector (v_x, v_y, v_z). More generally, we worked with the absolute velocity of the bow inferred from the coordinates of the bow frog marker:

$$VEL_{bow} = \sqrt{(v_x^2 + v_y^2 + v_z^2)} \tag{1}$$

This information could have been captured by simple accelerometers, but given that the experimental context primarily focused on the musician's postural aspects, we used the data collected by the motion capture system.

3.2   Acoustic Descriptors

In this paper, we tried to find acoustic descriptors, which at best could reveal the relation between the signal and the quality alteration perceived between notes played in normal and constrained conditions. This acoustic *harshness* phenomenon might correspond to a degradation of the perceived timbre, i.e. a change in the spectro-temporal features of the sound signal, for equal pitches and durations. Several timbre descriptors are potential candidates to suitably characterize such time-frequency transformations.

Temporal Domain. From a temporal viewpoint, a *harsh* note may differ from its *round* counterpart, by the way the energy rises during the onset of the sound. The kind of features that are likely to reflect this observation imply a prior extraction of the sounds temporal envelope, that for example can be obtained from the Root Mean Square (RMS) value [8] of each audio frame l composing the signal s:

$$Rms(l) = \sqrt{\frac{1}{N_w} \sum_{n=0}^{N_w-1} s^2(lN_{hop} + n)} \qquad (0 \leq l \leq L-1) \tag{2}$$

where N_w is the frame length, and N_{hop} the hop size in samples.

Attack Slope. The classical descriptor Attack Time could have been adopted as a temporal descriptor, but the Attack Slope (ATS) was preferred in the present case to overcome energy differences between signals. ATS represents the temporal increase or average slope of the energy during the attack phase [11]:

$$ATS = \frac{PeakValue}{AT} \tag{3}$$

where AT is the Attack Time, i.e. the time that the RMS envelope takes to deploy from 10% to 90% of its maximal value $PeakValue$.

Spectral Domain. From a spectral viewpoint, the shrill nature of the sound produced in the constrained situation would suggest energy reinforcement in high frequencies. Given the harmonic nature of cello sounds, harmonic spectral descriptors are believed to characterize this spectral transformation. We chose a total number of 25 harmonics to compute them.

Harmonic Spectral Centroid. We decided to focus on the Harmonic spectral centroid instead of the standard spectral centroid (SC), since the stochastic part of the signal seemed to be negligible with regards to the deterministic part. Hence, from the harmonic instantaneous features provided by subband decomposition, we computed the Harmonic spectral centroid (HSC(l)) to characterize the barycenter of the spectral energy distribution at each frame l. This descriptor is related to the perception of *brightness* in various acoustic studies on the violin [5]. HSC represents the mean value of HSC(l) [8]:

$$HSC = \frac{1}{L} \sum_{l=1}^{L-1} HSC(l) = \frac{1}{L} \sum_{l=1}^{L-1} \frac{\sum_{h=1}^{H} f_h(l) A_h(l)}{\sum_{h=1}^{H} A_h(l)} \qquad (0 \le l \le L-1) \tag{4}$$

where $f_h(l)$ and $A_h(l)$ are respectively the frequency and the amplitude of the hth harmonic in frame l.

Harmonic Tristimulus Ratio. To characterize more finely the spectral energy transfer, which may occur from a *round* sound to its *harsh* equivalent, we computed the harmonic tristimulus [12] at each frame. This descriptor considers the energy distribution of harmonics in three frequency bands and measures the amount of spectral energy inside each band relatively to the total energy of harmonics. The first band contains the fundamental frequency, the second one the medium partials (2, 3, 4) and the last one higher order partials (5 and more). Three spectral coordinates are hereby obtained for each frame l, corresponding to spectral barycenter distribution within each band:

$$TR_1 = \frac{1}{L} \sum_{l=1}^{L-1} TR_1(l) = \frac{1}{L} \sum_{l=1}^{L-1} \frac{A_1(l)}{\sum_{h=1}^{H} A_h(l)} \qquad (0 \le l \le L-1) \tag{5}$$

$$TR_2 = \frac{1}{L} \sum_{l=1}^{L-1} TR_2(l) = \frac{1}{L} \sum_{l=1}^{L-1} \frac{\sum_{h=2}^{4} A_h(l)}{\sum_{h=1}^{H} A_h(l)} \qquad (0 \le l \le L-1) \tag{6}$$

$$TR_3 = \frac{1}{L} \sum_{l=1}^{L-1} TR_3(l) = \frac{1}{L} \sum_{l=1}^{L-1} \frac{\sum_{h=5}^{H} A_h(l)}{\sum_{h=1}^{H} A_h(l)} \qquad (0 \le l \le L-1) \qquad (7)$$

where $A_h(l)$ is the amplitude of the hth harmonic in frame l. From here, we designed a more compact ratio focusing on the spectral transfer feature, which should increase for energy transfers towards higher partials:

$$TRIratio = \frac{1}{L} \sum_{l=1}^{L-1} TRIratio(l) = \sum_{l=1}^{L-1} \frac{TR_3(l)}{TR_1(l) + TR_2(l)} \qquad (8)$$

3.3   Validation of the Descriptors

To assess if these four descriptors, i.e. the bowing gesture descriptor and the three acoustic descriptors, are affected by the postural constraint, we performed statistical tests for each one, on the basis of the 8 *round/harsh* data pairs. Figure 2 presents the quartiles of the four descriptors between the two postural conditions. It was observed that in average, the postural constraint tended to reduce the bow velocity, while giving rise to a dual effect in the spectro-temporal acoustic features resulting in a decrease of the temporal attack slope coupled with an energy increase for high-frequency partials.

The relevance of each signal descriptor was evaluated by performing a simple paired two-tailed t-test, based on the null hypothesis that the means are the same between the normal and constrained conditions. Table 1 reports the results of these t-tests, which actually reveal that the null hypothesis can be significantly rejected and thus that the postural conditions can be discriminated for all signal descriptors. This signifies that the sound-bowing gesture relationship is significantly affected when the cellists are limited in their postural movements.

Table 1. Results of paired t-tests on the defined gestural descriptor and the three acoustic descriptors. The discrimination capacity between the normal and constrained groups of 8 data for each descriptor is given by the p-value: $^*p < 0.05$, $^{**}p < 0.01$, $^{***}p < 0.001$

Descs	Bow velocity	ATS	HSC	Triratio
t(7)	2.22	4.15^{**}	-4.21^{**}	-3.48^*

4   Correlating Bow Gesture to Sound Features

In this part, we focus on the global relation that exists between cellists bowing gesture and the resulting sound features. This connection is explored by means of raw linear and canonical correlations techniques.

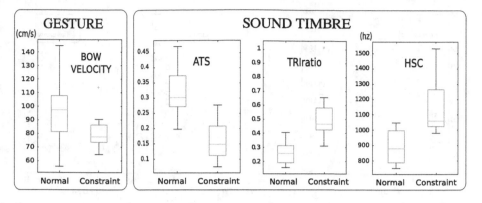

Fig. 2. Comparison of the mean gestural and acoustic features between the 2 types of postural conditions *Normal* and *Constraint*. The central marks are the medians, the edges of the boxes are the 25th and 75th percentiles

4.1   Raw Linear Correlations

Analysis. Assuming a linear relationship between the gestural and acoustic parameters, we computed the Pearson's linear correlation coefficient of the bowing velocity vector with each acoustic vector. Each feature vector was composed of 16 mean data, corresponding to the 8 pairs of {normal/constrained} mean descriptor data.

Results. Raw linear correlations revealed that the bowing velocity was strongly correlated to the attack slope (ATS) of the temporal envelope ($r^2 = 0.6^*$). By contrast, spectral descriptors such as harmonic centroid (HSC) and tristimulus ratio (TRIratio) surprisingly turned out to be weakly correlated to the bowing velocity ($r^2 = -0.11$ and $r^2 = -0.21$ respectively).

Discussion. Figure 3 depicts the three graphs of linear correlation between the gestural variable and each acoustic variable. The interpretation of these graphs becomes interesting if we consider pairs of variables {normal/constraint}. The first graph *(a)* highlights the influence of the postural constraint on the bowing velocity and temporal attack slope. It reveals that once the cellists were deprived of their postural adjustments, they showed a global tendency to combine a decrease in bow velocity with a less sharp way of attacking the string, reflected by a decrease of attack slope. The second and third graph, *(b)* and *(c)* highlight the influence of the postural constraint on the bowing velocity and spectral descriptors. They present similar interesting tendencies, in spite of the weak raw correlations obtained in the results: The reduced velocity induced by the postural constraint causes an energy shift towards high frequency components. A closer examination of the canonical correlations might allow confirming this effect on the spectral variables.

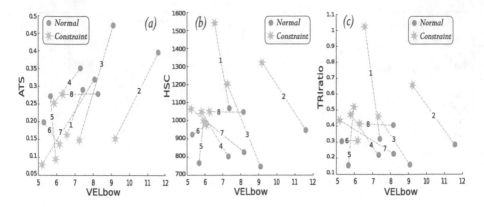

Fig. 3. Polar diagrams of the raw linear correlations obtained between the mean gestural bowing feature and the three mean acoustic ones over the 16 observations. Each {normal(N)/constraint(C)} pair is connected by a dotted line. The raw linear correlations are presented: *(a)* Between VELbow and ATS, *(b)* Between VELbow and HSC, *(c)* Between VELbow and TRIratio

4.2   Canonical Correlations

Analysis. We performed a Canonical Correlation Analysis (CCA) to assess and quantify the nature of the interaction between the bowing gesture and all the identified acoustic features. It consisted in finding two sets of basis vectors, one for the gesture and the other for the acoustic descriptors, such that the correlations between the projections of the initial variables onto these basis vectors are mutually maximized. Compared with the previous ordinary correlations, this technique offers the advantage of being independent of the coordinate system in which the variables are described. It actually finds the coordinate system optimizing their representation. We provided the CCA with the previously used feature vectors of 16 mean data, but organized differently: the 16 mean bowing velocities were contained in a vector $\mathbf{X}$, and the 3 variables (ATS, HSC, TRIratio) of 16 mean acoustic data in a matrix $\mathbf{Y}$.

Results. The Canonical Correlation Analysis between mean gestural and mean acoustic data ($\mathbf{X}$ and $\mathbf{Y}$) appeared to be highly significant ($r^2 = 0.74^*$). The analysis computed the canonical scores by projecting the initial variables $\mathbf{X}$ and $\mathbf{Y}$ on two matrices $\mathbf{A}$ and $\mathbf{B}$, which maximize the canonical correlation $corr(\mathbf{XA}, \mathbf{YB})$. We used the canonical loadings $\mathbf{A}$ and $\mathbf{B}$ to express each variate $\mathbf{U} = \mathbf{XA}$ and $\mathbf{V} = \mathbf{YB}$ as a linear combination of the initial gestural and acoustic variables respectively. It thus leaded to the 2 following equations:

$$\begin{cases} \mathbf{U} = -0.5 \times \mathbf{VEL_{bow}} \\ \mathbf{V} = -10 \times \mathbf{ATS} - 0.01 \times \mathbf{HSC} + 5 \times \mathbf{TRIratio} \end{cases}$$

Figure 4 presents the canonical scores (or variates $\mathbf{U}$ and $\mathbf{V}$) resulting from the method.

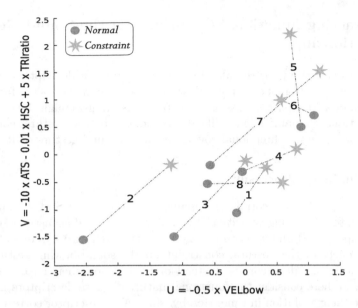

Fig. 4. Canonical variates of the CCA applied on the mean gestural and acoustic features. The variates U and V correspond to linear combinations of bowing gestures and acoustic features respectively. The canonical correlation between these two variates is $r^2 = 0.74^*$. Each {normal/constrained} pair has been represented by a dotted line.

Discussion. The canonical weights (or projection eigenvectors) **A** and **B** stand for the relative importance of each of the initial variables in the canonical relationships. We can hereby deduce from the first correlation equation that the gestural variable **VEL$_{bow}$** is negatively correlated to its variate **U** (**A** $= -0.5$). In the same manner, the second correlation equation indicates that the variate **V** is negatively correlated with **ATS** (**B(1)** $= -10$), positively correlated with **TRIratio** (**B(3)** $= 5$), and not correlated with **HSC** (**B(2)** $= -0.01$). By contrast with the raw linear correlation method, the CCA reveals a correlation with at least one spectral variable (**TRIratio**).

If we now consider data pairs of postural conditions, as it's represented on Fig. 4, we can get an interesting interpretation of the role played by each variate in the modification of the sound-gesture relationship. Along the gestural variate **U**, the constrained condition is rated higher as a whole compared to its normal counterpart, which indicates a global decrease of the gestural variable **VEL$_{bow}$**. Along the acoustic variate **V**, the constrained condition is also rated higher as a whole than its normal counterpart, which suggests a global dual effect of the two main acoustic correlated variables: A decrease of **ATS** coupled to an increase of **TRIratio**. This interpretation of the space built from the CCA variates, reinforces the results already obtained in Sect. 3. Furthermore, it is coherent with the results of Guettler [7], who demonstrated that the lowest bow speeds give the highest relative amplitudes for the upper partials.

5   Extracting Functional Covariates of the Sound-Gesture Relationship

The previous statistic tools revealed interesting results for descriptors averaged over the whole duration of each note. However, the examined data are functional by nature and in this part, we assess if the previous findings might be confirmed in the functional domain. The modifications induced by the postural constraint should allow extracting functional covariates of the sound-gesture relationship.

5.1   Preliminary Processing

By means of a canonical correlation analysis, we showed in Sect. 4 that a gestural descriptor of bowing velocity (VELbow) and two dual acoustic descriptors - attack slope (ATS) and spectral energy transfer (TRIratio) - were suitable to model the effect of the postural constraint on the sound-bowing gesture relationship within the data corpus. Instead of focusing on their mean values as previously, we here consider the functional nature of these descriptors, in order to compare their evolution in time. Hereby, since ATS descriptor corresponds to a discrete value, we rather consider the RMS envelope in the functional temporal domain.

Even though the musicians were asked to play the score at a fixed tempo, all the notes composing the corpus presented slightly different durations, because of deviations induced from the constraint or expressive intentions of the players. These temporal variations prevent the sequences of descriptors from being directly compared. A preliminary step thus consisted in synchronizing the temporal sequences of the corpus by time-warping process. The 8 {normal/constraint} pairs of descriptor curves were fitted to the duration of the longest one, which measured 56 data points (i.e. 45 ms in the mocap frame rate). This led to 16 time-warped temporal sequences for each one of the three functional descriptors: VELbow(t), RMS(t), TRIratio(t).

5.2   Analysis

The 3 groups of 16 time-warped curves were processed by Functional Data Analysis (FDA) techniques [13], which consisted in modeling each time-serie as a linear combination of equally spaced 6-order B-spline basis functions. We chose a semi-sampled basis with respect to the total number of data points in each curve, i.e. a basis of 28 (56/2) B-spline functions, to keep a fine-grained definition of each curve and limit the inner smoothing FDA mechanism.

This functional spline-based representation of time-point data turned out to be particularly suited to analyze the sources of variability encompassed within the sound-bowing gesture interaction. It was achieved by combining the FDA modelling to classical multivariate Principal Component Analysis (PCA), a technique known as Functional PCA (FPCA). We thus extracted the major modes of variability of this interaction by carrying out two *bivariate* FPCAs: The first one between the functional bow velocities VELbow(t) and the temporal sound envelopes RMS(t); The second one between the same bow velocities VELbow(t) and the functional descriptor of high-frequency spectral distribution called the TRIratio(t).

5.3   Results

The results of the two bivariate FPCAs are respectively presented Figs. 5 and 6. In each case, we focused on the first two principal components returned by the method, since they accounted for more than 90% of the overall variability among the bivariate set of 16 curves. A bivariate functional principal component was defined by a double vector of weight functions:

$$\begin{cases} \xi_m = (\xi_m^{VELbow}, \xi_m^{RMS}) & \text{for the first FPCA} \\ \eta_m = (\eta_m^{VELbow}, \eta_m^{TRIratio}) & \text{for the second FPCA} \end{cases}$$

ξ_m^{VELbow} denotes the principal m-variations of the bow velocity curves, relatively to ξ_m^{RMS}, the m-variations of temporal sound envelopes. η_m^{VELbow} denotes the principal m-variations of the bow velocity curves, relatively to $\eta_m^{TRIratio}$, the m-variations of high-frequency spectral distributions. The index m equals 1 or 2, since only two components are necessary to account for the principal variations.

For the first FPCA, we obtained two orthornormal bivariate eigenfunctions ξ_1 and ξ_2, respectively accounting for 72% and 21% of the variations. The effects of these bivariate eigenfunctions ξ_1 and ξ_2 are represented in Fig. 5, by specific perturbations of the mean functional variables $\overline{VELbow(t)}$ and $\overline{RMS(t)}$. These perturbations reflect the fact of adding or subtracting each eigenfunction to the two mean curves, i.e. $\overline{VELbow(t)} \pm \xi_m^{VELbow}(t)$ and $\overline{RMS(t)} \pm \xi_m^{RMS}(t)$. Interestingly, we notice that the first eigenfunction reflects a *positive* correlation, visible as an overall amplitude shift of the two functional means. The second eigenfunction correlates a distortion in the timing of the mean velocity profile with an amplitude shift of the mean sound envelope. The bivariate effect of these eigenfunctions is synthesized in polar diagrams (Fig. 5c1 and c2), which report the position of the mean function values $(\overline{VELbow(t)}, \overline{RMS(t)})$ by a dot in the (x, y) plane. Each point of the polar mean curve is linked to a line indicating the direction of the perturbation $(\overline{VELbow(t)} + \xi_m^{VELbow}(t), \overline{RMS(t)} + \xi_m^{RMS}(t))$.

For the second FPCA, we obtained two orthornormal bivariate eigenfunctions η_1 and η_2, respectively accounting for 71% and 20% of the variations. The effects of these bivariate eigenfunctions η_1 and η_2 have been represented Fig. 6 by specific perturbations of the mean functional variables $\overline{VELbow(t)}$ and $\overline{TRIratio(t)}$, as previously. Interestingly, we notice that the first eigenfunction reflects a *negative* correlation, visible as an opposed amplitude shift of the two functional means. The second eigenfunction correlates a distortion in the timing of the mean velocity profile with an amplitude distortion of the mean high-frequency spectral distribution. Polar diagrams of these two mean variables have also been reported with their eigenfunction perturbations (Fig. 6c1 and c2).

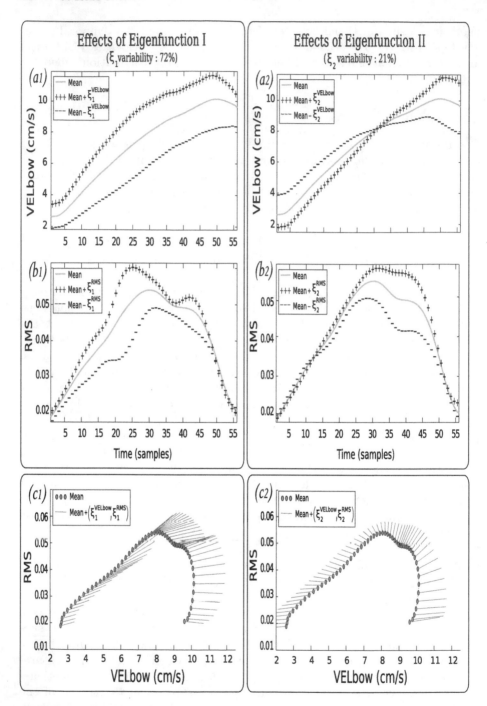

Fig. 5. *Left:* Effects of adding or subtracting the 1st bivariate eigenfunction ξ_1 to or from the mean curve of Bow velocity (a_1) and RMS (b_1). *Right:* Effects of adding or subtracting the 2nd bivariate eigenfunction ξ_2 to or from the mean curve of Bow velocity (a_2) and RMS (b_2). The covariate effect of each eigenfunction on both variables is presented in polar diagrams: (c_1) for eigenfunction I and (c_2) for eigenfunction II

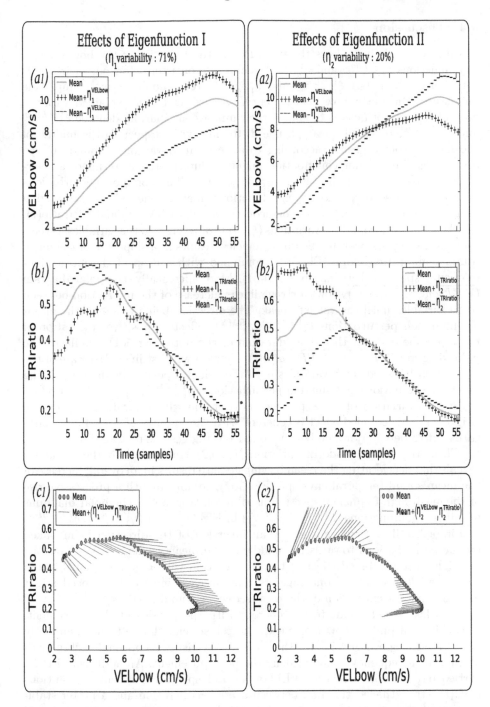

Fig. 6. *Left:* Effects of adding or subtracting the 1st bivariate eigenfunction η_1 to or from the mean curve of Bow velocity (a_1) and TRIratio (b_1). *Right:* Effects of adding or subtracting the 2nd bivariate eigenfunction η_2 to or from the mean curve of Bow velocity (a_2) and TRIratio (b_2). The covariate effect of each eigenfunction on both variables is presented in polar diagrams: (c_1) for eigenfunction I and (c_2) for eigenfunction II

5.4 Discussion

Results revealed that across the two FPCAs, the behavior of the bow velocity eigenfunctions ξ_m^{VELbow} and η_m^{VELbow} remained consistent. Indeed, their major contribution, denoted ξ_1^{VELbow} and η_1^{VELbow}, reflected an overall amplitude increase of the mean bow velocity curve, according to an explained variance around 70% in both cases. Similarly, their minor contribution, denoted ξ_2^{VELbow} and η_2^{VELbow}, reflected an amplitude distortion with respect to the middle of the mean velocity profile, according to an explained variance around 20% in both cases. This minor contribution might be interpreted in terms of accelerations/decelerations of the mean bowing gesture. The common perturbations induced by these bow velocity eigenfunctions, may be viewed as a leveraging tool to interpret the joint effects on acoustic variables RMS(t) and TRIratio(t).

First, the major mode of variations (ξ_1, η_1) transversal to the variables, reveals that increasing the overall mean bow velocity, results in a slope rise of the mean sound temporal envelope (Fig. 5b1), combined with a drop of the mean high-frequency spectral distribution (Fig. 6b1). More specifically, the polar diagram $(\overline{VELbow(t)}, \overline{RMS(t)})$ shows a strong linear increase of the interaction between these variables until the velocity peak. The direction being taken by the major eigenfunction perturbations $(\xi_1^{VELbow}, \xi_1^{RMS})$ reflects a positive covariation of these parameters over the whole duration of the note (Fig. 5c1). Similarly, the polar diagram $(\overline{VELbow(t)}, \overline{TRIratio(t)})$ shows a weakest linear decrease of the interaction between these variables until the velocity peak. The direction being taken by the major eigenfunction perturbations $(\eta_1^{VELbow}, \eta_1^{TRIratio})$ reflects a negative covariation of these parameters over the whole duration of the note (Fig. 6c1). This coupled effect is coherent with the findings of Sect. 4 and hence turns out to be a major trend of the sound-bowing gesture relationship.

Then, the minor mode of variations (ξ_2, η_2) transversal to the variables, reveals that accelerating the mean bowing gesture results in an overall increase of the mean sound temporal envelope (Fig. 5b2), combined with a progressive rise of the mean high-frequency spectral distribution (Fig. 6b2). The polar diagrams of minor eigenfunctions $(\xi_2^{VELbow}, \xi_2^{RMS})$ in Fig. 5c2, and $(\eta_2^{VELbow}, \eta_2^{TRIratio})$ in Fig. 6c2, reflect this tendency by an inversion of the direction being taken by the perturbations towards the middle of the mean sequences. The first one highlights the combined effect of bow acceleration with a gain of global sound energy, while the second one suggests that decelerating the bow speed might induce a quicker extinction of the high-frequency sound partials.

This last result seems to be coherent with the physics of the instrument, since within a pulling bow movement, the cellists can choose to independently accelerate the speed or reinforce the pressure, to ensure an optimal timbre quality and high-frequency content, along the bow movement. An additional FPCA carried out on bow velocities VELbow(t) and spectral barycenter evolutions HSC(t), strengthened this link between a bow acceleration and a better stabilization of the spectral barycenter. Nevertheless, further investigations should be conducted with other essential physical parameters like the bow pressure, to completely validate these assumptions.

6   Conclusion

This paper presented a contribution to a better understanding of the musician/instrument interaction in the case of cello playing. It aimed to better identify the connections between the cellists' motor control principles and the related expressive timbral features. More specifically, the role played by ancillary movements was investigated through a full postural constraint condition, which effects were assessed both on the cellist's bowing gesture velocity and spectro-temporal acoustic features of the produced sounds.

The results turned out to be coherent with bowed-string physics [7] and synthesis models [5]. Indeed, a canonical correlation analysis (CCA) performed on the mean values of the sound-gesture parameters, revealed that the discomfort caused by the postural constraint, was mainly linked to an overall decrease in bow velocity. This gestural variation was coupled to a *harsh* spectro-temporal acoustic transformation, combining a slope attack fall of the sound's temporal envelope, with an energy rise in high-frequency partials. Furthermore, a functional analysis of the descriptor data allowed to extract principal components (FPCs) characterizing the covariations of sound-bowing gestures in time. These eigenfunctions first confirmed the major trend already identified by the CCA. On the other hand, they also highlighted a minor influence of the postural constraint on the bow deceleration, coupled with a reinforcement in *brightness* (i.e. the upper partials in the spectrum) at the beginning of the sound.

Further investigations will consist in investigating more finely cellists' postural movements, to suggest an optimal coupling between their bow velocity and the preservation of spectro-temporal acoustic features.

Acknowledgments. This work was partly supported by the French National Research Agency and is part of the "Sonimove" project (ANR-14-CE24-0018).

References

1. Bianco, T., Freour, V., Rasamimanana, N., Bevilaqua, F., Caussé, R.: On gestural variation and coarticulation effects in sound control. In: Kopp, S., Wachsmuth, I. (eds.) GW 2009. LNCS, vol. 5934, pp. 134–145. Springer, Heidelberg (2010). doi:10.1007/978-3-642-12553-9_12
2. Caramiaux, B., Bevilacqua, F., Schnell, N.: Towards a gesture-sound cross-modal analysis. In: Kopp, S., Wachsmuth, I. (eds.) GW 2009. LNCS, vol. 5934, pp. 158–170. Springer, Heidelberg (2010). doi:10.1007/978-3-642-12553-9_14
3. Chadefaux, D., Le Carrou, J.L., Wanderley, M.M., Fabre, B., Daudet, L.: Gestural strategies in the harp performance. Acta Acustica United Acustica **99**(6), 986–996 (2013)
4. Chudy, M., Carrillo, A.P., Dixon, S.: On the relation between gesture, tone production and perception in classical cello performance. In: Proceedings of Meetings on Acoustics, vol. 19, p. 035017. Acoustical Society of America (2013)
5. Demoucron, M.: On the control of virtual violins-physical modelling and control of bowed string instruments. Ph.D. thesis, Université Pierre et Marie Curie-Paris VI; Royal Institute of Technology, Stockholm (2008)

6. Desmet, F., Nijs, L., Demey, M., Lesaffre, M., Martens, J.P., Leman, M.: Assessing a clarinet player's performer gestures in relation to locally intended musical targets. J. New Music Res. **41**(1), 31–48 (2012)
7. Guettler, K., Schoonderwaldt, E., Askenfelt, A.: Bow speed or bowing position - which one influence spectrum the most? In: Proceedings of the Stockholm Music Acoustic Conference (SMAC 03), 6–9 August 2003
8. Kim, H.G., Moreau, N., Sikora, T.: MPEG-7 Audio and Beyond: Audio Content Indexing and Retrieval. Wiley, Hoboken (2006)
9. Lartillot, O., Toiviainen, P.: A matlab toolbox for musical feature extraction from audio. In: Proceedings of the International Conference on Digital Audio Effects, pp. 237–244 (2007)
10. Leman, M.: Embodied Music Cognition and Mediation Technology. MIT Press, Cambridge (2008)
11. Peeters, G.: A large set of audio features for sound description (similarity and classification) in the cuidado project. Technical report, IRCAM (2004)
12. Pollard, H.F., Jansson, E.V.: A tristimulus method for the specification of musical timbre. Acta Acustica United Acustica **51**(3), 162–171 (1982)
13. Ramsay, J.O.: Functional Data Analysis. Wiley Online Library, Hoboken (2006)
14. Rozé, J., Ystad, S., Aramaki, M., Kronland-Martinet, R., Voinier, T., Bourdin, C., Chadefaux, D., Dufrenne, M.: Exploring the effects of constraints on the cellist's postural displacements and their musical expressivity. To appear in Post-Proceedings of CMMR 2015 - Music, Mind and Embodiment, Plymouth (2015)
15. Schelleng, J.C.: The bowed string and the player. J. Acoust. Soc. Am. **53**(1), 26–41 (1973)
16. Thompson, M.R., Luck, G.: Exploring relationships between pianists' body movements, their expressive intentions, and structural elements of the music. Musicae Scientiae **16**(1), 19–40 (2012)
17. Visi, F., Coorevits, E., Miranda, E., Leman, M.: Effects of Different Bow Stroke Styles on Body Movements of a Viola Player: An Exploratory Study. Michigan Publishing, University of Michigan Library, Ann Arbor (2014)
18. Wanderley, M.M., Vines, B.W., Middleton, N., McKay, C., Hatch, W.: The musical significance of clarinetists' ancillary gestures: an exploration of the field. J. New Music Res. **34**(1), 97–113 (2005)

Eclipse: A Wearable Instrument for Performance Based Storytelling

Ezgi Ucar[(⊠)]

Ezgi Ucar Design, 66 West 12th Street, New York, NY 10011, USA
Ezgiucar.design@gmail.com

Abstract. Eclipse is a dance performance telling the Altai Shaman story of a solar eclipse. Through movement of a dancer, a unique soundscape is created, to which the dancer moves. This feedback mechanism tries to achieve a multi-sensory interaction where the sounds created by movements are supplementary to the visual perception of the movements.

Keywords: New musical instruments · Wearable technology · Interactive storytelling · Multisensory perception · Altai Shamanism

1 Introduction

Eclipse is a project dedicated to exploring ways for technology to aid performative multi-sensory storytelling. The project revolves around four domains: new musical instruments, wearable technology, interactive storytelling and Altai Shamanism. The project contains a dance costume with embedded electronics, which act as a musical instrument.

Eclipse consists of two consecutive parts: ideation and design of the wearable instrument, and the improvised performance of dancers with the instrument. I decided to discuss each part separately since they address different users. The first part is meant to be used by the dancer as a creative tool, while the latter is meant to be experienced by the audience. Information regarding every step of the creation process can be found in corresponding sections of the paper.

2 Ideation

The purpose of this project is to explore how technology can be used to create audio-visual interactions and how technological advancements affect our perception of sound and music. The exploration not only works towards finding the connection between technology and performance arts, but also seeks to find the effects of the visual aspect of the performance in the audience's perception of the sound generated.

An inspiration that lead to the ideation of this project was the facial expressions or body movements that musicians make during a performance. As with every staged performance, musical performances have a visual aspect, and the musicians' expressions and movements are the most stimulating parts of the visuals. Durkin [1] touches upon this subject in Decomposition: A Music Manifesto.

© Springer International Publishing AG 2017
M. Aramaki et al. (Eds.): CMMR 2016, LNCS 10525, pp. 125–133, 2017.
DOI: 10.1007/978-3-319-67738-5_7

"We pay attention (with whatever degree of consciousness) to a musician's body movements, and through them we detect— or assume— certain "expressive intentions." Experimental subjects pick up on what Levity calls "an emergent quality"— something "that goes beyond what was available in the sound or the visual image alone." This "emergent quality" seems to be the result of a synergy between visual and audio stimuli, and consequently informs listeners' understanding of the music."

The "emergent quality" of musicians' body movements is an intended quality in this case. While a musician's body movement has no direct effect on the sound that is created by the traditional instrument, the dancer's movements are the driving force of creating the sound in Eclipse.

In Eclipse, I explore the paths between dynamic storytelling and multisensory perception. We perceive the world through different modalities. The information provided from multiple modalities are processed interdependently in our brains. The environment around us is dynamic; the visual, sonic, olfactory, tactile, and gustatory elements are constantly changing. So why should a story be limited to a static environment? It should be as dynamic as life is. Eclipse explores a dynamic storytelling environment where the sonic and visual elements change during a performance as well as in different performances.

2.1 Storytelling: The Altai Shaman Story

Altai Shamans worshipped the mother sun and the father moon as their gods. Sun and Moon gods would fight with evil spirits and protect their people from danger. Yet sometimes, evil spirits would capture the gods, causing solar and lunar eclipses. To save their gods, Altai people would shout, drum, and make incredible noises during the eclipse.

Eclipse introduces a new way of storytelling, through an interactive dance costume inspired by Altai Shamanism. The costume creates its own visual and sonic environment in response to the dancer's movements and tells the story of a Shaman Eclipse through its light play and dynamic soundscape. It goes beyond a dance costume, by becoming a performer itself, rather than merely existing as a prop during the performance. It has a personality involving a dynamic, yet unpredictable range of movements, over which the user has limited control.

The Shaman perceives a world of total aliveness, "in all parts personal, in all parts sentient, in all parts capable of being known and being used" [2]. They believe that everything that exists has life, including non-sentient objects. Drawing from this idea, the Eclipse dress was imagined as a non-sentient object that comes alive with the dancer's movements.

3 Technical Details

3.1 Sensory Data Processing

The audio interaction starts with sensor based data collection. Two proximity sensors located on the top hoop of the skirt provide relative location information of the dancer, with respect to the center of the dress. The purpose of having the dress as the starting point rather than a geographical location is to keep the interaction solely between the user and the dress.

Collected data are sampled into more manageable chunks of information, which is then translated into a MIDI control panel. To be more clear, each chunk of location information corresponds to a specific area within the 2D space inside the hoop. This 2D space acts as a MIDI control surface, with specific areas randomly assigned to specific controls such as pitch, panning, resonance, etc. The randomness only refers to the initial assignment; the control areas are fixed during the performances.

3.2 Wireless Communication

For the performer to have freedom in her movement, wireless communication between the wearable device and the sound source is essential. Computers with audio processing software and the loud speakers necessary for this project are neither compact, nor light enough to be integrated into a garment. Thus, the garment has to communicate with them remotely to provide data. In earlier prototypes, communication via bluetooth and wifi were eliminated for several reasons including delays in receiving the data and breaking communications. The final version of the dress uses Xbee [12] radios for wireless communication, which provide simultaneous gathering and processing of the data and creation of sound. Simultaneity between the visual and the audio is critical in a live performance; each movement that creates (and represents) a certain sound should occur simultaneously with the corresponding sound. As Newell argues, in order for us to interact with an object, the information we gather from it through different senses should come together as a coherent percept [7]. This will also help inform the audience that the sound is actually created by the movements and it will provide coherent feedback for multisensory perception.

3.3 The Feedback Loop

As the dancer moves, sensory data from the proximity sensors are collected with a Teensy [13] board embedded in the upper loop of the skirt and sent to another Teensy board connected to a laptop through an Xbee radio on each end. The first Teensy board is programmed to sample the data collected into manageable chunks that are then sent to the second Teensy board. In the computer, received data chunks are translated into MIDI commands for Ableton Live, where the sound is created. The sound outputted through external speakers is heard by the dancer who responds to it with reactionary movement.

3.4 Visual Enhancement

The visual aspect of the project consists of two parts. First is the actual dance performance with the aesthetic values added by the dress and the dancer's movements. Second is the projection of the top view of the performance, which creates the illusion of a solar eclipse. See appendix for the video link (Fig. 1).

Fig. 1. Two hoops of the skirt moving with the dancer

Visual design of the dress is fed by two main domains of this project. The first is Altai Shamanism and the second is storytelling, which come together in the Altai Shaman eclipse story. A Shaman's costume is believed to be created with the directions of spirits. It is uniquely decorated with characteristic traditional items such as bead-work, metals or feathers. Siberian Shaman costumes have symbols representing their travels to the Upper and Lower worlds. The guide spirits in their travels are represented by circular elements. Altai Shamanism, a relative of Siberian Shamanism, uses circular rings on their garments to represent the Sun and Moon gods [9].

Fig. 2. A view of the dancer testing the dress from above (Color figure online)

The skirt consists of two hoops attached to a bodice, which carries the weight of the dress. Two hoops made of metal wires symbolize the moon and the sun, as a reference to the Altai Shaman rings. Yellow LED strips embedded underneath the lower hoop create the illusion of a solar eclipse when viewed from above (Fig. 2).

4 Testing with Dancers

For the purpose of uniqueness, the dancers involved in the testing of the Eclipse dress were chosen to have expertise in different dance styles. They were all asked to improvise with the dress in whichever style they would please, keeping the Altai Shaman theme in mind. Visual and aural results of these improvised performances, as well as feedback from the dancers, guided me towards some critical decisions about the performance.

The first dancer, Qui Yi Wu, who considered her dance as "street style", found the dress to be limiting for the way she dances. Wu stated [10]:

"It is definitely a great design, I think it will fit more experimental and futuristic movement style. I do street dance so it's all about organic movements and freedom, and most of the time grooving to music. I feel like the design doesn't go with the momentum of spinning because of the way it attaches to the body and I don't know how to move without considering it will bump into my body frequently.

I really like the concept of having lighting around you and making music is always fun. Although sometimes it depends on what kind of music/sound you make. If it's complicated to conduct it might overwhelm the dancer."

This feedback was helpful in seeing the limitations that the dress creates for the user. In addition to the dancer's feedback, the performance showed the street dance style to be unfit for the story trying to be told, and the visual and aural elements did not match.

The second dancer, Betty Quinn, described her performance as "contemporary lyrical" [11]. In her feedback about the dress, Quinn observed:

"Feel was swaying, it made me feel like I was dancing with a partner, for sure. I had to navigate the natural movements and weight of the hoop with my body. Sound was otherworldly, mystical, it made the dress seem alive, which goes along with the partner aspect (Fig. 3)."

In the second user test, the dancer was more comfortable with the dress and its movements. The weight and shape of the skirt was not a limitation in this case, but a unique characteristic of the dress that the dancer can navigate. In her feedback, Quinn refers to the dress as a "partner" rather than a costume, which was the intention while creating the dress. With its weight, unique movements, and musical aspect, Eclipse dress has proven to be an active personality in the performance.

The third dancer, Kiki Sabater could not provide feedback but defined her style as Limón inspired modern dance. This dance style also visually fit the sound created (Fig. 4).

The takeaway from this study is that, as versatile as the dress was intended to be made to fit all styles of dance, it is more suitable to modern and experimental dance styles. Harsh movements or high jumps makes the dress hard to control for the dancer.

Fig. 3. Quinn performing Eclipse at Parsons School of Design

Fig. 4. Kiki Sabater performing *Eclipse* at Circuit Bridges Concert No. 35: UK Loop

Furthermore, modern and experimental styles created better cohesion between the visuals and the sound created during the performance. Since the sound created by the dress does not necessarily supply a consistent rhythmic base for the dancer, a flexible style will help the dancer improvise more comfortably.

5 Background and Related Work

Wearable technology can be classified under three main fields; fashion, data & communication, and performing arts. Wearable devices under the data & communication category have a higher practical and commercial use, while the other two usually have aesthetic and artistic concerns. Expanding DIY culture makes wearable technology accessible to a wider audience of makers and allows for cheaper resources and less costly experimentation. This resulted in the creation of several pieces of musical wearable technology in the past decade. The majority of these pieces involve micro-controllers, sensors, processing of the sensory data collected, and audio editing software to translate the processed data into sound/music. The Crying Dress [3] by Kobakant is a mourning garment that creates a weeping soundscape with a unique trigger; water dripping on embroidered sensors. The speakers embroidered out of conductive thread outputs the sound. This art piece is similar to Eclipse in terms of telling a story through a wearable technology piece creating a custom soundscape. The major distinction between the two projects is that Eclipse is meant for a large audience to observe is as a staged performance, while The Crying Dress is basically an expressive dress for a specified occasion; a funeral. The Crying dress is putting the wearer in a more passive role, by doing the job for the user, while on the other hand Eclipse needs the user to be active in order to function. Mainstone's body-centric devices such as Human Harp [4] and the collaborative work of Mainstone and Murray-Brown, The Serendiptichord [5], are examples of sensor based sonification of movement. Human Harp is not considered a self-contained wearable instrument, but rather a sound installation since it acts as an extension to a suspension bridge. However, the implementation of technology consists of sensors providing movement data, which is processed and translated into sound through audio editing software. The Serendiptichord, on the other hand, described by Murray-Brown as a "choreophonic prosthetic" [6], consists of fully mobile wearable components, including a headpiece and a pod for each hand. Sound is again created as an output of sensory data (movement and touch) processing.

Another precedent is Malloch and Hattwick's Les Geste [8], a performance with prosthetic digital instruments. The instruments are controlled by the performer through touch, movement, and location sensors.

All of these examples are similar to Eclipse in terms of their use of sensory data in creating sound. However, they do not have the storytelling aspect that is a critical part of Eclipse.

6 Future Work

This experimental project provided useful information for future prototypes or continuation of the project with multiple wearable devices. First of all, the user of the dress is narrowed down to modern, lyrical, and experimental dancers. With this information, other dresses fitting the same dance style can be created with the dancer's feedback during the process. Secondly, feedback from the dancers proved that this is an enjoyable experience for the creator, which can be enhanced by having multiple dresses - and therefore multiple dancers - interact with each other to create a soundscape.

The processes used in this project can be repeated to tell a different story. I would like this project to be a starting point for further multisensory storytelling explorations based on visual and aural interactions.

7 Conclusion

This paper outlines all steps of the experimentation towards creating a wearable instrument for interactive and performative storytelling. The ideation, purpose of the project, design process and implementations were covered in different sections of the paper. User test results, including feedback from dancers and observations of the author were provided.

This experimentation showed that it is possible to create a feedback loop of movement and sound, where the sounds created by the movements are coherent with the movements. The sonic environment created by the dress was a unique contribution of each dancer performing with it. The conception of a performer dress was successfully created on a wearable device with unique movements that needed navigation and unpredictable sound creation. This wearable "partner", as it was referred to by Quinn [10], turned out to be a dynamic character in the performance, telling the story of an Altai Shaman solar eclipse with its unique visual and sonic environment.

Acknowledgements. This project was executed as my thesis submitted to the faculty of Parsons The New School for Design, in partial fulfillment of the requirements for the degree of Master of Fine Arts in Design and Technology. Special thanks to Anezka Cecile Sebek, Barbara B. Morris, Katherine Moriwaki, Andrew Zornoza, Melissa Grey, Betty Quinn, Kiki Sabater, Qiu Yi Wu, Juno Liu, Kieun Kim, Daniel Mastretta Jimenez, Riley Kalbus, Marc Fiaux, Anna Meriano and Ryan Tunnell.

Appendix

The video of the Eclipse performance viewed from above is available at https://vimeo.com/133083095.

References

1. Durkin, A.: Do you hear what I hear? In: Decomposition: A Music Manifesto, p. 159. Pantheon Books, New York (2014)
2. Nicholson, S.J.: Shamanism: An Expanded View of Reality. Theosophical Publishing House, Wheaton (1987). Foreword
3. The Crying Dress. KOBAKANT. http://www.kobakant.at/?p=222. Accessed 11 May 2016
4. "About - Human Harp." Human Harp. http://humanharp.org/. Accessed Spring 2015
5. Murray-Browne, T., Mainstone, D., Bryan-Kinns, N., Plumbley, M.D.: The Serendiptichord: a wearable instrument for contemporary dance performance. Publication no. 8139. Audio Engineering Society, London (2010)
6. The Serendiptichord. Tim Murray Browne Interactive Sound Creative Code. http://timmb.com/serendiptichord/. Accessed Spring 2015
7. Solon, O.: Prosthetic Instruments Create Music through Body Movements (Wired UK). Wired UK. 8 August 2013. http://www.wired.co.uk/news/archive/2013-08/08/digital-instruments-gestes
8. Newell, F.N.: Cross- modal object recognition. In: Calvert, G., Spence, C., Stein, B.E. (eds.) The Handbook of Multisensory Processes, p. 123. MIT Press, Cambridge (2004)
9. Kostium, S.: Iz Kollektsii Irkutsk Go Oblast Nogo Kraevedcheskogo Muzeia = Shaman's Costumes, p. 17. Artizdat, Irkutsk (2004)
10. Wu, Q.Y.: User Testing Feedback. 10 April 2015. Online interview by author
11. Quinn, B.: User Testing Feedback. 2 June 2015. Online interview by author
12. "XBee® ZigBee." XBee ZigBee. http://www.digi.com/products/xbee-rf-solutions/modules/xbee-zigbee
13. Teensy USB Development Board. https://www.pjrc.com/teensy/

Music Composition, Public Spaces and Mobility

Sound Interaction Design and Creation in the Context of Urban Space

Julián Jaramillo Arango(✉)

Programa de Diseño y Creación, Universidad de Caldas, Grupo DICOVI,
Calle 65 No. 26-10, Manizales Caldas, Colombia
julianjaus@yahoo.com

Abstract. This paper reports current theoretical and creative results of a postdoctoral research study entitled Sound Design for Urban Spaces. It focuses on the design process of novel audio devices and on encouraging people in transit through the city to explore technology-empowered listening strategies. In this paper, the practice of urban sound design will be raised and some conceptual contributions concerning listening, acoustic analysis and sonic interaction will be discussed. We will extract some design insights that have been inspiring in the creation process of the Smartphone Ensemble, The AirQ Jacket and Lumina Nocte. These projects have been got under way along with MA students from the Design and Creation program at the Caldas University in Manizales, Colombia.

Keywords: Mobile music · Urban sound design · Sonic interaction design

1 Introduction

From the late 1960 portability has been introduced as a regular feature in audio devices and interfaces, promoting a generation of gadgets addressed to pedestrians and urban travelers. Since the commodification of audio gear suggest a complex economic and social processes [1] mobile audio determines a challenging scenario for the designer since it deals with both, technical and cultural aspects of sonic media. According to Hosokawa [2] the design success of the Walkman was not due to the technical innovation developed by Sony engineers. In fact, in terms of functionality the Walkman represented a sort of technological regression since it just permitted playback operations. However, in the sphere of urban everyday life the Walkman meant an important innovation in the technologies of the self, empowering the citizens with instruments to give shape to their singularities and extend their autonomy in the urban environment. Moreover it enriched the urban listening experience by allowing its user to construct and deconstruct musical meaning in relation with the urban space.

While recognizing an identifiable listening culture around portability, we also find a technological convergence for the design of novel devices. Long-term rechargeable batteries, Internet connection through 4 G, Wi-Fi and Bluetooth, GPS geo-referencing tools, sensors and touchscreens have inspired a new set of locative tools for the urban pedestrian whose prime representative is the smartphone. The distribution of computer software and hardware in the public space allows the passerby to explore the urban

© Springer International Publishing AG 2017
M. Aramaki et al. (Eds.): CMMR 2016, LNCS 10525, pp. 137–149, 2017.
DOI: 10.1007/978-3-319-67738-5_8

territory with unprecedented tools. The more urban technologies increase their scope, the more sound takes part in everyday human-computer interaction. In this context computer music expertise plays an important role in the design of applications addressed to the pedestrian. In our personal research and pedagogical experience in Manizales, we have gathered graduate and postgraduate students coming from Design studies, Music and Computer Science in order to put together a team of work around urban sound design. As the coordinator of such a team, I take this multidisciplinary context as an opportunity to engage new computer music practitioners.

After the introduction, Sects. 2 and 3 will present a high level discussion about urban acoustics, everyday listening and human-computer interaction from the perspective of design studies. While sound design is an emergent practice and there is not a shared consensus about its boundaries and limits, we will confront different directions in the urban sound design scenario. We will examine a series of authors coming from outside of the computer science that propose directions, assumptions and procedures in the subject. Firstly, the notion of sonic effect [3] will allow us to examine Pierre Schaeffer's sound object and Murray Schafer's soundscape. We will argue that urban studies interpretation of musical composition concepts stresses aspects of sound and listening relevant in the design practice, such as user experience and sustainability. We will also look through some insights in the field of human-computer interaction [4, 5] that introduces recent theories on human cognition, such as Embodiement and Enaction [6]. We also will discuss Behrendt's framework of mobile sound [7], which has been helpful to identify defined procedures for designers and creators interested in the pedestrian-computer sonic interaction.

The fourth section will be dedicated to review three design projects created under a two-years postdoctoral research study entitled Sound Design for Urban Spaces [8]. We will describe the design process and aims of the Smartphone Ensemble (2015) [9], a group of musicians and designers from Manizales that adopts mobile phones both as musical instruments and as social mediators. We will report some results of an experimental study we conducted examining which components and qualities of smartphones are more propitious for implementation on a musical environment. Then, we will discuss the AirQ Jacket (2016) [10], a wearable device that displays temperature and air quality data through light and sound. The portability of a tiny environmental station reporting relevant environmental data constituted a challenging interdisciplinary design project. The last part of this section will be dedicated to Lumina Nocte (2016) [11], a suggested trajectory by the Caldas University Campus guided by a smartphone application that triggers audio samples when the pedestrian reaches some GPS coordinates. Along the description of the design projects we will reflect in some of the design insight presented in the first section.

In the last section we will confront the different suggested definitions of urban sound design that were suggested along the text. Furthermore, we will propose a personal perspective of the urban sound design practice based on the concept of "informational territories" [12]. We will argue that the city has an informational layer that is complementary with a physical one. Under this perspective, the designer would be able to create a correspondence between the virtual and physical layer of the city.

2 Listening Experience in the Urban Context

In the Centre de Recherche sur l'espace sonore et l'environnement urbain (Cresson Centre) in Grenoble, It has been discussing sound and listening from the perspective of urban analysis. Notably the theoretic work by Jean François Augoyard and Henri Torgue [3] proposes a set of analysis tools adapted to the contingencies of contemporary cities, the sound effects. The study embraces concepts from XX century music composition theory, such as Pierre Schaffer's sound object and Murray Schafer's soundscape, in a way that some aspects, rarely discussed in music contexts, are highlighted. Under the authors' interpretation, the sound object and the soundscape become complementary tools in the analysis of the urban environment.

In the one hand, Augoyard and Torgue define the sound object as "...the interaction of the physical signal and the perceptive intentionality" [3]. The authors connect listening to the user experience problem, that gathers different concerns in contemporary design thinking. User experience based design research has developed diverse methodologies to extract user needs and habits [13]. In the case of sound, the approach to aural perception introduced by Pierre Schaffer provides answers and directions to the "problems" placed by the user, in this case the passerby. Furthermore, Augoyard and Torgue extract from Pierre Schaeffer the matter of sound subjective perception, discussing selective listening, memory and hallucination as current issues on auditory urban activity. Nonetheless, under this view the sound object is too narrow to analyze architectural and urban space acoustic phenomena. The out-of-context method of sound-by-sound examination provided by Pierre Schaeffer is compared with a linguistic analysis focused at the level of the words and syntagmas.

In the other hand, Cresson Centre researchers critically adopt the soundscape theory. While recognizing its expansive evolution, the soundscape theory is assumed as the main model to understand environmental acoustics. For designers the soundscape concept becomes a fruitful analysis tool since it faces sonic urban activity as a sustainable design problem. We would suggest that, unlike Pierre Schaeffer or John Cage approach to sound, listening and audio recording technology, the soundscape theory openly deals with the problem of sustainability [14, 15] from the perspective of design and creation. In the Murray Schafer conception of sound design, the musician is re-inserted into the society, playing the aesthetic role in a multidisciplinary ecological project. Augoyard and Torgue, for their part, argue that the soundscape theory blurs the analysis of the urban acoustic environment, leaving out a series of everyday urban situations that would belong to the Murray Schafer's "low-fi" category. Therefore, the authors place soundscape theory near the linguistic analysis tools that covers the whole structure of the text.

Augoyard and Torgue integrate Pierre Schaeffer and Murray Schafer theories in the inclusive concept of sound effect. To continue the linguistic analogy, the sound effects would correspond to an analysis at the level of the sentence. In order to restore a conceptual framework of the urban listening experience they assume that this analysis cannot be undertaken just from the Schaeffer's sound object and Schafer's soundscape theories. The whole picture of the urban listening analysis should take into consideration other fields of reference such as physical and applied acoustics, architecture and urbanism, psychology and physiology of perception, sociology and everyday culture and textual and media expressions. Another scholar from the Cresson Centre, Hellstrom, suggests that since it is not possible to embrace all these various disciplines, the sound designer "...operates within her/his own specialized knowledge field; thus sound design presupposes a disciplinary context and demands an approach to knowledge that emanates from a certain discipline" [16].

3   Sonic Interaction Design

Another contribution to the designer of portable audio devices for the urban context comes from Human-Computer Interaction studies, more specifically, from a group of scholars that identify and discuss the emergent practice of Sonic Interaction Design (SID). According to Franinović and Salter "...creative practices with sound are at the center of a broader shift in thinking about interaction" [5]. In a different way than Augoyard and Torgue, SID scholars extract Design insights from experimental musical knowledge.

Its worth mentioning that from 2001, New Interfaces for Musical Expression (NIME) conference has gathered sensor augmented sonic interaction research, and the evolution of such a research starts revealing both idiosyncrasies and contributions to other disciplinary contexts. According to SID scholars "...sonic interaction in the NIME orthodoxy is based on a highly codified model of musical expression..." that basically "...consists of the following formula: input (sensing) > mapping > output (sound synthesis) = musical expression" [5]. Besides NIME research orthodoxy, it is particularly useful in our discussion to think that interaction can be trivially adopted as a linear and out-of-context process.

A more complex scenario is raised when interaction is seen as a cyclic process. SID scholars propose that in sonic interaction phenomena, humans get into a feedback loop, where user actions govern the sound, and reciprocally, when the user listens to this sound, new decisions are demanded to take more actions. This model settles closer to the one of the musical improviser, since his/her practice can be seen as the adjustment of muscular tension in order to play expressive notes or sounds. In parallel, while there is not a prefigured musical structure, the sound feedback becomes the main expressive criteria in the preparation of the incoming note or sound. Rochesso et al. define Sonic Interaction Design as the "...practice and inquiry into any of various roles that sound may play in the interaction loop between users and artifacts, services, or environments" [4]. What SID theories suggest here is that the same interaction model that matches with musical improvisation can be fruitfully used to complete non-musical tasks.

The interdependence between the user and the environment is an important matter of discussion for Franinović and Salter [5], since they fill the gap between the sounding world and James Gibson's ecological approach to perception [17]. The biological metaphor of "structural coupling" [18] also becomes an inspiring resource to observe sonic interaction activity. Moreover, Franinović and Salter approach to cognitive studies by discussing embodiement and enaction as fundamental premises in the sonic interaction process. "Embodiement is the premise that the particular bodies we have influence how we think" and "Enaction is the idea that organisms create their own experience through their actions" [6]. In short: (en)actions with the whole intelligent body can only by guided by the own experience in the context. In such a reasoning perception is just a theoretical residue.

One of the claims of Franinović and Salter in the critique to the abstract approach to interaction is that it just takes into account a single variable. According to Hutchins "...attempts to explain complex cognitive accomplishments using models that incorporate only a tiny subset of the available resources invariably lead to distortions" [6]. Coherently, Franinović and Salter propose a multifaceted approach to interaction where the problem is situated in the following ways: "(1) a spatiotemporal-material process, (2) an act of poiesis or making that is an active process or formation, (3) situated, concrete, and embodied, (4) performative and emergent in that it constitutes itself in time through different agencies operating in tandem with each other, and (5) nonrepresentational (i.e., not reducible to an act of mimesis, imitation, or purely symbolic processing)" [5].

To close this section I would like to discuss Frauke Behrendt's classification of mobile audio since her study stresses aspects we are interested in, such as portability and mobility [7]. In addition, the study is openly affiliated with SID theory. Behrendt proposes a framework of mobile sound with four different directions in the creation of locative audio applications: musical instruments sonified mobility, sound platforms and placed sound. This taxonomy has been helpful to identify defined procedures for designers and creators interested in the pedestrian-computer sonic interaction. Furthermore, as we will see, the design projects we have developed in the Caldas University Design and Creation Program can be located in each of the categories proposed by Behrendt. Cognitive anthropologist Edwin Hutchins suggests that "...motion in space acquires conceptual meaning and reasoning can be performed by moving the body. Material patterns can be enacted as representations in the interaction of person and culturally organized settings. Courses of action then become trains of thought" [6]. For her part, Behrendt adresses "placed sounds", an emergent locative media practice where the "...audience can only access the located content when they are physically present in the specific geographic location" [7]. The premise of Embodiment, where the whole body takes part in the perceptual negotiation with the environment, became particularly meaningful in the urban context sonic interaction. As Hosokawa remarks [2], the act of walking have been transformed by portable sound media in a poetic one, engaging the pedestrian in novel technology empowered listening strategies.

4 Designing Prototypes for the Local Environment

The projects reported in this section were developed in the Universidad de Caldas Design and Creation program under a postdoctoral research study entitled Sound Design for Urban Spaces [8]. Funded by the Colombian science and technology research agency (Colciencias), the postdoctoral research study focuses on the design process of novel audio devices and seeks to encourage technology-empowered listening strategies for people in transit through the city. The *Laboratorio de Sonologia* has been the place where a group of designers, musicians and engineers have been developing design projects. We are identifying and evaluating alternative technologies available to designers and non-expert programmers in order to create both, devices and listening strategies for the main recipient and the end user of our research: the local passerby. In this concern, the projects have raised a set of questions such as: What is the role of sound in the human occupation of urban spaces? and How does sound act in the two-way link between the city passer and his/her mobile computer?

4.1 The Smartphone Ensemble

The Smartphone Ensemble (SE) [9] is a Manizales based group of musicians and designers leaded by Daniel Melán Giraldo and Julián Jaramillo Arango, exploring musical expressivity of mobile phones in urban contexts. Smartphones portability is taken as an opportunity to envision alternatives to the standard performance space, supporting the idea of a musical ensemble of non-traditional musical devices that travels while playing.

On the one hand, the group explores smartphones as musical instruments creating custom-made applications with different computer music synthesis methods. We have created audio processing software using Peter Brinkmann's libpd library [19] that allows sketching audio applications in the Pure Data Vanilla distribution. The GUI devices have been created with Daniel Iglesia's MobMuPlat, [20] which provides a GUI prototyping tool available to designers (Fig. 1).

On the other hand, the SE explores smartphones as social mediators performing public interventions in urban spaces. SE public presentations intend to be urban interventions, not traditional concerts, Therefore, improvisation based performances are structured according to short and defined tours around a specific public place

Fig. 1. Public intervention of the Smartphone Ensemble at the Gotera Park (Manizales) on November 13, 2015.

(the university campus, a neighborhood, a park, a building, a shopping mall, a market). In this spirit, atypical places can become a suitable performance space for SE musical interventions.

Since portable amplification is required in urban environments, we designed a wearable speaker system for SE outdoor interventions and rehearsals. The first SE performance was carried out in the Manizales Gotera Park on November 13, 2015, within the "electronic picnic", a regular event organized by governmental institutions Vivelab [21] and Clusterlab [22]. The group walked through the park following a trajectory while improvising over four different musical ideas.

One of the core ideas of the SE is that the music is guided by the experience of travelling through the urban space: the city operates as a sort of music score. The Enaction premise, where experience and situated activity in the particular context is put in the center of the user perception, encapsulates the spirit of the SE musical performance. As a technology-empowered improvisational music practice, SE urban interventions constitute a novel experience for both, the experimental musicians and the local listening audience.

In the *Laboratorio de Sonologia* we conducted an experimental study [23] examining which components and qualities of smartphones are more propitious for implementation on a musical environment and observing collaboration, intuition and interdependency phenomena [24]. The study was developed taking into account that musicians and non-musicians have different approaches. Instead of discussing the well-covered subject of smartphone capabilities [25, 26], our study is focused on usability. In this regard, we adopted some user-centered methodologies [27–29] that led us to a four phase process: (1) information and research where relevant data were gathered, (2) analysis where user needs were observed and identified, (3) synthesis in which possible solutions were proposed and (4) evaluation where proposals were valued. We conducted two sets of surveys; one of them requested general opinions about musical interaction with smartphones over a population of 21 non-experts. The other one, conducted over the 6 SE members, addressed the concept of musical expressivity, defined as the index among precision degree (P), action-response correspondence (C) and visual feedback quality (V). Being familiar with smartphone music making, the ensemble was requested to value musical expressivity playing rhythmic patterns and sustained notes in custom made applications that we developed for the study (Fig. 2).

There are different conclusions that we have drawn from the study results. In this paper we would remark that although touch screen and microphone seems to be more precise than the tilt sensor, they were comparatively less valued in the action-response correspondence appreciation. When visual feedback was rated, the tilt sensor was significantly better valued than the other tested input methods. It suggests that the freedom of the body movement, allowed by the tilt sensor and hindered by the touch screen and the microphone, is an important consideration in the design of mobile music applications. Moreover, the results support our intuition that mobility, in this case through the city, is an essential consideration in smartphone music making.

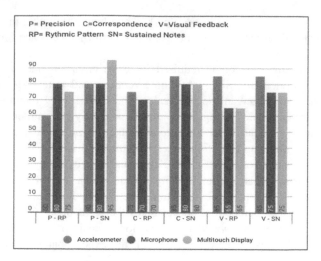

Fig. 2. Musical expressivity valued in different smartphone input methods by the six members of the Smartphone Ensemble.

4.2 The AirQ Jacket (2016)

The AirQ Jacket [10] is a wearable device that displays temperature and air quality data through light and sound. The jacket reacts to environmental conditions and notifies them to its user in a symbolic mode. While an active volcanic region emanating toxic gases surrounds Manizales, air quality becomes an important issue in the city everyday life. In this respect, the project aim to create a meaningful context for the passerby in the interpretation of scientific data about the city. The AirQ jacket is the MA degree project of fashion designer Maria Paulina Gutierrez.

The AirQ Jacket invites the passerby to interact with the environment in a feedback loop mode. By displaying environmental data, the jacket suggests deviations, redirections and particular detours in the pedestrian current track. The negotiation between environmental pollution and passerby location resembles the musical improvisation interaction model described above, which is implemented in the AirQ jacket to achieve a non-musical task (Fig. 3).

As well as other wearable technology pieces, the AirQ Jacket gathered crafting from programing and electronic prototyping on the one hand, and from sewing and dressmaking on the other. In this respect the interchange between audio and fashion design approaches leaded to a non-standard format: a wearable computer-jacket.

The circuit uses the Arduino microcontroller (pro version), an MQ-135 air quality sensor, a DHT-11 temperature sensor, four arrays of leds and a piezo-electric device. Because of the weight and comfort, the pattern making process was carried out taken into account the distribution of the circuit components on different parts of the jacket: the Arduino microcontroller behind the neck, the battery in a back-pocket, the piezo-electric hanging by the right shoulder and the arrays of leds in the front. In order to make the jacket washable, we attached the circuit components and cables in a way that they can be completely extracted.

Fig. 3. The first prototype of the AirQ jacket, a wearable computing design project developed in the Universidad de Caldas, Design and Creation Program.

The AirQ jacket creation process looked into the field of perceptualization [30], in this case, the mapping of scientific data to visual and auditory stimuli. On the one hand, temperature and air quality data are visualized by two arrays of colored leds attached to the upper and lower sides of the jacket. The circuit maps the information in a traditional symbolic way: blue-to-red to show temperature in the upper side, and green-to-red to show pollution in the lower side. On the other, the sonification system runs in a custom-made artifact attached to the jacket that was built with a piezo-electric device located inside a plastic cabinet that totally kills the sound, unless you approach the ear, such as telephonic equipment. Our sonification strategy demands an exploratory analysis process from the user and adopts a "reference" or contextual sound [31]. The user hears a couple of regular metronomic ticks. The first-one displays the temperature data changing the pitch and lets hear the pollution data changing the velocity. The second tick acts as a grid of reference, it represents "normal" state. When the user compares the two ticks he/she can appreciate the environmental conditions.

4.3 Lumina Nocte (2016)

The theoretical contributions coming from Cresson Centre have feed our aim to envisage new venues for computer music experiments and to find ways to engage new computer music practitioners. The complexity of sound depicted by Augoyard and Torgue [3] have influenced the view of our own urban environment. It has triggered discussions and novel thoughts about listening topics involving subjective sound perception, such as anamnesis, phonomnesis, asyndeton, synecdoche and perdition [3].

Lumina Nocte is a suggested trajectory by the Caldas University Campus guided by a smartphone application that triggers audio samples when the pedestrian reaches some

Fig. 4. The pathway of Lumina Nocte over the map of the Caldas University Campus.

GPS coordinates. More than an audio-guide, Lumina Nocte tells a horror story. Nine audio samples recreate old uses of the University buildings where a group of Catholic Church sisters directed a residential school for girls. The fictional narrative simulates terrific scenes the buildings might have witnessed. Local inhabitants statements were collected in the search of mysterious stories about past uses of the surrounding architecture, over these tales the fictional sonic tracks were inspired. Lumina Nocte deals with the perception of memory via the auditory channel, exploring sound as a link between affective activity and the urban structures. The work was developed during a seminar focused on interactive design, with students Vanessa Gañán, Hellen Zamudio y Carlos Zuluaga. Lumina Nocte was made with the Sonic Maps application [32] with which we efficiently solved the task needed to complete the project. Sonic Maps app allows the user to link sound samples to zones in a map and later hear them in the physical territory. The app invites the user to create his/her own experience by uploading original sound samples to a public audio server (Fig. 4).

Frauke Behrendt has discussed the design technique of associating samples or audio processes to GPS coordinates [7]. While recognizing several examples with multiple directions where geo-referenced audio has been used, she relates the practice of "placing sounds" to an Augmented Reality (AR) acoustic modality. The Lumina Nocte audience can only access the content when they are physically present in the geographic location, thereby walking becomes a mode of interaction, a sort of remixing. As Behrendt states, each passerby had his/her own listening experience depending on the decisions he/she makes in terms of direction, length of the walk, and time spent in specific locations [7].

5 Final Remarks

In the city the sound designer faces a challenging context, not only because an arsenal of technological resources is now available, but also because new conceptual directions are being discussed. On the shoulders of Pierre Schaeffer and Murray Schafer,

Augoyard and Torgue extract concrete urban listening situations for close examination. Their interpretation raises relevant topics in the design thinking, such as user experience and sustainability. They see urban sound design as a transdisciplinary practice oscillating in a group of fields of reference. Furthermore, Hellstrom suggests that the sound designer carries out his/her practice from one of these fields of reference, without losing sight of the multidisciplinary status of his/her practice. Conversely, Franinović and Sanders go into the interaction phenomenon supporting their discourse in cognitive studies and in the biological metaphor of organism-environment coupling. Refusing common assumptions in the linear model of interaction, they propose that the designer could be able to influence the interaction loop between the user and his/her environment. Moreover they propose a multifaceted model to sonic interaction taking into account the concepts of Embodiement and Enaction. For her part, Berhendt proposes concrete design procedures gathering projects in defined categories. Her classification of mobile music helps to recognize other projects goals and to identify truly original ideas from apparently spontaneous insights. The app prototypes developed for the Smarphone Ensemble would belong to the Behrendt musical instruments category. Since the mobile phone were not designed with a specific musical purpose, play an instrument with it could be considered a kind of "mis"-use; even more when the musical performance is being carried out in the public space. Lumina Nocte could also be considered in Behrendt taxonomy: in the placed sound category, "...artists or designers curate the distribution of sounds in (outdoor) spaces, often – but not exclusively – by using GPS" [7]. The AirQ Jacket could be an example of Behrendt notion of sonified mobility. This category comprises works "...where audience mobility is 'driving' or influencing the sound or music they hear while being on the move" [7].

The concept of "informative territories" [12], coined by Brazilian media theorist André Lemos, was another guiding concept in the creation of the three above-mentioned projects. Since it was not developed in the paper, we would like to insert it into the equation in the final section. According to Lemos, informative territories are "...zones of control of emission and reception of digital information for individuals who are circulating in the public space..." [12]. Lemos states that the urban environment is twofold; it has a physical layer and an electronic one. This layer not only comprises the Internet, but the whole compendium of data referencing the urban structures: "...a new layer of symbolism, a new way of defining ownership and meaning could be overlaid on the old. Invisible on the surface. New paths, new meeting places, new boundaries. New meaning associated with old structures" [33]. The image of a double-layered city transforms the passerby sense of place and suggests that he/she will be oscillating between these two layers. Portable audio devices enable the user to get in the virtual dimension the urban structures can provide while visiting them. On this scenario, the designer accomplishment would be the creation of a meaningful link between the urban space layers, enabling the user to find his/her own correspondences, reciprocities and equilibrium.

Acknowledgments. This research work has been funded by Departamento Administrativo de Ciencia, Tecnología e Innovación (COLCIENCIAS), Grant 2014-656.

References

1. Taylor, T.: Strange Sounds: Music, Technology, and Culture. Routledge, London and New York (2001)
2. Hosokawa, S.: The walkman effect. J. Pop. Music **4**, 165–180 (1984)
3. Augoyard, J.F., Torgue, H.: Sonic Experience, a Guide to Everyday Sounds. McGill-Queen's University Press, Montreal (2005)
4. Rocchesso, D., Serafin, S., Behrendt, F., Bernardini, N., Bresin, R., Eckel, G., et al.: Sonic interaction design: sound, information and experience. In: CHI 2008 Extended Abstracts on Human Factors in Computing Systems, pp. 3969–3972. ACM, Florence (2008)
5. Franinović, K., Salter, C.: The experience of sonic interaction. In: Franinović, K., Serafin, S. (eds.) Sonic Interaction Design. MIT Press, Cambridge (2013)
6. Hutchins, E.: Enaction, imagination and insight. In: Stewart, J., Gapene, O., Di Paolo, E.A. (eds.) Enaction. MIT Press, Cambridge (2011)
7. Behrendt, F.: Locative media as sonic interaction design: walking through placed sounds. J. Mob. Media **9**(2) (2015). http://wi.mobilities.ca/frauke-behrendt-locative-media-as-sonic-interaction-design-walking-through-placed-sounds/
8. Arango, J.J.: Sound design for urban spaces. https://sonologiacolombia.wordpress.com/
9. The Smartohone Ensemble. https://sonologiacolombia.wordpress.com/lab/ensamble-de-smartphones/
10. The AirQ Jacket. https://sonologiacolombia.wordpress.com/lab/airq-jacket/
11. Lumina Nocte. https://sonologiacolombia.wordpress.com/lab/limina-nocte/
12. Lemos, A.: City and mobility. Cell phones, post-mass functions and informational territories. J. Matrizes **1**, 121–138 (2007)
13. Norman, D.: The Design of Future Things. Paperback, New York (2005)
14. Gallopin, G.: Sostenibilidad y desarrollo sostenible: un enfoque sistémico. Cepal. Santiago de Chile (2003)
15. Manzini, E.: Design ethics and sustainability. Dis-Indaco-Politécnico di Milano. Milan (2006)
16. Hellstrom, B.: Noise Design - Architectural Modelling and the Aesthetics of Urban Space. Bo Ebay Forlag, Göteborg (2003)
17. Gibson, J.: The Ecological Approach to Visual Perception. Houghton-Mifflin, Boston (1979)
18. Maturana, H., Varela, F.: The Tree of Knowledge: The Biological Roots of Human Understanding. Shambhala Publications, Boston (1987)
19. Brinkmann, P., Kirn, P., Lawler, R., McCormick, C., Roth, M., Steinser, H.-C.: LibPD. Embedding pure data with libpd. In: Proceedings of the Pure Data Convention (2011)
20. Iglesia, D.: Mobmuplat, mobile music platform. http://mobmuplat.com
21. ViveLab Manizales. http://www.vivelabmanizales.com/
22. Clusterlab. http://clusterlab.co/networking/eventos/ii-picnic-electrnico-20
23. Arango, J.J., Melán, D.: The smartphone ensemble. Exploring mobile computer mediation in collaborative musical performance. In: Proceedings of the New Interfaces for Musical Expression Conference, Brisbane, pp. 61–64 (2016)
24. Weinberg, G.: Interconnected musical networks: toward a theoretical framework. Comput. Music J. **29**(2), 23–39 (2005)
25. Essl, G., Rohs, M.: Interactivity for mobile music making. Organised Sound **14**(2), 197–207 (2009)
26. Misra, A., Essl, G., Rohs, M.: Microphone as sensor in mobile phone performance. In: Proceedings of the 8th International Conference on New Interfaces for Musical Expression, Genova (2008)

27. Findeli, A.: Research through design and transdisciplinarity: a tentative contribution to the methodology of design research (2009). http://www.swissdesignnetwork.org/daten_swiss designnetwork/docs/04_Findeli.pdf
28. Moroni, S.: Apuntes Introducción Diseño (2008). https://disenoaiep.files.wordpress.com/ 2008/03/apunte_02-taller-de-diseno-ycreacion.pdf
29. Jones, J.C.: Design Methods. Wiley, London (1992)
30. Barras, S., Vickers, J.: Sonification design and aesthetics. In: Herman, T., Hunt, A., Neuhoff, H. (eds.) The Sonification Handbook. Logos-Verlag, Berlin (2011)
31. Walker, B., Ness, M.A.: Theory of Sonification. In: Herman, T., Hunt, A., Neuhoff, H. (eds.) The Sonification Handbook. Logos-Verlag, Berlin (2011)
32. Pecino, I., Climent, R.: SonicMaps: connecting the ritual of the concert hall with a locative audio urban experience. In: Proceedings of the International Computer Music Conference (ICMC 2013), Perth, Australia, pp. 315–320 (2013)
33. Russell, B.: Headmap Manifesto. www.headmap.org/book/get/headmap-manifesto.PDF

Increasing Pleasantness and Security Using 3D-Sound Design in Public Transport

Gaëtan Parseihian[1]([⊠]), Christophe Bourdin[2], Vincent Bréjard[3],
and Richard Kronland-Martinet[1]

[1] Aix Marseille Univ., CNRS, PRISM (Perception, Représentations, Image, Sound, Music), 31 Chemin J. Aiguier, 13402 Marseille Cedex 20, France
{parseihian,kronland}@prism.cnrs.fr
[2] Aix Marseille Univ., CNRS, ISM UMR, Marseille, France
christophe.bourdin@univ-amu.fr
[3] Aix Marseille Univ., LPCLS, Aix-en-Provence, France
vincent.brejard@univ-amu.fr

Abstract. A collaborative project aiming to improve the bus trip with auditory information is presented in this paper. This project took place in Marseille and involved several laboratories from Aix-Marseille University and the Marseille transit operator. This project consists in the study of three fundamental actions of the sound on the bus' passengers: designing sound announcement to inform passengers of the next stop in a playful and intuitive way, brightening up the route with spatialized soundscapes to increase the trips pleasantness, and using sound to alert passengers of emergency braking. For that purpose, a high quality multi channel sound spatialization system was integrated in the bus and a sonification software based on geolocation was designed. The overall concepts of this project are first presented, then the integration of the sound spatialization system and the implementation of the sonification software are described. Finally, an evaluation method of passengers satisfaction is discussed and first results of a laboratory experiment are presented.

Keywords: Sound design · Sonification · Sound spatialization · Mobility

1 Introduction

"Imagine yourself in a bus in an unfamiliar city. You leave the central station to reach the football stadium. Aggressive city soundscapes fade out as the doors are closing, uncovering an astonishing sound environment. At some stops, the sound of breaking waves comes brushing your ears then return to the front of the bus. Between the bus stops you imagine you can hear seagulls flying in the bus, a soft breeze brushing past your shoulder, and some boat masts knocking together far from you. A passenger informs you of the beaches' proximity and tells you that these are regularly heard in the bus. You continue your travel toward the stadium. While approaching, you hear a growing murmur, this doesn't seem to be

© Springer International Publishing AG 2017
M. Aramaki et al. (Eds.): CMMR 2016, LNCS 10525, pp. 150–168, 2017.
DOI: 10.1007/978-3-319-67738-5_9

due to the good atmosphere in the bus. Some sounds of soccer balls, of whistles, of roaring crowds, etc. The closer you are to the stadium, the more you have the impression of already being in the stadium. A "ola" wave is heard, coming from the front of the bus, reaching the back then returning back to the front of the bus, some passengers participate. It is followed by the stop announcement "Velodrom Stadium". This time you are sure that you have reached your destination."

This scenario fully illustrates Marseille transit operator (Régie des Transports Maseillais, RTM) vision of next generation of Marseille's buses. More than a way of transport, the bus can become a social and cultural meeting place. Sound ambiances and announcements can suggest places, open the bus onto the city, diminish the stress and transform a simple trip into a tourist and historic stroll, whereas sound alerts can increase passengers' security and prevent numerous accidents; all this in order to offer to the passengers a more pleasant trip. Indeed, nowadays, despite an increasing development of public transport in big cities, the use of personal cars is still dominant inducing many traffic-jams and is an important factor of air pollution. If the first reason is the lack of appropriate line and the difficulty of developing an homogeneous transport network, another frequent reproach to public transport is the lack of pleasantness of the trip. In the bus case, for example, the traffic-jams, the number of passengers or the temperature can transform a simple trip into a real ordeal.

The aim of this article is to present a collaborative project between the Marseille transit operator and several laboratories from Aix-Marseille University to further improve the bus trip using auditory information.

Sound could acts on humans in different ways: it informs [5,15], guides [16], but also influences the behaviour [8]. Considering these interactions, many potential applications might be developed in public transport sector. The sound can inform on the location of particular places, on points of interest along the route, or on the engine dynamic in the electric or hybrid vehicle cases. It can also be used to carry out a specific task (guide the passengers to the rear of the bus) and even influence passengers' behaviour, in term of subjective emotional valence and intensity (relaxation) and of posture (anticipatory postural adjustments), especially with the use of immersive sound methods.

The presented project consists in the study of three fundamental actions of the sound on the bus' passengers:

– Alert the passengers of the next stop in a playful and intuitive way: the goal here is to reconsider the sound alerts informing about the bus stops while illustrating those with typical auditory icons inspired from the places and the city history and geography.
– Brighten up the route with spatialized soundscapes to increase the trip's agreeableness: the goal here is to virtually open the bus on surrounding space by generating spatialized and progressive natural soundscapes (sounds of cresting wave, distant boats, seagulls, etc.) in order to positively impact passengers' behaviour and subjective emotional valence and intensity while informing them of potential points of interest along the route.

– Using sound to alert passengers of possibly destabilizing emergency braking: the goal here is to use spatialized and dynamic sounds in order to alert, in advance, the passengers (particularly those who stand up) of destabilizing emergency braking to avoid falls.

For this purpose, a high quality multi-channel sound spatialization system composed of ten loudspeakers was integrated in the bus and a sonification software based on geolocation was designed.

This article describes the different aspects of this project. First, the three fundamental actions of the sound on the passengers are succinctly described. Then, the integration of the sound spatialization system in the bus and the implementation of the sonification software are detailed. Finally, first works on the evaluation of the device by passengers are discussed.

2   Description of the Project

2.1   Playful and Intuitive Stop Announcements

Auditory Warnings in Public Transports. Clear and consistent on-board stop announcements are vital to ensure that buses are accessible to and usable by people with disabilities, as well as by visitors or others who may not be familiar with the service area. Without adequate on-board stop announcements some riders may have difficulty knowing when to get off the vehicle.

Traditionally, stop announcements are made manually by vehicle operators using a public address system or provided as part of an automated voice announcement system [3]. For automated voice announcement, vehicle operator can choose between using a text to speech software or pre-recorded voice. In both cases, the message must be clear and not misunderstood.

During the last few years, in addition to the vocal announcement, some vehicle operators have added different types of sounds to the stop announcement in order to increase its attractiveness and to distinguish their company from the others. For example, Paris' and Strasbourg' tramway stop announcements were designed by the sound artist Rodolphe Burger. They are made of musical jingles and voices. For each stop, a particular musical jingle and a pair of voices were recorded to design two different stop announcements for each stop (an interrogative announcement and an affirmative announcement). Evocative, playing with our musical memory, the musical jingles are inspired by the names of the stops and allow to introduce the voice announcement. For another example, the composer Michel Redolfi has introduced the concept of "sonal" for the tramways of Nice, Brest, and Besançon. Unlike the jingles (which suggest unchanging and monotonous stop announcement that sounds like a warning), the sonals are designed as musical sounds that can change over time. According to their designer, they discretely accompanies the riders on their journey and contains musical, vocal and historic elements linked to the specific features of the places and to the unconscious collective sounds shared by the local population. In Nice, the sonals vary randomly at each stop with a different night and day version.

Some of the announcements are dubbed in the Nice dialect (Nissarte). In Brest, the designers wanted to evoke, without exaggerating, the marine context. The sonals are pronounced by a women when the tide is coming in and a man as the tide is going out. Of course, the time of the day when it shifts is different everyday, but this design allows passengers to know where the sea is. As for Nice's tramway, the announcements are randomly dubbed in the local Breton dialect.

Our Approach. For this project, our intention is to design spatialized intuitive and playful auditory announcements (coupled with the traditional vocal announcement) having a semantic link with the bus stop. Hence, we want to rethink the sounds related to the bus stops by illustrating its with typical auditory icons of the places and of the city. For example, before arriving to the soccer stadium bus stop, a wave will be joined to the traditional announcement voice in order to notify to the passenger the stadium proximity. While the definition of typical sounds which can be easily identifiable and recognized by all the passengers is simple for few bus stops, the process of finding evocative sounds for all the stop is difficult or impossible. Thus, rather than looking for immediate correspondences between stops' names and sounds, our approach is to draw inspiration from the identity, the specificity and the history of the places crossed by the bus. In this way, a bike sound at Michelet Ganay stop can inform us that Gustave Ganay was one of the most famous cyclists from the 1920s and that he was native from Marseille. The sound of stream waters at Luminy Vaufrèges stop informs about the presence of an underground river. An extract of Iannis Xenakis music at Corbusier stop allows the passengers to discover the close links between music and architecture, etc. Linked to a dedicated website or application (detailing and adding supplementary information about the sounds used for each stop), these auditory icons tend to transform an ordinary trip from one place to another in a historic, tourist, and heritage visit.

With the spatialization of sound, auditory icons travel in the bus following the wave metaphor, giving the sensation of a sound that informs the passengers one by one, starting from the front of the bus and propagating to the back of the bus. In addition to the playful aspect, the use of the sound spatialization allows to attract the passengers attention by opposition to the usual announcement immobility. Different types of waves will be studied as a function of the auditory icon types. Indeed, the simple propagation from the front to back is of interest for some auditory icons while other will be easily perceived with a round trip trajectory or with a circular trajectory (e.g. starting from the right side of the bus and returning by the left side).

For a correct identification of the stop name by all the passengers, auditory icons are coupled with traditional voice clearly announcing the stop name. This vocal announcement is uniformly played on all the ten loudspeakers to ensure the most homogeneous diffusion in the bus and to guarantee the best hearing comfort and optimized intelligibility for all the passengers and in all the situations.

By convention, in the bus, a stop is announced twice: the first occur around 100 m after the previous bus stop, the second takes place around 30 m before reaching the stop. Depending on the transport company's or sound designer's choice, these two types of announcement are differentiated by the voice prosody or by the way they are introduced (using "next stop is..." or "stop:..." for example). This differentiation with auditory icons is based on the sound duration. First type of announces are associated to a long auditory icons (a sound between 5 and 10 s) while second type are associated to short auditory icons (between 1 and 2 s).

Finally, in order not to disturb and bother regular users, only a selection of few stops will be sonified to punctuate the trip. Selected stop and corresponding auditory icons can change according to the time (morning, afternoon, week-end), and to the traffic (peak or off-peak periods).

2.2   Designing Soundscapes for Trip Enhancements

Closed environment, high temperature during summer, direct contact with other passengers during peak periods, traffic jams, etc. In certain situations, a bus trip can become highly stressful for the passengers who are forced to undergo their uncontrollable environment and the foreign discomfort [9]. To reduce these problems, the idea here consists in enhancing the trip with spatialized soundscapes in order to virtually open the bus toward the surrounding space and to increase trip's agreeableness.

Effect of Environmental Sounds on Stress. Several studies have demonstrated restorative effects of natural compared with urban environments; these effects include increased well-being, decreased negative affects and decreased physiological stress responses [10, 22, 23]. In [23], Ulrich suggested that natural environments have restorative effects by inducing positive emotional states, decreased physiological activity and sustained attention. Considering the influence of natural sounds, a study by Alvarsson et al. [2] suggests that, after psychological stress, physiological recovery of sympathetic activation is faster during exposure to pleasant nature sounds than to less pleasant noise of lower, similar, or higher sound pressure level. Benfield et al. [4] highlight a better relaxation with natural sounds compared to no sound or to natural sounds mixed with human sounds (voice or motor). Watts et al. [24] describe the beneficial effects on anxiety and agitation of introducing natural sounds and large images of natural landscapes into a waiting room in a student health center. Other studies highlight the positive impact of music on stress reduction. In [7], the authors suggest that listening to certain types of music (such as classical) may serve to improve cardiovascular recovery from stress.

Our Approach of Soundscape Design for the Bus. In order to reduce passengers anxiety and to virtually open the bus, the project aims at enlivening the bus trip with:

- Spatialized contextualized natural soundscapes (composed with typical sounds from Marseille and its surrounding) and musical ambiances;
- Point Of Interest (POI) sound announcements (museum, monuments, parks, beaches, etc.).

Soundscapes and POI are geolocalized and triggered when the bus passes close to their position on the route. For the POI, as in augmented reality, the sounds are virtually placed on the object they are representing, that is the POI sound appears to come from the POI position. Hence, when passing by a church, the passengers will feel that the tinkling of the bells come from the church (the sound spatialization is based on the POI position with respect to the bus). The soundscapes are constructed to reflect a particular atmosphere or universe in coherence with the route or the neighbourhood, to give an overview of typical sounds surrounding the city, or to offer a trip based on musical ambiances. For example, in a city close to the sea, soundscapes might be composed of sea sounds (waves, boats, wind, seagull, etc.), and in highly urbanised area forests' sounds can be recommended. In addition to stress reduction, designed soundscapes will allow to divide the bus itinerary in several parts according to crossed neighbourhood and places.

Soundscapes design is based on a random reading of the preselected sound samples in order to avoid redundancy that could annoy and tire regular passengers. With this process, on one part of the route, soundscape ambiance is always the same but the sound events doesn't appear twice at the same time and at the same position. Sounds trajectory and frequency of appearance may vary as a function of the time of the day but also as a function of the traffic, the temperature, or the passengers number. It is also possible to design several similar soundscapes and to associate them to different periods of the week (morning or afternoon, week or week-end, for example).

2.3   Using Sounds to Secure the Passengers

The third part of the project aims at studying brief spatialized warning sounds designed to prevent bus passengers from emergency braking. The idea is to use dynamic and spatialized sounds in order to alert, in advance, the passengers (particularly those who stand up) of destabilizing emergency braking. In the bus, some of the passengers do not stand up in the same direction as the bus circulation and do not necessarily see the road. This results in an impossibility of predicting sudden vehicle movements and in an important postural destabilisation. Our objective is to analyse driver's foot behaviour to predict braking phases and produce an auditory warning allowing the subject to produce anticipatory postural adjustment.

High postural perturbations, such as those induced by emergency braking, endanger the body's stability. In order to preserve the equilibrium, as a function of the perturbation's predictability, humans can produce compensatory postural adjustment (CPA) and/or anticipatory postural adjustment (APA). In [19,20], the authors highlight the importance of APAs in control of posture and points out the existence of a relationship between the anticipatory and the compensatory components of postural control. It also suggests a possibility to enhance balance control by improving the APAs responses during external perturbations. In a study by [14] et al., the authors show that auditory precuing can play a role in modulating the automatic postural response. They demonstrate that a general warning signal, evoking alertness, can reduce automatic postural response latency but fail to give information about the perturbation direction with the auditory signal content [14].

For this part of the project, we are currently exploring the role of sound spatialization and of sound content as directionally specific pre-cue information for the execution of anticipatory postural adjustments and the reduction of automatic postural response latencies. This experiment will take place in laboratory rather than in a bus with an experimental setup composed of a force-controlled waist-pull perturbations system [21], three loudspeakers for spatial sound generation, a force platform for the measure of postural adjustments, and a PhaseSpace motion capture system for the analysis of protective stepping. To properly reproduce the perturbation, bus deceleration during emergency braking was measured with an accelerometer in a bus braking from 50 to $0 \, \text{km/h}^{-1}$. Several measurements were done. Mean decelerations duration during the braking was $1.37 \pm 0.37 \, \text{s}$ with a mean deceleration of $0.77 \pm 0.04 \, \text{g}$.

If the results of this experiment are conclusive, the advantage of sounds to accelerate automatic postural responses will be studied in real environment in the bus on a parking and finally the system efficiency will be evaluated with the statistics on passengers accidents.

3   Technical Description of the System

3.1   Integration of a High Fidelity Multichannel Sound Spatialization System in the Bus

One of the most innovative part of this project corresponds to the use of spatial sounds in the bus. Indeed, if bus and more generally public transports are equipped with several loudspeakers, the same acoustic signal is always emitted by all the loudspeakers. Here the three parts of the project are based on the use of spatial sounds and thus on the emission of different sounds by different loudspeakers. The integration of the high fidelity multichannel sound spatialization system is fully described in this section.

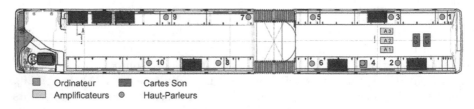

■ Ordinateur   ■ Cartes Son
▢ Amplificateurs   ● Haut-Parleurs

Fig. 1. Diagram of the integration of the different parts of the multichannel sound spatialization system in the bus.

This system is composed of:

- 10 loudspeakers
- 3 amplifiers (4 channels)
- 2 soundcards
- 1 computer Mac Mini.

The placement of each device is detailed on the diagram of Fig. 1.

For the first prototype, the system was set up in a hybrid articulated bus (CITARO G BlueTec Hybrid from Mercedes-Benz) which will serve the line 21 of Marseille's transport network. The ten loudspeakers were installed on the overhead panel (cf Fig. 2). Four loudspeakers were distributed at the back of the front part of the bus and six loudspeakers were distributed at the rear part of the bus. This distribution was chosen to ensure a sound diffusion as uniform as possible with spatialization fluidity while preserving half of the front part of the bus and the driver from the sound. The three loudspeakers and the two sound cards were installed on the ceiling's metallic frame, the computer was set up with silent block in an overhead panel. Amplifiers are supplied via traditional bus circuit in 24 V, computer is supplied with a specific socket in 220 V.

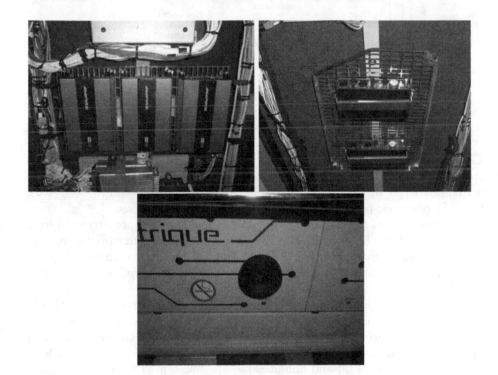

Fig. 2. Fixation of the amplifiers (top left), the sound cards (top right), and the loudspeakers (bottom).

3.2 Software Overview

The different objectives of the project will be attained by combining input data furnished by the bus system and geo-referenced data extracted from a geographic information system (GIS). Bus sonification will be provided using spatialized audio rendering with pre-recorded voice, auditory icons and soundscapes. An innovative system prototype has been built with an architecture divided into several functional elements. The general architecture of the system is shown in Fig. 3. Each part of the system is described below.

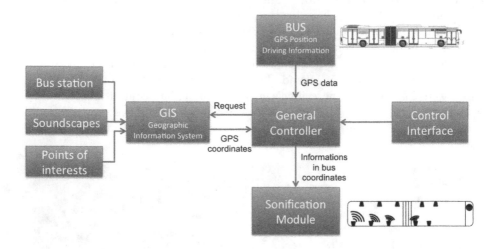

Fig. 3. General architecture of the system.

Geographic Information System. Geographic Information System (GIS) stocks, manages and returns the geographic data useful for the sonification. In actual prototype, three types of geographic information is necessary (see Sect. 2): bus stop positions, points of interest and soundscapes positions.

The positions of the bus stops that characterize the path are extracted from the RTM database. For each bus line, two separates paths (outward and return) are created and exported to GoogleEarth via kml files. For each bus stop the stop name is associated to the stop position (illustrated by yellow drawing pins on Fig. 4).

POI and Soundscapes data are created and positioned with GoogleEarth. For each position, tags are set for the object type (POI or Soundscape), the object name, and the range (in meter). With this information, the General Controller decides, as a function of the bus position in the path which information is to be sonified and how. POI and Soundscapes are represented with red and green drawing pins on Fig. 4, their ranges are represented with plain circles.

Information from the Bus. Several kinds of information need to be transmitted in real time from the bus to the General Controller for proper functioning of

Fig. 4. Screen capture of GoogleEarth representing a part of line 21's bus path. Drawing pins represent GIS information with bus stops in yellow, POI in red, and Soundscape in green. Red and green plain circles represent the ranges of each POI and Soundscape. (Color figure online)

the system. First, at the beginning of the trip, the number of the bus line and the driving direction (outward or return) are sent to the General Controller for the selection of the appropriate GIS information. During the trip, GPS bus position is sent each second to the General Controller for the trajectory following and the sounds triggering. Driving information required to detect emergency braking is currently under review. The first approach consists in the analysis of the brake pedal state, but a detection system only focused on this information might be too slow to permit an appropriate anticipatory reaction from the passengers. To tackle this problem, we are analysing feet movements with respect to acceleration and braking pedals states and inertial unit in order to detect emergency braking at least 200 ms before the deceleration. When available, this information is taken from the Controller Area Network.

Control Interface. The user interface allows the access to the sonification device setting. In normal conditions, the device works independently from any human intervention as a closed on-board system. In order to set-up the appropriate sounds, to adjust the levels of the different sound information (voice, stop sounds, soundscapes, and POI sounds), and to define the sound triggering laws (date and time slots of functioning), a user interface was created. It allows to remotely connect to the device computer and to adjust the settings with a WiFi connection.

General Controller. Central core of the system, the General Controller collects data from the GIS, the bus and the Control Interface to determine, during navigation, what notification messages are to be presented to the user. All the geolocalised data are converted into Cartesian coordinates and objects positions are calculated as a function of the bus position (for each new bus coordinate). Depending on the objects' distance and the settings, the central core identifies the information to sonify and send the appropriate messages to the sonification module.

Sonification Module. Developed with Max/MSP software, the sonification interface manages the sounds triggering and the spatialization. It consists in three modules for the control of the stop announcement, the soundscapes management, and the braking alert triggering. Each modules are constructed to run in real time as a function of bus position and information.

4   Passenger Evaluation of the System: Effect of Environmental Sounds on Stress

Designing such a project without taking into account passenger and driver general satisfaction seems totally useless. On one part, campaigns of client satisfaction assessment are planned by the transit operator with the bus prototype in order to evaluate the impact of the system, the feeling of monotony for daily users, the proper understanding of the auditory icons, and the correct intelligibility of the sounds. On another part, a specific experiment is required in order to measure the stress reduction due to the use of natural soundscapes during bus trips. As bus passengers may not be available for a long time (the mean trip duration in the bus is around fifteen minutes), it is important to design short evaluation procedures and to preliminary evaluate in laboratory the relaxing effect of several soundscape's types. For this purpose, a survey based on visual analogue scale has been designed. This section describes the design of this survey and the laboratory experiment implemented to validate the survey with traditional stress measurement methods (physiological measures of heart rate variability) and to evaluate the effect of three soundscape types (natural, urban, and musical) on stress reduction.

4.1   Design of the Survey

The impact of the soundscape on passengers must be evaluated with precise and relevent measurement tools in order to quantify its influence on the stress, the anxiety, the pleasure and the welfare of the participants. At least three different ways can be used to measure emotional responses: affective reports, physiological reactivity, and overt behavioural acts. The physiological or the behavioural measure can be relatively easy, in that technology or methodology will often dictate a clear preference of the subject, but they are not suitable for outside or travel status. On the other side, the use of affective reports fill in the previous criteria although the difficulty to find consistent answer with subjective assessment. Despite this difficulty, a survey has been constructed following several criteria:

- allowing the subject to do a self assessment of his emotional state, his perceived stress and anxiety,
- being filled within a reasonably short period of time,
- being presented in a visual form to control the bias due to verbal processing.

On the basis of these criteria, a survey composed of three visual analogue scales and two self-assessment manikins was created.

The measurement of transient and subjective psychological states related to anxiety, stress, and well-being is based on the use of visual analogue scales (VAS). These single-item measures, in which participants mark their subjective status on a visual scale (see Fig. 5 (top) for an example with anxiety), afford simple and rapid administration, and increased comprehension and completion rates [18]. For anxiety assessment, participants were instructed to draw a line on the scale position representing their current level of anxiety (between calm and anxious) in response to the question, "How anxious do you feel right now?". The anxiety VAS has been previously scientifically validated by [1], and the stress VAS by [13]. The VAS were realized in lines defined by two extremities representing the two extreme emotional states (calm/anxious, no-stress/high stress, feel good/feel bad). The line measures 10 cm and has no graduation in order to avoid some bias due to its discretization. Subjects are asked to report their emotional state by placing a mark on the line.

On another part, valence and arousal assessment are based on Self Assessment Manikins (SAM). The SAM is a non-verbal pictorial assessment technique that directly measures an emotional state associated with a person's affective reaction to a wide variety of stimuli [6]. The SAM range from a smiling, happy figure to a frowning, unhappy figure when representing the pleasure dimension (middle of Fig. 5) and range from an excited, wide-eyed figure to a relaxed, sleepy figure for the arousal dimension (bottom of Fig. 5). In the original version, the subject can place an 'x' over any of the five figures in each scale, or between any two figures, which results in a 9-point rating scale for each dimension. In the current survey, a horizontal line was placed under each SAM in order to allow a continuous rating of emotional states.

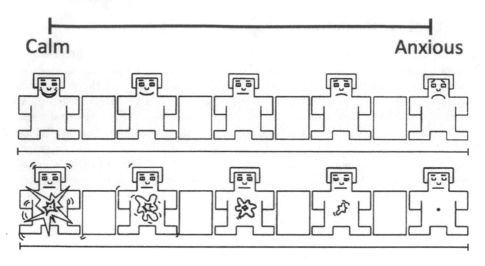

Fig. 5. Example of visual analogue scale (top) and self assessment manikins for pleasure (middle) and arousal (bottom).

4.2   Method

A laboratory experiment was designed with two goals: the first was to pre-evaluate the effect of typical soundscapes (natural, urban, and musical) on stress reduction; the second to validate the survey with traditional stress measurement methods (physiological measures of heart rate variability). To this end a three steps experiment was design:

- evaluation of the emotional state of the participant before the experiment (e.g. the baseline)
- stressor task to induce a specific subjective emotional valence and intensity to the participant (e.g. the stress)
- evaluation of the stress recovery due to the use of specific soundscapes.

Emotional state was measured with physiological measures and subjective questionnaires.

Participants. The study group consisted of 36 young and healthy subjects (20 men and 16 women, age: 21.4 ± 1.8 years, min 19 max 32). None of the subjects reported auditory loss. All of them participated on a volunteer basis; they signed an informed consent form prior to testing. This study was performed in accordance with the ethical standards of the Declaration of Helsinki (revised Edinburgh, 2000).

Stressor Task. The stressor task consisted in five minutes of mental arithmetic with harassment. This method was previously introduce and tested by [7]. Participants were instructed to count backwards out loud by 13 from 2397.

Thirty seconds into the task, the experimenter informed participants that their counting was too slow and that the task should be started again, but at a faster pace. Thirty seconds after the first interruption, they were informed their performance was still deficient. They were told to start again, but this time counting down by seven, instead of 13, since it would be less challenging. Similar interruptions continued every 30 s for five minutes.

Sound Selection and Presentation. Based on the studies described in Sect. 2.2, three different type of soundscape were used for the experiment:

- A natural soundscape based on forest with sounds of wind in the trees, insects and birds;
- An urban soundscape evoking a vegetable market with human voices (merchants and customers), cars and buses sounds;
- A musical soundscape composed with sound synthesis without specific tones, harmony, and rhythm.

Soundscapes were rendered over headphones at a low-medium volume (approximately 70 dB) and lasted five minutes.

Procedure. Experiment took place in a standard audiometric room. It took place in three steps. Participants were first asked to seat down and stand still and quiet during five minutes (for a baseline recording of physiological measures). After these five minutes, the stressor task was presented to the participant during three minutes. Finally, the last step consisted in a recovery phase. Participants were asked to stand still and quiet during five minutes. As a function of the condition, a soundscape (musical, natural, urban or no soundscape) was diffused in the room with two loudspeakers at a comfortable level. The soundscape condition was randomly assign to the participant in order to make four equal group of participants (the participants of one group only listen to one soundscape). At the end of the experiment, after the recovery phase, a happy video was presented to the participants in order to induce a positive emotional state before leaving the participant (no data were recorded during this step).

Data Recording and Analysis Procedures. The data measured for this experiment consisted in physiological measures and subjective measures.

The physiological measure consists in the heart rate which was acquired using a Biopac physiological data acquisition system[1]. Electrocardiogram (ECG) was measured between the chest using the standard two-electrodes configuration and the ankle using one electrode. ECG measures the heart activity through the electrical signal of the heart muscle. The number of beats per minute is called the heart rate and is typically between 70 and 80 bpm at rest. Inter Beat Interval (IBI) is the time interval in milliseconds between two "R" peaks in the ECG waveform. The evolution of the IBI is called the Heart Rate Variability (HRV) and is a sensitive and selective measure of mental stress [11]. HRV was extracted

---

[1] www.biopac.com.

from the ECG signal using Kubios[2] software. The ECG signal was recorded during the three steps of the experiment in order to evaluate the HRV between the three steps.

For each subject, the IBI was averaged over the five minutes of each of the three steps (base, stressor task, and recovery) and entered into a two-way repeated measures analysis of variance (ANOVA) with the soundscape type as within-subject factor (4 levels: natural, musical, and urban soundscape, and without soundscape). A Tukey test was used for all post-hoc analysis.

Subjective measures consisted in the previously described survey. The survey took place at the beginning of the experiment (before the first step) and at the end of the experiment (between the recovery phase and the positive video) in order to evaluate the correlation between the physiological measures and the survey responses.

4.3   Results

Influence of Soundscapes on Stress Recovery. The influence of the soundscape conditions as a function of the three steps of the experiment on the mean IBI is presented with boxplots on Fig. 6.

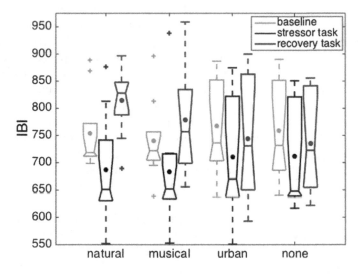

Fig. 6. Boxplot of the Inter Beat Interval (IBI) for each experimental step as a function of the soundscape condition. Mean in circle.

Globally, the mean IBI is 755 ± 80 ms for the base, 698 ± 100 ms for stressor task, and 768 ± 94 ms for the recovery. Statistical analysis of the IBI highlights a significant effect of the experimental step $[F(2, 64) = 28.134; p < 0.001]$.

---

[2] http://kubios-hrv.software.informer.com/2.2/.

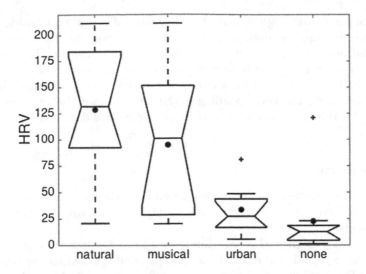

Fig. 7. Boxplot of the Heart Rate Variation (HRV) between stress and recovery step as a function of the soundscape condition. Mean in circle.

Post-hoc analysis revealed significant differences between the base step and the stressor task ($p < 0.001$) and between the stressor task and the recovery step ($p < 0.001$). There are no differences between the base and recovery step.

Considering the recovery step, the analysis highlights a significant effect of the soundscape type $[F(3, 31) = 8.512; p < 0.001]$ on the IBI. In order to take into account the different stress levels of each subjects during the stressor task, the analysis was processed with the HRV as covariate for a weighting adjustment. The mean HRV (between the stressor and the recovery task) are 128.3 ± 64.8 ms for the natural soundscape, 95.5 ± 72.1 ms for the musical soundscape, 33.7 ± 22.5 ms for the urban soundscape, and 22.8 ± 37.5 ms for no soundscape (see Fig. 7). The results highlight a significance of the covariate $[F(1, 31) = 87.839; p < 0.001]$. The good influence of the natural soundscape on stress recovery is highlighted by the post-hoc analysis which revealed a significant difference between this condition compared to no soundscape condition ($p < 0.005$) and urban soundscape condition ($p < 0.001$). The results also show a better influence of the musical soundscape condition over the urban soundscape condition ($p < 0.05$) and over the no soundscape condition (but without significant differences ($p = 0.091$)). There are no differences on stress recovery between natural and musical soundscape conditions on one part ($p = 0.453$), and between urban and no soundscape conditions on the other part ($p = 0.967$).

Correlation Between Physiological and Subjective Measures. To evaluate the survey efficiency in term of stress measurement, the auto evaluation scores measured during the first and the third step were correlated for each participant with the IBI measured for the same steps. Results show a positive and significant correlation between the score and the heart rate measurement

($r = 0.868$; $p < 0.001$), highlighting the pertinence of this item. Considering the other items, appropriate physiological data were not available to explore potential correlation between physiological and subjective measures. User responses for the second item (related to anxiety) are highly similar to the data related to stress, indicating that subjects were not able to make a difference between these two items. Results corresponding to the SAM and well-being items are not of interest for this in-lab evaluation, as no physiologicals data can be correlated with them.

4.4 Discussion

The objective of the presented study was to evaluate the effect of different soundscape type on stress recovery and to validate the stress survey with physiological measurements.

Results analysis showed a high influence of the soundscape type on stress recovery. As expected, the natural soundscape condition led to the best stress reduction. These results are in line with several studies which show that natural soundscapes, without sounds that directly threat the individual security, allow to faster achieve stress reduction compared to no soundscape [2,4]. Rather, the use of an urban soundscape condition (with humans' and motors' sounds) did not induce stress reduction and led to the same results as the absence of sound on stress recovery. This results suggests that the use of urban soundscapes must be avoided in the context of stress recovery. To go further, it will be of interest to deeply explore the soundscape content in order to highlight the most unpleasant sounds for the users. Finally, the musical soundscape induced more stress reduction than no soundscape condition although this result was not significant. To resume, in order to induce stress recovery to bus passengers with soundscapes, the best solution is to use natural soundscapes. Another option is to use musical soundscapes although this leads to minor reductions. The use of urban soundscape is not effective for stress reduction.

Naturally, these results are limited to certain soundscape types. Indeed for practical reasons it was not possible to test more than one sound material for each soundscape type. Then, for the natural soundscape, the correlation between the present results and the literature results suggests that the stress recovery might be observed with other sound materials than the forest sounds (such as sounds related to the sea, the mountain or the countryside). For the urban soundscape, in contrast, it is more difficult to extend the results obtained with the markets sounds as there exist no similar studies. However, it seems reasonable to avoid sounds related to motor engines or considered as noise pollution. Finally, the musical soundscape constructed for this study was deprived of any rhythmic and tonal content to be independent of any type of music (e.g. rock, rap, pop, classical. . .). As, the concept of musical soundscape is generally difficult to characterise, it is more interesting to consider the concept of relaxing music, which is characterized by slow tempo, repetitive rhythm, and gentle contours [12]. With this type of music, the present results are in line but less pronounced than the literature when considering the amount of stress reduction due to relaxing music [17]. It is also interesting to note that musical preference, previous music experience, age, and type of stress have a hight influence on the amount of stress reduction [17].

Considering the survey, the results show a high correlation between affective reports and physiological measurement validating the stress item of the survey. The results also suggest subjects' confusion between stress and anxiety, it is thus possible to suppress the anxiety item of the survey.

5   Conclusion

This paper introduces a collaborative project that aims at improving bus trip with auditory information. Thanks to the design of a high quality multi-channel sound spatialization system and the implementation of a sonification software based on geolocation, three fundamental actions of the sound on the bus passengers will be studied. We believe that the use of playful stop sounds announcement paired with spatialized natural soundscapes can de-stress the bus passengers and transforms a simple trip into a tourist and historic stroll. Furthermore, the use of sound to alert passengers of possibly destabilizing emergency braking can prevent of passengers accidents. Taken together, the three aspects of this project constitute a new approach for the design of sounds for public transport that may increase people's interest for the use of public transport. With such systems, it is also simple to transform a bus trip into a musical composition based on geolocation that could bring sound art to a new public.

Acknowledgments. This work was funded by the RTM and by Carnot Star.

References

1. Abend, R., Dan, O., Maoz, K., Raz, S., Bar-Haim, Y.: Reliability, validity and sensitivity of a computerized visual analog scale measuring state anxiety. J. Behav. Ther. Exp. Psychiatry **45**(4), 447–453 (2014)
2. Alvarsson, J.J., Wiens, S., Nilsson, M.E.: Stress recovery during exposure to nature sound and environmental noise. Int. J. Environ. Res. Public Health **7**(3), 1036–1046 (2010)
3. Barthe, P.: Announcing method and apparatus. US Patent 2,837,606, 3 June 1958. https://www.google.com/patents/US2837606
4. Benfield, J.A., Taff, B.D., Newman, P., Smyth, J.: Natural sound facilitates mood recovery. Ecopsychology **6**(3), 183–188 (2014)
5. Bezat, M., Kronland-Martinet, R., Roussarie, V., Ystad, S.: From acoustic descriptors to evoked quality of car-door sounds. J. Acoust. Soc. Am. **136**(1), 226–241 (2014)
6. Bradley, M.M., Lang, P.J.: Measuring emotion: the self-assessment manikin and the semantic differential. J. Behav. Ther. Exp. Psychiatry **25**(1), 49–59 (1994)
7. Chafin, S., Roy, M., Gerin, W., Christenfeld, N.: Music can facilitate blood pressure recovery from stress. Br. J. Health Psychol. **9**(3), 393–403 (2004)

8. Gandemer, L., Parseihian, G., Kronland-Martinet, R., Bourdin, C.: The influence of horizontally rotating sound on standing balance. Exp. Brain Res. **232**(12), 3813–3820 (2014)

9. Gatersleben, B., Uzzell, D.: Affective appraisals of the daily commute comparing perceptions of drivers, cyclists, walkers, and users of public transport. Environ. Behav. **39**(3), 416–431 (2007)

10. Grinde, B., Patil, G.G.: Biophilia: does visual contact with nature impact on health and well-being? Int. J. Environ. Res. Public Health **6**(9), 2332–2343 (2009)

11. Hjortskov, N., Rissén, D., Blangsted, A.K., Fallentin, N., Lundberg, U., Søgaard, K.: The effect of mental stress on heart rate variability and blood pressure during computer work. Eur. J. Appl. Physiol. **92**(1–2), 84–89 (2004)

12. Labbé, E., Schmidt, N., Babin, J., Pharr, M.: Coping with stress: the effectiveness of different types of music. Appl. Psychophysiol. Biofeedback **32**(3–4), 163–168 (2007)

13. Lesage, F.X., Berjot, S., Deschamps, F.: Clinical stress assessment using a visual analogue scale. Occup. Med. **62**(8), 600 (2012)

14. McChesney, J., Sveistrup, H., Woollacott, M.: Influence of auditory precuing on automatic postural responses. Exp. Brain Res. **108**(2), 315–320 (1996)

15. Merer, A., Aramaki, M., Ystad, S., Kronland-Martinet, R.: Perceptual characterization of motion evoked by sounds for synthesis control purposes. Trans. Appl. Percept. **10**(1), 1–24 (2013)

16. Parseihian, G., Gondre, C., Aramaki, M., Ystad, S., Kronland-Martinet, R.: Comparison and evaluation of sonification strategies for guidance tasks. IEEE Trans. Multimedia **18**(4), 674–686 (2016)

17. Pelletier, C.L.: The effect of music on decreasing arousal due to stress: a meta-analysis. J. Music Ther. **41**(3), 192–214 (2004)

18. Rossi, V., Pourtois, G.: Transient state-dependent fluctuations in anxiety measured using STAI, POMS, PANAS or VAS: a comparative review. Anxiety Stress Coping **25**(6), 603–645 (2012)

19. Santos, M.J., Kanekar, N., Aruin, A.S.: The role of anticipatory postural adjustments in compensatory control of posture: 1. Electromyographic analysis. J. Electromyogr. Kinesiol. **20**(3), 388–397 (2010)

20. Santos, M.J., Kanekar, N., Aruin, A.S.: The role of anticipatory postural adjustments in compensatory control of posture: 2. Biomechanical analysis. J. Electromyogr. Kinesiol. **20**(3), 398–405 (2010)

21. Sturnieks, D.L., Menant, J., Delbaere, K., Vanrenterghem, J., Rogers, M.W., Fitzpatrick, R.C., Lord, S.R.: Force-controlled balance perturbations associated with falls in older people: a prospective cohort study. PloS one **8**(8), e70981 (2013)

22. Ulrich, R.: View through a window may influence recovery. Science **224**(4647), 224–225 (1984)

23. Ulrich, R.S., Simons, R.F., Losito, B.D., Fiorito, E., Miles, M.A., Zelson, M.: Stress recovery during exposure to natural and urban environments. J. Environ. Psychol. **11**(3), 201–230 (1991)

24. Watts, G., Khan, A., Pheasant, R.: Influence of soundscape and interior design on anxiety and perceived tranquillity of patients in a healthcare setting. Appl. Acoust. **104**, 135–141 (2016)

Computer-Supported Interactive Systems for Music Production Performance and Listening

Using Pure Data for Real-Time Granular Synthesis Control Through Leap Motion

Damián Anache$^{(\boxtimes)}$

CONICET, Consejo Nacional de Investigaciones, Científicas y Técnicas,
UNQ, Universidad Nacional de Quilmes, Roque Saenz Peña 352,
B1876BXD Bernal Buenos Aires, Argentina
damian.anache@unq.edu.ar

Abstract. This paper documents the development of a granular synthesis instrument programmed on PD (*Pure Data*, Miller Puckette et al. (http://www.puredata.info) for being controlled by *Leap Motion* (https://www.leapmotion.com/), a computer hardware sensor that converts hands and fingers motion into simple data, ready for end-user software inputs. The instrument named *mGIL* (my_Grainer's Instrument for Leap) uses the *my_grainer* (Developed by Pablo Di Liscia, available at: puredata.info/Members/pdiliscia/grainer.) PD's external object as its GS (granular synthesis) engine and *leapmotion* (leapmotion external developed by Chikashi Miyama. Linux version available at: http://musa.poperbu.net/index.php/tecnologia-seccions-30/-puredata-seccions-45/129-installing-leapmotion-puredata-external-on-linux. Windows version at: http://jakubvaltar.blogspot.com.ar/2013/10/leap-motion-pure-data-external-for.html) external object as its local interface. This connection between software and hardware intends to reach expressive computer music sounds, with the performer's body imprints. The present status of that interplay (software + hardware) is a work-in-progress advance of the author doctoral thesis.

Keywords: Real-time synthesis · Pure Data · Leap Motion · Granular synthesis · Performance

1 Introduction

After Isaac Beekman [1], Dennis Gabor [2], Iannis Xenakis [3], Barry Truax [4] and Curtis Roads [1] himself, GS (granular synthesis) is fully documented by Roads on his book *Microsound* [1]. Nevertheless computer technologies are constantly improving and so are new approaches to this synthesis technique as *mGIL* (*my_Grainer's Instrument for Leap*) is an example of this nowadays. This instrument, *mGIL*, was developed on *Pure Data* to handle real time GS controlled by *LeapMotion*. In this development, GS focuses the timbral organization level in order to generate individual sound objects, instead of granular clouds. The aim is to create a group of grains as a sonic entity where the individual grains are integrated in a unique sound unit. Each grain has a meaning only inside that object. This can be described as a *short time granular sound* generated between a *packed* and a *covered fill* factor as Roads describe it[1].

---

[1] See [1], page 105.

© Springer International Publishing AG 2017
M. Aramaki et al. (Eds.): CMMR 2016, LNCS 10525, pp. 171–179, 2017.
DOI: 10.1007/978-3-319-67738-5_10

In the context of the author's doctoral thesis, the main motivation of using granular synthesis on this development was its capacity to allow a huge amount of parameters modifications in a short time scale, with a manifest spectral consequence. This aspect is of special interest in order to reach expressive sounds generated by synthesis.

The author's research is centered on the incidence of the interpreter/performer in computer music generated by synthesis means only. A first approach to the problem [5] suggests that granular synthesis could be an appropriate technique in order to imprint the performer bodily trace actions on every sound generated by a digital instrument. The reason of this is the huge amount of control data that it involves, which could exceed the thousand parameters in just one second[2].

According to the author's standpoint, if this feature is properly combined with the right device control, highly expressive synthesis sounds may be produced. Therefore, the lack of physical imprint[3] in computer music may be overcome. At this stage of research, the chosen device was *Leap Motion*. This device was considered an appropriate choice for the aim of this work, because it can acquire the position values for each finger of each hand (at least 36 outputs) with great accuracy at a user defined rate (among other useful data from movements and gesture analysis).

2 Framework

Many of the most important developments for GS can be found on Roads [1], from where the highlights are *CG – Cloud Generator* (by C. Roads), and the early real time developments by Barry Truax. On the other hand, if we focus on developments for the free and open source platform *Pure Data*, we find five synthesis units available as external objects. Some of the features of the mentioned externals is discussed in the next summary (Table 1) as well as in the following descriptions.

Table 1. Pure Data's externals for GS.

Name	Developer	Release	Output	G.Wf.[a]	G.Env.[b]
syncgrain[c]	Barknecht, F.	n.d.	Mono	Table	Fix
mill[d]	Keskinen, O.	n.d.	Stereo	Table	Hann
disis_munger1[e]	Ji-Sun, K., et al.	2007	Multichannel	Audio	Fix
granule[f]	Lyon, E.	2012	Stereo	Table	Table
my_grainer[g]	Di Liscia, O. P.	2012	Ambisonics	Tables	Tables

a-G.Wf. = Grain Waveform.
b-G.Env. = Grain Envelope.
c-https://puredata.info/Members/fbar (Last access: 02/2016).
d-http://rickygraham.net/?p=130474333 (Last access: 02/2016).
e-http://l2ork.music.vt.edu/main/make-your-own-l2ork/software/ (Last access: 02/2016).
f-http://www.somasa.qub.ac.uk/~elyon/LyonSoftware/Pd/ (Last access: 02/2016).
g-https://puredata.info/author/pdiliscia (Last access: 03/2016).

---

[2] See [1], page 87.

[3] This lack is marked by Anache [5] and is present on several authors of [6].

All of these objects implement the GS technique in a different way, offering advantages and disadvantages, different control parameters, possibilities and limitations. *syncgrain~* works only with synchronous GS and is a direct port of the *SndObject SyncGrain* by Victor Lazzarini. The grain waveform is obtained by reading a function table, meanwhile the grain envelope cannot be defined by the user. For *mill~* the grain waveform is also defined by user through a function table but the grain envelope is based on a *hanning* window with expanded sides possibilities. *disis_munger1~* is based on Dan Trueman's *munger~* (Computer Music Center, Columbia University). It doesn't generate grains by its own and needs an external audio input for working. Its grains envelope function is fix and the user can only change its duration. The output offers up to 64 intensity panning channels. *granule~* was developed at Department of Music and Sonic Arts Queen's University Belfast and it's included on the *LyonPotpourri* collection of externals together with other GS external object: *granulesf~*. Both, the grain waveform and envelope are defined by function tables but it only offers stereo output. Finally, *my_grainer~*'s latest version was released on 03/2016 and it can work with up to 24 different function tables at the same time for both the grain waveform and the grain envelope. Moreover it outputs an Ambisonics B-format signal (making 3D sound with full control feasible) and offers very detailed parameters in order to control the GS technique as its main reference literature explains: grain duration; gap between grains; pitch; amplitude level; spatial position; and auxiliary output level for external processing of each grain (like reverberation send.) The external also offers controls for a random deviation of each one of its parameters, different looping capacities for the audio tables read and may receive lists for specific random values choices.

3 Instrument Description

The instrument started as an improved version of Esteban Calcagno's patch called *Grainer_Dinamics*[4] but during the improvement process the patch achieved its own identity giving birth to *mGIL*. This new instrument keeps the original idea of being a programmable function-based controller for my_grainer~ with the addition of being triggered and further controlled through an external device. Nowadays the instrument is specially designed to operate with *LeapMotion* but it could be easily adapted to be used with other devices as well. Figure 1 below shows the instrument's main interface.

As explained before in Sect. 1, *mGIL* generates short time scale granular sounds, so its control function values are arbitrary limited in order to achieve this special kind of GS. For example, grains duration values are limited to 1–100 ms and *gap* (elapsed time between consecutive grains) values are limited to 1–500 ms. Also, as the synthesis engine allows it, *mGIL*'s parameter names are strongly related to Roads terminology [1], so it is designed for users who know the theory in advance. The user must handle carefully this interface, because some especial configurations may lead to undesired results. For example, a *gap* time smaller than the grain duration may produce overlapped grains, and therefore the audio output may be overloaded.

---

[4] Published on [8].

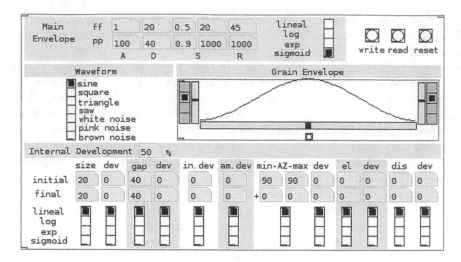

Fig. 1. *mGIL*'s GUI.

Each control function takes a starting value and an ending value, and a choice for the interpolation method to perform between these values. The interpolation methods must be chosen from the following options: linear, logarithmic, exponential and *S-shaped* sigmoid function.

The grain waveform is chosen from seven presets, divided in two groups: functions and noises; functions: sine, triangle, square and saw; noises: white, pink and brown. When using the functions waveforms, *mGIL* receives pitch values for transposing the original waveform, meanwhile noises ignores that input value (pitch control is explained on Sect. 3.1). The grain envelope is defined by a Bezier-based GUI, consisting of a sequence of two variable curves with an adjustable joint point. This offers many options for regular and custom envelopes, among them: bell-shaped, triangular, *expodec*[5], *rexpodec*[6], or any other two segment type shape.

Finally, the audio generated by the GS engine is controlled by the main ADSR[7] audio envelope, also defined by keyboard input values for a more precise control. This is different than the main envelope of most digital instruments, because in this case there must be two ADSR defined envelopes. One is for the higher intensity level and the other for the lower (normalized from 0 to 1, where 0 is *pp* and 1 is *ff*). So, the intermediate intensity values are generated by interpolation of the ones of the defined envelopes, according to four interpolation types: lineal, logarithmic, exponential and *S-shaped* sigmoid function. The main ADSR envelope also defines the total sound's duration. Because of this, the lengths of the transitions of all the *mGIL*'s control functions are defined proportionally to the length of the ADSR envelope (by *Internal Development* parameter on GUI).

---

[5] Exponentially decaying envelope, see [1], page 88.

[6] Reverse *expodec*, see [1], page 88.

[7] Acronym for *Attack, Decay, Sustain, Release*.

As shown in Fig. 2, in order to generate two outputs, *mGIL* needs two input values: pitch and intensity. The outputs are: one control-rate data package to control the GS of *my_grainer*~ and an audio-rate output to control the main amplitude envelope of *my_grainer*~ (the main ADSR envelope).

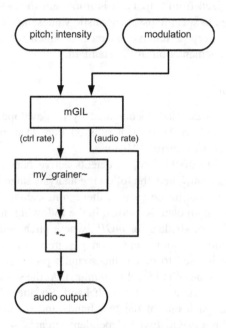

Fig. 2. *mGIL*'s connections scheme.

The remaining feature of *mGIL* is the modulation control. At this stage it just receives a value from 0 to 1 for scaling both the gap time and the bandwidth of the pitch variation (the later will only be taking in account if the defined GS configuration uses a random deviation of the main pitch). This will be the first feature to be improved in future *mGIL*'s versions, by adding more modulation inputs in order to achieve a more significant spectral influence.

3.1 Pitch and Dynamics

The design of *mGIL* offers two ways of pitch control: (A) specific frequency input (in hertz) with the option of normalized mode (from 0 to 1 for 20 Hz to 20 kHz); and (B) Bark Scale index input. For this last feature, *barkScale* was developed as a *PD*'s abstraction. It just allocates a table that receives a Bark Scale index as input and offers central frequency, bandwidth, low and high limits as outputs values. The input can also be normalized from 0 to 1 float values. On both cases, the received frequency values define the amount of transposition of the chosen grain waveform. In case that the chosen waveform is any kind of noise, the whole frequency input become meaningless and has no influence on the grain waveform.

In order to offer a balanced level audio output based on psychoacoustic data, an abstraction (*iso2262003*) was created based on the ISO 226:2003 international standard which documents the normal equal-loudness-level contours. The abstraction receives a frequency value (in hertz) and a loudness level contour (from 20 to 80 phon or normalize from 0 to 1) to compute the corresponding sound pressure level (from 0 to 120 dB SPL, or normalized from 0 to 1). It is important to notice that, as the digital domain cannot be related to specific psychoacoustic values, *mGIL*'s design assigned its internal values just to keep a relative balance of intensity across the spectrum, regardless of a strict implementation of the standard.

3.2   External Control

LeapMotion's operation is detailed documented by its developers team at its official website[8] and as anticipated on Abstract, it runs on Pure Data platform thanks to an external object developed by *Chikashi Miyama*.

The first analysis stage of this project detects active hands on each half of the interaction zone, left and right. Then, the following analysis stage is the detection of the closing/opening hands gesture inside each of these zones, done by comparison of the *sphereRadius*'[9] method output data. As shown in the following images (Figs. 3 and 4).

This gesture detection sends data for *mGIL*, where pitch and dynamics are determined by hands' elevation positions and open gesture's velocity, respectively. The hand elevation position is used to define the sound's pitch, and the velocity of the open-close gesture defines the sound level (*dynamics*). At the same time, the interaction zone is divided into two regions, one for each hand. So, the whole analysis scheme offers data outputs from each one of the two hands and is connected to two *mGIL* instances. Thanks to this design, two independent streams sound synthesis can be performed simultaneously (Figs. 5 and 6).

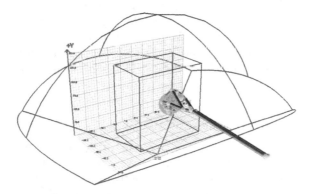

Fig. 3. Close hand gesture detection by *sphereradius* method.

---

[8] https://developer.leapmotion.com/documentation/ .

[9] See Leap Motion documentation.

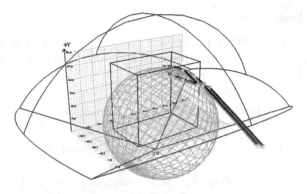

Fig. 4. Open hand gesture detection by *sphereradius* method.

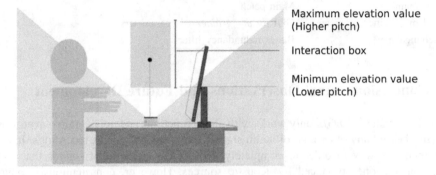

Fig. 5. Side view of the *interaction box*, and parameters' assignments for *mGIL*.

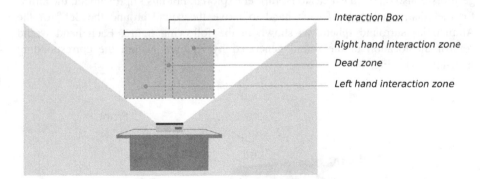

Fig. 6. Front view of the *interaction box*, and redefined interaction zones for *mGIL*.

3.3   Package Description

mGIL consists of a set of PD's patches and abstractions, some of them are flexible enough for being used in other instruments or even in general purpose projects. They all are listed below (Table 2).

Table 2. mGIL's patches and abstractions.

Name	Description
autopack2; autopack3	Packs two or three floats numbers in one list regardless of the order of receiving values
barkScale	Offers Bark Scale's values on demand, explained on Sect. 3.1
ISO2262003	Offers ISO 226:2003 data on demand, explained on Sect. 3.1
leapmotion-ctrl	Custom Leap Motion analysis for *mGIL*, needs *leapmotion* external object, explained on Sect. 3.2
mGILabstraction	*mGIL*'s core, GUI shown on Fig. 1
mGILmainPatch	Main patch
mGILmy_grainerParameters	GUI for *my_grainer*~'s parameters
OnebangTime	Bangs redundancy filter

4   Conclusions, Final Observations and Future Development

This first version of *mGIL* only works with audio functions and noisy grain waveforms, leaving behind any other kind of audio signals like acoustic sources recordings. It was designed this way in order to completely avoid the generation of sounds that may resemble the ones produced by acoustic sources. However, conscientiously explorations with acoustic sources recordings will be tested on next instrument's versions. The control of the *my_grainer* external 3D spatialisation capacities by performing gestures is also one of the areas to be further explored. For this improvement, the aim is for the relative position of each hand to move the sound around the 360° of the Ambisonics surround sphere, as shown in the following figure. Each hand would control the location of the sound generated by its own, within the corresponding right-left zone (Fig. 7).

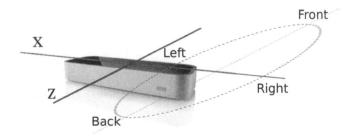

Fig. 7. Spatial control design for future versions.

This work also involved several suggestions of new features to Pablo Di Liscia (*my_grainer*'s developer). Some of them (for example, different looping capacities for grain waveform tables reading) are available in its last release (March, 2016) and some others maybe available on next versions.

One of the most important subject which was researched through this development is the influence of corporal gestures into the morphology of the generated sound in live performance. The actual state of this project allows the author to start his first studio compositions, performances and analysis in order to developed his doctoral thesis. At the same time, the source code, documentation and examples are freely shared on-line, so as other artists and programmers can be able to explore this research area.

References

1. Roads, C.: Microsound. The MIT Press, England (2004)
2. Gabor, D.: Acoustical Quanta and the Theory of Hearing. Nature **159**(4044), 591–594 (1947)
3. Xenakis, I.: Formalized Music. Pendragon Press, Columbia (1992)
4. Truax, B.: Real-time granular synthesis with the DMX-1000. In: Berg, P. (ed.) Proceedings of the International Computer Music Conference, The Hague, Computer Music Association (1986)
5. Anache, D.: El Rol del Intérprete en la Música Electrónica - Estado de la Cuestión. In: Actas de la Décima Semana de la Música y la Musicología, UCA, Argentina (2013)
6. Peters, D., Eckel, G., Dorschel, A.: Bodily Expression in Electronic Music – Perspectives on Reclaiming Performativity. Routledge, Abingdon (2012)
7. Paine, G.: Gesture and morphology in laptop music. In: Dean, R.T. (ed.) The Oxford Handbook of Computer Music. Oxford University Press, USA (2009)
8. Di Liscia, O.P. (ed): Síntesis Espacial de Sonido, CMMAS Centro Mexicano para la Música y las Artes Sonoras, Mexico, ebook with aditional files (2016)

Angkasa: A Software Tool for Spatiotemporal Granulation

Muhammad Hafiz Wan Rosli[(⊠)] and Andres Cabrera

Media Arts and Technology Program, University of California, Santa Barbara,
3309 Phelps Hall, Santa Barbara, CA 93106-6065, USA
{hafiz,andres}@mat.ucsb.edu

Abstract. We introduce a software tool for performing Spatiotemporal
Granulation called Angkasa, which allows a user to independently granulate space and time, through the use of spatially encoded signals. The
software is designed to be used as a creative tool for composition, real-
time musical instrument, or as an analytical tool. The current iteration
of Angkasa provides an interface for analysis and synthesis of both spatial and temporal domains. Additionally, we present a brief theoretical
overview of Spatiotemporal Granulation, and outline the possible, and
potential manipulations that could be realized through this technique.

Keywords: Microsound · Spatial sound · Analysis-synthesis

1 Introduction

The process of segmenting a sound signal into small grains (less than 100 ms), and
reassembling them into a new time order is known as granulation. Although there
are various techniques for manipulating these grains, almost all implementations
have some fundamental processes in common. Broadly speaking, the stages of
analysis (selection and sorting of input) and synthesis (constructing temporal
patterns for output) are always present in some form.

Articulation of the grains' spatial characteristics may be achieved by many
existing techniques, allowing one to choreograph the position and movement of
individual grains as well as groups (clouds). This spatial information, however,
is generally synthesized (i.e. artificially generated), unlike temporal information
which can be extracted from the sound sample itself, and then used to drive
resynthesis parameters.

Ambisonics is a technology that captures full-sphere spatial sound (periphonic) information through the use of Spherical Harmonics. This research aims
to use the spatial information extracted from the Ambisonics signal as another
dimension for granulation.

By extracting this spatial information, the proposed method would create
novel possibilities for manipulating sound. It would allow the decoupling of temporal and spatial information of a grain, making it possible to independently

M. Aramaki et al. (Eds.): CMMR 2016, LNCS 10525, pp. 180–191, 2017.
DOI: 10.1007/978-3-319-67738-5_11

assign a specific time and position for analysis and synthesis. Furthermore, temporal domain processes such as windowing, selection order, density, structure (pattern), higher dimensional mapping, as well as spatial trajectory and position, could be applied to the spatial dimension.

1.1   Related Work

The analysis, and extraction of grains from different positions in space is a research area that has yet to be explored. However, there has been a number of techniques used to disperse sound particles in space.

Roads outlines the techniques used for spatialization of microsound into two main approaches [8]:

1. Scattering of sound particles in different spatial locations and depths
2. Using sound particles as spatializers for other sounds via granulation, convolution, and intermodulation.

Truax, on the other hand, uses granular synthesis as a means to diffuse decorrelated sound sources over multiple loudspeakers, giving a sense of aural volume [11]. Kim-Boyle explored choreographing of grains in space according to flocking algorithms [5]. Barrett explored the process of encoding spatial information via higher-order Ambisonics, creating a virtual space of precisely positioned grains [1].

The techniques outlined above aims to position grains in a particular location in space– spatialization. On the other hand, Deleflie & Schiemer proposed a technique to encode grains with spatial information extracted from an Ambisonics signal [3]. However, this technique implements temporal segmentation, i.e. classical granulation, and imbues each grain with the component signals of the captured sound field.

In contrast, our method of Spatiotemporal Granulation segments the space itself, in addition to time, to produce an array of grains localized in azimuth and elevation, for each temporal window.

2   Theory

The granulation of sampled sounds is a powerful means of sound transformation. To granulate means to segment (or window) a sound signal into grains, to possibly modify them in some way, and then to reassemble the grains in a new time order and microrhythm. This might take the form of a continuous stream or of a statistical cloud of sampled grains - Roads (2001, p. 98).

The classical method of granulation captures two perceptual dimensions: time-domain information (starting time, duration, envelope shape) and frequency-domain information (the pitch of the waveform within the grain and the spectrum of the grain) [8].

The proposed method granulates space, and adds another dimension to this representation: Spatial-domain information. The fundamental premise of this method lies in the extraction of spatial sound information, and the segmentation of this space into grains which are localized in time, frequency, and space. These grains will henceforth be individually referred to as a *Spatiotemporal grain* (Fig. 1).

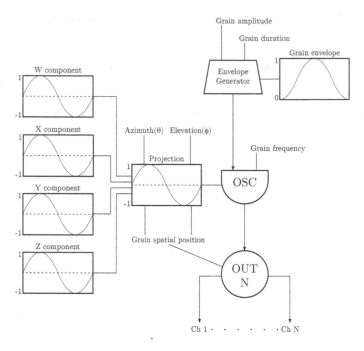

Fig. 1. Block diagram of a basic spatiotemporal grain generator

2.1 Encoding of Spatial Sound

There are several microphone technologies that allow the capturing of spatial information, such as *X-Y/Blumlein Pair*, *Decca Tree*, and *Optimum Cardioid Triangle*. However, these technologies do not capture the complete full-sphere information of spatial sound.

On the other hand, *Ambisonics* is a technique that captures periphonic spatial information via microphone arrays, such as the "SoundField Microphone" [4]. It is important to note that using this technique, sounds from any direction are treated equally, as opposed to other techniques that assumes the frontal information to be the main source, and other directional information as ambient sources.

The spatial sound field representation of *Ambisonics* is captured via "Spherical Harmonics" [4]. Spatial resolution is primarily dependent on the order of the Ambisonics signal, i.e. order of Spherical Harmonics. A first-order encoded signal is composed of the sound pressure W, and the three components of the pressure gradient X, Y, Z, representing the acoustic particle velocity (Fig. 1). Together, these approximate the sound field on a sphere around the microphone array.

2.2 Decoding of Spatial Sound

One of the strengths of Ambisonics is the decoupling of encoding (via microphone & virtual), and decoding processes. This allows the captured sound field to be represented using any type of speaker configuration.

In practice, a decoder projects the Spherical Harmonics onto a specific vector, denoted by the position of each loudspeaker θ_j. The reproduction of a sound field without height (surround sound), can be achieved via Eq. (1).

$$P_j = W(\frac{1}{\sqrt{2}}) + X(\cos(\theta_j)) + Y(\sin(\theta_j)). \tag{1}$$

2.3 Spherical Harmonics Projection

Consider the case where we have N number of loudspeakers arranged in a circle (without height). In the case where N is 360, we are essentially playing back the sounds to reconstruct the captured sound field at 1° difference. Instead of playing back the sounds from 360 loudspeakers, we can use the information as a means to specify different sounds from different locations.

This forms the basis for extracting sound sources in space for the spatiotemporal grains. If we were to look at the frequency content of these extracted grains

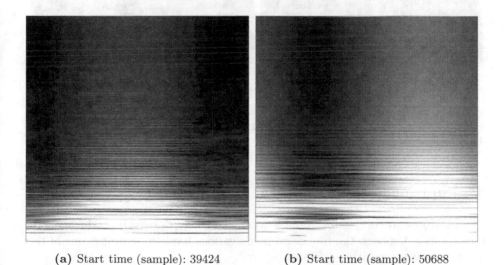

(a) Start time (sample): 39424   (b) Start time (sample): 50688

Fig. 2. X-axis = azimuth (0–360°), Y-axis = frequency bin, Intensity = magnitude of bin, Window size = 512. Sample = fireworks, first-order Ambisonics

in the same temporal window (Fig. 2), we can deduce that each localized grain contains a unique spectrum. Additionally, the direction of a particular sound object could also be estimated.

Periphonic Projection. Equation 1 can be extended to include height information, i.e. extracting every spatiotemporal grain (Fig. 1) in the captured sound field (Eq. 2).

$$P_j = W(\frac{1}{\sqrt{2}}) + X(\cos(\theta_j)\cos(\phi_j))$$
$$+ Y(\sin(\theta_j)\cos(\phi_j)) + Z(\sin(\theta_j)). \tag{2}$$

The result of this decomposed sound field can be represented as a 2 dimensional array (azimuth & elevation) of individual spatiotemporal grains, in the same temporal window (Fig. 3).

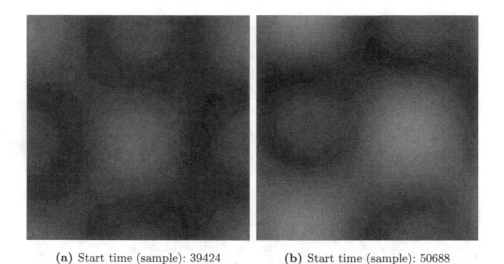

(a) Start time (sample): 39424   (b) Start time (sample): 50688

Fig. 3. X-axis = azimuth (0–360°), Y-axis = elevation (0–360°), Intensity = energy of localized spatiotemporal grain, Window size = 512. Sample = fireworks, first-order Ambisonics

3   Implementation: Angkasa

The word *Angkasa* originates from the Malay language, derived from the Sanskrit term *Ākāśa*. Although the root word bears various levels of meaning, one of the most common translation refers to "space".

In the context of our research, Angkasa is a software tool which allows a user to analyze, visualize, transform, and perform Spatiotemporal Granulation. The software is designed to be used as a creative tool for composition, real-time musical instrument, or as an analytical tool. The current iteration of Angkasa was developed using openFrameworks (C++ toolkit) on a 2015 Mac Pro (OSX 10.10.5). Video documentation of the software can be accessed at http://vimeo.com/157253180.

3.1 Analysis/Synthesis

Potentially every parameter used for classical granulation [8] can be adapted to Spatiotemporal Granulation. One of the parameters [13] that acquire a different context is *Selection Order–* It is expanded to include not only the temporal layout, but also the spatially encoded layout of the captured sound field.

Selective Granulation. Specifying only a certain region to be granulated allows us to selectively granulate the sound field. For example, one could granulate only a single quadrant (of space), and temporally stretch the grains that fall within that area, while allowing the other quadrants to progress at a different time speed. In effect, a moving sound object would retain its spatial trajectory, but assume a different temporal structure as it moves through these selected areas of space. The areas could be selected via different techniques, including (but not limited to):

1. Regions of the frame, such as quadrants, sections
2. User defined selection of grains [12]
3. Statistical algorithms for quasi-random selection
4. Audio features, as in Concatenative Synthesis [10].

Spatial Read Pointer. Because navigating space as a compositional parameter can be complex, an automatic way of moving through the space was designed. In addition to the ability to select a single grain in space, we implemented a technique to select a sequence of grains called the "Spatial Read Pointer". Analogous to the read pointer in classical (temporal) granulation, the spatial read pointer orbits around a specified trajectory, and extracts grains that fall within the path.

To ensure that the spatial read pointer is able to extract grains at the correct position in space, the orbit needs to be updated at a rate that is at least as high as the trigger rate. This is achieved by calculating the orbit trajectory in the audio callback (at audio rate). As such, not only are the grains extracted from the correct position in space and time, but the movement of the orbit could be increased to audio rate.

Algorithmic/Generative. As discussed, the spatial read pointer is one technique for specifying a selection pattern. This functions as a starting point for further investigations in extracting, and triggering spatiotemporal grains. Other algorithms that would be explored in the near future include fractal based, physics based (swarm & flocking), statistical, stochastic, and cellular automaton.

Space-Time Representation. The representations shown in Fig. 3 can be thought of as individual slices, or frames of a specific moment in time. If all the frames are successively lined up, we would gain a representation of the full space-time decomposition. This would open up to the possibility of traversing through both dimensions, allowing us to simultaneously extract and synthesize grains from different points in space and time. For example, the Spatial Read Pointer can be used not only to extract grains based on each frame (frozen time), but could also be used to navigate seamlessly to extract any spatiotemporal grain in space and time. One could also create a dynamic manipulable cloud containing only spatiotemporal grains extracted from a section of space, in a specific time period.

Spatial Windowing. A temporal grain is generated by multiplying a 1 dimensional audio signal (less than 100 ms) with a specified window (hanning, hamming, blackman, etc.). In other words, the algorithm takes a snapshot of a number of samples in time, and removes certain parts of the signal. Through Spatiotemporal Granulation, we can apply a 2 Dimensional window to select only a portion of grains to be triggered (or 3 Dimensional in the full space-time representation). Properties of the window such as window type [7] can be customized, akin to the temporal domain counterpart [14].

Spatial Trajectory. The location and motion of sound objects in a spatial scene could now be extracted from a soundfield recording. For example, we could extract the motion of a moving object, and impose a different path, or change the course of its original trajectory. Alternatively, we could retain the original motion, but change the content of the sound object. An example of this would be to analyze the motion of a flying insect (such as a bee), and use the extracted path as a trajectory for the sound of a moving train. Additionally, we can spatially disintegrate a sound object based on real-world models, such as smoke or fluid simulation.

As we now have independent control over both the temporal, and the spatial segmentation, we are able to customize and manipulate one domain, without affecting the other. For example, imagine a scene with an exploding sound object, followed by grains traveling outwards in 360° from the initial burst. We can reverse time, causing the sound to be played backwards, and the grains to spatially coalesce, instead of the radial outwards dispersion. Additionally, we can allow only the spatial dimension to travel backwards, but allow the temporal dimension to progress normally (or vice versa). The perceived effect would resemble the space collapsing into a single point at the origin, but the sound to move through time at normal speed.

Extracting the trajectory of motion not only allows us to transform, and customize the motion of a sound object, but it also allows us to map the information to other granulation parameters. For example, we can map the speed of movement to the pitch of the grain, or a grain's temporal length (or spatial size)– the faster the motion, the smaller the size, or vice versa.

Spatial Cross-Synthesis. As discussed in Sect. 2.1, spatial resolution is primarily dependent on the order of the Ambisonics signal. Additionally, the contents of captured signal, and the space where the sound was captured determines how correlated the spatiotemporal grains are. For example, transient sounds such as fireworks tend to produce unique spatiotemporal grains, compared to long, sustained sounds. Similarly, the sounds captured in an acoustically dry space tends to produce grains that are more distinct, compared to a reverberant space.

By performing cross-synthesis, one can "compose" the space-time palette, in order to create a desired space. For example, we can impose the spectral envelope of a spatiotemporal grain to another grain from a different spatial position, temporal position, or a grain from a different sample. The resulting palette can be directly encoded into B-Format as frames for the spatial scene, or used as a platform to extract individual spatiotemporal grains. Examples of algorithms for performing cross-synthesis include convolution and Dictionary Based Methods [9].

3.2 Spatialization

Individual decomposed spatiotemporal grains could now be assigned to different locations in space through the use of various spatialization algorithms. At the time of writing, we have explored the positioning of grains by re-encoding them into Ambisonics. Further explorations in spatialization of spatiotemporal grains will be carried out in the near future. Space now becomes an additional expressive parameter through maintaining, breaking or contrasting the original space with the transformed space.

Example of techniques that could be used include clustering algorithms to statistically position the grains around a specified point in space. Additionally, a random deviation may be applied to the original position of selected spatiotemporal grains, in order to displace their presence in space.

Exploring Space. In classical granulation, when we freeze the time (where the grain is extracted from), we hear the grains from that moment in time. Through Spatiotemporal Granulation, we now have the ability to explore the spatial dimension of sounds. The extreme case would be to freeze time, and "scan" the captured space, which would result in spatially exploring a moment frozen in time. Examples of algorithms that could be used to trigger these grains include those that are mentioned in Sect. 3.1.

Spatial Stretch. Analogous to the stretching of temporal grains, spatial stretching would allow us to control the source width, and *smear* the spatial position of a sound object. This is achieved by increasing the grain density, and overlapping the decorrelated grains in a specific position. Additionally, one can increase the decorrelation of grains via random modulation of its sinusoidal components [2]. The process of decorrelating grains, and resynthesizing the sound field could potentially reduce comb filtering effects when a lower order Ambisonics file is decoded over a large number of loudspeakers.

The spatial stretching, in addition to temporal stretching can be used to transform a noisy spatial scene into an ambient-like environment. For example, the discrete grains from a noisy recording can be transformed into an enveloping ambient space by spatially stretching, and overlapping the spatiotemporal grains.

Spatial Warping. The spatiotemporal grains in a given frame (Fig. 3) can be rearranged, and concentrated in a particular area (spatial density), or spread across a particular region of the frame. By controlling the spatial density over time, we are able to simulate the effect of warping space, without affecting the temporal domain of the sound material. Selection techniques for the grains to be controlled are similar to those described in Sect. 3.1.

Spatial Descriptor. The analysis of discretized grains in space and time could lead to the possibility of spatial audio descriptors. For example, one could analyze the spatiotemporal grains of a single frame, and determine the spatial centroid of a given space. The spatial features could also be combined with other temporal, or spectral features, such as spectral spread, skewness, kurtosis, harmonic and noise energy, which would allow us to measure the spatial distribution of specific features.

By analyzing the spatial scene, we would be able to spatially segregate sound sources based on their location. This could lead to the potential of instrument separation/extraction via spatial properties– Spatial source separation. For example, we could analyze the position of specific instruments/performers in a spatial recording, and separate the instruments based on their spatial location, in addition to spectral qualities. Furthermore, this information could also be used as a template to spatialize non-spatial recordings. An example case would be to train a machine learning algorithm with a database of instruments performed around a sound field microphone. We can then input the system with instrument tracks, and have the algorithm place these sounds using the trained information.

Allosphere. We plan to use Angkasa in the UCSB Allosphere [6], where the spatiotemporal grains can be spatialized via 54 loudspeakers. Additionally, the Allosphere also provides 360° realtime stereographic visualization using a cluster of servers driving 26 high-resolution projectors, which would allow the spatiotemporal grains to be acoustically, and visually positioned in its corresponding location [14].

3.3   Interface

The Graphical User Interface for Angkasa features a section for temporal decomposition (classical granulation), and a section for spatial decomposition. When used simultaneously, the resulting extraction forms a *Spatiotemporal Grain*.

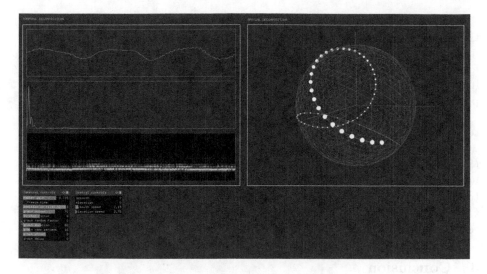

Fig. 4. Screenshot of "Angkasa"

Temporal Decomposition. Visualization of the temporal decomposition includes temporal, and frequency domain plots, as well as a spectrogram to monitor the extracted grains in real time (Fig. 4 - top left).

Users are able to control parameters such as position in file, freeze time (static temporal window), grain voices, stretch factor, random factor, duration, window type, offset, and delay via GUI sliders.

Spatial Decomposition. The spatial decomposition is visually depicted using a geodesic sphere, which represents the captured sound field. Users specify a value for azimuth and elevation to extract grains from that position in the captured sound field.

The spatiotemporal grains are visualized as smaller spheres, placed in the position where the grains are extracted from, on the bigger geodesic sphere (Fig. 4 - top right). Selection of locations on the sphere could be done via:

1. Independent GUI sliders for azimuth and elevation
2. Point picker on the surface of the sphere
3. Algorithmically (discussed in Sect. 3.1).

3.4 Future Work

We plan to improve the visualization so that each grain's energy is mapped to the size, or opacity of the smaller spheres, representing the energy content of each grain (from that location in space).

Furthermore, we plan to map the representation shown in Figs. 2 and 3 on to the geodesic sphere shown in Fig. 4. This would allow a user to analyze the palette in real-time, before extracting, and triggering the spatiotemporal grains.

The ability to select grains for analysis and synthesis allows a user to use the software tool for real-time performance. However, a limitation that presents itself is the ability to control the overall meso or macro structure of the performed/composed piece. One of the future directions in interface design is to implement a controllable automated timeline, which would allow a user to compose the sequence of change over time.

The spatiotemporal frame (Fig. 3) allows a user to navigate within the frozen temporal window. In order to change the temporal location of the window, a user would have to change the position in file from the Temporal Decomposition GUI (Sect. 3.3). As an extension to this representation, we plan to develop an interface where each spatiotemporal frame is lined up in the Z-dimension, allowing a user to select, and navigate around the full space- time representation. An external OSC [15] controller will be designed as a means to navigate the fully decomposed representation.

4   Conclusion

We presented a brief theoretical overview of Spatiotemporal Granulation, and outlined the possible, and potential manipulations that could be realized through this technique. We introduced a new software tool for performing Spatiotemporal Granulation called Angkasa. Development of the tool will proceed in different directions, including (but not limited to) analysis, extraction, transformation, synthesis, spatialization, and visualization of Spatiotemporal Granulation.

Acknowledgments. The first author would like to thank his advisors, Curtis Roads, Clarence Barlow, JoAnn Kuchera-Morin, Andres Cabrera, and Matthew Wright for their guidance, and assistance in this research project. His gratitude is also extended towards *Staatliche Hochschule für Gestaltung*, and *Zentrum für Kunst und Medientechnologie*, Karlsruhe, Germany, for hosting him during the "Space-Media-Sound" research exchange program. Their encouragement, and assistance has proven to have had an extensive impact on the research implementation. This work was partly sponsored by Universiti Sains Malaysia, Ministry of Education Malaysia, and the Baden-Württemberg Foundation.

References

1. Barrett, N.: Spatio-musical composition strategies. J. Organ. Sound **7**, 313–323 (2002)
2. Cabrera, A.: Control of source width in multichannel reproduction through sinusoidal modeling. Ph.D. dissertation, Queen's University Belfast (2012)
3. Deleflie, E., Schiemer, G.: Spatial-grains: imbuing granular particles with spatial-domain information. In: The Australasian Computer Music Conference, ACMC 2009 (2009)
4. Gerzon, M.A.: Periphony: with-height sound reproduction. J. Audio Eng. Soc. **21**, 2–10 (1973)
5. Kim-Boyle, D.: Spectral and granular spatialization with boids. In: International Computer Music Conference, ICMC (2006)

6. Kuchera-Morin, J., Wright, M.: Immersive full- surround multi-user system design. Comput. Graph. **40**, 10–21 (2014)
7. Roads, C.: The Computer Music Tutorial. MIT Press, Massachusetts (1996)
8. Roads, C.: Microsound. MIT Press, Massachusetts (2001)
9. Sturm, B.L., Roads, C., McLeran, A., Shynk, J.J.: Analysis, visualization, and transformation of audio signals using dictionary-based methods. In: International Computer Music Conference, ICMC (2008)
10. Schwarz, D.: A system for data-driven concatenative sound synthesis. In: Digital Audio Effects (2000)
11. Truax, B.: Composition and diffusion: space in sound in space. J. Organ. Sound **3**, 141–146 (1998)
12. Rosli, M.H.W., Cabrera, A.: Gestalt principles in multimodal data representation. IEEE Comput. Graph. Appl. **35**, 80–87 (2015)
13. Rosli, M.H.W., Roads, C.: Spatiotemporal granulation. In: International Computer Music Conference, ICMC (2016)
14. Rosli, M.H.W., Cabrera, A., Wright, M., Roads, C.: Granular model of multidimensional spatial sonification. In: Sound and Music Computing, SMC (2015)
15. Wright, M., Freed, A.: Open sound control: a new protocol for communicating with sound synthesizers. J. Organ. Sound. **10**, 193–200 (2005)

User Experience in an Interactive Music Virtual Reality System: An Exploratory Study

Thomas Deacon$^{(\boxtimes)}$, Tony Stockman, and Mathieu Barthet

School of Electronic Engineering and Computer Science,
Centre for Digital Music (Room Eng 111), Queen Mary University of London,
Mile End Road, London E1 4NS, UK
{t.e.deacon,t.stockman,barthet}@qmul.ac.uk

Abstract. The *Objects VR* interface and study explores interactive music and virtual reality, focusing on user experience, understanding of musical functionality, and interaction issues. Our system offers spatiotemporal music interaction using 3D geometric shapes and their designed relationships. Control is provided by tracking of the hands, and the experience is rendered across a head-mounted display with binaural sound presented over headphones. The evaluation of the system uses a mixed methods approach based on semi-structured interviews, surveys and video-based interaction analysis. On average the system was positively received in terms of interview self-report, metrics for spatial presence and creative support. Interaction analysis and interview thematic analysis also revealed instances of frustration with interaction and levels of confusion with system functionality. Our results allow reflection on design criteria and discussion of implications for facilitating music engagement in virtual reality. Finally our work discusses the effectiveness of measures with respect to future evaluation of novel interactive music systems in virtual reality.

Keywords: Creativity support · Design research · Flow · Interaction analysis · Interactive music systems · Thematic analysis · User experience · Virtual reality

1 Introduction

Virtual Reality (VR) is now an accessible medium for music interaction, that could transform consumption and production of music, if designed systems can capitalise on the unique possibilities of VR. For those without musical experience it could provide new forms of creative engagement while for those more experienced the medium offers new possibilities for creating and interacting with music. New media formats have continually, and drastically augmented the music creation and listening landscape [10]. As a new medium VR needs adoption, requiring effective design of the technology to foster a constructive dialogue around music interaction as a non-specialist pastime. Changing the relationship between producer, consumer, and creator alters our relationship to music and

© Springer International Publishing AG 2017
M. Aramaki et al. (Eds.): CMMR 2016, LNCS 10525, pp. 192–216, 2017.
DOI: 10.1007/978-3-319-67738-5_12

could build towards increased engagement in music with those without extensive musical experience [4].

As a medium VR is visual, sonic and inherently interactive. Designing an interactive music system for this medium requires new understanding given the potentially unique characteristics of musical interactions occurring within VR, "warranting their own performance practices, approaches and taxonomies" [17]. Of the research conducted into direct control of interactive music systems in VR categories include: (i) virtual object manipulation with parametrised sound output [24], (ii) controlling musical characteristics of a pre-existing composition [26], (iii) virtual instrument representations [15], (iv) spatial audio interfaces [38], (v) multi-process audio environments [6] that are combinations of the previous categories (this includes *Objects VR*). Many of these implementations offer novel interaction methods coupled with creative feedback and visualisation but give little analysis of user skill levels, and how this alters individual experience and results.

Our *Objects VR* interface design explores music interaction in an interactive music system in virtual reality (VR). In *Objects VR* the user interacts with an object-based interface to control three tracks of music (drums, bass and synth) and track-based effects, see Sect. 3.2. Hand actions are captured through a Leap Motion device attached to an Oculus Rift DK2 head-mounted display (HMD) that renders the VR environment. We investigate users' natural exploration and formation of understanding to be able to interact creatively in the proposed virtual environment. We use an exploratory mixed methods assessment of user exploration behaviours, subjective experience and understanding. The study compares users' expertise with music technology and sound synthesis using thematic analysis [9], interaction analysis [23], a creativity support metric [11], a spatial presence survey [18] and a sonic interaction survey. Discussion puts forward relevant research directions to support creative engagement with interactive music systems in VR by understanding different groups experience; this informs design by understanding how users naturally engage and understand a VR interactive music system. Though this design research can only address the proposed music interfaces particular functionality and chosen musical genre, further developments could inform design principles for other novel interactive music applications. Effective evaluation facilitates design development of prototypes and artefacts, and more generally, research into key theories around music interaction.

2   Related Works

A common factor in measuring the effectiveness of VR is the concept of presence. An operational definition of Spatial Presence is that it is a binary experience, where perceived self-location, action possibilities and mental capacities are connected to a mediated spatial environment instead of reality [37]. Further analysis of the Spatial Presence theory highlights that if affordances of virtual objects activate actions then a feeling of presence is fed back [29]. This means that within an experience it is not only the spatial environment that a user feels present but also the virtual object framework.

Encouraging creative music engagement is a suitable goal for any interactive music system. The theory of flow describes states of optimal experience that can improve engagement [12]. Attaining a state where users can perform supremely and effortlessly involves balancing of motivation and skill; based on the design of: challenge, learning, and functionality [27]. So, for new interactive music systems in VR, at any skill level, flow should be actively positioned in design and evaluation phases. Flow states have the following conditions: (i) clear goals, (ii) unambiguous feedback on performance, (iii) balance of challenge and ability; and effects: (i) action and awareness merge, (ii) total concentration, (iii) sense of control, (iv) self-consciousness disappears, (v) distorted sense of time, (vi) autotelic experizence.

The exploratory nature of this work means qualitative methods are suitable for developing understanding within the design space, such as discourse analysis of live music-making using interactive systems [34]; research of new musical instrument design using grounded theory [22]; and use of thematic analysis to analyse design decisions effects on sonic exploration and manipulation [1]. We deem it important not to focus purely on usability, as this does not account for the diverse nature of experience with musical interfaces. In the design of user experience studies, using professional musicians, Johnston suggests three important questions [22]: *Do instruments meet design criteria identified during design? How do musicians experience them? What is the relationship between the instrument and the musician's experience?*

In this study, the performance of the rendered environment is evaluated using spatial presence conceptualisations. Flow theory is used a heuristic to analyse users' situated interactions and conceptual understanding using interaction analysis, interview thematic analysis, and survey self-report.

3   Design Space

The formulation of problems and solutions in the creation of the system is the design space, and inside this space all the competing theories and influences merge. The design space is a conceptual tool to accommodate multiple disciplines and approaches in representing the design work. But the design space cannot be fully described here because of its complexity and size. We used a user-centred research through design methodology [39] for the production of prototypes and artefact[1]. The design process is based on research and practise of prototyping [20], testbed comparisons [8], heuristic evaluation [35] and user experience testing [14]. Similar approaches have been used to design music technology for a gesturally controlled operatic-lead signal processor [13] and a digitally augmented cello [2].

---

[1] We define prototype as any representation of a design idea, regardless of medium, and artefact as the interactive system being designed [20].

3.1   Design Criteria

The design criteria were that the VR experience should: (i) Be accessible and fun for novices of music technology, musical education, and VR; (ii) Allow 'physical' experimentation and interaction with musical content; (iii) Lead to high levels of presence; (iv) Allow users to experience flow states. The focus on novice engagement means levels of musical control must be carefully considered. It looks to provide novice users the ability to learn purely within the experience, and maintain coherent musical output e.g. stable harmony and well fitted rhythm. Body-based interaction can provide an immersive presence enhancing interaction in VR [32], while engaging users in embodied musical interaction [16]. Also engaging with fluid arm motions has been shown to improve creativity [33], making body-based spatial interaction a field of worthwhile development for musical engagement. By positioning flow in the design space we are hoping to create a quality of interaction that promotes learning for novices but can also provides experts with new ways of interacting or feeling creative. For novices we want "good flow" [28], experiences that can scaffold towards deeper musical engagement and experience, not just an immediate feelings of pleasing perceptual stimulus and enjoyment.

3.2   Artefact

Designing the relationship between geometry, motion and sound is essential to *Objects VR* interface. Understanding of sonic functionality is gained while exploring a VR environment, where the environment is the interface. The system allows control of playback of short repetitive musical phrases of a 2-step UK garage and dubstep style. This is combined with spatial audio panning, and timbral control utilising gestural interaction and direct interface manipulation. A composition was commissioned to be easily layered in many different ways[2].

The system utilises grabbing and contact interactions in an object-based interface to control three tracks of music (drums, bass and synth) and track-based effects. Users' actions are captured through a Leap Motion device attached to an Oculus Rift DK2 head-mounted display (HMD) that renders the VR environment. The VR application sends OSC data about user action, objects, and system states to Ableton Live and Max/MSP. Audio loops are triggered directly through the LiveAPI using javascript commands, while object parameters are remotely controlled through various mappings, discussed in the next paragraph. Ambisonic to binaural panning is rendered using the Higher Order Ambisonics library for Max/MSP [30].

Interface Objects. The visual design of object form represents context of music interaction: effects control or loop playback. Colour represents content relationships to track type, indicated in Fig. 1. A **Grid Unit Menu (GUM)** is a container object with a series of buttons that allow triggering of loop content.

---

[2] Content produced by production duo Commands, assets available on SoundCloud.

(a) Green Synth Grid Unit Menu with Prism Explosion Feedback

(b) Red Drum Prism Grab Attempt with Ray casting Beam

(c) Blue Bass Loop Cube being manipulated by user

Fig. 1. Comparison of interface sections (Color figure online)

The GUM requires docking of a loop cube to allow audio playback via buttons. A **Loop Cube (LC)** is an object for placement within a GUM; each face of the LC has unique visual representation that pertains to a loop of music. **Sphere** objects control binaural panning and distance based volume attenuation of their track given position in 2D (XZ) space. **Prism** objects are parameter space widgets for controlling track effects, mapping is unique to each object. Mapping strategies are in two forms: scaled mapping of object position to Ableton Macro controls and interpolated parameter spaces utilising Manifold-Interface Amplitude Panning [31]. Track effects include: (i) *Drum* - Interpolated convolution reverb amount and type. 3D (XYZ) VR space to 2D (XZ) effect mapping. The further away the object the wetter the signal mixture. Position in the VR space blends size of reverb, going clockwise: front-right = cavernous, back-right = large hall, back-left = room, front-left = small tight space. (ii) *Bass* - Filter cut-off, 3D (XYZ) VR space to 1D effect mapping. Object distance from user sets frequency, further from user sets higher frequency. (iii) *Synth* - Duration and timbre of notes. 3D (XYZ) VR space to many dimensional mapping with complex relationship of spatial parameter to sonic output. Approximately, distance changes length of notes and height alters timbre.

Interaction Features. Two distinct interface metaphors are present in the artefact: (a) *Docking* metaphor where users must place objects within other structures to yield further functionality, (b) *Spatial interaction* metaphor, objects control audio modulation parameters based on mappings of hand and head movement in the space.

Various interaction dynamics are present to improve usability and aesthetic enjoyment: (i) Magnetic objects and grabbing gestures to expand interaction space on top of direct object contact. Objects are selected and hyper-realistically [25] grabbed using iconic pinch or grab gestures that only select objects available

Fig. 2. Magnetic grabbing gesture and bounding rules. Hatched area indicates selectable objects boundary. Closest object will be grabbed, in this case the cube not the heptagon. Shaded area is approximate HMD field of vision.

within a certain bounding box based on the visual field (see Fig. 2). Expanded depth of interaction space is gained at the cost of users having to learn behaviours and their issues; (ii) Gaze-based movement of GUMs was implemented to have them move back and forward only when looked at; (iii) Object-based gravity was implemented to ameliorate interaction errors, where if an object is flung beyond the range of direct control a force is applied to the object to always bring it back to within grabbing range; (iv) A 3D matrix of points appears on grabbing a prism, this indicates the boundaries of possible spatial interaction; (v) Light-streams indicate the object that is currently closest and available for grabbing, Fig. 1b.

Though challenging in music interfaces, audio feedback of action is implemented for: (i) Loop Cube (LC) grabs, using single note of C minor triad with note being mapped to object group, Drums = C3, Synth = D#3, Bass = G3; (ii) Successful *docking* of a LC in a Grid Unit Menu (GUM); (iii) Audio and visual explosion feedback occurs when a Sphere or Prism makes contact with the centre of the GUM, indicating that it does not belong there, Fig. 1a.

Incremental introduction of environment objects is utilised so that functionality is explored one piece at a time. At the start of the experience only one LC is presented to user while other objects are hidden, once this object has been grasped another object will appear, this process continues one by one till all objects are available.

4   User Evaluation

The evaluation of the system uses a mixed methods approach based on semi-structured interviews, surveys and video-based interaction analysis. The methodology evaluates experience, interaction, and knowledge representation, by triangulated analysis of multimodal data.

4.1 Participants and Setting

Twenty-three participants (9 female, average age 28) were recruited from Queen Mary University of London email lists and special interest groups (music, technology, VR) from meetup.com. Demographic data was collected alongside Likert-based self-assessments. Novice and Expert groups were based on response to the self-assessment item[3]: *I am experienced at using music software and sound synthesis.* The response scale had 5 points pertaining to experience level (Not at all - Very much) points 1 and 2 are aggregated as Novice (N = 8) and points 4 and 5 were grouped as Expert (N = 9); with point 3 being assigned as Moderate (N = 6).

All sessions and interviews were conducted in the Media and Arts Technology Performance Lab in Queen Mary University of London. Study was carried out following ethical review by the Queen Mary Ethics Committee (Approval ID QMREC1522a), all participants provided informed consent.

4.2 Experimental Procedure

Participants engaged in two uses of *Objects VR*, the *Explore* session and the *Task* session. Interviews were conducted after each session and survey metrics were completed after the second interview. The testing procedure was adapted from [34], where process of data collection was purposeful to obtain the most subjective representations of experience before questionnaires were issued that may introduce bias to self-report. In the *Explore* session no training or indication of function was provided before the session, and the concept of a musical loop and effects controllers was not introduced. Participants were told to just play with the interface and see what they could learn and how they felt using it. The *Task* session came after a functionality briefing about the environment dynamics and interaction gestures, but no details of sonic or musical function were divulged. The task of that session was to use the interface again to accomplish more musical ideas. No formal performance goals were set, the task was to just make music. The experiment had the following procedure, average or approximate times per section indicated:

1. Explore Session (*M(SD)* = 8 min 30 s (1 min 26 s));
2. Interview A (*M* = 6 min 02 s (2 min 25 s));
3. Functionality Briefing (3–5 min);
4. Task Session (*M* = 6 min 10 s (3 s));
5. Interview B (*M* = 6 min 38 s (2 min 11 s));
6. Surveys (5–15 min).

As of incremental learning rules the *Explore* session had a longer session time. Overall the whole process took between 40–45 min.

---

[3] Other groups self-assessment items were included for VR experience and interactive sensor experience, but group numbers of novice and expert were highly skewed so are not evaluated here.

To locate meaning within the qualitative data, inductive thematic analysis was used based on Braun and Clarke's six step process: familiarise with the data, generate initial codes, search for themes, review themes, define and name themes, and produce a report [9]. In an inductive revision and organisation of codes, categories and themes emerge from the data. Coding of VR interface interactions is based on the annotation of phases of action using Interaction Analysis (IA) [23]. IA offers a structured approach that has been used previously for analysing musical interaction [5]. IA de-marks ordered units of activity, signified by: *shifts in activity, shifts of attention, use of spatial alignment and posture, spatial organisation of activity.* Useful categories for bounding actions include observation of patterns such as: *how sections of action begin and end, levels of repetition and variability of actions, entry and exit strategies of interaction.*

5   Qualitative Results and Analysis

5.1   Behavioural Data

Data included video of HMD screen-grab of VR interactions, two video perspectives of body actions in the physical testing space, audio recordings of a voice mic and the music created, and video of interviews. To work with the multimodal data, content was arranged for combined analysis using Final Cut Pro 10 to synchronise and layer all data sources. This combined perspective data was then imported into MAXQDA 12 for analysis, where VR and physical interactions were evaluated using IA and interview self-report was analysed using thematic analysis.

The following notation is used to indicate what data sources a summary of occurrences or quote came from. Grab(x) means code "Grab" was observed x times. (Px): participant number e.g. (P7) is participant seven; (N = x): participant occurrences in a theme or explanation. In theme summaries instances of observation are counted once per participant e.g. *Play*(6) six different users refer to theme *Play*. Moderates were excluded from qualitative analysis due to insufficient group numbers and the focus on comparing novice and expert results.

5.2   Explore Session Interaction Analysis

Through IA coding of the Explore session a coding system was developed. Relevant codes are included in Table 1.

Interaction Analysis Themes. The following analysis highlights features of user interaction with *Objects VR* in the explore session before interview A (users' first contact with the interface). Vignettes and codelines were used to exemplify common or interesting cases, as for many issues a deep level of detail is needed to unpack user behaviour.

Table 1. Subset of interaction analysis code system from explore session

Operational (1534): itemised interactions with the interface

Code (n)	Group	Brief description
Button success (279)	Actions	User presses button on purpose
Grab LC (143)	Actions	User grabs loop cube
Put LC (68)	Actions	User places loop cube in GUM
Prism feedback (50)	Actions	Prism enters GUM space
Sphere feedback (25)	Actions	Sphere enters GUM space
Eject LC (21)	Actions	Purposeful ejection of LC from GUM
Sticky object (114)	Problems	see *Sticky Objects* theme
Button error (111)	Problems	Unsuccessful button press, or accidental press
Grab error (61)	Problems	Unsuccessful grab action
Utterance (87)	Interactions	Statement or vocal sound
Posture (20)	Interactions	Embodied interaction to stimulus
Gesture (18)	Interactions	Interesting use of hands and arms

Interpretive (262): theories around micro-phases of user action

Code(n)	Group	Brief description
Change of focus (31)	Attention	Natural change in action pattern
Unexpected > CoF (34)	Attention	Surprise causing change in action patterns
Observe after action (21)	Attention	Pausing after action or feedback
Probing for functionality (37)	Physical	Systematic pattern of actions with interface element
Discovery (37)	Conceptual	First time feedback or function witnessed, often with embodied reaction

Strategies (106): assumptions about macro-phases of user actions

Code(n)	Brief description
Exploring (39)	Unstructured phases of interaction
Experimenting (54)	Systematic or repetitive phases of interaction

Sticky Objects. Due to magnetic grabbing implementation not working well, many users struggled with objects attaching themselves to their hands. Marked by code *Sticky Object*, and frequently with *Unexpected > CoF*. Sticky objects had the impression of being quite frustrating, marked by distressed or volatile release attempts and various utterances. But by interrupting users focus sticky objects maybe allowed opportunities for learning. Examples of such issues are detailed in Table 2 and are described further in the theme *Surprises*.

Repetitive Actions. The *Probing for functionality* and *Experimenting* codes
annotated inferences related to determining functionality often based on repetitive actions. Common patterns included: filling GUMs with each different type
of object one after another, systematic button pressing either individually or in
dual button holds (Fig. 3), and trying to join cubes together. The actual goal of
such experimentation was subjective and better left to triangulated analysis.

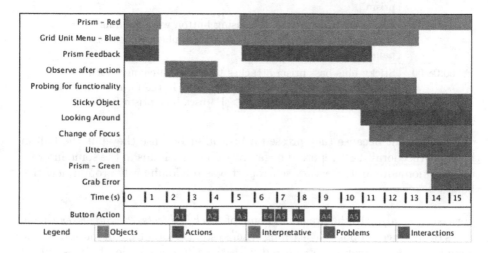

Fig. 3. Novice P3 *Probing for Functionality.* Systematic button pressing without audio
playback (no LC in GUM).

Audio Feedback. When trialling elements to determine functionality, as in *Repetitive Actions*, many objects only provided musical feedback when the track was
running, this may lead to incorrect assumptions of system function as of ambiguous feedback. It is important to distinguish **without audio** and **with audio**
probing. A comparison is made between P3 in Fig. 3 and P4 in Table 2. In the
without audio playback case, P3 quickly moves through GUM buttons, finds
little happening, and moves to exploring other objects. For the **with audio** case,
a different pattern of probing was seen; P4 switched on and off the buttons with
associated musical loops switching on and off. Pattern of action is broken by a
Sticky Object attaching to them.

   Many users experienced the prisms and spheres as feedback objects (*Prism
Feedback* and *Sphere Feedback*) either accidentally or on purpose. While the
feedback does provide adequate indication of negative operation, and stimulating audio-visual effects, if the track is not active its musical function may not be
determined. As an example, during a phase of probing, P1 was holding a sphere
and error feedback effects were caused while trying to use buttons. From the
video it appears as if P1 was more interested in determining the function of the
buttons, and then feedback noise happens. Potentially, this sequence of actions
confused their mental model of function, as reliable links between actions, reaction and stimulus were not clearly made. The user was left wondering whether

Table 2. Novice P4 *Probing for Functionality* with audio playback and *Sticky Objects*

Timecode	Sequence of action (Interpretations)
00:07:30	Trialling buttons: switching on and off, repeats for different buttons
00:07:46	Sticky green prism attaches to hand -> change of focus to green prism
00:07:51	Ejects LC from green GUM using button while holding prism -> tries to put prism into GUM, causing explosion Feedback -> P4 pauses for 1 s
00:08:00	Sticky blue bass prism attaches to hand, P4 changes focus to it -> movement yields new audio feedback in the form of distinct filter parameter modulation -> P4 uses blue prism for 35 s

sound is present because they pressed a button or because they put the ball in the box. Anecdotally, P1 reported negatively on many items in the sonic interaction questionnaire and interview self-report was predominantly around negative themes.

Surprises. Relating to the previous theme of *Sticky Objects*, the *Surprises* theme marks occurrences of possible learning from system error, often annotated by the *Discovery* code. *Discovery* intersected with the *Utterance* code 11 times, where an 'out-loud' signalled their reaction to the stimulus. An out-loud can be considered to render 'private' activity 'public' and visible [19]. Through action, elements interplay may cause realisation of function or new possibility to users, who make visible their reaction. Also, noticeable focus shifts and altered interaction phases potentially mark a discovery. The link of verbal utterance, gestures and posture in isolating possible moments of discovery proved a useful technique. An example of an accident leading to interface exploration can be seen in Table 2, at time-code 00:08:00 where a *Sticky Object* bass prism attaches to their hand while audio is playing and changes interaction pattern for significant period of time.

5.3   Explore Session Interview Themes

Analysis of the *Explore* session interviews highlighted a series themes within self-reports across Novice and Expert groups. High-level themes include **Comprehension, Confusion, Engagement, Frustration, Interface, Interaction, Altered states of perception (ASoP), Goals and models (GaM).** Thematic analysis results are separated into Novice (Table 3), Expert (Table 4) and Shared (Table 5) themes.

An important theme that disambiguates Novice from Expert users is **Comprehension**. The theme marks self-report of understanding components of their experience and the interface. The **Confusion** theme describes how levels of uncertainty manifest in self-report. A common theme with high levels of uncertainty in interface and interaction in general, but the content of what was

Table 3. Novice interview analysis themes

Theme (n)	Description	Theme relations
Varied conceptual models (7)	Highly varied interpretations of system as their conceptual model	Comprehension, confusion, GaM
Interface Feedback (5)	Objects fed back subjectively useful information about what was possible	Comprehension, GaM
Colours and groups (4)	Visual relationships made sense, but not as track or audio function	Comprehension, interface
Empowered interaction (4)	Control and interaction felt "physical", "immersive", "powerful", "magical"	Engagement, interaction
Not getting it (4)	Feeling of missing some level of understanding that was annoying	Frustration, interface
Objects (4)	Uncertainty of what objects did and their relationships	Confusion, GaM
Body (3)	Experience of altered perception of self or perceptual incongruence: "dream-like"; feeling of not having a body; "floating" and "weird"	ASoP, enjoyable, strange but I like it
Hearing differences (3)	Confusion in distinguishing musical changes	Confusion
Playful exploration (3)	Description of playful discovery, exploration and reward	GaM, self-learning, playing
Purpose (3)	Feeling "lost" or uncertain in general of what to do	Confusion, GaM
Learning issues (2)	Taking a long time to learn gestures and how to interact	Frustration, interaction

confusing varies across groups. The **Engagement** theme draws attention to highly varied representations of what was engaging for individuals in the experience with many shared components across groups. The only aberrant case is Novice P1 who experienced only **Confusion** and **Frustration**. The **Frustration** theme marks self-report around levels of frustration with their experience. All users struggled with gestural interaction, interaction dynamics and the way objects worked hence this theme couples extensively with the **Interaction** theme in both groups. How and to what level frustration was reported indicates slight difference in emphasis between groups.

Table 4. Expert interview analysis themes

Theme (n)	Description	Theme relations
Functional understanding (9)	Detailed description of system, with links to audio functionality	Comprehension, confusion, interface
Colour and sound (8)	An understanding of colour and shape relationships to tracks	Comprehension, interface
Frustrated interaction (6)	Frustration with interaction at lack of adequate control	Frustration, interaction
Intention (6)	Their goal was to make music	GaM
Novel (4)	Descriptions of the novelty of musical interface and experience as enjoyable; despite frustration and uncertainty	Engagement, GaM
Metaphors (2)	An awareness of interface metaphors in self-report	Comprehension, interaction

The **Interface** theme relates to the functionality of the environment objects. Analysis is grouped by the functionality category: Loop playback objects (GUMs, LCs and Buttons) or effects control objects (Spheres and Prisms). The **Interaction** theme relates to control, gestural interaction, and interface dynamics. It highlights some important differences in Novice and Expert participants. Novices talked more positively about their feeling of interaction and control than the Expert group, though still citing similar errors such as *Sticky Objects*. Whereas the Expert group highlighted their interaction with mostly frustration at the lack of adequate control. The **Altered states of perception** theme was often related to the **Engagement** theme and may link to flow and spatial presence theories. Novice altered states were described as enjoyable and bodily oriented. In contrast, the Expert group described altered states of perception with less of an emphasis on a relationship to their bodies, instead report related to task immersion in music but with equally evocative terms. The **Goals and models** theme highlights how participants conceptualised the system and their purpose in using it, rather than discrete levels of system function.

5.4   Task Session Interview and Interaction Analysis

Similar patterns of activity and interview topics were observed in the Task session. Key themes of difference, reflection and change are presented in Table 6 (Users with moderate experience were excluded from the analysis). Of the persistent issues that occurred, Novices had continued problems with *Hearing Differences* in musical content, and general confusion over the conceptual model of function. Both groups continued to report uncertainty around what the spheres

Table 5. Shared interview analysis themes

Theme	Description	Group and Theme relations
Enjoyable (22)	Used of positive vocabulary to report aspects of experience, across all but one participant (P1)	Engagement, ASoP, strange but I like it
Strange but I like it (10)	Use of "strange", "weird" or "odd" to describe experience but the clarifying the term as enjoyable	Engagement, ASoP, enjoyable
Self learning (9)	Report of self-learning through interface affordances and feedback. Includes encouragement to learn, moments of discovery, and "intuitive" interface dynamics	Engagement, GaM; novice: playful exploration; expert: immersed in sonic interaction
Loop playback objects (8)	Understanding of functionality varies by group	Interface; novice: confusion; expert: comprehension;
Effects objects (7)	Prisms and spheres were confusing	Confusion, interface
Play (6)	Interaction was "playful" or "playing"	Engagement, GaM
Immersed in sonic Interaction (5)	Description of being immersed in sonic interaction as creative musical engagement, task immersion or feelings of connection to sound	ASoP; novice: engagement; expert: engagement, GaM

purpose was, and in one anomaly an Expert user forgot sphere functionality across sessions. There was continued errors around implementation and sensor issues, such as *Sticky Objects*. The *Improved experience* theme collects instances of more effective probing and gestural control seen in Task session, except for two aberrant cases: (i) gestural control was worse (P19), (ii) did not play any audio using GUMs in second session (P2). Barring these exceptions, instances of enjoyable experience with music and interaction were reported. The following sub-themes highlight improvements:

- *Being more aware of surroundings*: Users interacted with more objects, possibility due to functionality briefing indicating that other objects existed;
- *More focused* (5): Self-report of being more focused on getting an understanding to make objects to do something they wanted.

Table 6. Task session thematic analysis

Theme	Description	Group
Changing strategies (8)	Early in the task session there are more instances of direct and immediate sound actions with LC and GUM elements to trigger sounds, compared with their previous interaction in the explore session	Shared
Less frustrating (6)	Instances of more confident gestures and sets of actions. Self-report of still being difficult to interact, but better in general	Shared
More sonic control (5)	IA observation of improved control and self-report of feeling more in control	Novice
Need more time (3)	Persistent levels of confusion, indicting that they needed more time	Shared
Opaque mappings (3)	Difficulty of reproducing sonic effect with prism mappings, self-report attributes parameter mappings as quite unclear, though they understood overall function	Expert
Plateau of possibilities (3)	Statement that the system lacks depth of function for extended use	Shared

6   Quantitative Results and Statistical Analysis

Quantitative data relating to user experience was obtained through a series of post-experience questionnaires, where responses relate to the whole experience. These are: (i) *Sonic Interaction Design (SID)* questionnaire a five-point Likert assessment of flow and sonic interaction, designed for the study based on items from [5]. SID item statements are presented with their results in Sect. 6.1; (ii) *Creativity Support Index* [11] *(CSI)* was used to determine the value of the interface as a creativity support tool (CST) for music. CSI item statements can be found in publication [11]; (iii) *Spatial Presence Experience Scale* [18] *(SPES)* was used as a presence metric that integrates concepts of spatial presence [37], it functions as a diverse media measure of presence. SPES item statements can be found in [18].

Moderate group results were used within statistical analysis, but most comparisons were conducted to look at the difference between Novice and Expert groups.

6.1   Sonic Interaction Questionnaire Results

The median (Mdn) and interquartile range (IQR) for all Sonic Interaction (SID) items can be seen in Fig. 4.

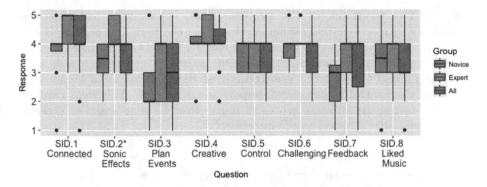

Fig. 4. Sonic interaction questionnaire box and whisker plots. Asterisk marks items with significant differences. Y axis response scale values: 1 = I do not agree at all; 2 = I do not agree; 3 = Neither agree or disagree; 4 = I agree; 5 = I fully agree.

- **SID.1 I was connected to the sound changes through my actions.** A Mann-Whitney's U (MWU) test found a near significant result for independent factor Group when comparing Novice and Expert, $U = 19.5$, $Z = -1.72, p = 0.09, r = 0.36$. Despite the lack of significant difference between groups, the general trend is of strong agreement that users had agency over sound. This puts emphasis on the interview analysis to determine what level of sonic agency was experienced.
- **SID.2 I could relate my actions to specific sonic effects.** A Kruskal-Wallis H (KWH) test revealed a near significant effect of Group on SID.2 response ($\chi^2(2) = 4.81, p < 0.09$). A MWU test and found a significant difference between Novices and Experts ($U = 15.5, Z = -2.16, p < 0.05, r = 0.45$), with the mean ranks of Novices and Experts being 3.38 and 4.22. While both groups overlap between neutral and agreement, the expert group had a more positive tendency to relate action to sonic effects. This finding could corroborate the thematic analysis theme of *Hearing Differences*, indicating that Experts and Novices appreciation of action and sonic effect was not observed to be the same in this study.
- **SID.3 I could plan sonic events using objects.** No significant result was found comparing all groups (KWH test) or comparing Novices and Experts (MWU test). The results average around neutral but with groups having differing trends, Novices ($M = 2.5(1.2)$) tend to disagree more than Experts ($M = 3.44(1.13)$) that they could plan sonic events.
- **SID.4 I felt part of a creative process.** The dominant trend was that all users agreed that they felt part of a creative process.
- **SID.5 I felt in control.** Positive result where responses tended towards neutral and agreement.
- **SID.6 It was challenging.** Novice and Expert responses tended to agree that they found the process challenging. To link to flow conceptualisations about challenge and reward, a more detailed analysis of what was challenging is required.

- **SID.7 The feedback in the system made sense.** Item had a netural tendency with no significant difference found for comparing all groups (KWH test) or comparing Novices and Experts using a MWU test, despite different distributions of positive and negative tendencies.
- **SID.8 I liked the music I created.** Given the fixed nature of the musical content the neutral to agreement responses are positive. This item requires further testing in different genres of music to determine whether stylistic boundaries alter reaction to the interface.

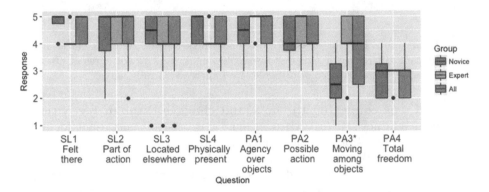

Fig. 5. Spatial Presence Experience Scale box and whisker plots. Y axis is response scales same as Fig. 4.

6.2 Spatial Presence Experience Scale Results

Self-location (SL) Items. There is strong agreement that participants felt "there" in the virtual environment (SL1), and were actively taking part in action (SL2), and that they felt like they were located in a different environment from the physical testing area (SL3). Also results indicate predominantly agreement for feeling physically present in interface environment (SL4). No significant difference for group was observed across SL items.

Possible Actions (PA) Items. There is strong agreement that participants felt they had agency over objects in the environment (PA1), and agreement that there was possibility for action within the environment (PA2). There is a significant difference for group in responses to 'feeling like they could move among the objects in the environment' (PA3) ($\chi^2(2) = 6.76, p < .05$). MWU pairwise comparisons using Holm-Bonferroni adjustments indicate a moderately significant effect of group Novice ($M = 2.63(1.06)$) and Expert ($M = 4.11(1.05)$) ($U = 11.5, Z = -2.42, p < .05, r = 0.51$). So Novices felt less possibility to move throughout objects in the virtual environment than Experts. On average participants were neutral about having total freedom to do whatever they wanted in VR (PA4) with no significant differences present across groups.

6.3   Creativity Support Index Results

The CSI is a psychometric survey designed to evaluate a Creativity Support Tool (CST). It measures user, tool and task by weighting factors to their importance in the task. Factors evaluated include: Exploration, Expressiveness, Immersion, Enjoyment, Results Worth Effort (RWE), and Collaboration[4]. CSI results contains the following features:

- Average Factor Count (AFC) indicates what is important to users in a creative task. Counts are based on 15 pair-wise comparisons of CSI factors. AFC therefore scores task importance and weights the average factor scores and final CSI score.
- Average Factor Score (AFS) is the average responses to two Likert scale questions for each factor. It indicates the direct response of the user to the tool for the task to that factor.
- Weighted Average Factor Score (WAFS) is sensitive to the relative importance of factors reflecting the relationship of tool, task and user.
- Overall CSI score is an index score out of 100, where a higher score indicates better creativity support.

Table 7. Table of CSI factor comparisons

Factor	Average factor count Mdn (IQR)	Average factor score M (SD)	Weighted average factor score M (SD)
Enjoyment	3 (2–4)	8.13 (1.52)	48.61 (23.16)
Exploration	4 (2 4)	5.98 (2.05)	40.7 (19.75)
Expressiveness	3 (3–5)	5.7 (2.08)	41.48 (22.74)
Immersion	3 (2.5–4)	7.3 (2.23)	46.96 (28.01)
Results Worth Effort	1 (1–2)	6.76 (1.76)	20.22 (19.05)

Results Summaries. See Table 7 and Fig. 6 for factor results[5].

- **CSI scores.** The general tendency of the population for the combined CSI scores place ObjectsVR in a positive light with a high average score ($M = 65.94(14.45)$), no significant effects were observed based on Group and distributions were similar. Compared to other CSI scores in literature this is good result [3, 21, 36] and is a useful benchmark for future iterations.

---

[4] Although collaboration is not a feature of *Objects VR*, the factor must be kept to preserve the CSI scoring structure.

[5] Lack of normality in the data means non-parametric statistics were chosen for all tests of significance. It was considered to transform the data, but the sample sizes per group in the sample would question the validity of any results. Collaboration factor is not discussed.

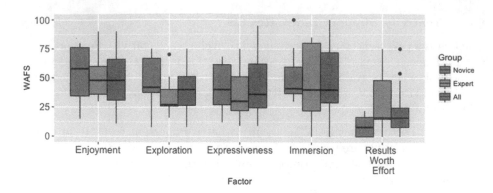

Fig. 6. Creativity Support Index ox and whisker plots of weighted average factor scores.

- **Enjoyment.** The WAFS for the enjoyment factor was the highest average across the whole population; with no significant differences present across groups. Enjoyment is a moderately important task factor given AFC.
- **Exploration.** AFC indicates exploration of ideas and possibilities is an important feature in a making music task. No significant results were observed between groups. The WAFS for Exploration was higher for the Novice group than the Experts (Table 6), but with no significant difference.
- **Expressiveness.** The AFS for expressiveness of the tool scored average to well across the whole population. WAFS show a moderate tendency across the sample with no significant results for group.
- **Immersion.** Average values for AFC highlight Immersion with moderate importance (Table 7), but as with expressiveness the variance of the Expert results are of interest ($M = 3.0(1.36); Mdn = 4; IQR : 2-4, Min = 0, Max = 5$). Moderately important AFC with high AFS produced a WAFS of moderate importance, but with high variance; with no significant differences were observed for groups.
- **Results Worth Effort.** Compared to the relatively low AFC, the RWE AFS was quite positive (Table 7). The WAFS exhibited a near significant result for group (KWH test: $\chi^2(2) = 4.19, p = 0.12$). A MWU test of Novice and Expert groups was not significant ($U = 18, Z = -1.74, p = 0.09, r = 0.36$), but again near significant. The WAFS has comparatively low average to other factors.

7   Discussion

We discuss in this section of how well the *Objects VR* artefact satisfied its original design criteria. By reflecting on results and their means of observation, we can evaluate our design method to determine implications for the design and research of interactive music systems in VR. Additionally, the analysis and advice offered is case-based and should be understood to be provisional and exploratory.

7.1 Design Criteria Assessment

Accessible and Fun for Novices. Despite the brief time in the environment across both sessions, novices tended to find it an engaging and enjoyable experience of interacting with musical content, barring aberrant cases. Self-report marked high levels of enjoyment and engagement (*Enjoyable, Playful, Strange but I like it*) despite difficulties of interaction. The IA marked noticeable improvement in interface use across both sessions (*More sonic control*). The experience was predominantly considered to make them feel creative (SID.4) and the highest WAFS from the CSI was Enjoyment. But, high levels of confusion and frustration were observed in self-report (*Not getting it, Objects, Hearing differences*) with IA themes marking persistent issues with interaction (*Sticky Objects, Button Error, Grab Error*). Findings offer many implications for design improvement to enhance creative engagement by improving comprehension of musical function (*Varied conceptual models*) to scaffold understanding of musical function to explore creative goals.

Allow 'Physical' Experimentation and Interaction With Musical Content. The highest CSI AFC was for Exploration. This highlights that exploring ideas and possibilities is an important feature of a music making task. Positive average results include all user groups feeling "connected to sound changes" (SID.1), being part of a creative process (SID.4), feeling in control (SID.5), and liking the music they made (SID.8). Based on IA, most of the interaction clustered around use of the button-based menus for content playback (*Button Success, Grab LC, Put LC, Button Error*) to achieve this. When the spatial objects were found they were of interest, and for some the level of feedback produced noticeable changes of focus (*Discovery*). But comprehension of their function was poor (*Objects, Effects objects, Opaque mappings*), and usage patterns were often brief and constrained in their use of space. Though in two cases (P4, P23) the movement patterns using prism objects were highly varied, using a large space around them to influence the sound and their interaction. Engagement with a different physical space for making music is still a interesting direction of research to expand the interaction space and achieve the design criteria. But it leaves a challenge: in a medium that affords spatial interaction how do we structure rich and diverse interactions in space with appropriate levels of depth and feedback to the experience?

Obtain High Levels of Presence. From SPES results, high levels of presence were achieved. Self-report and CSI factor Immersion highlights task immersion as a topic of further investigation at whether presence is correlated in VR interactive music systems. The Immersion factor has a large range across the whole population. Large differences were observed in individual cases for the task of making music. The results range means further analysis is needed to determine how users interpreted the task of making music in a VR environment, to resolve whether the immersive nature of VR is being reported on or if levels of task immersion are achieved for creative tasks. An interesting comparison would be to test similar functionality across media types to determine whether musical tasks are equally as immersive outside of VR.

Allow Users to Experience Flow States. Within self-report there are many examples of musical engagement, but the extensive feature of frustration and confusion indicates that potential for flow might be hindered by basic interaction problems. Following is a breakdown of conditions for flow in relationship to this study and artefact.

The initial goal of the first session was exploration and understanding, then music-making is the only goal set for the Task session. So perhaps goals set in the experiment did not provide an optimal condition for flow. Novice self-report highlights some instances feeling lost in initial exploration (*Purpose*) that could corroborate this assertion. A more directed experiment design that sets direct goals for users using the VR interface may provide a sufficient level of challenge and goals that direct the initial learning of the interface.

The system was considered to have sufficient feedback (SID.7, *Interface and Feedback*) but the many errors of interaction (*Problems* and *Frustration*), incorrect models of function (*Varied conceptual models*) and misuse of error feedback (*Audio Feedback*) mean that feedback is unclear. The ambiguity of what feedback applied in exploratory inspection means incorrect assumptions of function could be developed, limiting this condition for flow. Complex and mysterious environments need to contain constructive breakdown of interaction [27], or risk distressing Novices. Environment items should be context-dependent; if a track is not running then it's effectors should not be available. This may help build conceptual models of what can be done but still maintain a playful and magical character to the environment.

The artefact and study determined that users enjoyed their experiences (CSI Enjoyment) while finding it challenging (SID.6). But development of skills in the environment to maintain suitable challenge is potentially limited by a shallowness of system functionality (*Plateau of possibilities*) and for novices a lack of comprehension to establish confident use. Improvements could be found in less rigid forms of musical content interaction e.g. rather than playing back samples you assemble compositions yourself. But a balance of expressive capability and immediate engagement needs to be addressed. It is feasible that well scaffolded complexity in initial engagement could still allow exploration of rich musical possibilities without too much explicit instruction or knowledge dissemination before use.

One effect of flow is to experience an activity as intrinsically rewarding. Much of the self-report across all groups was about levels of enjoyment and engagement. Linking results from 'feeling part of a creative process' (SID.4), 'liking the music created' (SID.8) and CSI factor RWE; interaction was worthwhile regardless of musical output. This is a positive result for both groups as it positions VR music spaces as engaging experiences. Some assume that Experts desire highly expressive systems [7], but our findings for Expressivity CSI factor suggest a more nuanced understanding. Add to this the near significant results for the RWE factor, and it warrants further understanding of how users frame music making when approaching a novel interactive music system. This prompts questions of whether actionable results are more important than ideation or play, and does the nature of the medium alter expectation in this regard. Maybe Experts judge the medium of the system into what they expect from an experience; they interpret VR as non-task oriented and do not impose a need for thinking about "good" results. Given this line of reasoning and RWE AFC finding, it is worth trialling the CSI on more traditional computer music software to determine whether the medium of experience alters results for expert users in similar tasks.

7.2 Methodology Commentary

The mixed methods study looked to probe initial behaviours, feelings and thoughts of individuals using *Objects VR*. This details design issues for new users but also highlights more general design issues around Novice or Expert music systems. The IA and interview themes highlight important features of experience for designing user interaction within the *Objects VR* design space. The CSI and SID surveys were useful triangulation metrics to explore important concepts around flow and user engagement. But, the disambiguation around sonic and task immersion requires further investigation to look for any differences between Novice and Expert groups in relation to flow in VR interactive music system. The question that grouped novice and expert users, while being imprecise, did provide useful categories for comparison but future studies should use validated measures such as the Goldsmiths Musical Sophistication Index[6]. Also further controls need to be put in place to moderate groups based on VR experience.

7.3 Design Implications for Novice VR Interactive Music Systems

Use Natural Behaviours. Study and implement gestural behaviours that relate to users natural understanding. Multiple selection and manipulation taxonomies should be supported, just as in real life, we can pull, push, shove, or cradle an object. Though this makes creation of environments more difficult, the depth of possible interaction could improve presence, experience and performance.

Design for Sensor Frailty. Sensor field of vision (FOV) and fidelity issues govern design of consumer grade interaction experiences. FOV changes how elements need to be presented in an environment for interaction. In *Objects VR* magnetic grabs resulted in extensive interaction errors. So, design interfaces to actively understand how and when the FOV is a potential hindrance to action, and design system feedback for user action with the sensor space to learn how to interact optimally.

Expression vs Engagement. Balancing a low entry fee with sonic depth is troublesome for music novices, and therefore understanding how a novice approaches

---

[6] http://www.gold.ac.uk/music-mind-brain/gold-msi/.

and learns is fundamental to designing experience in VR interactive music systems. In *Objects VR* the audio functionality presented was often too opaque for users to understand, so, keep it simple! The novice theme of *Hearing Differences* relates to other research on novice music interface design [5,7]; where musical content should be diverse enough to clearly hear the differences of musical contributions.

Be Careful With Divergent Metaphors. The *Objects VR* interface utilised multiple interaction metaphors for action-sound relationships. This was confusing to Novices, as signification of function and effect was not clear. We are not advising to avoid using multiple metaphors, rather that clear boundaries, signifiers and transitions are used to guide users through their use.

Create Vivid and Matching Connections. Object groups should be visually and behaviourally cohesive to a user. Colours and shapes need to be correctly assigned to allow understanding across the interface. If possible connect features to functionality, but limit overall complexity.

8　Conclusion

Designing VR interfaces for creative musical applications provides significant challenges for HCI, requiring a different approach to traditional task-based design of systems. *Objects VR* is an example of working with the trade-off of expression and engagement to determine the appropriate balance of complexity and expressivity in a virtual reality interactive music system for novice users. It provided most users with an enjoyable experience of interacting with musical content, despite levels of frustration witnessed in many interaction accounts. Repeated instances of confusion witnessed after exploratory interaction pose many design implications for consideration in novice and expert systems for interactive music in VR. Addressing these issues could allow for creating spaces with high conditions for flow, with expressive experiences free from situated distractions.

Future research directions based on findings that would benefit the domain of VR interactive music systems include: (i) Scalable frameworks for interaction analysis, such as an automatic logging system utilising human-in-the-loop machine learning; (ii) Spatial interaction related to music interfaces; (iii) Development of understanding in problem areas for music interfaces that effect flow, potentially linking flow and presence conceptualisations using physiological data; (iv) Development of questionnaires to quickly assess VR interactive music systems prototypes and artefacts.

Acknowledgements. We would like to give thanks to Stuart Cupit and the development team at Inition for guiding the initial technical development of the interface. This project was funded by the EPSRC and AHRC Centre for Doctoral Training in Media and Arts Technology (EP/L01632X/1), and the EU H2020 research and innovation project Audio Commons (688382).

References

1. Adams, A.T., Gonzalez, B., Latulipe, C.: SonicExplorer: fluid exploration of audio parameters. In: CHI, pp. 237–246 (2014)
2. Andersen, K., Gibson, D.: The instrument as the source of new in new music. In: Research Through Design, pp. 25–27 (2015)
3. Andolina, S., Klouche, K., Cabral, D., Ruotsalo, T., Jacucci, G.: InspirationWall: supporting idea generation through automatic information exploration. In: Proceedings of the C&C, pp. 8–11 (2015)
4. Barthet, M., Thalmann, F., Fazekas, G., Sandler, M., Wiggins, G.: Crossroads: interactive music systems transforming performance, production and listening. In: Proceedings of the CHI Workshop on Music and HCI (2016)
5. Bengler, B., Bryan-Kinns, N.: Designing collaborative musical experiences for broad audiences. In: Proceedings of the C&C, p. 234. ACM Press, New York (2013)
6. Berthaut, F., Desainte-Catherine, M., Hachet, M.: DRILE: an immersive environment for hierarchical live-looping. In: Proceedings of the NIME, pp. 192–197 (2010)
7. Blaine, T., Fels, S.: Collaborative musical experiences for novices. J. New Music Res. (2010)
8. Bowman, D.A., Johnson, D.B., Hodges, L.F.: Testbed evaluation of virtual environment interaction techniques. Presence: Teleoperators Virtual Environ. $10(1)$, 75–95 (2001)
9. Braun, V., Clarke, V.: Using thematic analysis in psychology. Qual. Res. Psychol. $3(2)$, 77–101 (2006)
10. Byrne, D.: How Music Works. Canongate Books, Edinburgh (2012)
11. Cherry, E., Latulipe, C.: Quantifying the creativity support of digital tools through the creativity support index. ACM TOCHI $21(4)$, 1–25 (2014)
12. Csikszentmihalyi, M.: Flow: The Psychology of Optimal Experience, 1st edn. Harper & Row, New York (1990)
13. Elblaus, L., Hansen, K.F., Unander-Scharin, C.: Artistically directed prototyping in development and in practice. J. New Music Res. $41(4, SI)$, 377–387 (2012)
14. Forlizzi, J., Battarbee, K.: Understanding experience in interactive systems. In: Proceedings of the DIS, pp. 261–268 (2004)
15. Gelineck, S.: Virtual reality instruments capable of changing dimensions in real-time. In: Proceedings of the ENACTIVE (2005)
16. Godøy, R.I.: Gestural-sonorous objects: embodied extensions of Schaeffer's conceptual apparatus. Organ. Sound $11(02)$, 149 (2006)
17. Hamilton, R.: Mediated musical interactions in virtual environments. In: CHI Workshop on Music and HCI (2016)
18. Hartmann, T., Wirth, W., Schramm, H., Klimmt, C., Vorderer, P., Gysbers, A., Böcking, S., Ravaja, N., Laarni, J., Saari, T., et al.: The spatial presence experience scale. J. Media Psychol. (2015)
19. Heath, C.C., Luff, P.: Collaboration and control: crisis management and multimedia technology. CSCW $1(1–2)$, 69–94 (1990, 1992)
20. Houde, S., Hill, C.: What do prototypes prototype. In: Handbook of Human-computer Interaction, 2nd edn., pp. 367–381 (1997)
21. Jacob, M., Magerko, B.: Interaction-based authoring for scalable co-creative agents. In: Proceedings of the ICCC, pp. 236–243 (2015)
22. Johnston, A.: Beyond evaluation: linking practice and theory in new musical interface design. In: Proceedings of the NIME (2011)

23. Jordan, B., Henderson, A.: Interaction analysis: foundations and practice. J. Learn. Sci. **4**(1), 39–103 (1995)
24. Mulder, A., Fels, S.S., Mase, K.: Mapping virtual object manipulation to sound variation. IPSJ Sig Notes **97**(122), 63–68 (1997)
25. O'hara, K., Harper, R., Mentis, H., Sellen, A., Taylor, A.: On the naturalness of touchless: putting the interaction back into NUI. ACM Trans. Comput.-Hum. Interact. **20**(1), 1–25 (2013)
26. Rodet, X., Lambert, J.P., Gaudy, T., Gosselin, F.: Study of haptic and visual interaction for sound and music control in the phase project. In: Proceedings of the NIME, pp. 109–114 (2005)
27. Ryan, W., Street, E., Siegel, M.A.: Evaluating interactive entertainment using breakdown: understanding embodied learning in video games. In: Proceedings of the DiGRA (2009)
28. Salisbury, J.H., Tomlinson, P.: Reconciling Csikszentmihalyi's broader flow theory: with meaning and value in digital games. ToDIGRA **2**(2), 55–77 (2016)
29. Schubert, T.W.: A new conception of spatial presence: once again, with feeling. Commun. Theory **19**, 161–187 (2009)
30. Sèdes, A., Guillot, P., Paris, E., Anne, S., Pierre, G., Eliott, P.: The HOA library, review and prospects. In: Proceedings of the ICMC, vol. 2014, pp. 855–860 (2014)
31. Seldess, Z.: MIAP: manifold-interface amplitude panning in Max/MSP and pure data. In: Proceedings of the AES, pp. 1–10 (2011)
32. Slater, M., Usoh, M.: Body centred interaction in immersive virtual environments. Artif. Life Virtual Real. **1**, 1–22 (1994)
33. Slepian, M.L., Ambady, N.: Fluid movement and creativity. J. Exp. Psychol. **141**(4), 625–629 (2012)
34. Stowell, D., Robertson, A., Bryan-Kinns, N., Plumbley, M.: Evaluation of live human-computer music-making: quantitative and qualitative approaches. Int. J. Hum.-Comput Stud. **67**(11), 960–975 (2009)
35. Sutcliffe, A., Gault, B.: Heuristic evaluation of virtual reality applications. Interact. Comput. **16**(4), 831–849 (2004)
36. Vinayak, R.D., Piya, C., Ramani, K.: MobiSweep: exploring spatial design ideation using a smartphone as a hand-held reference plane. In: Proceedings of the TEI, pp. 12–20 (2016)
37. Wirth, W., Hartmann, T., Böcking, S., Vorderer, P., Klimmt, C., Schramm, H., Saari, T., Laarni, J., Ravaja, N., Gouveia, F.R., Biocca, F., Sacau, A., Jäncke, L., Baumgartner, T., Jäncke, P.: A process model of the formation of spatial presence experiences. Media Psychol. **9**, 493–525 (2007)
38. Wozniewski, M., Settel, Z., Cooperstock, J.: A spatial interface for audio and music production. In: Proceedings of the DAFX, pp. 18–21 (2006)
39. Zimmerman, J., Stolterman, E., Forlizzi, J.: An analysis and critique of research through design: towards a formalization of a research approach. In: Proceedings of the DIS, pp. 310–319 (2010)

Image/Sound Interaction - Digital Games

VORPAL: An Extensible and Flexible Middleware for Real-Time Soundtracks in Digital Games

Wilson Kazuo Mizutani$^{(\boxtimes)}$ and Fabio Kon

Department of Computer Science, Institute of Mathematics,
University of São Paulo, Rua Do Matão, 1010, São Paulo 05508-090, SP, Brazil
{kazuo,kon}@ime.usp.br
http://compmus.ime.usp.br/en/vorpal

Abstract. Real-time soundtracks in games have always faced design restrictions due to technological limitations. The predominant solutions of hoarding prerecorded audio assets and then assigning a tweak or two each time their playback is triggered from game code leaves away the potential of real-time symbolic representation manipulation and DSP audio synthesis. In this paper, we take a first step towards a more robust, generic, and flexible approach to game audio and musical composition in the form of a generic middleware based on the Pure Data programming language. We describe here the middleware architecture and implementation and part of its validation via two game experiments.

Keywords: Game audio · Game music · Real-time soundtrack · Computer music · Middleware

1 Introduction

Digital games, as a form of audiovisual entertainment, have specific challenges regarding soundtrack composition and design [10]. Since the player's experience is the game designer's main concern, as defended by Schell [13], a game soundtrack may compromise the final product quality as much as its graphical performance. In that regard, there is one game soundtrack aspect that is indeed commonly neglected or oversimplified: its potential as a *real-time*, procedurally manipulated media, as pointed out by Farnell [3].

Even though there is a lot in common between game soundtracks and other more "traditional" audiovisual entertainment media soundtracks (such as Theater and Cinema), Collins [2] argues that there are also unquestionable differences among them, of either technological, historical, or cultural origins. The one Collins points as the most important difference is the deeply nonlinear and interactive structure of games, which make them *"largely unpredictable in terms of the directions the player may take, and the timings involved"*. Because of this, many game sounds and music tracks cannot be merely exposed through common playback (as happens with prerecorded media): they also need some form

© Springer International Publishing AG 2017
M. Aramaki et al. (Eds.): CMMR 2016, LNCS 10525, pp. 219–228, 2017.
DOI: 10.1007/978-3-319-67738-5_13

of procedural control to be tightly knit together with the ongoing narrative of the game. However, this is seldom fully explored. Except in a few remarkable cases, most game musical soundtracks tend to have little real-time connections between what is happening in the game and what is going on with the music, for instance.

The ways with which real-time soundtracks are typically dealt with are poor and do not scale well. Basically, the development team needs to find a common ground for musicians, sound designers, and programmers where they can reach an agreement on how to introduce real-time behaviour into the game source code modules related to audio reproduction and sound assets management. Farnell [3] explains that the common approach is to produce as many assets as needed and then list all event hooks that must go into the game code to timely play the corresponding sounds and music (perhaps with one or two filters applied to the output). This is not only a waste of memory and a disproportional amount of effort, but also a very limited way of designing a game soundtrack. Farnell goes as far as to say that even advanced and automated proprietary middleware systems fail to provide a satisfactory solution, since they *"are presently audio delivery frameworks for prerecorded data rather than real 'sound engines' capable of computing sources from coherent models"*.

In our research, we provide an alternative to such excessively asset-driven solutions by empowering the musicians and sound designers with a tool able to express procedurally how a game soundtrack is to be executed, and by embedding it into a cross-platform programming library that can be easily integrated into the development workflow of digital games. As such, we present, in this paper, the *Vorpal Open Real-time Procedural Audio Layer* (*VORPAL*[1]), an opensource, extensible, and flexible middleware system for the development of real-time soundtracks in digital games as the result of our research. The middleware implementation is available at https://github.com/vorpal-project/vorpal under the MPL 2.0 open source license.

2   Soundtrack Implementations in Digital Games

Matos [9] states that soundtracks are essentially the union of all sound effects, voices, and music that are played along with a visual presentation. In the traditional asset-driven approach, each audio element from these soundtrack parts is implemented in the game code by specifying a playback trigger consisting mainly of [3]:

1. *Which* sample assets are to be played.
2. *How* they are to be played (that is, what filters should be applied).
3. *When* they are to be played.

As an example of this pattern, consider a gunshot sound effect. Using a prerecorded gunpowder explosion sound, one could produce different firearms

---

[1] A recursive acronym.

sounds by applying multiple filters to it and then mapping the corresponding configuration whenever a weapon is shot. This way, when the player's character wields a specific type of pistol, its respective sound effect is triggered.

Being able to synchronize an audio element playback achieves an initial level of real-time behaviour on its own. It is often further expanded by allowing the other two parameters (the *which* and the *how*) to change according to the game state. In the game *Faster Than Light* (*Subset Games*, 2012), every musical piece in the soundtrack has two versions – one for exploration and one for combat – and they are cross-faded between each other whenever the game situation changes from exploration to combat and vice-versa. This consists of both a modification in the sample used (the *which*) and a real-time control over the filters, responsible for fading out the previous version of the music while fading in the next one (the *how*).

However, since this method specifies only whole samples to be played, it excludes from the sound design space other forms of audio construction, notably symbolic representation (e.g., MIDI) and Digital Signal Processing (DSP) audio synthesis. The *IMuse* system [8] was an example of how to use symbolic representation to allow music changes in real-time. Essentially, it provided if-then-jump commands among the other typical music score based messages, bringing symbolic representation closer to a programming language of its own. Regarding DSP audio synthesis, there are quite a few works on physically based real-time audio synthesis [1,4,6], which could contribute to many unexplored ways of dealing with sound effects in games using no sample files, but at a greater computational cost.

3 Real-Time Restrictions in Game Implementation

To be considered a real-time application, digital games rely on the **Game Loop** architectural pattern [5,12]. It guarantees that the time difference between the continuous input processing and output generation is so short that the user experiences it as being instantaneous. This is accomplished by dividing the program execution into very short steps between each input handling and output rendering, then finely controlling the process rate of these cycles inside an endless loop.

Nystrom [12] shows how the Game Loop frequency is related to the Frames Per Second ratio (FPS) of the game, i.e., the ratio of how many graphical frame buffers are fully rendered per second. Ideally the FPS should be greater than or equal to the Game Loop frequency, which means that its visual output may change and adapt at least as often as changes are made to the game state. On the other hand, conventional asset-driven audio implementations in games provide a slower feedback mechanism, since they load as many audio samples as possible from the assets to the computer sound card (where they can no longer be promptly accessed) in each game cycle. The samples are transferred in chunks that are typically too big, causing effects applied to the game soundtrack to come with a perceptible delay, thus not satisfying the desirable real-time requirements. Essentially, it incurs in too much *latency*.

For instance, in the $L\ddot{O}VE$ game framework[2], the default audio stream buffer contains 4096 samples, which, with an audio sample rate of 44100 Hz, leads to soundtrack changes being able to occur only every 93 ms, approximately. The simple solution to this is to reduce the size of the audio buffers sent to the sound card, which actually means processing less audio in each game cycle. If a game is to be executed at 60 FPS and its audio is sampled at 44100 Hz, then each game cycle must provide only $44100/60 = 735$ audio samples. In the more general case, one cycle may actually have a variable time length. If we let f_{audio} be the audio sample rate (in Hertz) and Δt be the time difference (in seconds) between the current game cycle and the last, then the number N of maximum audio samples allowed for the current cycle would be:

$$N = f_{audio} \cdot \Delta t \qquad (1)$$

As a matter of fact, the DSP graphical programming language *Pure Data*[3] has a standard cycle buffer size of merely 64 samples. That would be precise enough for a game running at approximately 689 FPS. The drawback of reducing the audio buffer size is that if the computations needed to fill it actually last long enough to make a perceptible time gap between each buffer update, then the sound might come out chopped by the sudden lack of samples to play. There is also an increased overhead in having a larger number of smaller data copies sent to the sound card. Thus, even though reducing the buffer size is important to decrease latency, a point of equilibrium must be found or the audio quality may be compromised [7]. This depends on how much computation time the Game Loop has available for handling audio processing and on the technical capabilities of the sound hardware at our disposal. Weiner [15] proposes a possible audio pipeline that based on lazy evaluation, for instance.

4   Proposed Architecture

The main purpose of the *VORPAL* middleware is to bridge soundtracks and game engines. As such, we understand that its main user is the sound designer, although the programmers that bind the game code to the middleware must also be taken into consideration. This is commonplace for game audio middleware, requiring the division of the tool into two separate but complementary interfaces[4]. The first is a "soundtrack editor" – a visual application through which sound designers author audio content that can be later exported to the game. The second is a programming library exposed through an Application Programming Interface (API) that is capable of loading the media exported by the editor and playing it during the game execution (see Fig. 1).

---

[2] love2d.org.

[3] puredata.info.

[4] See *Firelight*'s *FMOD Studio* (www.fmod.org), *Audiokinetic*'s *Wwise* (www.audioki netic.com/products/wwise), and *Elias Software*'s *Elias* (www.eliassoftware.com).

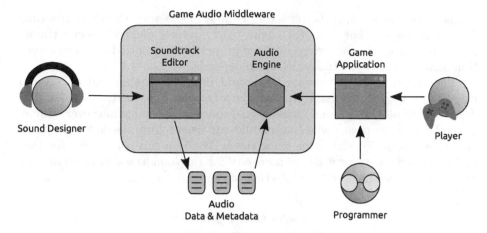

Fig. 1. Standard overview architecture for game audio middleware.

VORPAL follows this general architecture. However, instead of focusing the soundtrack editor in audio assets management, we chose to develop a procedure-oriented tool. We designed a collection of high-level abstractions in the Pure Data programming language, called the **Soundtrack Creation Kit**, that sound designers can use to produce Pure Data patches as part of a game soundtrack specification. The game engine can then link to *VORPAL*'s **Audio Engine** (a programming library) to load and *execute* the soundtrack patches authored this way. Our intention is to focus on giving sound designers full control over the sonic behaviour instead of just rigid sonic scheduling, since they can *program the soundtrack themselves* with an accessible, community-approved language such as Pure Data.

4.1   Pure Data Integration

Pure Data originally comes as a stand-alone application capable of creating, editing, and executing patches by itself, promptly serving as our soundtrack editor. However, even though it is capable of communicating with other applications through sockets or MIDI channels, ideally one would not want to have multiple applications launched when playing a digital game. The solution would be to run Pure Data's DSP *from inside the game*. There is a community developed programming library called libpd[5] that provides access to Pure Data's core implementation, allowing its host program to load and execute Pure Data patches without the Pure Data application.

However, when using libpd, there is no audio output handling. The host application is only given the processed signal and is responsible for sending it to the sound card or doing whatever it wants with it. Additionally, the processed signal is provided in blocks of 64 stereo samples, as mentioned before. Our audio

---

[5] libpd.cc.

engine must synchronize the retrieval of these blocks with the game run-time flow as in Eq. (1). For that, the engine API routines demand precise timing information from the game execution *and* properly synchronized evocation, since time management is controlled by the game code.

The communication between the sound designer patches and our Audio Engine consists of two main types of data transfer. The first, which we just described, results from libpd's audio signal computation happening every frame. The other transfer occurs when our middleware must inform the designer's patch of a relevant change within the game state. Based on this communication, the patch may do whatever it deems necessary for the soundtrack to follow up the game narrative. The overall architecture of our engine can be seen in Fig. 2.

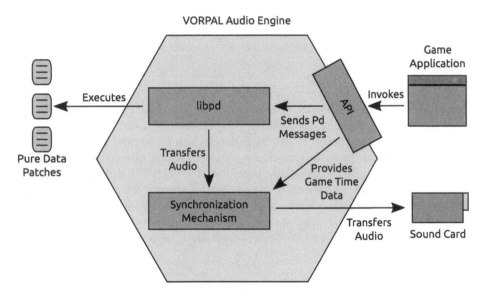

Fig. 2. *VORPAL* Audio Engine's architecture.

4.2   Middleware Abstractions

Finding a good model that links soundtrack elements to game elements depends mostly on how the latter are designed. But, aside from the Game Loop pattern, there is not much one can assume about the software architecture of a game without losing compatibility or discouraging users by imposing unwanted conventions. Thus, in this work we choose a rather weak assumption that within the code base of a game there is the concept of *game objects*, ideally implemented through Object-Oriented Programming. Game objects range from obvious candidates such as the player's avatar, the items lying on the floor, or a blazing fireball falling from the skies, to implicit or merely bureaucratic elements like the camera, a monster spawning spot, or an inventory interface button. The job assigned to the *VORPAL* middleware is, then, to map real-time soundtrack events to each game object – even a music track, which could be traced to an invisible auxiliary game object called "Player's Headphone".

This is done through the **Soundtrack Event** abstraction we introduce with the *VORPAL* middleware. Each Pure Data Patch the sound designer creates using the Soundtrack Creation Kit describes a Soundtrack Event type (like a class in Object-Oriented programming languages). When the programmer loads these patches through the Audio Engine API, he or she can create Soundtrack Event instances. Soundtrack Events are supposed to roughly present a one-to-one mapping with game objects. A character avatar could have a Soundtrack Event assigned to it to play its voice and dialogue, just as a door could carry a Soundtrack Event for when it creaks due to a player opening it.

The real usefulness of this abstraction lies in the concept of *messages* from Object-Oriented Programming. When a piece of code invokes a method on an object, we say that it is sending that object a message. Analogously, since our abstraction is based off on Object-Oriented Programming, Soundtrack Events can be sent **Commands**, which trigger real-time effects in them. For instance, the Soundtrack Event we previously assigned to a character avatar could respond to the Commands "shout", "speak dialogue line 322", "step in mud", etc. Each of these would then be sent to the Pure Data patch that implements the Soundtrack Event type, where it could be used to perform the corresponding real-time DSP effect the sound designer defined. An example for music themes would be a Soundtrack Event that responds to Commands like "play", "increase tension", "roll dramatic transition", "finish up in at most 8 s", etc.

5   Implementation Decisions

For the sake of game engine compatibility and performance [5,12], we chose to develop our middleware in C++, except for the parts that must be made in Pure Data. The Audio Engine uses *OpenAL*[6] for cross-platform open-source-friendly access to the sound card, enabling us to produce proper playback of the desired audio. It also comes with convenient spatialization features that are explored by the system.

5.1   Audio Engine

To satisfy the real-time restrictions described in Sect. 3, the *VORPAL* Audio Engine strongly relies on *OpenAL*'s buffer queueing mechanism. It enables the allocation of multiple buffers whose purpose is to send audio data to the sound card in First-In-First-Out order. Each buffer can have arbitrary sizes, but we fit them to Pure Data's cycle block size (64 samples). Then, *OpenAL* automatically switches the current buffer to the next one when it has finished playing. That way, even when the game cycles do not match Pure Data's cycles, we can schedule the next block. Doing so increases latency, but since the block is very small the difference is minimal and allows us to reduce the previously discussed overhead.

---

[6] See www.openal.org and kcat.strangesoft.net/openal.html.

The actual audio transfer from a patch to the engine uses the Pure Data array API instead of its standard output, since this simplifies the use of multiple simultaneous audio buses. The engine recognizes the audio buses thanks to a naming convention. The Soundtrack Creation Kit then wraps it, hiding this and other implementation details needed to properly synchronize the filling of the arrays with the engine cycles.

Still on the engine side, we implemented the Command abstraction as follows. It relies on the messaging mechanism from Pure Data, accessed via libpd. With a single routine call, a message is sent to the sound designer's patch containing as much information as desired, so long as it can be represented by a list of numbers and character strings (Pure Data symbols). Besides, each patch is represented by a C++ class designed after the Soundtrack Event abstraction. That is, each instance of that class is a Soundtrack Event instance, and it provides the API for sending Commands to the corresponding Pure Data patches.

5.2 Soundtrack Creation Kit

For a Pure Data patch made by the sound designer to actually work properly with the *VORPAL* middleware, it must contain at least one specific object from the Soundtrack Creation Kit. We developed an abstraction patch called **Audio Bus**, which captures a signal produced inside Pure Data and sends it to the corresponding Soundtrack Event instance in the Audio Engine. Each patch is then responsible for sending to its Audio Buses the corresponding sound signal. The captured signals are managed and mixed by the Audio Engine, then played when the game application demands so. Besides the Audio Bus, there other auxiliary abstraction patches the Soundtrack Creation Kit provides. Their intention is to guide the sound designer's workflow when using the middleware, but they can be ignored if one wishes to work directly with the low level mechanisms of the Pure Data language.

6   Results

To validate our proposal, we used our middleware to create soundtracks for two very different games. First, we forked the open-source game *Mari0*[7] and replaced its default soundtrack for one entirely produced by our middleware. The game is a parody of two other famous games: *Super Mario Bros.* (*Nintendo*, 1985) and *Portal* (*Valve*, 2007). The focus was the music track, and we experimented only with Koji Kondo's "Overworld Main Theme", the music track for the first stage of the game. By dividing the music in its three voices – melody, bass and percussion – and the score bars into a few sections, we were able to add the following real-time behaviours to the game soundtrack:

1. The music advances through the bars as the player progresses through the stage, so that each of its parts has a particular music segment associated.

---

[7] stabyourself.net/mari0.

2. Mario's size directly influences the bass voice. The stronger he gets, the louder the bass line becomes.
3. The quantity of enemies nearby also increases the percussion volume, in an attempt to suggest that the situation became more action-intensive.

The second validation is a soundtrack for an original title we created in partnership with a professional sound designer. The game developed was called *Sound Wanderer*, and has been accepted as a demonstration in an international conference on computer music [11]. We also evaluated the tool's usage by potential users during that process. The source code of both games is available under an open source license at http://compmus.ime.usp.br/en/vorpal/games.

7   Conclusion

There are many details regarding our research that we had to skip over here. A detailed account of our findings and a throughout description of the *VORPAL* middleware can be found in the first author Masters Thesis available at the *VORPAL* web site. But we can say that there are many interesting challenges in this research area. First, as widespread as Pure Data is, it lacks a simple user interface that would be appealing to sound designers and composers with no programming experience. Second, with a new soundtrack composition workflow comes a whole new skill set for sound designers and composers to reach out to – an unavoidable cost of breaking well established paradigms [14]. Our expectations are that, with this work, we will at least open the way for new methods of producing soundtracks for digital games that actually try to exploit the dynamic and interactive nature of the medium, avoiding further waste of this game design space.

References

1. Bonnel, N., Drettakis, G., Tsingos, N., Viaud-Delmon, I., James, D.: Fast modal sounds with scalable frequency-domain synthesis. ACM Trans. Graph. **27**(3), 24:1–24:9 (2008). doi:10.1145/1360612.1360623
2. Collins, K.: Game Sound: An Introduction to the History, Theory, and Practice of Video Game Music and Sound Design. The MIT Press, Cambridge (2008)
3. Farnell, A.: An introduction to procedural audio and its application in computer games (2007). http://cs.au.dk/~dsound/DigitalAudio.dir/Papers/proceduralAudio.pdf
4. Farnell, A.: Designing Sound. The MIT Press, Cambridge (2010)
5. Gregory, J.: Game Engine Architecture. A.K. Peters/CRC Press, Boca Raton (2014)
6. James, D.L., Barbič, J., Pai, D.K.: Precomputed acoustic transfer: output-sensitive, accurate sound generation for geometrically complex vibration sources. In: ACM SIGGRAPH 2006 Papers, pp. 987–995. SIGGRAPH 2006. ACM, New York (2006). doi:10.1145/1179352.1141983
7. Lago, N.P., Kon, F.: The quest for low latency. In: Proceedings of the International Computer Music Conference, pp. 33–36 (2004)

8. LucasArts: Method and apparatus for dynamically composing music and sound effects using a computer entertainment system. United States Patent 5315057 (1994)
9. Matos, E.: A Arte de Compor Música para o Cinema. Senac, Brasília (2014)
10. Meneguette, L.C.: Situações Sonoras e Jogos Digitais. Simpçõrio Brasileiro de Games, pp. 30–33 (2013)
11. Mizutani, W.K., Vicente, D., Kon, F.: Sound wanderer: an experimental game exploring real-time soundtrack with openda. In: Demonstration at the 12th International Symposium on Computer Music Multidisciplinary Research, São Paulo (2016)
12. Nystrom, R.: Game Programming Patterns. Genever Benning, Mahwah (2014)
13. Schell, J.: The Art of Game Design: A Book of Lenses, 2nd edn. A.K. Peters/CRC Press, Boca Raton (2014)
14. Scott, N.: Music to middleware: the growing challenges of the game music composer. In: Proceedings of the 2014 Conference on Interactive Entertainment, pp. 34:1–34:3. IE 2014. ACM, New York (2014). http://doi.acm.org/10.1145/2677758.2677792
15. Weiner, K., DiamondWare Ltd.: Interactive processing pipeline for digital audio. In: DeLoura, M. (ed.) Game Programming Gems II, pp. 529–538. Charles River Media, Revere (2001)

New Atlantis: Audio Experimentation in a Shared Online World

Peter Sinclair[1]([⊠]), Roland Cahen[2], Jonathan Tanant[3], and Peter Gena[4]

[1] Ecole Superieur d'Art d'Aix. Locus Sonus Research Unity, Rue Emile Tavan,
13100 Aix-en-Provence, France
peter.sinclair@ecole-art-aix.fr
[2] Ecole Nationale Superiere de Creation Industrielle (ENSCI les ateliers),
48 Rue Saint-Sabin, 75011 Paris, France
roland.cahen@ensci.com
[3] Independant Software Engineer, Jon Lab., Tilly, France
jonathan@free.fr
[4] School of the Arts Institute Chicago (SAIC),
36 S. Wabash Ave., Chicago, IL 60603, USA
pgena@artic.edu

Abstract. Computer games and virtual worlds are "traditionally" visually orientated, and their audio dimension often secondary. In this paper we will describe New Atlantis a virtual world that aims to put sound first. We will describe the motivation, the history and the development of this Franco-American project and the serendipitous use made of the distance between partner structures. We explain the overall architecture of the world and discuss the reasons for certain key structural choices. New Atlantis' first aim is to provide a platform for audio-graphic design and practice, for students as well as artists and researchers, engaged in higher education art or media curricula. We describe the integration of student's productions through workshops and exchanges and discuss and the first public presentations of NA that took place from January 2016. Finally we will unfold perspectives for future research and the further uses of New Atlantis.

Keywords: Audiographic creation · Audio for virtual environments · Sound spatialisation · Networked music

1 Introduction

New Atlantis is a shared (multi-user) online virtual world dedicated to audio experimentation and practice. Unlike most online worlds where image is the primary concern, in NA sound comes first. NA provides a context for new-media students to showcase research projects that explore the relationship between sound, virtual 3D image and interactivity. It offers a pedagogical platform for audiographic animation, real-time sound synthesis, object sonification and acoustic simulation. It is a place to organize virtual sound installations, online concerts, Soundwalks and other audiovisual art experiences.

© Springer International Publishing AG 2017
M. Aramaki et al. (Eds.): CMMR 2016, LNCS 10525, pp. 229–246, 2017.
DOI: 10.1007/978-3-319-67738-5_14

The name New Atlantis comes from the title of an unfinished 1628 utopian novel by philosopher Francis Bacon [1], which describes a legendary island somewhere in the ocean, doted with extraordinary audio phenomena that might be considered as premonitory of today's electronic and digital audio techniques. We have adopted some of Bacon's ideas and nomenclature to create classes for the virtual world such as "Sound Houses", "Sound Pipes", "Trunks" and "Helps". In NA all elements are intended to have audio qualities: spaces resonate, surfaces reflect and collisions activate the multiple sounds of the objects involved. A collection of purpose built scripts implement low level sound synthesis and multiple parameter interactivity, enabling the creation of complex sound sources and environments linked to animation or navigation in the visual scene.

NA can be accessed via a web viewer or as a standalone application. It is organized as "spaces" that can be accessed independently but that share the same basic principles of navigation and specific scripts. Multi-user, it can be shared by several players at the same time making it suitable for group playing in both the gaming and the musical sense of the word. Every registered user can create and host individual or shared spaces which he or she can decide to make persistent or not. At the time of writing, we are working on a limited number of public "spaces" that contain multiple "Sound Houses" (architectural elements with specific acoustics) and other sound objects. These can be visited by navigating through the scene or created within the scene. The audio "mix" of these different sources varies with distance, so placing and navigating between sound objects can become a musical experience. In public spaces, players can interact with one another and with shared objects potentially playing together.

New Atlantis project is not only about creating a multi user virtual universe, but also about making it together while learning. It is experimental, creative and educational. New opportunities for further development in NA are created through the organization of workshops, courses or events that group art students in different locations, working together at a distance. It is a way to encourage ubiquitous working

Fig. 1. Students showcasing their projects in New Atlantis. ENSCI les ateliers, September 2015

groups of students to share immaterial and non-local (international) art projects. Most sound and music education schemes tend to be oriented towards established disciplines. NA on the other hand encourages experimental design projects and the exploration of new or emerging creative fields. Francis Bacon's *New Atlantis* proposed a model for the role of science and art in society that placed education at the heart of culture. Our project emphasizes discovery, cultural exchange, experimentation, learning and furthering of knowledge in an educational and creative environment (Fig. 1).

2 Context and History

"We have also sound-houses, where we practise and demonstrate all sounds and their generation. We have harmony which you have not, of quarter-sounds and lesser slides of sounds. Divers instruments of music likewise to you unknown, some sweeter than any you have; with bells and rings that are dainty and sweet. We represent small sounds as great and deep, likewise great sounds extenuate and sharp; we make divers tremblings and warblings of sounds, which in their original are entire. We represent and imitate all articulate sounds and letters, and the voices and notes of beasts and birds. We have certain helps which, set to the ear, do further the hearing greatly; we have also divers strange and artificial echoes, reflecting the voice many times, and, as it were, tossing it; and some that give back the voice louder than it came, some shriller and some deeper; yea, some rendering the voice, differing in the letters or articulate sound from that they receive. We have all means to convey sounds in trunks and pipes, in strange lines and distances" [1].

The origins of the NA project go back to 2005 when the Locus Sonus, ESA-Aix (Ecole Superieur d'Art d'Aix-En-Provence) and SAIC (School of the Art Institute of Chicago) were awarded FACE [2] funding for an academic and research exchange program. The original impulse occurred through collaboration between teams of the 3d and sound departments of the partner establishments, which led to the observation that there was scope for research into the area of audio in games and other virtual environments.

That NA refers to a Utopian model can be interpreted in several different ways. Firstly as the above citation demonstrates, the original text by Francis Bacon describes an island territory that was home to numerous extraordinary audio phenomena. Beyond this novel predicts the principles of the contemporary research university as seen in the description of "Salomon's House" which promotes international exchange: *"For the several employments and offices of our fellows, we have twelve that sail into foreign countries... who bring us the books and abstracts, and patterns of experiments of all other parts"* [1] and trans-disciplinary research: *"We have three that collect the experiments of all mechanical arts, and also of liberal sciences, and also of practices which are not brought into arts"* [1]. These ideas, combined with the fact that we are indeed engaged in creating a utopian world that might be considered as situated (albeit in our imagination) somewhere in the ocean – between Europe and America – combine to make NA a suitable reference.

Since the ESA-Aix/SAIC partnership was separated by the Atlantic Ocean, we rapidly adopted networked solutions for our collaborations: video conferencing and remote desktop were used to exchange lessons and conferences and an interconnected 3d cave were set up with an interface in both Aix and Chicago. The first experiments in

3d audio-graphy took place in Second Life [3], using Pure Data [4] as an audio engine. The process involved sending html commands from second life to an external server that did the audio synthesis and streamed the result back to second life; the project was presented in 2009 at the "Second Nature" festival in Aix-En-Provence [5]. This system worked well enough to convince us that it was worthwhile pursuing the development of sophisticated audio features for virtual environments, however, it was difficult to implement and the delay due to streaming was problematic.

The decision was made to build our own multi user world using Panda 3d [6] with Pure Data [4] bundled as an audio engine. Ecole Nationale Superieure de Creation Industrielle (ENSCI, les ateliers) became associated with the project at this point. This first version of NA was developed during multiple workshops that took place in Chicago and Aix en Provence between 2007 and 2011. The project involved a relatively complex path finding system used to calculate acoustics and custom-built client server software [7]. Although a working version was tested successfully during a workshop at ENSAB in 2011 [8], it was decided to abandon the development based on Panda/Pd in favor of Unity3d [9], a more recent and efficient platform offering greater scope for audio programming and possessing built in networking capabilities.

3 New Atlantis Project Aims

There are multiple aims associated with the NA project: as mentioned above the project emerges from an international exchange program and one of its first ambitions is to provide a platform for international academic, artistic, cultural and scientific exchange. The more specific aim is to further research into audio for virtual environments with the precise goals of providing an educational tool for students and a synchronized platform for remote music and sound art practices.

3.1 Research into Audio for Virtual and Networked Environments, Background

The history of audio development in game environments is relatively short and, at least when this project was initiated, somewhat lacking in substance. Arguably, this might be put down to competition between audio and visual requirements in terms of processing power on personal computers or game boxes. If in recent years companies such as AudioGaming [10] that are specialized in audio for game environments have started to appear, for the essential they provide sound design services for the commercial game market, rather than considering the virtual world as a possible audio interface. Therefore the historical origins of this project might be considered from several other angles. One approach is that of visual interfaces for musical compositions such as *UPIC* [11] originally developed by Iannis Xenakis or navigable scores such as *Fontana Mix* 1958 by John Cage [12]. Distant listening, remote performance and other streamed and networked art forms are another thread that has been largely investigated by Locus Sonus [13]. Experiments with remote musical presence started as early as 1992 when during an event organized by Michel Redolfi; Jean Claude Risset and Terry Riley in Nice played with David Rosenboom and Morton Subotnick in Los Angeles using

Disklaviers and a satellite connection [14]. In 1967, the late Maryanne Amacher conceived of and produced *City Links*, in Buffalo, NY. The 28-h performance took live microphone feeds from five different locations in the city. Victor Grauer and Max Neuhaus were involved in the Buffalo production and Neuhaus subsequently did similar work that came to be known as "telematic performance". The rapidly developing discipline of sonification [15] is equally useful when reflecting on the sound of virtual objects. In effect the different members of the research team have pursued these different lines of investigation over the past decades.

We should not however ignore early forays into audio-graphic creation an example being Ivan Chabanaud[1] and co-author Roland Cahen's *Icarus* [16]. When this virtual reality project was started in 1995, sound synchronization techniques where cumbersome: a Silicon graphics machine rendering visual objects was connected to *Opcode Max 3* (MIDI only) using an external MIDI expander and the IRCAM's spatialisation system. More recent audio-graphic projects that R. Cahen has been involved in include *BANDONEON* [17], *PHASE* [18], *ENIGMES* [19], and *TOPOPHONIE* [20].

Other recent research initiatives focusing on shared virtual environments such as *UDKOSC* [21] use the OSC protocol to associate external audio engines such as Pd or Supercollider with a virtual environment. Although the original version of NA followed this line of investigation we have switched to the using the audio engine incorporated in Unity for the sake of simplicity and versatility on the user side (see Sect. 6). *The Avatar Orchestra Metaverse*, formed in 2007, is another Interesting experimental project led by American Sound Artist, Pauline Oliveros: "*The Avatar Orchestra Metaverse* is a global collaboration of composers, artists and musicians that approaches the virtual reality platform Second Life as an instrument itself" [22]. However this approach is very different to that adopted for New Atlantis in the sense that it is dependent on the resources of the existing virtual world Second Life. Proteus by Ed Key and David Kanaga [23] is a rare example of a virtual world where the combination of low-resolution graphics and generative composition create an ever-evolving landscape/soundscape, offering a delicate interaction between the audio and visual components.

3.2 Fields of Investigation

Interactive Sound and Music with Virtual Objects

Audiographic design is a multimodal approach that consists of coordinating graphical form and behavior with auditory events in the design of virtual objects. These objects, although they are visual images, can incorporate physical simulation so they can interact with us and between themselves. While artists and designers often have a limited culture of multimodality, creating audiographic objects or compositions requires interconnections between various domains of expertise such as sound design, graphic design, 3D animation, real time interaction and coding. New Atlantis has been conceived to provide an adequate platform for this type of training. Designing

---

[1] Ivan Chabanaud, was a fascinating french digital artist who gave wings to his audience as they became icarus for the space of a visit. Our friend Ivan died the 4th September 2015.

multimodal interactions and implementing them in a virtual world is more complex than creating simple visual representations or video. It obliges the author to resolve more design issues and to give objects deeper consistency, bringing them close to a physical reality, even if they remain immaterial. At a certain point, the simulated object becomes the object in its own right and the notion of "virtual" is modified. Arguably, virtual objects are somehow non-material objects that incarnate their own reality. This has long been the case in music as well as with other abstract artistic activities, when an initial manipulation of representation ceases to be the finality.

Since the audiographic relationship is constructed, it can also be fictitious. An object's sound can be modified to become quite different from the "real life" original, while paradoxically appearing very real or possibly more than real (hyperreal). An early example of this phenomenon can be found in Jacques Tati's film *Mon Oncle* where "retouched" audio recordings focus attention unnaturally on specific banal visual objects [24]. We consider that this bending, schematizing or *detournement* of the relation between the visual object and its associated sound is a fruitful terrain for investigation. Virtual composition also allows us to interact with sound objects using a variety of expressive devices such as physical modeling, avatar form and behavior, fictional scenarios and gameplay, opening a multitude of new forms of narration.

We are currently developing new tools for New Atlantis in collaboration with FRE PRISM that will incorporate LMA's intuitive synthesizer control system. The system is based on a principal of control by metaphorical description of material qualities and physical actions. It is thus highly suitable for the creation of virtual objects in particular since the simulated object does not necessarily require a real-world model.

Spatialization, Sound Navigation and Virtual Acoustics

Sound navigation consists of browsing through different sound sources placed in a spatialized sound scene, thereby composing a musical form from the mix produced by movements relative to these sources. It is an artistic transposition of our sound experience in the physical world [25]. In virtual worlds, sounds are mainly spatialized through orientation and distance. The simple act of navigation allows us to create spatial mixes or canons as well as subject and object motion sequences. Spatial acoustics are another important part of our audio perception and indeed they participate in our natural audio interactions as we activate reverberant spaces through our own actions such as footsteps or vocalizations [26]. This praxeology [27] of sound space can also be developed in virtual environments and the juxtaposition of different acoustic responses as we navigate while generating sounds or listening to sounds generated by other players, provides an original approach to real-time audio signal processing. Short simple sound sources such as clicks or collision sounds can be used to activate and compare virtual acoustics and continuous sound sources can be multiplied to create complex harmonics. Such indeterminate forms of navigation, inspired by SoundWalking or other Soundscape related activities (see *The Tuning of the World* by Schafer [28]), are alternatives too more permanently authored audiographic forms.

3.3   A Synchronized Platform for Remote Music and Sound Art Practices

Networked Playing and Performance

In the case of NA "playing" may mean "gameplay" i.e. in general video games parlance "the specific way in which players interact with a game" [23], or it can equally be used to designate musical playing. In the preceding section, we approached NA as a compositional tool but it can also be considered as an audio "sandpit", as a shared instrument, or as a stage for public performances. The fact that these activities are synchronized online means that NA also opens a line of investigation into remotely shared musical and sound art practices. This in turn invites speculation as to the possibility of a creating a new paradigm in musical practice and distribution, a question that we wish to investigate in future research.

Networked music performances have existed since the beginning of the Internet and even before through the use of telephone and radio (see examples in Sect. 3.1). Until now however, such activities have, for the most part, focused on mixing networked (streamed, midi or OSC controlled sounds) with locally sounding instruments an example is Jean Claude Risset's use of the Disc Clavier, another is French musician Eric M's practice of using Locus Sonus' "open microphone" live audio streams [29] to introduce indeterminate sounds into his DJ sets. With NA however, the virtual sound space is distributed, and co-users share events, functions, triggers, controllers and audio recordings (made on the fly) through a dedicated server. The fact that all connected users share the "current state" of a space (see technical explications in Sect. 3) means that as long as an instance of a space is active, they experience the same evolving situation from wherever they are (within the limits of the network's capabilities). There is no distinction per se between musician and audience, this allows for inventive approaches to shared performance (for example, if one player introduces a sound source object or makes a recording, other players can hear it, move it or modify its parameters).

3.4   An Educational Tool

Locus Sonus [30] is a research unit based at ESA - Aix and funded by the French ministry for culture. Its main concern is practice-based research into sound art. Locus Sonus' research investigates virtual and acoustic sound space in a permanent exploration of "new auditoriums" [13]. ENSCI les Ateliers, have worked on numerous sound design projects including sounding objects, industrial sound design, audiography, sound spatialization, auditory interfaces but also sound art, electronic music, radio broadcasts, soundtracks for films, and various research projects [31]. The School of the Art Institute of Chicago's Art and Technology department teach virtual and augmented reality, gaming, 3d modeling, computer imaging, live performance audio and immersive audio [32]. Between them, these three structures provide the multidisciplinary expertise, creative and educational context that the NA project is founded on. The recent addition of the FRE PRISM as a new partner adds elements of fundamental research in the domain of digital audio to this rich consortium.

Teaching Sound in Art and Design Schools

Over the last 20 years sound education in France has progressively shifted from the *conservatoires* (music academies) to schools of art and design. The main reason for this is that, apart some rare exceptions, conservatoires were designed to teach solely classical music theory and instrumental practice and have therefore experienced difficulty in adapting to the challenges of XXth and XXIst century music and sound art production. As a consequence sound arts, sound design, some performing arts and sound for multimedia are now taught in many art and design schools including ENSCI and ESA-Aix. Most of the students concerned are consequently visual artists and rarely trained musicians. On the one hand this is a drawback, because they have a limited sonic culture, and on the other it is an advantage because they don't have preconceived models or cultural bias. Similarly, unlike traditional composers who arguably consider music as a result of relationships between pitch and rhythm, artists tend to use sound as material. Since their culture is primarily visual, these students have a tendency to create sounds in relation to images and to be concerned with multimedia and interaction.

Working and Creating Online in Virtual Workshops, Complementary Skills and Delocalized Working Groups

Creating and playing music together and by extension audiographic composition and performance are a great way to link people; this holds for artists, designers and students as well as the game audience. NA "bridges people with and through sound" since it is a group project within which participants with different skills and different degrees of expertise can come together and cooperate. Thus although the permanent team of NA is constituted of experienced developers, researchers, artists and teachers, this team has been completed from the outset of the project by successive generations of post graduate students. The architecture of NA has been designed in such a way as to encourage a variety of artistic approaches and methodologies, a creative participant can easily build a new and unique space (or level) however different propositions can also be easily combined into a single space. This method of creating content is gradually enlarging and enriching the scope of the project through a process of experimentation, feedback and exchange. On another level, as described above, creating content for the world is also be a challenging pedagogical exercise. Students are encouraged to work in teams pooling skill sets and sharing experience. The NA team is spread over several geographic locations, rather than this becoming a handicap it has turned into a fundamental characteristic of the project. NA is progressively becoming the place where we meet to work and remote collaboration is in the process of becoming second nature.

4 Architecture and Development

The particular aims of New Atlantis, described above, imply that certain decisions have been made regarding the architecture and other parameters of the world. To give some examples: the world needs to be shared online, it should be easy to use by a wide range of players (including those creating content) and audio performance – including synchronization between players – is paramount.

4.1   System Architecture

New Atlantis consists of three main software components:

The first is a MySQL database/PHP backend. The second is a standalone app (Mac OS X/Windows), named the Viewer, which allows the player to navigate the world, host multiplayer sessions, manage his account (spaces, assets…) and upload content. The third (optional) component is the SDK, which allows the advanced participant to build a viewer and to create components and contents using Unity3D authoring software (Fig. 2).

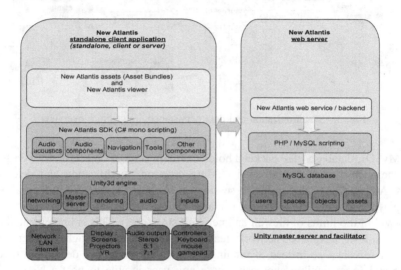

Fig. 2. System architecture overview

Entities and Related Concepts

A **Space** is an independent New Atlantis world. It is not necessarily related to the Bacon Sound Houses concept: several Sound Houses could exist in one Space, or one Sound House could be split in several Spaces. The absolute rule is that one Space is totally independent: nothing communicates with, exits to or enters from the outside.

An **Object** is a composite-audio-graphic-3d-interactive object created by a participant (designer/artist/developer) in Unity and uploaded to a Space in the form of an "Asset Bundle". Objects have qualities (in particular audio capabilities) and consist of a data packages with associated states. These include the updating position, orientation, and other related parameters in the currently activated space. When not in a space, an object is referred to as an **asset**.

A **player (user** or **visitor)** is a human user of the New Atlantis platform. The system holds parameters related to the players, such as email, login, password and a list of assets.

The **viewer** is the multi-purpose application that is the main tool a player has to use to visit and navigate a space.

4.2 Synchronization and Data Persistence

As a shared audio world, New Atlantis has stringent needs when it comes to synchronization since, as described above, we wish players to be able to play together musically. This requires that what each player hears on different connected computers is as close as is possible to the same thing (Fig. 3).

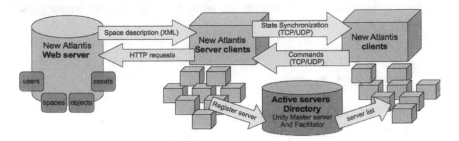

Fig. 3. Synchronization and data persistence architecture overview

A MySQL database/PHP backend holds the main state of objects and a web service allow the access to this database, including creation, modification and deleting of objects. Any player is able to host a session on his/her personal computer and accept other players running the same viewer application, from virtually anywhere in the world (within the limits of firewall and network structures). This is implemented using Unity's built-in advanced network features (NAT punchthrough, Master server, Facilitator server) – so instead of running a dedicated server, we decided to take this simpler and more flexible approach where any user is able to host a New Atlantis session with a chosen Space (this method is used by most multiplayer video games).

We have had to define and implement the way Unity's network system manages synchronization, when several players are connected together in a session. We decided to use an authoritative server scheme, meaning that the server runs the entire simulation and sends objects *states* to the clients that are running the scene without the logic (solely the rendering). The only exception to this is the avatar position, which is not sent by the server but generated by each client to guarantee good local fluidity (to avoid lag in the avatar's own position). The number of objects that need to be synchronized has a direct effect on performance and we tried several variations on "depths" of synchronization, from every single object to only a few main ones. There is inevitably a compromise that has to be made between performance and accuracy in simultaneity between clients (largely dependent on bandwidth). We should insist here on the special needs of working with sound: principally good temporal synchronization. To sum up, in the viewer application, two types of synchronization occur:

1. A synchronization of the objects contained in a given space: the viewer app connects to the web service and downloads an XML manifest (list) of all objects in the space with their initial state (position, orientation, name). Each object is an Asset Bundle that is then downloaded by the viewer and held in cache for future retrieval.

2. A client/server synchronization with Unity Network engine: synchronization of avatars positions, created objects, audio recorded during playing... The Unity Network engine implementation works with TCP/IP and UDP/IP messages sending with a proprietary format including synchronized parameters serialization. We have had to implement RPCs (Remote Procedure Calls) functions to handle special cases and audio-graphic synchronization.

4.3 Content Creation: Tradeoff Between Simplicity and Features

As described in Sect. 2, NA has several levels of usage. Technically, the system needs to be used by a wide range of players with skills that range between basic gaming and professional design and programming. Advanced players, such as students in workshops, can use the NA SDK package in Unity, while a player without such skills is still be able to run the viewer app and access the spaces without doing any programming. It should be mentioned that some of the students during the workshops and throughout the duration of project development have even programmed substantial improvements and add-ons to the platform.

We have identified the following users:

1. Simple player/visitor – visits and navigates a space.
2. Advanced player/visitor – creates spaces with existing assets.
3. Builder – builds new assets to be used and shared.
4. Core developer – creates new standard NA components.

Unity is used both as a content creation platform and as the game engine. This means that while it is tempting to allow the builder to use Unity's authoring tool with as few restrictions as possible, it is necessary to forbid practices that could lead to issues, such as bad synchronization or malfunctioning components.

The Need to Standardize Accepted Scripts

For security and design reasons, builder created scripts cannot be included in Asset Bundles. User-created Objects can reference existing scripts, but a new script (at the time of writing), needs to be included in the viewer to be available in the system. A workaround would be to build a .NET assembly using Mono Develop or Microsoft Visual Studio and use .NET reflection to make it available at runtime. However this is still in development and is not a perfect solution since it would also enable potentially unlimited access to scripting with the implied security problems.

Performance Considerations

Resources are a major concern when it comes to user-generated content: a player could potentially build a highly complex object that is too "greedy" with the resources of visiting computers (including video rendering performance, download time, CPU processing and memory). We have decided to manage this in two ways. Firstly, by defining "good practice" guidelines, these include: limiting the number of simultaneously playing sound sources; reducing the number of physical collisions and rigid bodies; reducing the size of audio clips; avoiding triggering too many audio sources too frequently; being careful with the use of custom DSP processing. In addition to these guidelines, we have limited the Asset Bundle upload size to a maximum of 7 MB.

The second approach is via the implementation of active optimization schemes, such as dynamic audio sources management as well as dynamic components (distant audio sources and objects in general are deactivated).

4.4   The Viewer App and the Standard Tools and Navigation

As we aim for high coherency between spaces and the player's experience, we decided to introduce some standard concepts.

1. Navigation: after a few early discussions and tests concerning a user-definable avatar and navigation system, we finally decided to provide a standard navigation system, that includes a few cameras and standard controls (with keyboard and mouse or with a dedicated gamepad).
2. Interactions and tools: we designed all interactions as "tools", that are selectable in the viewer by the player. A large number of these tools have been suggested many of which concern variations on modes of audio interaction (rubbing or dragging as well as simply colliding). At the time of writing roughly half of these ideas are implemented including sound-playing tools, an object thrower, physical interactions, flashlight, sunlight, trunk creation (audio recorder)...

Audio Components
We have built a library of audio components to be used on audiographic objects in New Atlantis, these include:

1. Audio synthesis: noise generation, oscillators, FM synthesis, loopers, wave terrain synthesis...
2. Audio triggering: play/stop an audio source based on specific events, such as a collision, a volume intersection (named a trigger), a threshold distance with the listener...
3. Audio parameter modulation: pitch, volume, panning...
4. Experimental audio filtering: implementation of Bacon's audio helps.
5. Audio recording: with content synchronization over the network (the "trunk").

   This list of audio components continues to augment with the ultimate intention of providing a comprehensive toolbox for DSP interaction and sound generation.

Other Standard Components
Because in New Atlantis designers can only use built-in scripts, it has also been necessary to provide a wide range of other standard components, including animations, visuals, move and rotate, teleport, GUI, particles triggering, physics...

4.5   Audio Spatialisation and Virtual Acoustics

A standard approach to audio spatialisation divides perception into three classes: the direct path, the early reflections and the late reverberation. As most 3D game engines today, Unity has a simple 3D audio sources management, which we used to spatialize an audio source's direct path. Unity also has a concept of Reverb zones with dedicated parameters (such as presets, level, reverb time…), but the Reverb effect is applied to the final mix and is triggered by the listener position – this means that by default, it is not possible to have sources in different spaces and have each source/space resonate independently since all sources are reverberated simultaneously. To compensate for this we have introduced the possibility for an Audio source to make its immediately surrounding space resonate (NAReverbEffector/Resonator) by using volume triggering, this allows us to have more complex shapes than standard Unity reverb zones (simple spherical volumes). This is a workaround since instead of the listener it is the audio source that is reverberated (we found this to be a better compromise) (Fig. 4).

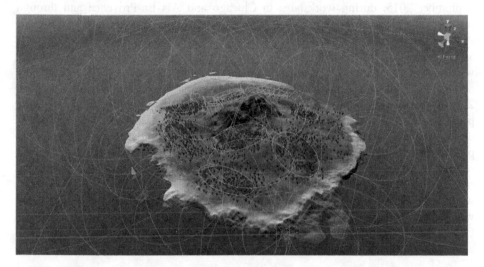

Fig. 4. New Atlantis space "Ljubljana Island" showing reverb zones.

First Reflections

We have conducted some experiments concerning first reflections, that consisted of sending rays in all directions around the audio source, determining which rays hit a colliders (corresponding to an audio reflecting surface in our approximation), and then calculating the distance source-to-collider and collider-to-listener to define the audio delay for this path. The audio delay for each ray is then introduced in a multitap delay System (a FIR (Finite Impulse Response) filter) and applied to the audio source (using C# OnAudioFilterRead() custom DSP code). Although still an approximation, this gave interesting results – a sense of scale, small spaces (with a short slap back echo) and big spaces (cliffs, canyons etc.). However at the time of writing we have not yet included this as a standard feature in NA.

Audio Sources Directivity and Roll-off

By default, the Unity audio engine does not provide management of audio source directivity. We have introduced the possibility to set a curve defining the source volume depending on the angle (similar to a polar diagram). Sound attenuation is implemented either by manual adjustment of roll off curves, where the builder defines how the sound attenuates over distance, or by using a physically accurate model for sound attenuation, (the well known inverse square distance law) where the builder simply defines the Sound Pressure Level at 1 m in dB (dB SPL).

5   First Results - Student Workshops Public Presentations

5.1   Period September 2014 - January 2016 Description and Method

New Atlantis design and development took place between September 2014 and September 2015, during workshops in Chicago and Aix-En-Provence and through regular online (skype) meetings. Subsequently a workshop was organized in ENSCI les Ateliers in Paris that included a group of 15 students and the whole team of researchers, artists from Aix, Chicago, Troy and Paris. Within a week, students who had never worked with either sound or 3D environments were able to create a set of audiographic objects. At this point we programmed the 2016 performance (see below). From October 2015 to January 2016 the team worked separately but connectedly to prepare this performance: in Paris, another group of 10 students created their own objects, helped to design graphic interface elements such as the avatar and prepared for the upcoming performance. At the same time a Masters student from ESA-Aix (Alex Amiel) was in residence in SAIC Chicago, helping to build the Chicago space, a group of Masters students were working in ESA-Aix to create the Aix space and Ben Chang was working in RPI-Troy to create his own space. From January 10 to 15 another workshop with a fresh group of students from design art and gaming schools took place at Le Cube. This time, the framework was more advanced and the group was able to work and produce results much faster.

5.2   Presentations January 16th 2016

For the performance on January 16th 2016 participants and audience were gathered in four different venues: Le Cube (Issy les Moulineaux, Paris France), the Vasarely Foundation (Aix en Provence), SAIC (Chicago) and Rensselaer Polytechnic Institute (Troy - New York state). The sound was played over 7.1 or 5.1 surround systems. As well as being connected via NewAtlantis the participants in different venues were connected via Skype during the performance and the audience was able listen to their commentaries and exchanges live. Five NA spaces were visited during the 80-min performance that started at 9 pm in Paris and 2 pm in Chicago. The audience reaction was enthusiastic and there was a positive reaction towards the prospect of continuing development.

6 Conclusions and Further Research

One of the aims of NA is to provide a platform for international academic, artistic, cultural and scientific exchange. In this sense the project has indeed succeeded in creating a robust bridge between the American and French research teams and students. The remaining challenge is for New Atlantis to become a real-time tool or platform for international artistic and musical collaboration. Hopes are high however since music and sound are after all internationally comprehensible. Possibly the most important step, that of making the app publicly available has yet to be made.

6.1 Game Architecture and Development

With the ultimate goal of making all things audio in NA (i.e. that all visual elements have an audio counterpart) the concept of *acoustic materials*, could allow us to define the way a 3D surface interact with incoming sound, with parameters such as absorption at several audio frequencies, audio diffusion and reflection. We intend to implement audio path-finding using Unity's ray casting capabilities – precisely calculating the contribution of each source to each space and applying a chain of audio effects based on the traversed space's characteristics. This was implemented in the previous Panda3D/Pd version of NA it now has to be ported to Unity. Other advanced topics will be addressed in the future, such as accurate sound occlusion (possibly using ray casting between the source and the listener), and more advanced audio spatialization algorithms with the Unity Spatialization SDK. It is our intention to incorporate audio streaming capabilities into NA permitting the real time inclusion "real world" captured sounds. This would enable a voice object for example whereby a visitor could detach his or her voice (from navigation) and use it to make a distant space resound.

6.2 Integration of and Intuitive Synthesizer

Locus Sonus has recently joined with the audio group of the CNRS Laboratory LMA, now FRE PRISM with a program (accord cadre) funded by MCC (Ministry for Culture and Communication) and CNRS (Centre Nationale pour la Recherche Scientifique). In this context it is planned to integrate the LMA's research into intuitive synthesizer interaction. In effect this synthesizer that is controlled by "semantic descriptions of sound events" [33, 34], including non-existent ones, would appear to be an ideal solution for audio graphic experimentation in NA.

6.3 Interface and Graphic Design

Before releasing a public version of the New Atlantis app in is necessary to improve the ergonomics of the user interface. The design process is programmed and we hope to achieve this goal within the coming months (Fig. 5).

Fig. 5. New Atlantis performance synchronized between: Le Cube, Vasarely Foundation, SAIC and RPI. January 2015. Photo: Le Cube.

7 New Atlantis Team 2016

Coordination
Peter Sinclair (Locus Sonus - ESAAix), Peter Gena (SAIC), Roland Cahen (ENSCI).

Development
Jonathan Tanant (JonLab): lead developer and software architect, Components developement: Alexandre Amiel (ESAAix).

Faculty/Research
Mark Anderson (3d Graphics SAIC), Robb Drinkwater (Audio programming SAIC), Michael Fox (3d GraphicsSAIC), Jerome Joy (Audio Locus Sonus).
     Ben Chang (Programming, 3d Graphics).

Students
Daan De Lange, Théo Paolo, Alexandre Amiel, Antoine Langlois (ESAAix) Adrien Giordana, Luca Notafrancesco, Marion Talou, Dorian Roussel, Valentin Moebs, Anaïs Maurette de Castro, Thomas Signollet, Oscar Gillet, Juliette Gueganton, Mathilde Miossec, Gamzar Lee, David Guinot, Paul Barret, Gaëtan Marchand, Aristide Hersant, Louis Fabre, Blanche Garnier, Lucas Dubosque, Alexandra Radulescu.

Organization
Anne Roquigny (Locus Sonus), Julie Karsenty (ESAAix).

Partners
Locus Sonus ESAAix Ecole supérieure d'art d'Aix-en-Provence.
   ENSCI Les Ateliers, Rensaler Polytechnic Institute, Troy, School of the art Institute of Chicago, Chicago USA.

Previous Participants
Ricardo Garcia, Gonzague Defos de Rau, Margarita Benitez, Anne Laforet, Jerome Abel, Eddie Breitweiser, Sébastien Vacherand.

References

1. Bacon, F.: The New Atlantis. No publisher given, United Kingdom (1628)
2. French-Americain Cultural Exchange. http://face-foundation.org/index.html. Accessed June 2017
3. Second Life official. http://secondlife.com/. Accessed June 2017
4. Pure Data – Pd community. https://puredata.info/. Accessed June 2017
5. LS-SL Seconde Nature. http://www.secondenature.org/LS-SL-LOCUS-SONUS-IN-SECOND-LIFE.html. Accessed June 2017
6. Panda3D – Free 3D game Engine. https://www.panda3d.org/. Accessed June 2017
7. NA version1. http://locusonus.org/w/?page=New+Atlantis. Accessed June 2017
8. LaForet, A.: New Atlantis, un monde virtuel sonore. In: Locus Sonus 10 ans d'expérimentation en art sonore. Le Mot et Le Reste, Marseille (2015)
9. Unity Game Engine. https://unity3d.com/. Accessed June 2017
10. AudioGaming. http://www.audiogaming.net/game-sound-design. Accessed June 2017
11. UPIC. https://en.wikipedia.org/wiki/UPICÒ. Accessed June 2017
12. Cage, J.: Fontana Mix. Peters, New York, no. EP 6712 (1960)
13. Sinclair, P., Joy, J.: Locus Sonus 10 ans d'expérimentation en art sonore. Le Mot et Le Reste, Marseille (2015)
14. Polymeneas-Liontiris, T., Loveday-Edwards, A.: The Disklavier in networked music performances In: ATINER, 4th Annual International Conference on Visual and Performing Arts 3–6 June 2013, Athens, Greece (2013)
15. Sinclair, P.: Sonification: what where how why artistic practice relating sonification to environments. AI Soc. **27**(2), 173–175 (2012). Springer
16. Installation Icare de Ivan Chabanaud. http://www.musicvideoart.heure-exquise.org/video.php?id=2151 Accessed June 2017
17. Bandoneon. http://roland.cahen.pagesperso-orange.fr/bandoneon/Bandoneon.htm, http://www.edit-revue.com/?Article=200. Accessed June 2017
18. Cahen, R., Rodet, X., Lambert, J.-P.: Sound navigation in phase installation: producing music as performing a game using haptic feedback. In: Subsol, G. (ed.) ICVS 2005. LNCS, vol. 3805, pp. 41–50. Springer, Heidelberg (2005). doi:10.1007/11590361_5
19. ENIGMES. http://projetenigmes.free.fr/wiki/index.php?title=Accueil. Accessed June 2017
20. Topophonie. http://www.topophonie.com. Accessed June 2017
21. UDKOSC. https://ccrma.stanford.edu/wiki/UDKOSC. Accessed June 2017
22. Avatar Orchestra Metaverse. http://avatarorchestra.blogspot.fr/. Accessed June 2017
23. (Between 22 and 23) Ed Key, Kanaga, D.: Proteus – A game by Twisted Trees. http://twistedtreegames.com/proteus/. Accessed June 2017
24. Tati, J.: Composing in Sound and Image. https://www.criterion.com/current/posts/3337-jacques-tati-composing-in-sound-and-image. Accessed June 2017

25. Cahen, R., Rodet, X., Lambert, J.P.: Virtual Storytelling: Using Virtual Reality Technologies for Storytelling: Third International Conference, ICVS 2005, Strasbourg, France, 30 November–2 December 2005. Springer, Heidelberg (2005)

26. Sinclair, P.: Inside Zeno's Arrow: Mobile Captation and Sonification Audio Mobility, vol. 9, no. 2 (2015). http://wi.mobilities.ca/

27. Thibaud, J.P.: Towards a praxiology of sound environment. Sensory Studies - Sensorial Investigations, pp. 1–7 (2010)

28. Schafer, R.M.: The Tuning Of The World. Alfred Knopf, New York (1977)

29. Locus Sonus Sound Map. http://locusonus.org/soundmap/051/. Accessed June 2017

30. Locus Sonus. http://locusonus.org. Accessed June 2017

31. Cahen, R.: Teaching Sound-Design @ENSCI les Ateliers. In: Proceedings from the Virtuous Circle – Cumulus Conference, Milan, Italy (2015)

32. SAIC. http://www.saic.edu/academics/departments/ats/. Accessed June 2017

33. Conan, S., Thoret, E., Aramaki, M., Derrien, O., Gondre, C., Kronland-Martinet, R., Ystad, S.: An intuitive synthesizer of continuous interaction sounds: rubbing, scratching and rolling. Comput. Music J. **38**(4), 24–37 (2014). doi:10.1162/COMJ_a_00266

34. Pruvost, L., Scherrer, B., Aramaki, M., Ystad, S., Kronland-Martinet, R.: Perception-based interactive sound synthesis of morphing solids' interactions. In: Proceedings of the SIGGRAPH Asia 2015, Kobe, Japan, 2–5 November 2015

Estilhaço 1 and 2: Conversations Between Sound and Image in the Context of a Solo Percussion Concert

Fernando Rocha[1,2]([⊠]) and Eli Stine[2]

[1] Federal University of Minas Gerais (UFMG), Av. Antônio Carlos, 6627,
Pampulha, Belo Horizonte, MG 31270-901, Brazil
fernandorocha@ufmg.br
[2] McIntire Department of Music, University of Virginia (UVA),
112 Cabell Dr, Charlottesville, VA 22904, USA
ems5te@virginia.edu

Abstract. This paper discusses the pieces *Estilhaço 1 and 2*, for percussion, live electronics, and interactive video. The conception of the pieces (including artistic goal and metaphor used), the context in which they were created, their formal structures and their relationship, the technologies used to create both their audio and visual components, and the relationships between the sound and corresponding images are discussed.

Keywords: Interactive music · Interactive video · Percussion music · Visual music · Hyper-instruments · Hyper-kalimba

1 Introduction

Estilhaço 1 and 2 were created as part of a project undertaken by percussionist and composer Fernando Rocha called: 'The concert as a work of art: A holistic approach to the creation and performance of a full length solo percussion concert'. The goal of this project was to create a full-length concert for solo percussion and electronics which includes video and other interactive technologies. The concert was conceived as an integrated performance, one which includes individual pieces but which is presented as a connected whole. The project will contribute to an auto-ethnographic study considering how we program contemporary music and how we can consider the trajectory of a concert as a whole, rather than simply putting a series of pieces together. *Estilhaço 1 and 2* were written by Rocha to open and close this concert.

Estilhaço 1 and 2 are two related works that can be presented as individual pieces or as a set (preferably with one or more pieces in between them). Despite their very different sound palettes, the two pieces are conceptually quite similar. They both explore the idea of creating long resonances from short notes and extracting short notes from long resonances. The forms of the two pieces are generated by exploring and combining these two layers of sounds (short and long). The electronic part provides a structure over which the performer is free to improvise. Estilhaço 1 also exploits the melodic potential of the kalimba. The two works dialogue with videos created by Eli Stine. In the first, the video is created in real time, following the performer's sounds and gestures. In the second, the same video is projected and used as a guide for

© Springer International Publishing AG 2017
M. Aramaki et al. (Eds.): CMMR 2016, LNCS 10525, pp. 247–255, 2017.
DOI: 10.1007/978-3-319-67738-5_15

the performer's improvisation. Thus the two works play with the relationships between image and sound. (Program note written by Fernando Rocha for the premiere of the pieces on Feb 5th, 2016).

The name 'estilhaço' (originally in Portuguese) means fragment, splinter, or shard. It relates to the process of breaking the long metal resonances into sharp fragments in *Estilhaço 2*. Similar processes also occur in *Estilhaço 1*. Both pieces use custom made patches in Max. The video component of the pieces utilizes Jitter and Processing. In this paper we will present how the pieces were conceived and explain some details of their audio and video components. We will also discuss how the relationship between sound and video was explored.

2   The Audio Element and Formal Structure of *Estilhaço 1* and *2*

The main compositional idea in both pieces was to explore the dichotomy between long and short sounds; we extended the instruments' capabilities to create, in real time, extremely long resonances as well as short attacks and complex, dense rhythmic structures. *Estilhaço 2* was composed first, and its instrumentation asks for triangles, crotales, bells and gongs (or other metals of long resonances). The objective here was to shift the attention of the audience from the natural, long resonances of the instrument to dense structures, created by a series of short attacks. Formally, the idea was to create a kind of ABA' structure, beginning with a sparse, soft and relaxed texture, moving gradually to a section of greater density, volume, and tension, and then going back to another relaxed structure, somewhat modified from the beginning as a reflex of the natural trajectory of the piece.

In terms of technology, all the processes used in the piece were created by recording samples (from 90 ms to 450 ms, depending on the effect to be achieved) after every instrumental attack detected by the system. This made it possible to create a system with no need to touch the computer during the performance. As stated by violinist and electronic music performer Mari Kimura, "in order to convey to the audience that using a computer is just one of many means to create music, I wanted to appear to use the computer as seamlessly as possible on stage" [4]. The 'bonk ~' object [5] was used to detect attacks. After an attack is detected, a gate closes for 300 ms and no new attack can be detected during this time. A sequence of effects is built into the patch, and each attack sends a sample to a corresponding effect according to this sequence.

There are six types of effects (each one with 6 to 8 variations), all based on different ways of playing back the recorded samples. The first effect is created by looping three versions of the sample with cross fades, thus creating smooth resonances. Effects 2 to 4 create resonances that are less and less smooth, until they are heard as a series of attacks. This is accomplished first by using imperfect cross fades, and then by using amplitude modulation. Effects 5 and 6 are created with shorter samples (90 to 150 ms) that are not looped, with envelopes that make the attacks very clear. Each sample is played using different random rhythmic lines at different tempi, and some of the samples are played at different speeds, resulting in variations of length and pitch.

The sequence of these events in the patch guarantees the formal structure of the piece. They correspond to three sections: (A) a long and gradual crescendo in volume, density and complexity beginning with natural sounds and then adding artificial resonances that are increasingly modified as the piece moves on; (B) a climactic section in which all the different effects occur at the same time. A complex texture is created by using many short samples with sharp attacks; (A') a gradual decrescendo, moving back to the original state, while keeping some elements of the climax (specifically, two layers with short and articulated sounds from effect 6).

The performer is free to improvise during the piece without necessarily altering the larger structure. This illustrates another layer of dichotomy in the piece: the action of the performer versus the result of the system. For example, the performer can continue playing only long notes throughout the piece, but even in this case the climax section (between 1/2 and 3/4 of the length of the piece) will create a busy, complex texture that is full of short attacks. However, there are ways to interfere with the opening and closing crescendo and decrescendo. In the first sections of the piece, the system creates only long resonances without generating any rhythmic structure. But if two attacks are played with an interval of less than 300 ms, the second one will be recorded into the buffer created by the first one. Thus the loop of this sample will create a texture full of short attacks instead of one stable resonance.

Estilhaço 2 also uses a surround system in order to better engage the audience and to highlight each of its multiple rhythmical lines. While most of the samples recorded are sent only to one or two speakers, the samples that are played at different speeds from the original move around the audience. This is particularly effective when two very long resonances are played midway through the piece. At this moment, one of the resonances is slowly pitch shifted to a major third below, while the other goes to a tritone below. Each of these two processes takes about 20 s, during which the sounds circle around the audience. This is a very noticeable effect that helps to mark the beginning of the climax section of the piece.

Estilhaço 1 was composed for hyper-kalimba, a thumb piano extended by the use of sensors[1]. While the piece similarly explores the dichotomy of long vs. short sounds, it also highlights another contrast: noise vs. melody. The kalimba is traditionally a melodic and harmonic instrument. In this piece its sound palette was expanded in order to create a dialogue between the melodic aspect and noisier, less harmonic sounds (in both the acoustic and the electronic domains).

For the performance of *Estilhaço 1*, a new mapping for the hyper-kalimba was created. This mapping kept some features explored in earlier pieces for the instrument, such as pitch shift (controlled by a combination of tilt and applying pressure to the right

---

[1] The hyper-kalimba was created by Fernando Rocha with the technical assistance of Joseph Malloch and the support of the IDMIL ("Input Devices and Music Interaction Laboratory"), directed by Prof. Marcelo Wanderley at McGill University. It consists of a kalimba (a traditional African thumb piano) augmented by the use of sensors (two pressures sensors, three-axis accelerometer and 2 digital buttons) which control various parameters of the sound processing. An Arduino Mini microcontroller board 2 was used for sensor data acquisition and data were communicated to the computer over USB. The instrument has been used in concerts since October 2007, both in improvisational contexts and in written pieces [6].

pressure sensor), while adding new possibilities. Two of the new features are essential for the piece, since they help to explore the two dichotomies (long vs. short notes and melodic vs. noisy sounds); (1) the possibility of creating artificial resonances of the acoustic sounds; (2) the transformation of the traditional 'melodic' sounds of the instrument into 'noisy' and unpredictable sounds.

In order to prolong the sounds of the kalimba a modified version of an object called 'voz1' (created by Sérgio Freire and used in his piece, *Anamorfoses*) was used [3]. As in *Estilhaço 2*, this object creates artificial resonances by recording a fragment of the natural resonance and playing it back in three loops, mixed with crossfades. In this mapping, pressing the right button attached to the instrument opens or closes a gate which allows for the recording of the excerpts. When this gate is open, each attack detected by the 'bonk ~' object is recorded into a buffer, and the new resonance is played. To avoid recording and reproducing part of the attack of the sound, the recording begins 100 ms after the attack is detected. As in *Estilhaço 2*, the performer can also create 'dirty' buffers (by playing two consecutive attacks with a short interval between them: the second attack will be recorded into the buffer created for the resonance of the first one). By using the left pressure sensor, the performer is able to cut the artificial resonances into shorter fragments that are played randomly in different speakers of the system at different tempi.

To be able to change the characteristic, melodic sound of the kalimba, the granular synthesis object 'munger1 ~' was used [1]. There are two ways of turning on or off the munger effect: turning the instrument upside down or shaking it vigorously for a few seconds. Shaking stimulates a more dramatic change, since it also adds some distortion to the sound.

Compared to *Estilhaço 2*, the form of this piece was expanded in order to leave room for melodic exploration and transformations with pitch shift. However, one could still consider the form of the piece to be ABA', where A correspond to sections 1 and 2, B to 3 and 4; and A' (or C) to 5 and 6 (Fig. 1). The following is a brief description of the material explored in the six sections of *Estilhaço 1*.

1. Exploration of natural noisy sounds of the instrument (scratching and hitting) and artificial 'noisy' sounds created by the munger1 ~ object (high pitched overtones).
2. Exploration of melodies played in the original range of the instrument. At the same time a layer of long resonances of the noise from the first section are chopped into shorter and shorter envelopes until they disappear, and a new layer of long resonances of notes is created, generating a harmonic background texture.
3. Dramatic change in texture using the munger1 ~ object with a preset that allows for great variation of grains and pitch.
4. The munger effect is turned off, but the performer explores the pitch shift feature of the mapping, generating a wide variation of pitch around the sounds produced.
5. The munger effect comes back with a preset that showcases high overtones, similar to the first section of the piece.
6. A dramatic gesture of shaking followed by a punching gesture, then placing the kalimba upside down, triggers the last part of the piece. This consists of two layers made by long and short sounds, similar to the last part of *Estilhaço 2*. One layer is created with the munger1 ~ object, which continues to process the last sound

produced and generates different fragments that contrast in terms of length, separation, and pitch. Long, artificial resonances of high-pitched notes which are recorded into the buffers in the previous section create a second layer of sound; both layers fade out to the end.

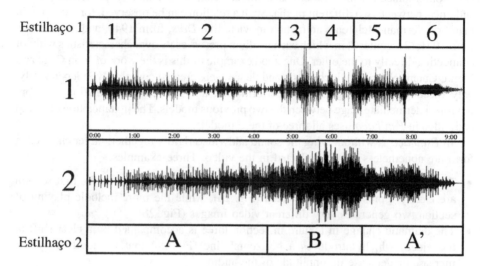

Fig. 1. Representation of overall stereo waveforms of *Estilhaço 1* (top waveforms) and 2 (bottom) with corresponding formal sections.

3   The Video Element of *Estilhaço 1* and *2*

The video component of *Estilhaço* utilizes Cycling 74's Jitter and the Processing programming language. The system is as follows: data from the Max patch that is being used to process the sounds of the hyper-kalimba and also data extracted from the audio analysis are sent via OSC messages (over UDP) either remotely (using two laptops) or locally (from program to program) to a Jitter patch, which parses the data and sends it to Processing (again over UDP). The data is used to affect a program in Processing (a flocking simulation) whose frames are sent *back* to Jitter using the Syphon framework. The video is then processed inside Jitter (applying colors, background videos, etc.) and displayed on a projector beside the performer.

   In order to create the video for *Estilhaço 2* one can either record the video created during the performance of *Estilhaço 1* and play it back for the final piece, or record the data from the hyper-kalimba during the performance of *Estilhaço 1* and play it back through the system for the final piece. Due to randomization the latter method will reproduce the exact timings of gestures of the first piece, but not the exact same visual gestures.

   Lastly, in the creation of the video component a parallel was made between the dichotomy of the accompanying acoustic instruments being manipulated through digital means and the use of a completely synthesized, animated image (the flocking algorithm) being combined with real-world video recordings.

4 Connecting Audio and Video in a Collaborative Project

Nicholas Cook describes a multimedia work as "a distinctive combination of similarity and difference" [2]. He goes further to identify three models of multimedia interaction: (1) 'conformance', which describes a direct relationship, clearly perceived by the audience, between two different media. Such a relation can be observed, for example, in many of Norman Mclaren's animation movies, like *Dots*, from 1940, and *Synchromy*, from 1971; (2) 'contest', in which each medium preserves its own characteristics without connecting directly to the other. One good example of this is the work of John Cage and Merce Cunningham, in which music and dance were created completely independently, only meeting on the stage for the performance; and (3) 'complementation', a more flexible, intermediate stage between the two previous models. The juxtaposition of sound and video in *Estilhaço* uses all three of these models.

In *Estilhaço 1*, without tying the sound and video rigidly together, larger changes in form are nonetheless clearly reflected in the video. Three examples:

- The noisy sounds produced by short high overtone grains used in the first section are clearly represented in the video (Fig. 2a), while the more melodic playing of section two generates very different video images (Fig. 2b).
- The dramatic change in texture in section three is accompanied by a clear shift in the video, which introduces a horizontal line (Fig. 2c) that is modified by the increase or decrease in amplitude of the audio.
- One of the sound layers of section six is a series of sound fragments produced by granular synthesis. The video mirrors the change in these fragments, increasing in brightness to follow the increase in amplitude, and finally fading out together with the audio.

2a   2b   2c

Fig. 2. Images of the video of *Estilhaço* in (a) section 1; (b) section 2; (c) section 3

The 'complementation' model is presented in two variants: (1) Images may be mapped from the sound avoiding a one-to-one relation (thus one not necessarily perceived by the audience); or (2) the algorithm for the video includes some random component (again the relation is not necessarily perceived by the audience).

In *Estilhaço 2*, the sounds of the performance originally do not interfere with the video, and so for much of the piece the music and video happen simultaneously without connecting to one another (like the 'contest' model). However, the performer can choose to read the video as a 'score' to guide improvisation. For example, different images can influence the choice of timbre. In my performances, the lower gongs (which have a distinct timbre compared to the others used in the piece) are only used when the image of a horizontal line appears in the video, creating a noticeable shift in the sound world of the piece. The performer may also choose to mimic the sudden appearance of new images in the video with musical attacks.

Since there are similarities in the musical form of the two pieces (as described earlier) it is not surprising that an examination of their waveforms shows parallels between them (Fig. 1). In both pieces there is a climax section between 4 min 45 s and 6 min 50 s and a clear fade-out after 7 min 40 s. However, the opening sections are more distinct. In *Estilhaço 2*, we hear a very gradual crescendo from the beginning to the climax (section A), while *Estilhaço 1* includes more variations. Since the video used for *Estilhaço 2* is created by the performance of *Estilhaço 1*, there is a disconnect between the music and the video in the opening of the second piece that did not exist in the opening of the first (at this moment *Estilhaço 2* asks for sparse, soft attacks, whereas the video created by *Estilhaço 1* reflects its more active texture). After the premiere, we re-discussed this issue and decided to find a way to better connect the music and the video of the section. Our solution was to map the first 18 attacks of *Estilhaço 2* to the video, so that each attack would change the contrast of the video and generate a flash effect, as if the video had been turned on and off again. These flashes become progressively longer, so that by the last of the 18 attacks the contrast is back to normal and the video is fully "on".

The presentation of the same video in a different sonic context (in *Estilhaço 2*) asks the audience to directly engage with their memory and to re-contextualize both the video and the sonic gestures that are being presented alongside it. A work of visual art that was generated by the sounds of the hyper-kalimba is torn away from that setting and placed in the context of very resonant metal instruments. This provokes the audience to make connections between the video and the hyper-kalimba gestures, the video and its relationship to the gestures of *Estilhaço 2*, and then between the structures of *Estilhaço 1* and *Estilhaço 2*.

It is also interesting to note that the use of the same video helps to give a form to the concert as a whole, one which follows the main structure of each Estilhaço: A B A', where A is Estilhaço 1 with the video, B are the other pieces included in the program and A' is Estilhaço 2 with the same video created by the first piece.

5   Final Considerations and Future Work

Estilhaço is the result of a collaboration between performer/composer Fernando Rocha and video artist/composer Eli Stine. The piece was conceived for a specific concert, one which included both electronic and acoustic elements, and which was designed to hold together as an artistic whole. It was important to us that the system we created served an aesthetic, musical purpose, supporting the overall performance. The fact that the system created for the pieces does not require the performer to touch the computer during the performance aids to make the computer more invisible to the audience, becoming 'just one of many means to create music' [4].

The piece's relation to the context of the concert influenced some ideas used in its composition; for example, the overall structure of the concert mirrored the form of the two versions of *Estilhaço* (ABA'). The compositional process was guided by a very clear idea about musical materials and the trajectory of the piece's form—one which is indicated by its name, which means "fragment" or "shard". "Estilhaço" is a metaphor for the process of breaking the long, metallic resonances of the opening into small, sharp fragments[2]. *Estilhaço 2*, conceived first, uses this process to explore a dichotomy between short and long notes. Following a quiet, calm opening section, there is an increase in density, dynamic, and complexity, building tension and leading to a climax; then the piece gradually returns to a more 'relaxed' texture.

The video element of the piece not only helps to engage the audience but also adds another layer of interest and drama to the works. It opens up an exploration of the possible relationships between music and video (another dichotomy), since, while the two pieces use the same video, they have very distinct sonic palettes.

Estilhaço was premiered on Feb. 5th, 2016, and it has been performed in four other concerts since then (updated in Dec. 15, 2016). After the premiere, a few details related to the audio/video connection were edited, such as the addition of an interactive aspect at the beginning of the video of *Estilhaco 2*, as described in Sect. 4 of this paper. As a future goal, the authors intend to make the video even more intimately tied to what's going on in the hyper-kalimba patch. The work has also inspired us to consider other ways in which video (and repeated viewings of the same/similar videos) can be used in the concert format, and to research other possible hyper-instruments for the control of video systems.

Currently the authors have been working on a new project: a real-time video element for the performance of *Starboard*[3], an instrument made of wood, nails, springs, strings, a piezo-contact microphone, and light sensors. The first performance of *Starboard* to include the video element took place at CMMR 2016; it is an ongoing project with more performances scheduled for 2017. In the work, video is projected onto the instrument itself, creating a unified visual spectacle that encompasses both the movements of the performer and the reactive video projection. The video is mapped to a circular shape and projected directly onto a circular wooden board that is mounted on the back of the instrument (Fig. 3).

---

[2] As stated by Wessel and Wright, in the creation of interactive works, "metaphors for control are central to our research agenda" [7].

[3] *"Starboard* (2016) is a collaboration between Fernando Rocha and instrument creator/multimedia artist Peter Bussigel. Sensors hidden within the instrument allow for the creation of two different textures… one dense and messy, like a cloud of sounds, and the other dancing and rhythmic. Moving in and out of time with sounds that may or may not return, creating at some point a feeling of groove that is ready to dissolve, Starboard is an instrument for navigating between the promise of the computer and the truth of nails sticking out of a board." (Program note written by Fernando Rocha for the performance of the piece on July 5th, 2016 at CMMR).

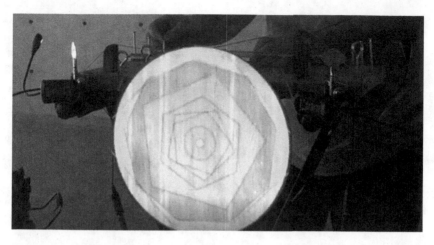

Fig. 3. Image of *Starboard* performance.

Acknowledgements. Project undertaken with the support of the Brazilian federal agency CAPES (Coordenação de Aperfeiçoamento de Pessoal de Nível Superior).

References

1. Bukvic, I.I., Kim, J.-S., Trueman, D., Grill, T.: Munger1 ˜: towards a cross-platform Swiss-army knife of real-time granular synthesis. In: Proceedings of the International Computer Music Conference. International Computer Music Association, Copenhagen (2007)
2. Cook, N.: Analysing Musical Multimedia. Oxford University Press, Oxford (1998)
3. Freire, S.: Anamorfoses (2007) para Percussão e Eletrônica ao Vivo. In: Revista do III Seminário Música Ciência e Tecnologia, pp. 98–108, São Paulo (2008)
4. Kimura, M.: Creative process and performance practice of interactive computer music: a performer's tale. Organ. Sound **8**(03), 289–296 (2003). Cambridge University Press
5. Puckette, M., Apel, T., Zicarelli, D.: Real-time audio analysis tools for Pd and MSP. In: Proceedings of the International Computer Music Conference, pp. 109–112. International Computer Music Association, San Francisco (1998)
6. Rocha, F., Malloch, J.: The hyper-kalimba: developing an augmented instrument from a performer's perspective. In: Proceedings of 6th Sound and Music Computing Conference, pp. 25–29, Porto - Portugal (2009)
7. Wessel, D., Wright, M.: Problems and prospects for intimate musical control of computers. Comput. Music J. **26**(3), 11–22 (2002)

Interactive Music Production

The Qualities of the Perceived Sound Forms: A Morphological Approach to Timbre Composition

Danilo Rossetti[1,2(✉)]

[1] Institute of Arts, University of Campinas, Campinas, Brazil
danilo_rossetti@hotmail.com
[2] MUSIDANSE/CICM Université Paris 8 Vincennes-Saint-Denis,
Saint-Denis, France

Abstract. In this article, we present and discuss timbre and sound morphology in live electroacoustic and instrumental music from a compositional standpoint. We approach interaction and convergence issues in live electroacoustic music, related to the idea of sound morphology, based on the undulatory and granular sound paradigms. In instrumental composition, we analyze instrumental synthesis based on frequency modulation so as to generate pitches and enable timbre interpolation. Timbre fusion is also addressed, based on concepts of jitter, permeability and timbre of movement (*Bewegungsfarbe*). For these purposes, some examples of our compositions are addressed to illustrate these sound properties. In order to analyze the generated timbres, we apply time-varying audio descriptors to reveal some characteristics of the generated timbres. We conclude by comparing the analyzed operations with the emerging form of these works considering both the micro and macro temporal aspects. This article is an extended version of the paper "Interaction, Convergence and Instrumental Synthesis in Live Electronic Music", presented on the 12th CMMR.

Keywords: Timbre composition and perception · Live electroacoustic music · Interaction and convergence · Instrumental synthesis · Timbre fusion

1 Introduction and Contextualization

The act of composing has always been an art which deals with the articulation of sound objects in time. During different periods, different techniques were applied to produce this articulation. Among these techniques, we mention the more general ones, such as harmony, rhythm, counterpoint and orchestration. In the 20th century, when technical objects from radio studios started to be used in experimental composition (i.e. the advent of concrete and electronic music), the internal universe of sound could be accessed. In this sense, the act of composing music involved dealing with microtime operations (linked to time scales under the limit of the note). This concerns, for example, the manipulation of frequency partials or grains, in addition to the traditional composition techniques. Through this changing paradigm, a number of questions emerged from this practice. In the music of our time, how can forms be constructed and articulated with other forms? How can one think and analyze this process with the aid of computing environments?

© Springer International Publishing AG 2017
M. Aramaki et al. (Eds.): CMMR 2016, LNCS 10525, pp. 259–283, 2017.
DOI: 10.1007/978-3-319-67738-5_16

When one thinks about live electroacoustic[1] music, one of the first problems that arises is the interaction between the instrumental acoustic and electroacoustic parts of a work. That means to imagine how to make these two sound sources merge together and sound as a unity of form, as one single timbre. This interaction can be analyzed by considering several aspects related to electronic treatments.

At least two time conceptions are considerably important in the field of electroacoustic music combined with acoustic instruments: deferred time and live electronics [2]. In deferred time compositions, the electroacoustic part is previously composed in studio and then fixed in a support (generally known as tape). This modality is usually assigned to the first experiments with instruments and electronic sounds—as verified in the works *Musica su due dimensioni* (1952), by Bruno Maderna, for flute, plates and tape, and *Kontakte*[2] (1958-60), for piano, percussion and tape, by Karlheinz Stokhausen—although even today works with these characteristics continue to be composed. During the performance of electroacoustic tape music, interpreters of acoustic instruments must follow the tempo and the events of the electroacoustic part. The result is that less space for interpretative nuances is predicted.

Another possibility is live electronics or live electroacoustic music, in which there is a more prominent interaction between acoustic instruments and electroacoustic sounds. In this modality, instrumental sounds are captured by a microphone and treated by electroacoustic processes during the performance and, at the same time, the resultant electroacoustic sound is diffused. The instrumental sounds can also be recorded in a support (a buffer) during the performance for subsequent electroacoustic diffusion. Because of this intrinsic connection between these two universes, in live electroacoustic music, musicians have more temporal liberty in their interpretation, also interfering in the resultant electroacoustic sounds. Real-time systems are sensitive to external information (instrumental sounds) and interact by producing sound morphologies that are dependent upon the kind of the interpreter's performance.

Live electroacoustic music (live electronics) emerged in the 1960s as we can see in works such as *Mixtur* (1964), for orchestra, and *Mantra* (1970) for two pianos, crotales and woodblocks, both by Stockhausen, in which the instrumental sounds are manipulated live by ring modulators. The appearance of *Ircam*, in 1977, also contributed to the development of live electronics possibilities. These new implementations can be seen in works of composers such as Pierre Boulez, Jonathan Harvey, Emmanuel Nunes, Philippe Manoury, and Horacio Vaggione, among others who passed through this institute.

It is worth mentioning the question about multichannel spatialization of the generated sounds. One possibility is to conceive them as punctual sources that perform trajectories in the acoustic field, one of the first implemented spatialization techniques in multichannel works. Another possibility is to imagine the diffusion space as sound immersive. For this purpose, we can use ambisonic tools of spatialization. Ambisonics [3] is an ensemble of synthesis techniques, recording and reproducing sound fields,

---

[1] We adopt the term electroacoustic as the convergence of both concrete and electronic music into one practice [1].

[2] *Kontakte*, in addition to the mixed version, has an acousmatic version for tape solo.

which surround the listener, based on the decomposition of the acoustic field in spherical harmonics, similar to sound decomposition in frequency partials. This acoustic field corresponds to a sphere where the center is the listener. In the case of electroacoustic music, ambisonics offers spatial treatments such as rotation and translation of sound fields as well as the synthesis of diffused sound fields.

Next, interaction aspects from the sound morphology standpoint will be addressed. The word interaction is defined as a kind of action that occurs as two or more objects have an effect one upon another, where the idea of a two-way effect is essential, as opposed to a one-way casual effect. Another characteristic is that interaction systems lead to the idea of emergent phenomena. In this sense, the acoustic sound generated by different instrumental techniques can be combined with the chosen electronic treatments. In compositional processes, it is possible to converge acoustic sounds and electronic treatments in relation to similar sound models. Convergence, in turn, can be thought as the act of converging and the motion toward union or uniformity, the independent development of similar characters often associated with similarity of environment, and the merging of distinct technologies or devices in a unified whole. As a result, we expect that this idea of convergence will amplify the instrumental possibilities, thus generating new sonorities to be diffused.

Our sound morphology view is based on composition and sound analysis considering both the undulatory (continuous) and granular (discontinuous) paradigms of sound, which will be discussed later. This approach is slightly different from the notions proposed by Schaeffer [4], Smalley [5] and Menezes [6], which are based on a sound object *solfège,* a listening typology (auditory description), or an interaction morphology. Our approach is mainly focused on the compositional process, which can be a live electronics process, seeking to converge the instrumental and electronic parts, or an instrumental composition process, seeking, in a metaphorical way, to transfer a number of properties of electroacoustic treatments to instrumental writing.

We do not think of the undulatory and granular models as the only possibilities to build instrumental and electronic timbres, nor as dialectically opposed. Rather, we think about these two models as complementary, i.e. as a tool that can guide us in processes of timbre fusion. Concerning these paradigms of sounds, we will analyze a few examples (scores and sonograms) from our live electronics works *Oceanos* [7], for alto sax, and *Poussières cosmiques* (2014–15), for piano.

The electronic part of the analyzed works is conceived in Max, working with objects of HOA (High Order Ambisonics) Library, developed by the *CICM* (*Centre de recherche Informatique et Création Musicale*) of *Université* Paris 8. By using the *hoa. process* ~ object of this library, and choosing a mono source file as input (pre-recorded or captured live with a microphone), we can address treatments such as reverb, delay, granulation, ring modulation, microtemporal decorrelation and convolution, combining them with an ambisonic multichannel spatialization. More specifically, this paper will discuss ring modulation, granulation and microtemporal decorrelation examples.

We assume that technicality is related to live electroacoustic music from these two standpoints: the construction of computing environments and the technique related to musical instruments *lutherie*. As an epistemological reference for this universe, we mention the second part of Gibert Simondon's doctoral thesis *Du mode d'éxistence des objets techniques*[8]. For Simondon, a high degree of technical development is achieved not from automation, but from the existence of a margin, which permits the machines to be sensitive to external information (keeping an interface). In these "open" machines, man would be the interpreter and organizer of the processes, having a coordination and invention function in these systems. In this regard, there is an analogy between the mode of existence of the concretized technical objects (which are established due to their well-defined internal architecture) and the living organisms, which are stable and viable. As Simondon states, machine and society developments occur in the sense of naturalization of their structures and not in the sense of humanizing nature.

Regarding sound forms, we bring the concept of enaction attributed to Francisco Varela [9], to enact, to give the conditions to the emergence of a form. This concept arises from the criticism of the idea of representationalism, and is based on the statement that nothing in the world is preconceived. Considering baroque, classical, romantic and even some works of modern music, form is predefined in a certain manner, if we refer to sonatas, suites, concertos, symphonies, etc. Obviously, a symphony by Mozart has different characteristics from a Beethoven symphony, in the same way that both differ from a Mahler symphony. However, from an analytical standpoint, the same structural elements can be found in all those symphonies.

On the other hand, in live electroacoustic music, for instance, we assume that form is constructed during the processes of composition and interpretation of the works, and is variable in certain aspects considering each performance. In an enaction model, the perceptible whole (perceived form) cannot be decomposed in the totality of its parts. This configures an emergent process based on open systems, in which their microstructures connect and interfere with each other from the organized internal networks. Since we focus on the processes of composition and interpretation of live electroacoustic music and timbre fusion processes in instrumental works, we can also refer to the allagmatic method of Simondon [10], a theory of operations, a study and analysis of the processes and dynamic transformations, which lead to individuated forms.

We will also analyze Gérard Grisey's concept of instrumental synthesis [11], which is closely connected with the works of spectral composers from the 1970s. Generally, in acoustic or live electroacoustic music, instrumental synthesis would be the simulation of electronic compositional procedures in instrumental composition. In the examples that will be presented, frequency modulation synthesis [12] will be addressed in the instrumental context. Our analysis also includes the use of irrational numbers as indexes of modulation, to generate new inharmonic spectra and timbres. Such examples concern compositional procedures of our work *Diatomées* (2015), for instrumental ensemble and live electronics.

Timbre fusion, which, in our view, is also an allagmatic process [13], occurs when different structures in perception merge into a single timbre. This process will be firstly approached from an acoustic standpoint, mentioning the existence of jitter, the fluctuations in frequency that occur in the sustained part of the instrumental sounds [14, 15]. We will also approach timbre fusion from the compositional experience, mentioning György Ligeti's concepts of permeability and timbre of movement [16]. Aiming to illustrate these concepts linked to timbre fusion and focusing on the transference of some procedures from electroacoustic to instrumental music, we will present other examples of our works *Diatomées* and *Le Vide: Trois Réflexions sur le Temps* (2015), for four soloist voices and instrumental ensemble. Finally, we will analyze the timbres produced by instrumental combinations with the aid of parametric audio descriptors. These descriptors provide numeric data which allow us to understand and interpret the perceptual characteristics of the generated timbres.

Our final considerations will address the interaction and convergence in live electroacoustic music, including the interaction produced between micro and macro events so that musical form is generated. In addition, we will discuss the result of the instrumental synthesis processes applied to our compositions, the achievement of timbre fusion, and the characteristics of the generated timbres as per the further proposed definitions.

2 Undulatory and Granular Paradigms of Sound

The undulatory paradigm is related to continuous structures, considering that the sound pitch is defined relatively to the sustained part of the sound envelope. In the 19th century, modern psychoacoustics was structured having, on the one hand, the research of Hermann Von Helmholtz and Georg Simon Ohm and, on the other hand, the research of August Seebeck. Helmholtz [17] presented an undulatory model based on the Fourier series. Fourier's theorem states that any form of regular and periodic vibration can be considered as the addition of single pendular vibrations whose durations are once, twice, three, four (etc.) times longer than the frequency of the referred movement (the fundamental frequency), also differing from each other in phase. Likewise, when the human ear perceives a sound, it performs a real-time spectral analysis where the lowest partial defines the pitch. Each single partial would be perceived by a determined nerve ending, which means that different pitches excite different nerve endings. Ohm's Acoustic Law, also adopted by Helmholtz, states that every movement of the air, corresponding to a specific mass of air, can be decomposed into a sum of simple pendular vibrations. The ear perceives these simple vibrations and their pitch depends on the duration of the correspondent vibration.

In 1841, based on his experiments with a siren sound, Seebeck did not observe the existence of the phenomena described in Ohm's Acoustic Law. Nevertheless, he observed the presence of another phenomenon, a "periodicity pitch", in sounds formed by a superposition of partials. The periodicity pitch means that even when the fundamental frequency of a given sound is missing, we can still perceive it as having the same pitch. Seebeck concluded that not only does the fundamental frequency determine the sound pitch, but also the upper partials [18]. As this law states, pitch perception is the result of a harmonic fusion of periodic partials into a single sound.

Jan Frederik Schouten, in 1940, while working on his concept of residual pitch [19], corroborated Seebeck's conclusions concerning the periodicity pitch. According to Schouten, Ohm's Law is only valid for the lower partials of a sound with periodic oscillations. Higher partials are perceived as an amalgam, in a single unity called residue, whose pitch is identical to the fundamental frequency. Thus, the ear does not perform a spectral analysis of a sound to discover its qualities, but perceives it from the fusion of the periodic partials (the fundamental frequency and upper partials). In fact, only a minority of the lower partials is perceived separately.

In the 1950s, Werner Meyer-Eppler [20] conducted research, observing the triple pitch quality and the presence of an effect called "formant pitch". Considering the triple pitch quality, the first is its absolute pitch, running parallel to the frequency; the second is the chroma, a quality which recurs cyclically within each octave (for frequencies of up to 4.500 Hz); the third is the residual pitch. If, in a residual pitch experiment, the continuous "mutilated" note (without the fundamental) is interrupted for approximately one second, the sensation is completely altered. Instead of the "residual tone", we hear a new pitch which lies in the region of the strongest remaining partials. This new perceived structure is the formant pitch.

In the 1970s, Ernst Terhardt [21] carried out research defining the terms "virtual pitch" (which corresponds to Seebeck's periodicity pitch and to his synthetic mode) and "spectral pitch" (which corresponds to Helmholtz and Ohm's analytical mode). The pitch of a single oscillation would be a spectral pitch, while the pitch of a complex sound (formed by a sum of partials) would be a virtual pitch. Related to these categories, there are two perception modes: the analytic mode, resulting in a spectral pitch, and the synthetic mode, resulting in a virtual pitch. Virtual pitch is considered as an attribute of an auditory perception based on *Gestalt*, since we perceive a contour, even when it is not present (as in the case of the missing fundamental frequency).

The granular paradigm is associated with discontinuity having Gabor's acoustic quanta theory [22] as basis, whose heritage is the wave-corpuscle duality of quantum physics. Gabor conceived a sound description method that combines two other methods normally employed for this purpose: time-function description of sound and Fourier frequency analysis. The first method operates from well-defined time instants while the second method operates from sequences of infinite waves, which have well-defined frequencies. According to Gabor, the Fourier method carries an internal contradiction once the term "frequency", in a mathematical sense, only refers to sequences of infinite waves. In fact, this is not the case of the sounds we hear, which have finite durations.

Gabor presented the hypothesis that a sound is composed of innumerous quanta of information, which are described from time and frequency variables. His hypothesis is defined by analogy with the corpuscular theory of light, which states that a stream of light is formed by a continuous, granular texture. Under this approach, the information theory posits that the acoustic signal can be divided into cells, with each cell transmitting one datum of information. Any acoustic signal can be divided into cells, and the whole of this representation corresponds to the totality of the audible area, in terms of time and frequency.

Iannis Xenakis, inspired by Gabor's theory, developed a granular theory in music domain [23] as a part of his Markovian stochastic music. According to Xenakis's stochastic music theory, traditional musical notions such as harmony and counterpoint are not applied. They were replaced by notions such as frequency densities (considering a given period of time), grain durations, and sound clouds. In the second chapter of *Musiques Formelles* (1962), Xenakis presented a hypothesis about the nature of sound. Every sound is an integration of grains, which are elementary sound particles, sound quanta. These grains have a threefold nature: duration, frequency and intensity. Every sound, every sound variation (even the continuous ones) is conceived as an assemblage of numerous elemental grains, disposed in terms of frequencies and durations.

It is important to emphasize that, in our opinion, there is a paradox between the granular sound theory and compositions with a granular sonority. The main characteristics of the granular theory were addressed in the paragraph above and are related to both stochastic music and Xenakis's criticism to serialism. Xenakis's first composition applying the granular method was *Analogique A & B* (1958–59). It is interesting to notice that this work does not have an overall granular sonority. On the other hand, *Concret PH* (1958), a *musique concrète* work from this composer based on recordings of burning coals and developed on the *Groupe de Recherches Musicales*, has a remarkable granular sonority.

In our compositional process discussed next, we assume that the most important variables related to the granular paradigm are mainly based on temporal structures (e.g. grain size, grain delay and feedback, cloud density) and linked to ideas of time and rhythm, which can be synchronous or asynchronous. The undulatory paradigm, nonetheless, is mainly connected with the frequency universe, since its most important variables control frequency values such as the organization of partials in a certain sound. However, this does not mean that there are no frequency variables related to the granular paradigm (we can define, for instance, the frequency band of a sound cloud) or that there are no temporal definitions concerning the undulatory paradigm (for instance, we can define the duration of each partial of a sound).

3   Interaction and Convergence in Live Electroacoustic Music

Here we will present some examples of our pieces *Oceanos* and *Poussières cosmiques* considering ideas of interaction and convergence, based on the undulatory and granular paradigms of sound. In both works, instrumental sounds are captured by microphone and processed in real time in Max patches (electronic treatments and spatialization) running objects from HOA Library.

3.1   Undulatory Paradigm

In the first example, we address a fragment of the piece *Oceanos* (2014), for alto sax and live electronics. Figure 1 shows a multiphonic played by the saxophonist[3], which is combined with the electronic treatment known as ring modulation [24]. This combination between instrumental writing and the chosen electronic processes is conceived to achieve a morphologic interaction between these two means. The multiphonic has a spectral configuration represented by a superposition of partials above a fundamental frequency. The ring modulation is an electronic process based on the interaction of two sound waves (carrier and modulation frequencies). The result of this operation is the generation of new frequencies whose values are the sum and the subtraction of the carrier and modulation frequencies.

---

[3] In this recording, the piece was performed by José de Carvalho.

In our example, the carrier frequency is the sound of the saxophone (captured by the microphone), while the modulation frequency is set at 13.36 Hz. This value corresponds, in terms of octaves, to the G three quarters of tone higher, which is the multiphonic basis pitch[4]. In ring modulation, when modulation frequencies under 20 Hz are used (the lower limit of audible frequencies in humans), we perceive a rhythmic effect known as *tremolo*, due to the produced amplitude modulation. This rhythmic perception is equivalent to 13.36 oscillations per second. Below, in Fig. 1, we can observe the score and sonogram of said fragment of the piece. In the score, we have the multiphonic writing including the produced pitches; in the sonogram (performed on *AudioSculpt*) we can observe the time and frequency distribution of the resulting sound (instrumental sound and its electronic modulation).

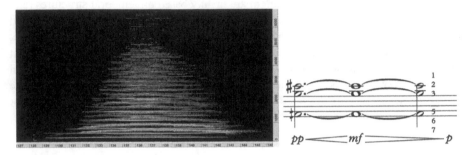

Fig. 1. Combination of a multiphonic with a ring modulation process (sonogram and score)

In our second example concerning the undulatory paradigm, the third part of our work *Poussières cosmiques* (measures 61–72)[5] is addressed. In this example the pianistic writing is mainly based on chords which are perceived as color and timbre. These chords do not have a harmonic directionality as it occurs in tonal music. However, we adopted as a strategy for their construction the superposition of dissonant intervals. Although there is no harmonic directionality in this part, other kinds of directionalities can be found. Among them, we mention the register change, which moves from low to high, and the dynamics differences, which evolve from *piano* (*p*) to *fortississimo* (*fff*) in this passage. These directionalities are not exactly linear but in an overall scope they are perceptive evolutions. In measure 68, we can observe a metric modulation. The tempo changes from a quarter note equal to 75 to 94. In fact, there is an equivalency between these two tempi. A five against four triplet in a tempo of 75 is equivalent to a tempo of 94. This metric writing is located in measure 67, anticipating this metric modulation to the pianist.

In the electroacoustic part of this example, we also use ring modulation, combined to delay lines. The sound of the piano is considered as the carrier wave, while the values of the modulating wave are stipulated under 20 Hz, as in the former example.

---

[4] Transposed score.

[5] Performed by Alexandre Zamith (live recording).

The delay time does not exceed 240 ms and feedback rates do not exceed 0.35. The converging sonority that emerges from the interaction between instrumental and electroacoustic parts is the presence of a "shadow" in the acoustic attack and resonance of the piano (due to the delay utilization) as well as the addition of frequencies in the spectral envelope of the modulated sounds (due to ring modulation). In this discussed part of the work, there are three electroacoustic presets that control the operating values of the electronic treatments: 3.4, measures 61 and 62, 3.5, measures 64 to 68, and 3.6, measures 70 to 72. The numeric values of these variables are gradually interpolated in time. These interpolations occur in measure 63 (3.4 to 3.5) and measure 69 (3.5 to 3.6). The score and the sonogram of this part are shown below, in Fig. 2.

Fig. 2. Combination of piano chords with ring modulation and delay processes (score and sonogram)

3.2   Granular Paradigm

The first example of granular paradigm intends to show an idea of interaction and convergence between instrumental writing and electronic treatments in our work

Poussières cosmiques[6] considering the granular model of sound. Figure 3 shows in the piano writing that the pitches are concentered in the extremely high register (measures eight to eleven). Sixteenth notes with slightly different rhythms are written for both hands so as to produce minimal temporal offsets between the two voices. The tempo, in this passage, starts with a quarter note equal to 48 and goes up to 90. As we can notice, the left-hand rhythm is maintained constant with sixteenth notes whereas the right hand executes rhythmic variations such as 5:4, 6:4, 7:4, 9:8, 11:8 and 13:8.

The minimal temporal variations between these two voices produce an asynchronous perception in listening, similar to granular synthesis processes (with larger grains compared with the grains of an electronic granular synthesis). In convergence with this pianistic writing, we addressed microtemporal decorrelation and delay as treatments to create a diffused sound field. This procedure emphasizes the generation of a granular and discontinuous resulting sonority. In the sonogram below, we can observe some characteristics of the granular paradigm such as the presence of a sound mass whose density evolves in time. Considering the global perception, this granular mass is fused with the pitches played by the pianist.

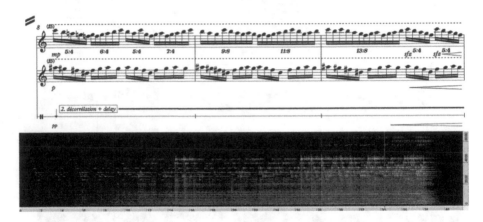

Fig. 3. Sonogram and *Poussières cosmiques score* (measures 8 to 11)

The microtemporal decorrelation [25] is an electronic treatment similar to the delay which generates microtemporal offsets in space and time between the produced audio tracks, which are diffused in a multichannel system. Through these minimal offsets, and depending on the sound phase (considering a 360° plan), changes on the spatial perception can be produced, creating a diffused sound field. Taking an ambisonic diffusion space into consideration, microtemporal decorrelation is one of the techniques of diffused field synthesis. In order to promote the interaction of acoustic and electroacoustic sounds, we converge the granular writing of the piano with electronic treatments such as the microtemporal decorrelation and the delay. This operation results in an amplification (in terms of quantity of information in space and time) of the morphologic qualities found in the piano sound.

---

[6] Performed by Sophia Vaillant (live recording).

In the second example concerning the granular paradigm, we address the final part of our work *Oceanos*[7] [6] (p. 7). Here, we intend to develop an interaction between the instrumental writing emphasizing saxophone techniques that produce granular sonorities (such as *frullato*, *tremolo*, slap tongue, *staccato*, and trills) and the granulation electroacoustic process. Among these instrumental techniques, we can have fast variations in near pitches (trills) or an addition of noise to the played pitch (*frullato*). Slap tongue and *staccato* produce very short sonorities with almost no resonance, emphasizing the attack transients of the played notes. Another applied variation mode in the score is the presence of discontinuous figures with different speeds (*accelerando* and *rallentando*). In Fig. 4 we show the score and the sonogram of this part of *Oceanos*.

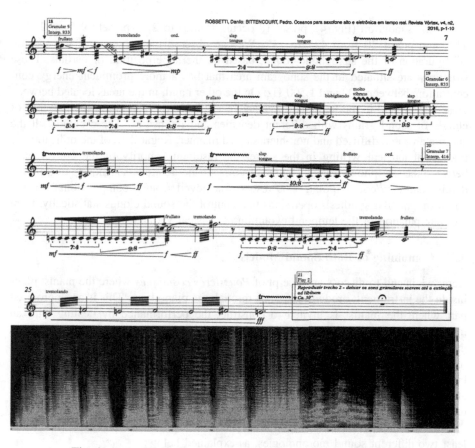

Fig. 4. Score [6] (p. 7) and sonogram of the final part of *Oceanos*

---

[7] Performed by Pedro Bittencourt (studio recording).

The electroacoustic treatment, converging to the proposed saxophone writing, is the granulation. In the addressed part of the score, three presets were assigned to control the following granular synthesis variables: grain size, delay time, feedback and rarefaction rate. These variables are associated to the HOA object *hoa.syn.grain ~*. Considering the three presets of this part of the piece (18 to 20), the grain size changes from 80 to 30 ms, the delay time evolves from 1 to 3 s, the feedback rate remains stable on 0.95, and the rarefaction rate changes from 0.5 to 0.8. It is necessary to explain that on the *hoa.syn.grain ~* object, the rarefaction rate, whose values are distributed between 0 and 1, indicates the increasing of discontinuity in the perceived electroacoustic sound. Value 0 means total continuity while value 1 indicates total silence. As a manner to equilibrate the resultant sonority, if we want to obtain a more discontinuous sound, it is interesting to have more elevated values of delay time and feedback rates.

In the sonogram (Fig. 4), preset 18 occurs from 0 to 27", preset 19 from 29" to 41", and preset 20 from 42" to 73". We can observe the presence of the spectral configuration of the saxophone sound, based on the superposition of partials. These structures are situated in the sonogram area that has a more prominent energy concentration, between 200 and 1,500 Hz. On the other hand, in the areas located between these partials and in the frequency area above 1,500 Hz, we can notice the presence of clouds of sound grains with different densities and intensities. These clouds fill the audible area in a diffused and non-hierarchized manner. Regardless of the utilization of traditional musical writing in the score, the resultant sonority of the convergence between the saxophone sounds and the electroacoustic treatments stands apart from the duality harmony/counterpoint. This result is achieved from a compositional process based on granular synthesis operations that control the sound clouds statistically, from the manipulation of the temporal evolution of musical variables.

3.3   Combining of Both Sound Models

Here, we intend to discuss an excerpt of *Poussières cosmiques* where the pianist plays inside the instrument, producing sounds through the piano harp. This is an improvised part where the pianist is invited to construct the performance by dealing with an instruction to produce different sound morphologies and, at the same time, interact with the electroacoustic response. This part lasts approximately one minute and these are the instructions presented in the score: "slightly hit the wood and piano harp, from low to high register, making circular movements with the hands. Try to alternate between fast attack percussive sounds and slow attack more resonant sounds (for the latter sounds, use drumsticks)".

Our intention, considering these instructions, is to invite the pianist to produce at least two different sound morphologies, as explained below:

(1) Percussive sounds on the piano woods with prominent attack transients, and continuous circular hand movements on the low strings, seeking to produce "noisier" sounds with no defined pitches.

(2) More resonant sounds produced with drumsticks or fingers from the percussion of the strings, seeking to generate sounds with well-defined pitches. Although these are pitched sounds, their timbre is different from the traditional sound of piano notes, which are generated from the hammer mechanism of the piano.

The chosen electroacoustic treatment to modulate this improvised part is the granulation, which operates from three presets having different numeric variable values. In Fig. 5, we present the score and the sonogram of this excerpt. In the sonogram, we can visualize the sounds of the first categorization placed in the low frequency area, having more energy. Punctual sounds with harmonic spectra are related to the second category. We can observe the presence of these kinds of sounds in 14", 21", 30", 34", and 42". They have a considerable duration due to the granulation delay. We observe, as a result, that these two resultant sonorities are contrasting in terms of morphology. As to the first one, we can describe them in terms of continuity, density and energy, whereas in the second one, they are punctual sonorities that have a well-defined pitch.

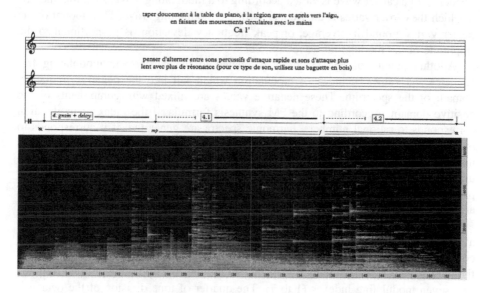

Fig. 5. Score and sonogram of the improvised part of *Poussières cosmiques*

4   Instrumental Synthesis and Timbre Interpolation

The definition of instrumental synthesis (*synthèse instrumentale*) can be found in the well-known text by Grisey [11] ("A propos the la synthèse instrumentale", 1979, 35–37). In relation to this concept, Grisey states that the advent of electroacoustic music enabled composers to explore and manipulate the morphology of sound in its interior, and then to manipulate the sound in different time scales (from microphonic to macrophonic).

According to Grisey, access to the microphonic universe is only possible through electronic or instrumental synthesis. The electronic synthesis is a microsynthesis because from its different techniques (additive synthesis, amplitude, ring or frequency modulation, etc.) we can generate the internal components (partials) of a resultant sound. Instrumental synthesis involves a modelization process where the instrument is used to play each internal component of an analyzed synthetic timbre. In this process, each partial of the analyzed sound is played as a pitch by a determined instrument. Consequently, a new series of partials is produced for each acoustically performed pitch.

In order to describe the instrumental synthesis process employed in our work *Diatomées*[8] (2015) for violin, bass clarinet, harp, percussion and live electronics, we address some considerations of frequency modulation synthesis, according to John Chowning [12]. Frequency modulation is a kind of modulation between two signals (a carrier and a modulating frequency) that produces spectral modifications in the generated timbre along its duration. As Chowning explains, "In FM, the instantaneous frequency of a carrier wave is varied according to a modulating wave, such that the rate at which the carrier varies is the frequency of the modulating wave. The amount of the carrier varies around its average, or peak frequency deviation, is proportional to the amplitude of the modulating wave" (p. 527).

Another quality of FM synthesis is related to the carrier and modulating frequencies and values of index of modulation which fall into the negative frequency domain of the spectrum. These negative values are mixed with components of the positive domain. According to the FM synthesis formula, if the index of modulation corresponds to rational numbers, harmonic spectra are generated, if it corresponds to irrational numbers, inharmonic spectra are generated. In our view, irrational values of indexes of modulation can generate very interesting timbres and constitute a huge universe to be explored. In *Diatomées*, we employed FM instrumental synthesis procedures from both rational and irrational values of indexes of modulation, which are described below.

In order to generate the main scale of the piece (used in A to C parts), we performed a FM instrumental synthesis from the interval between Bb4 (464 Hz) and A2 (110 Hz), considering the Bb4 as the carrier and the A2 as the modulating wave. The following figure (Fig. 6) shows the obtained frequencies (and the corresponding pitches) from the first seven modulating indexes (1 to 7). The quarter of tone division of the octave is employed. The arrows indicate slight deviations in the corresponding pitches (around one eighth of tone).

In the D part (last part of the work), the idea was to apply the concept of degree of changing (*degré de changement*) as proposed by Grisey [10] in his article "Structuration des timbres dans la musique instrumentale" (1991). This is a method to gradually interpolate different timbres in time. The pitches obtained in the first instrumental FM procedure are considered as having an index of modulation value of 1. We gradually distorted the original spectrum from the multiplication of its frequencies by irrational numbers such as $2^{1/5}$ (1.15), $2^{1/4}$ (1.25), $2^{1/2}$ (1.41) and $2^{4/5}$ (1.74). The

---

[8] Performed, in this recording, by the Ensemble *L'Itinéraire*.

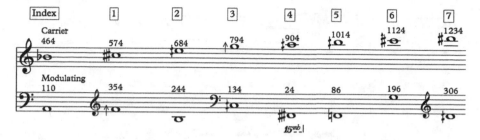

Fig. 6. Main *Diatomées* scale, generated by FM instrumental synthesis

new obtained spectra, shown in Fig. 7, are vertically organized and separated in semitones and quarters of tone to provide better visualization. The moment of timbre transition in the piece is highlighted by the presence of Thai gong notes. This transition also involves pitches from some precedent and posterior measures in order to achieve a gradual interpolation between timbres.

Fig. 7. New timbres obtained from gradual inharmonic distortions of the original spectrum

As an example of timbre interpolation, we present the interpolation between timbres generated by the multiplication factors 1.25 and 1.41, related to measures 82 to 84 of *Diatomées*'s score. Pitches A, D#, B and B@ (in measures 82 and 83) produced by the Thai gong announce new timbre arrival. They are related to factor 1.41. In Fig. 8 we highlight the sustained pitches and their correspondence with the involved modulation factors. The F one quarter tone higher played by the violin in measure 82, and later played by the bass clarinet in 83 belongs to factor 1.25. Also in measures 82 and 83, the *tremolo* E – D and its inversion to a major ninth (an octave higher), both played by the harp, also belong to this factor. In measure 83, the D played by the violin belongs to the 1.41 factor. In measure 84, all the sustained notes from the harp chord and the artificial harmonic of the violin (which has the C one quarter note higher as the base note) refer to the 1.41 factor. As we can notice, in measure 83 there are pitches from both modulation factors, constituting timbre interpolation.

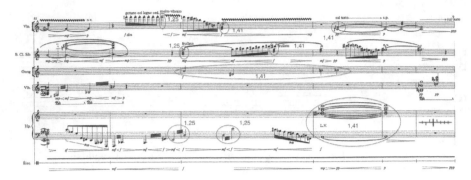

Fig. 8. Timbre interpolation between factors 1.25 and 1.41 of FM instrumental synthesis

5 Timbre Fusion

In this section, we discuss some features about timbre fusion, trying to illustrate these processes with examples of our compositional works. As we affirmed before, we consider timbre fusion as an allagmatic process. This means that we focus on operations that enable the fusion of different structures into single timbres. First, from an acoustic standpoint, timbre fusion by jitter will be discussed. Briefly, jitter is understood as the fluctuations or aperiodicities related to the sustained part of instrumental sounds. A difference between the notions of timbre and texture will also be proposed. In reference to the compositional praxis, we will discuss the concepts of permeability and timbre of movement (*Bewegungsfarbe*) by György Ligeti. These concepts came from this composer's experience with electronic music in the 1950s, influencing his latter approach to instrumental composition.

Finally, we will analyze timbre fusion results from two examples of our works *Diatomées* and *Le Vide: Trois Réflexions sur le Temps*. This analysis is based on a combination of parametric audio descriptors, such as loudness, fundamental frequency, harmonic energy, inharmonicity, noise energy and noisiness, from which we intend to identify a few features of the generated timbre structures.

5.1 Jitter

Jitter phenomenon is defined as the aperiodic fluctuations of the sustained part of instrumental sounds, being one of the important factors for the fusion of different structures into a single timbre. According to McAdams [15], timbre fusion by jitter occurs from a modulation frequency which gives coherence (from constant proportions) through the spectral components of a sound, and grouping them into a single perceptive auditory image. Different jitter waveforms can be extracted from musical sound sources, whether they be voices or instruments. Mentioning Dubnov, Tishby and Cohen [14], these instrumental sound fluctuations are related to microtemporal sound scales between 100 and 200 ms. Their control by the musicians is not possible. In fact, jitter is originated from the acoustical mechanism of the instruments, which enable sound production. Its presence is mainly noticed on brass, woodwinds and strings.

Meyer-Eppler [20], in the 1950s, had already noticed jitter presence in aleatoric modulation experiences, a kind of aperiodic modulating wave that operates simultaneously in frequency and amplitude. The aleatoric modulation, in electronic music context, would be the fusion factor for different sine waves into a single timbre. These aleatoric oscillations can be produced from the utilization of an aleatoric noisy signal (in frequency and amplitude) established in a frequency range from 10 to 100 Hz. This aleatoric oscillation would be a modulating wave that amalgamates other distinct waves, promoting frequency and amplitude modulations in them.

5.2 Permeability

Assuming that jitter is one important acoustic feature of timbre fusion, we now move on to the discussion of experimental compositional processes, which can provide timbre fusion. In his article "Évolution de la Forme Musicale" [16] (1958, French translation) Ligeti proposes the notion of permeability. This notion addresses the simultaneous development of two or more structures of different natures, and their possibility to impregnate or merge each other. Permeability can be investigated through an interpenetration study of different sound structures, forming heterogeneous layers. For instance, Ligeti performed this kind of interpenetration study in the composition of his electronic work *Artikulation* (1958). From this experiment, he concluded that the higher the number of the performed operations with the organized material, the higher the flatness degree of the generated sounds.

In this study, Ligeti aimed to interact sound materials with different aggregation states. This process was accomplished from sound morphologies that had different textural characteristics in their internal organization. This study allowed the composer to know which materials would merge and which ones would segregate in listening. As we observed from our own permeability studies, sounds with different morphologies have the tendency to merge each other. On the other hand, sounds with similar morphologies or closer spectral features, when developed simultaneously, tend to mask some of their low intensity structures. This masking phenomenon is linked to the idea of hearing saturation. When saturation level is attained, our ear cannot distinguish new sounds that are added to such combination.

As an application of the permeability notion in our compositional process, we approach the measures 75 to 80 of *Diatomées*. In this excerpt, we intend to discuss a timbre fusion process based on the complementarity of undulatory and granular structures developed together by superposition and juxtaposition. In reference to instrumental synthesis, we applied instrumental techniques that generate undulatory sonorities (morphologically organized from a superposition of partials) and techniques that produce granular sonorities. As we can see in Fig. 9, among the instrumental techniques related to undulatory paradigm, we mention the chords written for the harp, in which the sustained part is highlighted from the presence of their resonance. There is also the multiphonic assigned to the bass clarinet that results in five different superposed pitches, besides the vibraphone part where, from the pedal utilization, sound resonance is detached. We observed that the spectral fusion of the played pitches is promoted through jitter, occurring in the sustained resonances of the chords and single notes simultaneously performed.

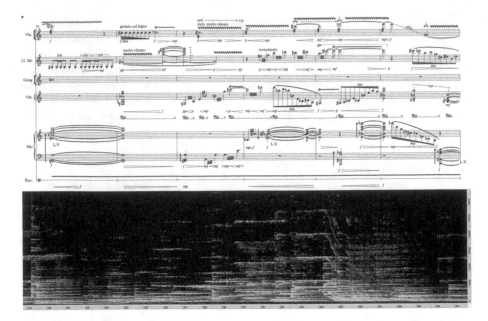

Fig. 9. Permeability and timbre fusion by complementarity of sound models in *Diatomées*

As instrumental granular sonorities, we mention the violin techniques of *gettato col legno*, bass clarinet *tremolo* and trills, and *staccato*. There is also the *écrasé* effect, which generates noisy sonorities from the overpressure of the violin string with the arch. This technique results in the addition of granular features to the violin sound, moving our perception to a sound mass sensation, mostly when the *écrasé* is combined with other granular techniques. Generally, this overpressure sonority is more pregnant in audition than the undulatory spectral characteristics related to the pitch of the played note.

An interesting instrumental technique to be discussed is the *tremolo* played by the violin, combined with the *molto vibrato* effect (measures 77 to 79), and the arch position varying from *ordinario* to *sul ponticello*. The *tremolo* produces a moderate granular sonority, which is emphasized by the *écrasé* presence. The *vibrato*, on the other hand, generates a kind of frequency modulation controlled by the speed movement of the player's finger that raises and lowers periodically the string. With the combination of these techniques, we obtain in a single instrument a granular sonority modulated by an undulatory effect.

Considering the permeability notion, this excerpt of *Diatomées* is considerably impermeable, due to the superposition of different structures that merge each other into one unique timbre. This fusion produces a spectrally dense timbre, from different morphologies that impregnate each other without masking their individual features. These individual morphologies have heterogeneous spectral characteristics that, once superposed, generate one unique aggregation state, a new timbre. An unstable equilibrium is achieved from the assemblage of different structures into one unique timbre, which is perceived as a single structure. In Fig. 9 we can see the score and the sonogram of this excerpt of *Diatomées*.

5.3   Timbre of Movement

Another experimental category that emerged from Ligeti's experience with electronic music was named timbre (or color) of movement (*Bewegungsfarbe*). In his article "Musique et Technique: Expériences Personnelles et Considérations Subjectives" [16] (1980, French translation) he states, based on information theory studies, that we are well able to distinguish individual sound events over 50 ms of duration (1/20 s). Faster events, on the other hand, merge each other in time. Analogous to images, if a film is registered with 16 frames per second, we can still perceive each frame individually. If it is recorded with more than 20 frames per second we start having the impression of a continuous movement of the image.

Timbre of movement notion was conceived during the time Ligeti assisted Gottfried Michael Koenig in his electronic composition *Essay* (1957–58). In this composition, Koenig wanted to manipulate sounds on the border between polyphony and melody fusion into a single timbre. In this work, there are moments when we distinguish pitches as melody lines or polyphony but when the number of melody lines rises considerably, going beyond the fusion (or saturation) limit, another sound quality emerges, denominated timbre of movement. In this operation, a rhythmic phenomenon such as a sound sequence that alternates in fast time intervals becomes one unique and constantly changing timbre phenomenon. More specifically, the sound objects are not anymore perceived as rhythmic movement but as a stationary event. The movement is transferred into the sound interior, through constant changes in its quality, like a polyphony that takes place inside the timbre. This technique was later applied to Ligeti's instrumental works such as *Apparitions* (1960) and *Atmosphères* (1961), earning the name of micropolyphony. In these works, a complex polyphony is constructed, overcoming the limit of event segregation in listening and resulting in a complex structure varying in time.

We intended to apply the timbre of movement notion in our work *Le Vide: Trois Réflexions sur le Temps*[9] for four soloist voices, flute, clarinet, tuba, percussion, viola, violoncello and double bass. Here, we present a spectrally dense part of this work, in which at some moments the saturation limit of listening is exceeded (measures 84 to 92, rehearsal mark E). In this excerpt there are several instrumental and vocal events with different techniques, contributing to the modulation of timbre evolution. The orchestration was conceived intending to emphasize these continuous transformations and instrumental interpolations.

In this section, in measure 84, we mention the *accelerando* of the ascending string figures, holding the metric of 9 against 8 triplets, in sixteenth notes. These figures result, in measures 85 and 86, in high notes and fast trills. Beginning in measure 85, this idea imitation is held by the vibraphone, finishing with a C#–E *tremolo*. The resonance of this phrase is sustained through the pedal until the end of measure 86. In this passage we perceive a timbre fusion of the string trills and the vibraphone *tremolo* and resonance. Over these instrumental undulatory figures, spoken voice figures are superposed, beginning in measure 86. The sentence *"le fil du temps est couvert de noeuds"*, synchronously spoken by the four voices without a defined pitch, produces a unique

---

[9] Performed by Soli Tutti Vocal Ensemble and Bobigny Conservatoire Contemporary Music Instrumental Ensemble, under the direction of Denis Gautheyrie.

sound with noisy spectral features. In measure 87, these voices become gradually ordinary sung notes, passing through *frullato* and returning to *ordinario*, in measure 88.

In measures 87 and 88, inasmuch as the voices turn into pitched notes, the vibraphone performs arpeggiated chords. Beginning in the third beat of measure 87, the strings play artificial harmonics in *molto vibrato* and *sul ponticello* techniques, alternating between *ordinario* and *tremolo* modes. In this section, we can perceive the fusion of vibraphone, voice and string sounds into a single timbre modulated by the employed extended instrumental techniques. Beginning in measure 89, flute, clarinet and vibraphone perform the same mentioned *accelerando* ascending figures, in imitation, resulting in sustained notes with trills and *frullato*. These effects in the woodwinds are sustained until measure 91, while the vibraphone resonance is maintained through the pedal, until measure 92. The voices, from measures 89 to 91, perform an alternation of *ordinario* pitched notes and *frullato*. The strings maintain the mentioned effects until 89, changing to *pizzicato* in 91 and 92. As an overall sound result of measures 89 to 92, we perceive a fusion of the produced structures of woodwinds, vibraphone, voices and strings that change morphologically in time. In Fig. 10 it is possible to see the score and the sonogram with the described events of this part of *Le Vide*.

Fig. 10. Score and sonogram of *Le Vide*, rehearsal mark E, measures 84 to 92

5.4   Timbre Fusion Evaluation

In this topic, we searched to construct a model for the analysis of timbre fusion, considering both compositional excerpts we came to present. This model, which is based on Peeters *et al.* [26], is formed by the following time-varying audio descriptors: loudness, fundamental frequency analysis, harmonic energy, inharmonicity, noise energy, and noisiness, which are defined below according to Peeters *et al.*, (*Op. Cit.*) and Fastl; Zwicker [27].

(1) Loudness belongs to the category of intensity sensations, which is variable in terms of frequency. The correspondence of loudness in terms of frequency and intensity is given through Fletcher and Munson curves.
(2) Fundamental frequency is estimated from digital algorithms.
(3) Harmonic energy is the energy of the signal explained by the harmonic partials. It is obtained by summing the energy of the partials detected at a specific time.
(4) Inharmonicity measures the departure of the frequencies of the partials from purely harmonic frequencies. It is estimated as the weighted sum of deviation of each individual partial from harmonicity.
(5) Noise energy is the energy of the signal not explained by harmonic partials, obtained through the subtraction of the harmonic energy from the total energy.
(6) Noisiness is the ratio of the noise energy to the total energy. High noisiness values indicate a signal that is mainly nonharmonic.

The choice of different audio descriptors illustrates our systemic approach to timbre, which is considered as a complex structure. The multiple characteristics of timbre cannot be described by few variables. They can, however, be revealed by the choice of determined descriptors that provide us with information we desire to analyze. We do not consider our model as one unique system because the descriptors were chosen from timbre fusion characteristics we wanted to emphasize. In further works and analyses, other types of descriptors can be implemented.

In our fusion timbre analysis model, we can see the correlation between some audio descriptors, such as loudness, harmonic energy and noise energy. On the other hand, descriptors such as harmonic energy and inharmonicity are opposite since they measure opposite features. The analysis of the presented excerpt of *Diatomées*, considering the mentioned audio descriptors is shown below in Fig. 11. They were performed by *Orchids* software.

Through the interpretation of the graphics, we highlight the following points. In the loudness graphic (which in overall view is similar to the noise energy graphic), we observe an energy peak in the beginning, relative to the attack of the B Thai gong, in measure 75. After this point, the intensity sensation returns into the low level, increasing gradually to new peak values, among which we mention values 9.7 (arpeggiated chord from the harp in measure 78) and 10.9, (F6 one quarter of tone higher, with *tremolo* and *écrasé* effects followed by a *glissando* within two octaves low, measures 79–80). We also notice the presence of an overall inharmonic timbre, comparing the inharmonicity and harmonic energy values. Despite its variation, there are inharmonic peaks such as 0.68 and 0.8, corresponding to the A5 *tremolo molto vibrato* and the mentioned F6 one quarter tone higher, both performed by the violin, in

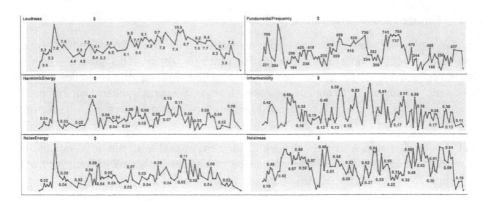

Fig. 11. Audio descriptor analysis of *Diatomées* excerpt

measures 78 and 79. Finally, the noisiness ratio has peaks throughout this excerpt, indicating the existence of a high degree of noise components in the generated timbre. We highlight the 0.86, 0.84 and 0.95 peak values, corresponding respectively to the beginning of measure 77 (several synchronous events), the mentioned F6 one quarter tone higher (measure 78) and F4 *molto vibrato écrasé*, both from the violin, in measure 80. On the other hand, the *tremolo* chord of the vibraphone, measure 76, has a noisiness value of 0.03, which is extremely low.

In Fig. 12, we can see the graphics for the audio descriptors of the analyzed excerpt of *Le Vide*. In this analysis, we can observe that the loudness, harmonic and noise energy graphics have similar developments in time, which means that these perceptive features are correlated. When the energy increases (be it harmonic or noise) we have the increase of loudness level perception, which is a global intensity perception measurement. The loudness values of 12.8 and 12.2 correspond to measures 85 and 86 (string and vibraphone trills, and spoken voices), while the values 13.4 and 13.8 correspond to measures 89 to 91 (flute and vibraphone trills, in addition to clarinet and voice on *frullati*). This latter part presents a higher level of harmonic and noise features.

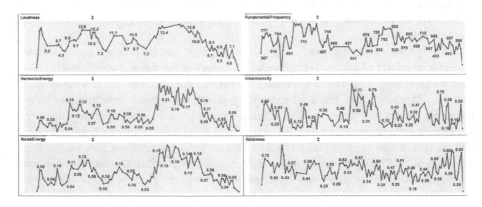

Fig. 12. Audio descriptor analysis of *Le Vide* excerpt

Upon comparing the harmonic level and inharmonicity, we notice that they are more equilibrated when compared to the former example. High harmonic features emerge between measures 89 and 91 (with peak values of 0.27 and 0.25). Inharmonicity is higher between measures 87, 88, and at the beginning of 89. In this part the strings are performing artificial harmonics in *tremolo molto vibrato sul ponticello*. Artificial harmonics produce high pitches (two octaves higher than the base note) that, when combined with these modulation effects, produce high inharmonic sonorities (values of 0.97 and 0.79). The same phenomenon appeared in the example of *Diatomées*. It indicates the correlation between high pitches in strings (modulated through different instrumental techniques) and a high degree of inharmonicity. Finally, the noisiness descriptor has an overall constant value, close to 0.6, with the exception of a few peaks. The first peak appears at the end of measure 84, with a value of 0.97, due to the ascending *accelerando* figures of strings. Their artificial harmonics in measure 88 produce a noisiness ratio of 0.67. The latter noisiness peaks (values 0.82 and 0.83) are related to the *pizzicati*, in measures 91 and 92.

6 Operations in Micro and Macrotime

First, in this article, we intended to present different possibilities of interaction and convergence in live electronic music. Based on the interaction and convergence between instrumental and electroacoustic universes, live electronic music provides innumerous possibilities of new sound generation with aesthetic qualities. These new sound morphologies are the result of timbre fusion between different structures that are perceived as a single unity. Micro and macrotime issues were approached by taking into consideration the operations presented and discussed herein so as to produce a formal coherence in the analyzed works. Micro events interfere with each other by means of close contacts between sound particles (grains or partials). At the same time, the macro form is being constituted by means of a continuous modulation, which constitutes the perceived musical form in listening.

Our view of the undulatory paradigm in microtime domain (formed by events whose duration is inferior to the note limit) is that the interaction between acoustic and electroacoustic means is focused on frequency operations. These operations, which always consider a continuous timbre, intend to reinforce some partials that are common to both means as well as add new ones to the resultant sound.

In relation to the granular paradigm, the interaction is based on discontinuous events, which are mainly modulated by time values. For instance, we can combine a granular electroacoustic texture (with grains up to 100 ms of duration) with instrumental grains whose duration is longer. For this purpose, we must imagine instrumental techniques that produce discontinuous sonorities such as *staccato* and trills, *jeté col legno* on strings, or *frullato* and slap tongue sounds, on aerophonic instruments.

Considering macrotime events (notes and their combination in time), it is possible to apply instrumental synthesis procedures aiming to generate pitches and scales that will be used in the composition process. In terms of form generation, we can apply the idea of timbre interpolation as discussed in *Diatomées*'s compositional process.

Aesthetically interesting timbres can be produced from irrational values of frequency modulation indexes. These spectra can be distributed in different ways in the score so as to allow timbre interpolation.

Sound forms—be they provided from the convergence of instrumental and electroacoustic sounds or from the fusion of different instrumental sounds—were conceived from the enaction concept. Those generated sound forms (timbres) are not predetermined, however, they are the result of an emergent process, meaning that their form is constructed along compositional and performing processes. This confirms the objective of this research of generating new sound forms from experimental processes.

The combination of different timbres in time and space brings the idea of timbre fusion, an operation we have approached based on the allagmatic method, from excerpt analyses of our works *Diatomées* and *Le Vide: Trois Réflexions sur le Temps*. The merging of different structures into a single timbre was approached by jitter (acoustical point of view) and hearing saturation (perceptive point of view). Furthermore, we conceived a model based on audio descriptors to analyze the acoustic features of the generated timbres, which was applied to our composition excerpts. We imagine, for further works, expanding this description model, considering the characteristics of the analyzed timbres we desire to discuss.

Acknowledgments. São Paulo Research Foundation - FAPESP - for the support of this research through the processes 2013/00155-4 and 2014/9548-9.

References

1. Couprie, P.: Musique électroacoustique. http://ears.pierrecouprie.fr/spip.php?article3110. (Accessed Jun 2017)
2. Menezes, F.: Fusão e contraste entre a escritura instrumental e as estruturas eletroacústicas. In: Atualidade Estética da Música Eletroacústica, pp. 13–20. Editora Unesp, São Paulo (1999)
3. L'Ambisonie d'Ordre Supérieur. http://www.mshparisnord.fr/hoalibrary/ambisonie/ambison ie-ordre-superieur/ (Accessed Jun 2017)
4. Schaeffer, P.: Traité des Objets Musicaux. Seuil, Paris (1966)
5. Smalley, D.: Spectromorphology: explaining sound shapes. Organized Sound **2**, 107–126 (1997)
6. Menezes, F.: For a morphology of interaction. Organized Sound **7**(3), 305–311 (2002)
7. Rossetti, D; Bittencourt, P.: Oceanos para saxofone alto e eletrônica em tempo real. Revista Vórtex **4**(2), 1–10 (2016). Score and audio
8. Simondon, G.: Du Mode d'Éxistence des Objets Techniques [1958]. Aubier, Paris (1989)
9. Varela, F.: Conhecer: As Ciências Cognitivas, Tendências e Perspectivas. Instituto Piaget, Lisboa (1994)
10. Simondon, G.: L'Individuation à la Lumière des Notions de Forme et d'Information [1958]. Jérome Millon, Grenoble (2005)
11. Grisey, G.: Écrits ou l'Invention de la Musique Spectrale. Éditions MF, Paris (2008)
12. Chowning, J.: The synthesis of complex audio spectra by means of frequency modulation. J. Audio Eng. Soc. **21**(7), 526–534 (1973)
13. Rossetti, D., Ferraz, S.: Forma como um Processo: Do Isomorfismo ao Heteromorfismo. Revista Opus **22**(1), 59–96 (2016)

14. Dubnov, S., Tishby, N., Cohen, D.: Polyspectra measures of sound texture and timbre. J. New Music Res. **26**, 277–314 (1997)
15. McAdams, S.: Spectral Fusion, Spectral Parsing and the Formulation of Auditory Images. Doctoral thesis, CCRMA Department of Music. Stanford University (1984)
16. Ligeti, G.: Neuf Essais sur la Musique. Contrechamps, Genève (2010)
17. Helmholtz, H.: On the Sensations of the Tone. Dover, New York (1954)
18. Seebeck, A.: Beobachtungen über inige Bedingungen der Entstehung von Tönen. Analen der Physik und Chemie **53**, 417–436 (1841)
19. Schouten, J.F.: The residue: a new component in subjective sound analysis. Proc. Koninklijke Nederlandse Akademie van Wetenschappen **41**, 1083–1093 (1940)
20. Meyer-Eppler, W.: Statistic and Psychologic Problems of Sound. Die Reihe **1**, 55–61 (1958)
21. Terhardt, E.: Pitch, consonance, and harmony. J. Acoust. Soc. Am. **55**(5), 1061–1069 (1974)
22. Gabor, D.: Theory of communication. J. Inst. Electr. Eng. **93**(3), 429–457 (1945)
23. Xenakis, I.: Musiques Formelles. La Revue Musicale Richard Masse, Paris (1962)
24. Bode, H.: The multiplier-type ring modulator. Electron. Music Rev. **1**, 9–15 (1967)
25. Kendall, G.S.: The decorrelation of audio signals and its impact on spatial imagery. Comput. Music J. **19**(4), 71–87 (1995)
26. Peeters, G., et al.: The timbre toolbox: extracting audio descriptors from musical signals. J. Acoust. Soc. Am. **130**(5), 2902–2916 (2011)
27. Fastl, H., Zwicker, E.: Psychoacoustics: Facts and Models. Springer, Berlin (2007)

Event-Based Ubiquitous Music Interaction with MCMM: A Musical Communication Modeling Methodology

Flávio Luiz Schiavoni(✉)

Computer Science Department, Federal University of São João Del Rei,
São João Del Rei, MG 36307-352, Brazil
fls@ufsj.edu.br

Abstract. This paper introduces Musical Communication Modeling Me-thodology (MCMM): a theoretical framework to develop context-aware interaction in music applications with ubiquitous devices. Music is changing its context everyday and many applications are being developed without an easy way to define the interaction and the semantics. The framework uses the event-driven model to drive user-to-user interaction based on the device-to-device communication. The framework itself is a set of activities and can orient developers to create collaborative and cooperative music applications.

Keywords: Ubiquitous music · Theoretical framework · Context-aware music application

1 Introduction

In the past we had the idea of one machine to one person. Since then, Computer Science is changing its paradigm from the 1980's and nowadays it is a common situation that many people have many devices embedded in a rich environment [3]. One can say that Mobile devices are everywhere and the idea of being "always on" is now part of our daily routine. This situation is explored by ubiquitous music [9], a research field where everyday devices are used to make music.

Music making is a human activity that involves social collaboration and it can be used as a good metaphor for interaction. Ubiquitous music intends to explore these natural features of music and the ubiquitous feature of devices in a integrated way, putting together multiple users, devices, sound sources, music resources and activities [9]. The ubiquitous devices can provide several types of interaction: GUI, wearable, mobile, ubiquitous, continuous and discrete. All these interactions can be thought as sensors perceiving the environment [11] that can trigger different actuators. Powered by computer networks, it can be used to expand music making activity creating new models for music interaction [8].

© Springer International Publishing AG 2017
M. Aramaki et al. (Eds.): CMMR 2016, LNCS 10525, pp. 284–298, 2017.
DOI: 10.1007/978-3-319-67738-5_17

To connect different devices to create collaboration in music is not an easy task. There are several issues on this subject and to help one to trespass common problems that are already solved, we did a formalization of how to communicate event based music devices.

In this paper we propose a theoretical framework to create event-based music interaction based on the idea of several devices connected to sensors and actuators. The theoretical framework presented here is free of architecture, programming language, device type or implementation, and can be used as a guide to musical application development. The proposed framework is focused on event-based communication but it can be easily expanded to data stream communication like audio or video. Data stream commonly demands more network bandwidth, data transformations to integrate heterogeneous systems (like sample rate, endianness or bit depth change) and buffering implementation to synchronize network packets. More on network music and audio transmission can be found on [12].

After some research, development and experiments, initial results of the project was presented at the 12th International Symposium on Computer Music Multidisciplinary Research (CMMR). This paper is a complementary publication with some step forward research on this subject.

The remainder of this paper is organized as follows: Sect. 2 presents related works and fundamentals, Sect. 3 presents the proposed framework activities, Sect. 4 presents the framework draft and Sect. 5 presents the conclusion.

2   Related Works and Fundamentals

There are many works about music interaction in computer music research. The most discussed ideas have a focus on the interaction of a musician and a device. This scenario is important because it raises several discussions about how a user can interact with a device and make music [5,10,15]. Some activities may permit musical interaction through the sound emitted by devices at an acoustic environment without exchanging data or meaning. In this scenario one user's action hardly affects directly how other users are playing their own device. In our research, we plan to go further and focus on user-to-user musical interaction regarding the device-to-device communication. This model can also be extended to several musicians and several devices.

The main aspects of network music were already discussed in two seminal works from Barbosa and Weinberg. The first is Barbosa's classification of collaborative music using computer technologies [1]. The second work is Weinberg's concept of Interconnected Musical Networks, and topologies of networks in the scope of music [13].

In contrast to application or implementation, in which case the development can reflect a single and closed model, our approach emphasizes an open model to integrate different applications in a distributed music environment. It does not consist of a single unified model but a way to map cognitive actions to music in a collaborative way. This approach implies that the mapping outreaches the simple idea of exchanging raw data between two points, and aims at more meaningful messages.

3   The Framework Overview

The proposed framework starts trying to answer a question: "If I want to develop a collaborative musical instrument using portable devices, what should I do?". We enumerated several activities to help answering this question dividing the development into simple activities that can be realized in group or individually.

In this work, we divided the development of an event-based music interaction application in a set of activities to address implementation issues in an independent form. This is, in our point of view, a basic set of activities to develop a context-awareness application for devices and sensors. Our framework work flow is based on 6 different basic parts, as presented on Fig. 1.

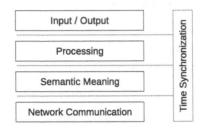

Fig. 1. The framework layers

Like the TCP/IP stack, we arranged different parts of the framework into layers that are responsible for different activities and abstractions. So, it is possible to describe each activity and each layer as a small problem to be solved locally. Furthermore, like the TPC/IP stack, every device would have the same layered architecture to grant a communication stack and facilitate the message exchange.

As depicted on Fig. 1, we enumerated 6 activities: Input, Output, Time Synchronization, Processing, Semantic Meaning and Network Communication. In this representation we have only one Input and Output to make it clean and easy to understand although some devices can have diverse sensors and also outputs. Time Synchronization are an optional task and some application development will not need to use all these activities. The idea of this workflow is to describe the full path to dispatch an event from one device to every device connected to a environment every time a new event occurs on the Input.

3.1   Communication Roles

In computer networks, communication is initiated by one party and another party responds. Network communication uses two terms to define these roles: server and client. The client program initiates the conversation while the server responds. Together, server and client creates a distributed application [4, p. 7].

Despite the terms, these roles are associated only with communication start up. Servers wait for a client connection while clients need to know the server address to connect to. Once the connection is done, these roles are replaced by an application protocol that defines the data flow and how resources will be shared through a network.

Once the communication started, these roles are not important anymore but it is important to understand and map the data flow between musicians and devices. The computer implementation of this data flow leads one to decide who should send data and who should receive the data as well as how many participants should send and receive data simultaneously.

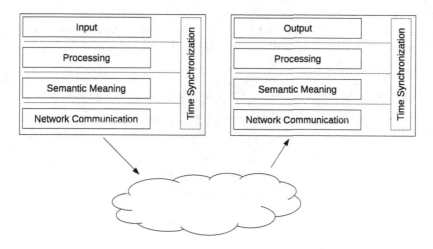

Fig. 2. The framework roles: input and output devices

In our proposed framework, it means who will use inputs to understand and interact with the environment and who will use outputs to change the environment. It is possible that every device on the environment can provide inputs and outputs but we will divide the roles **input** and **output** to be more clear when describing the activities. This division is depicted on Fig. 2.

Inputs and outputs can be set up as one wish to create a **musical environment**. A musical environment can be a stage, a rehearsal, a laptop orchestra, an installation or any situation of music collaboration with mobile devices. The musical environment can be fixed or vary with audience participation.

4   The Framework Activities

The framework activities, described on last Section, can be divided into the proposed roles of the environment. Even if Input and Output have a Processing activity, for instance, this activity is different because of the data flow.

4.1 Input (Sensors)

Since we intend to have human interaction, the basic Input in our framework is a sensor listener. Sensors are used to map users' gestures and environment activities. It would be possible to have a software input created by an algorithm, another software, or a file, indeed. Since we intend to have users, a sensor is a computational way to capture or listen to states or changes in user's activities in the environment in analog or digital sampling. Sensors can be found embedded on mobile phones, notebooks, notepads, tablets and also can be attached to different devices like Arduino, Galileo or Raspberry Pi [7].

Different devices may have different sensors and the same sensor can have different configurations and constraints. An example for this statement is a touchscreen that can be found in different sizes depending on the device. The size of a touchscreen is a sensor constraint and it will have computational effects on the data communication, as we will see at Subsect. 4.5.

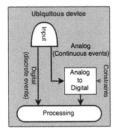

Fig. 3. Input activity

The idea of using a sensor to create and dispatch an event also follows the paradigm of monitoring a sensor to create reactive applications [6]. An observation of a sensor can bring at least two values: what changed on a sensor and when it happened. It is important to notice that a sensor value can be a parameter or a set of parameters. A touchscreen, for instance, brings X, Y position of the latest touch event while an accelerometer can have X, Y, Z values regarding the acceleration on three dimensional axes. The identification of the owner of the sensor can be a relevant data to report in some cases. Thus, we can monitor what, when, and where an event took place in the environment.

Electronically, a sensor can have a continuous or discrete signal. In the case of an analog sensor, it will need a conversion to discrete values based on some constraints before sending an event to a digital system, as presented on Fig. 3. The sensor observation captures discrete instances of these parameters every period of time, or better put the sensor sample rate. Sensors with a high sample rate are normally more accurate and also more expensive than other sensors. We consider that the conversion from analog to digital is an extension of the input. This conversion is not managed at the Processing activity because this activity acts as monitor of digital events, as we will present at Sect. 4.4. Moreover, most of the analog sensors can be found as digital sensors, and in this case they will dispatch the events in some discrete scale.

4.2   Output (Actuators)

A device uses its output actuators to locally reflect a change in the environment. It is also possible to consider logical components in the Output activity such as an event recorder software, so one can have a score from the local sonic environment. Common actuators like sonic feedback, haptics feedback and visual feedback can be used as a context-awareness feedback for the application from the output point of view.

It is clear that different devices can have different actuators. Also, just like the sensors, actuators can have different constraints that influence the outcome. It leads us to some local decisions about how to react to some received message. One application can choose to have a sonic output to a message while another application can have only a visual output to the same message. The example depicted on Fig. 4 illustrate some possibilities of actuators output in a certain device.

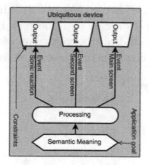

Fig. 4. Output activity

Output is also used to give feedback to the user's own actions. User's interaction with the device can be reported with some feedback to the user and this feedback can also be merged with the environment messages.

4.3   Time Synchronization

Music can be explained as sound events organized in time. Since our focus is musical interaction, time synchronization can be necessary. This layer appears several times on Fig. 1 because Time Synchronization activity can be necessary to synchronize different data. The basic idea of time sync is to have event ordering. In several scenarios, the order of the events is important and it is undesirable to have the second event before the first [3].

If the timing of users' action or environment changes is critical, the time synchronization needs to occur right before the Processing. In this framework proposal we assumed that the Processing can have multiple threads or dispatch events in different order. On the other hand, if the timing is not so critical, and the Processing is expected to change the sampling rate or discard some events, it is better to have a Time Synchronization activity after the Processing or avoid using this activity.

Since network communication can bring latency and jitter to the application, it can also be necessary to synchronize event messages on the sender/receiver and keep the order of the events when necessary. A time-stamp field can also be used with a local ring buffer to synchronize received events with different latency (jitter). In musical interaction through the network, the packet loss is a common drawback of unreliable connections and the medium can be the source of most noise and interference at the communication process. One can imagine a message to start a sound and another message to stop a sound as a common Use Case to play a musical note, but if the second message is lost, the note will be played forever. We can also illustrate the same result if the Network Communication delivers the second packet before the first one. On the other hand, some applications may not have this problem if the events are independent, like *play A4 for 1s*, and the sonic result is not time aligned.

Another important point is the necessity of defining a clock for the synchronization process. Synchronization can be done based on a local clock, a global clock, a relative time clock, and also a virtual clock adjusted on periodically. A single representation of Time Synchronization activity is presented at Fig. 5.

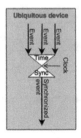

Fig. 5. Time synchronization activity

Furthermore, message ordering can be done using an auto-increment for every new event or attaching a time-stamp field on the event. This activity can hold events on a buffer before sending in order to assure the synchronization.

4.4   Processing

Sometimes, an Input sensor will keep the same value for a long period of time. In this situation, it can be necessary to avoid the generation of several messages to the environment with the same value. For this reason, a processing of the input value can help to guarantee a new event to update the environment only if the change in the value is really significant, for example.

Also, it is possible to (a) convert a continuous value to a discrete value, (b) convert a discrete value into a constrained value based on some rules, (c) generate an event only if a change is really significant, (d) apply the input constraint to a value to decide if it is possible to react to an environment change. From digital signal processing research we can grab plenty of filters that may be used here in case the data from an event differs from the type of data required to be sent.

A threshold can be applied to a sensor value to estimate a minimum change that will be reported. A Low Pass Filter can be used to avoid reporting drastic changes of a value and to create a smooth event output. In this way, the Processing is responsible to map every user interaction to an event or a group of events, independently of the interaction model [7]. A representation of the Processing activity in two different situations is presented on Fig. 6.

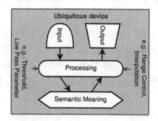

Fig. 6. Processing activity

This activity can fit better after an Input or Semantic meaning, depending on the application context in each device. The events dispatched from Semantic Meaning activity can also be filtered by Processing activity since a message may need an adjustment before being sent to the Output. The Processing may be used to redefine the range of values that an Output will receive after some point. A drastic pitch change, for instance, can create a glitch effect on the sound, and for this reason, even when every message changes the pitch value, it can be necessary to have an interpolation ramp between the previous value and a new one.

4.5 Semantic Meaning

The Semantic Meaning activity will map the received message to the specific end for each actuator to assure a local reflection of this environment change, and in the end we will have only final meaningful events. This final event must have a semantic meaning instead of a raw value because an isolated event discards its original context and lacks a semantic meaning. For this reason, a semantic model is necessary to associate a particular user interaction and a desired sonic result. This association is required to: map one or more event to an acoustic result; create a message with semantic meaning, and; normalize or standardize the data representation [8]. In addiction, semantic models are more abstract than notations and can decouple the gesture from the acoustic result creating a common agreement to the environment [3].

Another reason to use a semantic meaning layer considers the device constraints. If a drum set is played in a touchscreen, for instance, the touch position

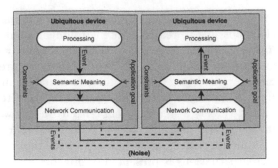

Fig. 7. Semantic meaning activity

must be mapped to the desired drum pad and this message must be sent to the network and not a single two-dimensional parameter because the drum position on the screen can vary depending on the device size settings. So far, it is necessary to give locally a semantic meaning because only the user's device knows its own settings.

Since a device can have several sensors, a semantic model can also group several events from one or more sensors into one single message in order to generate a new unique event. Using this fusion paradigm it is possible to have a more accurate vision of the environment and reflect a more accurate sonic result. It means that one can acquire user's position, gesture, localization and other events from available sensors and merge in one single message in the end. This single message can be used to change the audio volume of an instrument in another point and therefore change the environment with a sonic result.

Another reason to use a semantic meaning layer is related to the application constraint. A touch position from one device can be used to play the piano, the drums, the xylophone or to control a sequencer, an audio effect or any other musical instance in other devices. These messages can eventually be interpreted by the second device without any additional mapping since the network message has semantic meaning and not X, Y positioning.

From the communication point of view, the event needs to be interpreted by the Semantic Meaning activity considering the application context at the receiver environment. Although all participants need to talk in the same language to ensure the communication, the semantic meaning can be used to adapt the message to another context at a specific environment. In this case, the Semantic Meaning activity at the receiver may or may not share the same semantic model from the sender, but will act in the same way, receiving and mapping several events.

It can also use different techniques to respond softly to an environment event. Imagining a common instrument played by several musicians, the note pitch can be defined as an average of the actual value and a received value or it can change its value on every received message. Altogether, the Semantic Meaning activity will define a **group of messages** and send different events through the network in order to notify the whole distributed environment. Figure 7 presents an overview of this activity in some possible situations.

Once the group of messages is defined, it is also necessary to define a network format to exchange these messages. A network message should be encoded in common formats, like text-plain, JSON, XML and OSC, before being sent. The latter is considered the most used network data format in music context [14] since it is supported by different music programming languages like Pure Data, CSound or Supercollider and several music applications. Other formats may be applied, like the byte chunks used by MIDI or any serialization method.

At this point, the codification of the message can also include any cryptography depending on the medium used. The receiver should be aware of the message format, decode the event, interpret the message based on its own semantic model, and create another event to be dispatched by the Semantic Meaning activity.

4.6 Network Communication

We need to exchange messages to other users to notify the environment about some new event. In the presented framework, the network communication layer is responsible to exchange messages on the environment. As our aim is to ensure communication between many users, a group communication paradigm should be used to fulfill our proposal with specific solutions depending on the communication medium.

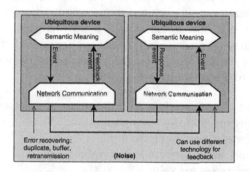

Fig. 8. Network communication activity

In Local Area Networks (LAN), a Broadcast or Multicast addressing methodology can be used, and for World Area Networks (WAN) communication, a central relay server is a common solution. Hybrid solutions can mix different network addressing methodologies depending on the desired performance structure. The *buzzword* Cloud Computing can be another specific solution that extends the functionality of WAN with the addition of distributed servers and cloud services. The Network Communication activity can also be used with technologies that interconnect devices in a more direct way. One can cite the wired connections, or the wireless options like Infrared, Bluetooth, and the Wi-Fi Direct.

Network communication turns out to be a critical part of any framework when a performance using a musical instrument controlled through the network requires very precise timing. Thus, network latency and jitter can interfere adversely on the application usage. Normally, LAN has lower latency and jitter than WAN but it varies depending on the network infrastructure, number of devices, protocol choice and others implementation choices.

All of these alternatives have their own constraints. The selection of the technology depends on the interfaces supported by devices at the sonic environment, and some devices may have more than one interface that can be used at the same time. Figure 8 shows the main characteristics of Network Communication activity.

5   The Framework Draft

In this section we present a draft of the MCMM activities. Here we will present a guideline to start a new application based on this framework. It is necessary to describe each activity details prior to start developing. In this way you can have an open view of the constraints of the musical environment, evaluate the application goal, come up with solutions for the issues, and have a general representation of the application developed beforehand.

This theoretical framework comprises a group of ideas that can support the study and development of applications for music interaction based on events. We can have some graphical representation like the ones on Fig. 9 in order to better presenting the applications, and we need to use textual descriptions based on the draft below if we need to specify the details regarding each activity included in the framework We may need to describe other applications that can be connected or interact with the musical application during a performance in case we want to suggest possible ubiquitous interaction.

1. **Input**: Read and dispatch values from a sensor or a set of sensors that can monitor user's gesture and the environment.
   - To Define: Sensors and Devices.
   - Input: Continuous or discrete sensor value.
     Output: Discrete sensor value.
2. **Output**: Use actuators to reflect an environment change or a user's action.
   - To Define: Actuators.
   - Input: Discrete value.
   - Output: Discrete or continuous value.

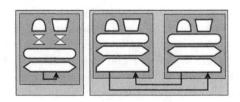

Fig. 9. Examples of graphical representation using the framework

3. **Time Synchronization**: Synchronize events based on a clock. Incoming events can be buffered in order to wait for a specific time.
   - To Define: Time sync clock. Buffer type. Localization of the syncs.
   - Input: Event with or without timing information.
   - Output: Event with or without timing information. Event on time.
4. **Processing**: Filter and monitor values.
   - To Define: Threshold, ramps and filters.
   - Input: Raw data in discrete format.
   - Output: Raw data in discrete format.
5. **Semantic Meaning**: Transform a raw data into a musical message associating a semantic meaning to an event, or decode a musical message into raw data before sending to an output. This activity is also called **mapping** and depends on the application goal.
   - To Define: Application goal. Message format. Message mapping. Context.
   - Input: Raw data, Message with meaning.
   - Output: Message with meaning, Raw data.
6. **Network Communication**: Send and receive messages from and to the environment.
   - To Define: Network addressing methodology. Network transport protocol.
   - Input: Message event.
   - Output: Message event.

Additionally, some skills may be required by the developers and users of this framework. For input reading, some skills on sensors and microelectronic may help to deal with the technical aspects of the electronics components. Experience with message packing syntax may help at the mapping activity, and a good knowledge on network implementation will be necessary to assure a good communication between devices. Depending on the application goal, the developers may need some skills in synthesizer implementation. In addition, the output manipulation depends on the expertise regarding the actuators, while the processing will be mostly based on DSP fundamentals.

5.1   Case Study I: Sensors2OSC

Some applications from music interaction field can be described using this theoretical framework. In order present our theoretical framework applied in a real case, we are going to describe an application named Sensors2OSC [2] already developed by the authors.

Sensors2OSC is a mobile application that sends all sensors events using OSC through the network. A user just needs to select the sensors and set an IP and Port in order to start sending the new events. At another point, we can receive the OSC messages using any program and use the values to control whatever we want.

Figure 10 presents the application structure with two instances of Sensors2OSC on each side, and a computer music program in the middle. The final context of an interactive application using Sensors2OSC is described on Table 1. We believe that both representations are sufficient in any case.

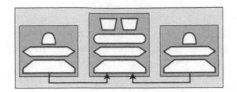

Fig. 10. Sensors2OSC presented with this framework

Table 1. Sensors2OSC description using MCMM

Input	To define	The sensor
	Input	Continuous values
	Output	Digital events
Semantic meaning	To define	OSC address correlated to the sensor
	Input	The sensor ID and value
	Output	Message with OSC address
Network communication	To define	Unicast or Multicast
	Input	TCP or UDP packets
	Output	TCP or UDP packets
Semantic meaning	To define	Interpret OSC addresses
	Input	Message with OSC address
	Output	Raw value of the sensor event
Processing	To define	Optionally the user can filter the value
	Input	Value of the sensor event
	Output	Value of the sensor event
Output	To define	Any synthesizer or program
	Input	OSC messages
	Output	Continuous audio signal or program update

5.2   Case Study II: Orchidea

The Orchidea is a project focused in the development of an Orchestra of Mobile (Android) Devices, presented in Fig. 11. This project is using MCMM as a base to the development.

Orchidea Input, initially, is a cellphone touchscreen. Other sensors can be used but our initial development used only the touchscreen. The output is the sound and uses libpd and Puredata patches as the synthesizer. Thus, it was possible to detach the sound design from the programming. There are a message mapping by semantic meaning by instrument development and the network communication uses OSC and multicast.

The development of a new instrument in Orchidea depends on (a) the creation of a touchscreen, (b) the message definition, (c) the synthesizer creation on Pure Data.

MCMM activities helped this project definition and development and worked as a guide to the application development.

(a)

(b)

Fig. 11. Orchidea GUI

6 Conclusion

In principle, mobile phones were developed for people communication purpose. Once they became pocket computers, they have being used to music making activities. Several music making applications were developed focused on a single user activity and progressively taking advantage of the communication capability of devices.

This paper presented MCMM, a theoretical framework to develop Event-based music applications with a communication layer to allow user-to-user interaction based on device-to-device communication. This framework enumerated a group of activities, defined a development workflow and presented some technical issues in every activity.

Since our goal was not focused on implementation details, this framework can be used with any programming language, device type or music application type. Moreover, it can put together in the same musical environment different applications and devices, from desktop application to notebooks, mobiles or other devices. It is also important to notice that we can also use this framework to describe most of the applications already developed for musical interaction. Authors encourage the idea that this framework will serve as an starting point for instructing developers and musicians on modeling and sharing the structure of their applications with lay audience and users in a near future.

References

1. Barbosa, A.: Displaced soundscapes: a survey of network systems for music and sonic art creation. Leonardo Music J. **13**, 53–59 (2003)
2. De Carvalho Junior, A.D., Mayer, T.: Sensors2OSC. In: Sound and Music Computing Conference, Maynooth, pp. 209–213 (2015)
3. Dix, A.: Towards a Ubiquitous Semantics of Interaction: Phenomenology, Scenarios, and Traces. In: Forbrig, P., Limbourg, Q., Vanderdonckt, J., Urban, B. (eds.) DSV-IS 2002. LNCS, vol. 2545, pp. 238–252. Springer, Heidelberg (2002). doi:10.1007/3-540-36235-5_18

4. Donahoo, M.J., Calvert, K.L.: TCP/IP Sockets in C Bundle: TCP/IP Sockets in C, 2nd ed., Practical Guide for Programmers (Morgan Kaufmann Practical Guides). Morgan Kaufmann (2009)
5. Flores, L.V., Pimenta, M.S., Keller, D.: Patterns of musical interaction with computing devices. In: Proceedings of the III Ubiquitous Music Workshop (III UbiMus). Ubiquitous Music Group, São Paulo (2012)
6. Hinze, A., Sachs, K., Buchmann, A.: Event-based applications and enabling technologies. In: Proceedings of the Third ACM International Conference on Distributed Event-Based Systems, DEBS 2009, pp. 1:1–1:15. ACM, New York (2009)
7. Kernchen, R., Presser, M., Mossner, K., Tafazolli, R.: Multimodal user interfaces in ubiquitous sensorised environments. In: Intelligent Sensors, Sensor Networks and Information Processing Conference, pp. 397–401 (2004)
8. Malloch, J., Sinclair, S., Wanderley, M.M.: Libmapper: (a Library for Connecting Things). In: CHI 2013 Extended Abstracts on Human Factors in Computing Systems, CHI EA 2013, pp. 3087–3090. ACM, New York (2013)
9. Pimenta, M.S., Flores, L.V., Capasso, A., Tinajero, P., Keller, D.: Ubiquitous music: concepts and metaphors. In: Proceedings of the 12th Brazilian Symposium on Computer Music, Recife, Brazil, pp. 139–150 (2009)
10. Radanovitsck, E.A.A.: mixDroid: compondo através de dispositivos móveis. Ph.D. thesis, Universidade Federal do Rio Grande do Sul (2011)
11. Realinho, V., Romão, T., Dias, A.E.: An event-driven workflow framework to develop context-aware mobile applications. In: Proceedings of the 11th International Conference on Mobile and Ubiquitous Multimedia, MUM 2012, pp. 22:1–22:10. ACM, New York (2012)
12. Schiavoni, F.L., Queiroz, M.: Network distribution in music applications with Medusa. In: Proceedings of the Linux Audio Conference, Stanford, USA, pp. 9–14 (2012)
13. Weinberg, G.: Interconnected musical networks: toward a theoretical framework. Comput. Music J. 29, 23–39 (2005)
14. Wright, M.: Open sound control: an enabling technology for musical networking. Organised Sound 10, 193–200 (2005)
15. Young, J.P.: Using the Web for live interactive music. In: Proceedings of International Computer Music Conference, Habana, Cuba, pp. 302–305 (2001)

New Digital Instruments - Multisensory Experiences

A Virtual Musical Instrument for 3D Performance with Short Gestures: Exploring Mapping Strategies with Virtual Reality

André Montes Rodrigues[1]([⊠]), Marcelo Knorich Zuffo[1],
Olavo da Rosa Belloc[1], and Regis Rossi Alves Faria[2]([⊠])

[1] Electronic Systems Engineering Department, Polytechnic School,
University of São Paulo, Av. Prof. Luciano Gualberto, 158 – Butantã, São Paulo,
SP 05508-010, Brazil
{andre.montes.rodrigues,mkzuffo}@usp.br,
belloc@lsi.usp.br
[2] Laboratory of Acoustics and Music Technology,
Music Department - FFCLRP, University of São Paulo, Ribeirão Preto, Brazil
regis@usp.br

Abstract. We present a new digital virtual instrument designed, built and played using 3D interactive technologies, with interest in reducing both learning time and difficulty in playing musical phrases and chords across the musical scale. Design concepts stress on a smart note mapping, rely on bi-manual interaction, and intend an optimized gestural performance on a virtual keyboard to shorten playing trajectories. The proposed keyboard is built stacking note keys in multiple lines, and the note mapping allows performing typical musical intervals and patterns with short gestures. This implementation employed an Oculus Rift head-mounted display and a Razer Hydra for gesture input. The combination of 3D visualization, natural interaction and the proposed mapping is meant to contribute to ease musical performance by allowing fast execution of specific note sequences. The instrument concept encapsulates complexity by creating a fluid way for musicians to perform gesture patterns that would otherwise require non-trivial motor skills.

Keywords: 3D virtual musical instrument · Short gesture performance · Alternative keyboards

1 Introduction

Factors associated to the difficulty of learning new instruments include physical limitations and the logical, spatial and mechanical complexity in mapping sound to musical patterns. It is assumed that the more clear and intuitive is the mapping, the less time it takes to learn the instrument. With traditional musical instruments, physical and geometric constraints are naturally present. Piano, for instance, despite its clear and simple layout, is one of the most difficult instruments to master due to its particular mapping [1].

© Springer International Publishing AG 2017
M. Aramaki et al. (Eds.): CMMR 2016, LNCS 10525, pp. 301–315, 2017.
DOI: 10.1007/978-3-319-67738-5_18

Musicians often mention the high impact and the relevance of execution mechanics on the pleasure to play. Some instruments like the flute, violin and guitar rely almost only on the hands while piano and harp calls for higher amplitude movements. In fact, players of big instruments are usually characterized by their gracious execution, when music comes closer to dance and choreography. The harp is a typical example where movement mechanics is critical for performance. Moving in space is also a powerful way to remember songs and to boost both motivation on learning and joyfulness on execution.

Interaction modes are expanded in many degrees with virtual reality resources. Beyond buttons and sliders, gestural capture and trajectory tracking in natural space offer unlimited new possibilities to explore. The adoption of three-dimensional interactive virtual interfaces is also a cost-effective and fast approach to design, build and test new concepts towards optimization of note mappings in a moment that virtual reality is experiencing a "revival" due to the advent of low-cost head-mounted displays (such as the Oculus Rift) and many 3D interaction devices. Such technologies can definitely contribute to modernizing of paradigms in music creation and performance and to promote integration with other art forms.

Given this scenario, in the near future one may expect the rise of new musical instruments using immersive technologies and newer generations will likely prefer to use contemporary technologies with which they are familiarized. However, before such "paradigm" can pose a real alternative for professional musicians, advancements in performance techniques and instrument controllability will be necessary. Therefore, the capabilities, potentials and constraints of such technologies must be adequately assessed.

The main contribution of this research is exploring new possibilities of 3D interactive technologies in order to create a musical instrument that enables easier and faster learning by connecting musical theory to note mapping in an intuitive manner and allowing anyone to play regardless of musical proficiency or physical characteristics.

The rest of this paper is structured as follows. First we'll review some concepts and references in virtual musical instrumentation. In sequence, we present the main concepts of our approach and comprehensive implementation details. The article is wrapped up with preliminary feedback from experts, a discussion about current limitations, possible improvements and promising lines of investigations for future work.

2   Issues in Virtual Musical Instrument Design

A review on the available literature suggests that several developers put a lot of effort packing virtual instruments with several features, often resulting in higher learning difficulty and instability, whereas new interfaces should be harmonized to human minds and bodies [1]. Recommendations to greatly improve mapping transparency include the adoption of well-designed interfaces, visual and tactile feedbacks and offering a physical piece to handle, preferably portable and aesthetically designed [2].

Interactive instruments may allow for anyone to participate in musical creation and performance processes, from the most talented to the most unskilled out of the large public [3]. However, as some players exhibit "spare bandwidth", new instruments should have a "low entry fee" with no limits on virtuosity [4]. Still, according to Cook, full freedom is not a virtue, and customization should be controlled [5].

Gesture-based instruments stand out as a promising approach to tackle the major issues and to conform to some of the best practices identified above. A review of NIME proceedings (the international conference series on new computer interfaces for musical expression) reveals several projects that explore gestures to control sound [6]. Airstick [7] and Termenova [8] are Theremin-style instruments, and the latter introduced laser guides as an improvement to offer the user a perceivable spatial structure. Future Grab [9] employs a data glove and Poepel *et al.* relies on mouth expressions and arm gestures to control a vocal synthesizer [10]. The Leap Motion controller (www. leapmotion.com) is adopted on AirKeys [6] and Digito [11] uses depth cameras to capture tap gestures, so that the user can choose discrete notes of a chromatic keyboard in 3D space. As one can see, such projects are focused in developing and testing specific interaction methods, not comprehensive solutions for the aforementioned issues. As far as instrument feedback mechanisms are concerned in those references, whenever visual feedback is provided, it is accomplished in two dimensions with conventional monitors. It should also be noticed that mapping doesn't seem to be a relevant concern. However, research suggests that mapping is accountable for most of the difficulty to learn and play an instrument [12].

Hunt *et al.* recommends that mapping should preserve flow and fun [12]. However, the multiple dimensions involved makes designing a good mapping a hard task. Many note mappings, keyboards and interface layouts have been proposed throughout the history of musical instruments, so to overcome limitations such as the difficulty to stretch beyond octaves (due to the large distance of the keys) and to transpose without changing the fingering (resulting in each chord having the same shape and same fingering regardless of musical key). The harmonic table note layout, for instance, known since the 18th century [13], is a tonal array of notes disposed in a symmetrical hexagonal pattern, where the musician can play a sequence of minor thirds ascending along the diagonal axis at left, a sequence of major thirds along the diagonal axis at right, a sequence of fifths along the vertical axis, and a semitone sequence moving on the horizontal (Fig. 1).

Another example is the Wicki-Hayden layout [13], also a hexagonal lattice with stacks of major scales arranged in a manner that octave intervals are played along the vertical axis; the left-diagonals cross sequences of fourths; the right diagonals cross fifths intervals; and the notes on the horizontal are separated by a whole-tone. A famous hexagonal isomorphic keyboard is the Jankó's layout, patented in 1885 [13]. With a different combination of the CDE and FGAB groups of notes, this layout may have 4-row up to 6-row implementations, and there is no change in the use of white keys for representing natural tones and black for sharps and flats. Its neighboring keys on the horizontal row are distant a whole tonal step, and on the vertical row they are distant a half step (semitone).

These layouts bring advantages in facilitating learning, composing and playing specific music styles, however, they also present some disadvantages, such as costly mechanical implementations and paradoxically vicious playing behavior, as found in the literature and beyond the scope of this paper. However, counting with the inherent configurability and cheap implementation allowed by digital virtual instrumentation, one should reconsider this balance nowadays. When designing new musical instruments one should pursue improvements and expansion in playability and musical

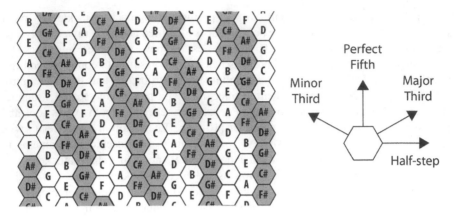

Fig. 1. Harmonic table note layout.

expression. None of the aforementioned gesture-based instruments proposed proper solutions for visual feedback or simpler mapping schemes. In this context, we believe that virtual reality methods can tackle feedback issues, which could facilitate mastering some incredible instruments that did not succeed in the past due to, among other things, the required amount of time and effort to master them.

A prospection on the relation of body gestures and sound gestures reveal an interesting and rich research area dedicated to the analysis and the design of mapping strategies. Perez has recently compiled and correlated several studies on the meaning and mapping of musical gestures and the use of physical (digital) interfaces for live electronics [14]. In his study, Perez approaches the characterization of body and sound within the musical gesture context, tracing relations and mapping existing between both. A method for gestural analysis in performances that use interfaces like DMIs (Digital Musical Instruments) may consider two axes: to evaluate the interface use characteristics, and the instrumental mode. In the case of a virtual instrument with an interface designed as an instrument type (multidimensional gestural control) operating in an instrumental mode, one finds a causal mapping between gestures at the interface (physical movements) and the generation of sounds. Additionally, considering the point of view of the audience in a performance, the visual role of the gestures is highlighted.

Analyzing also the strategy of mapping of gestures into sounds, from the studies of Caramiaux *et al.* (2014 *apud* Perez 2016) mapping strategies can rely on listening modes and on gestural descriptive modes. According to them, listening modes can be of two types: causal (related directly to sound sources) and acoustic (related to the listening of sound parameters, e.g. dynamics). Gestural descriptive modes can be of two types: mimicking (iconic) and tracing (analogic) [14]. For the present case, our proposed virtual instrument reveals an instant mapping strategy, relating to a causal listening mode linked to a sound source (e.g. a synthesizer or a specific timbre) and adopts a gestural strategy for direct mapping of touchable space points to musical notes.

A unique contribution here to the improvement of gestural instruments is in the explicit and designed combination of 3D visual feedback and a mapping optimized for continuous movements. Our approach was to conceive a reconfigurable virtual instrument to test alternative keyboard layouts that can facilitate traversing intervals across the scale, minimizing the path or gestural trajectories in playing phrases and chords, and to achieve a particular note mapping that can leverage low-level music knowledge by providing a high-level interface.

In the next section the main concepts of the proposed system are presented in detail, followed by a complete description of the current implementation.

3 Design and Operational Concepts

Assuming that reducing the complexity of learning and performance depends on a good correspondence between execution patterns and musical patterns, the main directive for our proposal is that an instrument should be *more musical than mechanical*, strengthening the concept of pattern as foundation for musical representation. An essential assumption is that there are finite musical patterns, obvious in chords and arpeggios, but not so obvious in sequences of single notes. The patterns are finite, but their combination provides varied musical results. Thus, our proposal approaches an 'interpreted' virtual musical instrument, which incorporates low-level musical knowledge, accessed by a high-level interface.

3.1 Design Foundations

The first stage of development was characterized by an intense dialogue with the major stakeholders of the project, including VR developers, musicians and programmers. This iterative process led to the adoption of three design pillars that guided the implementation of the virtual musical instrument, which are presented below.

Bi-manual Interaction
Traditional instruments usually embed physical references to avoid the musician getting lost while playing. The adoption of two 3D cursors, each controlled by one hand, was the choice for realizing a bi-manual operation. Despite the possibility of using arm, legs, torso and head movements, we did not come across coherent proposals that would use such movements at this stage and the development team suggested that it could easily incur into undesired complexities and cognitive loads, due to several degrees of movement to deal with. These choices were sought to reduce any cognitive load for positioning in space, reducing the need for physical reference elements.

Note Mapping to Simplify the Execution of Musical Patterns
Considering single notes, in practice, musical expressiveness is directly dependent on the execution fluidity of several patterns of single notes, from fast scale sequences to intervals and arpeggios. One need to be able to execute jumps with consistency, speed and precision. Considering that transitions between individual notes (e.g. in intervals, octaves and arpeggios) may be difficult to perform with successive gestures, the choice was to locate notes in space so as to maximize movement continuity in the execution of patterns, i.e., avoiding large jumps and abrupt gestural transitions.

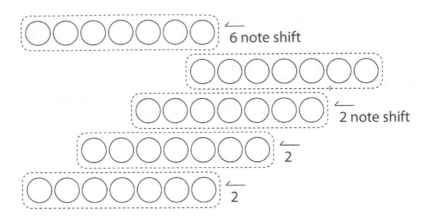

Fig. 2. Stacking note keys in multiple lines. The second line is the base octave. The first line is shifted backwards by six displacements and the third and other lines below are cumulatively shifted backward by two displacements.

The first decision to achieve this was to use stacked and shifted redundant keyboards, a recurrent idea in the design of isomorphic keyboards. However, different from usual isomorphic keyboards, our implementation deals with a square lattice where a note has other eight as neighbors.

The second decision is based on the assumption that traditional western music strongly adopts a single heptatonic scale. While other scales with five notes (pentatonic), six notes, eight notes (diminished) and other modes for heptatonic layout exist, they were left for future explorations. In fact, despite variations in the number of notes in a scale, most traditional songs around the world adopt specific scales and their execution benefits from a specific layout. This assumption allows for a simplification of the keyboard layout. Further, the removal of unused notes reduces jumping frequency during the execution of a specific song, even though it restricts the instrument to the chosen scale.

In this experimental implementation, the scale and tonal distance between notes follow the pattern of a diatonic major scale and we opted to stack five keyboard lines. As shown in Fig. 2, a 6-note shift was chosen for the first line and 2-note shift for the three bottom lines in order to maximize the amplitude of intervals that can be played in continuous movements.

As shown in Fig. 3, the kernel is a diatonic major scale (natural tones, the white notes on a traditional keyboard) and the distances are shown in diatonic tone shifts for this scale. One can clearly see that the choice for the number of shifts can minimize the path to play distant notes.

This phased replication of such scale kernel allows executing various intervals and sequences of notes only by crossing a spatial cursor throughout neighboring notes, reducing therefore the need for jumps (Fig. 4). Figure 4 compares gestural tracks of phrases played on the piano keyboard and on our keyboard implementation. Notice the shorter and continuous path to play some intervals due to the arrangement of keys.

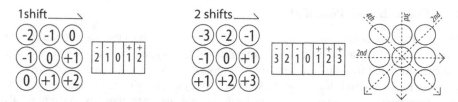

Fig. 3. The impact on playability, considering the number of shifts. One shift (left) gives a 5 tone continuous reach (left) from any note. Two shifts (center) allow greater reach and preserve two different ways to play second intervals: along the horizontal and diagonal lines (left).

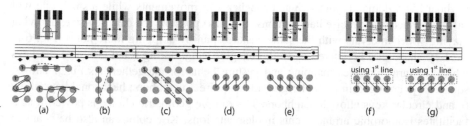

Fig. 4. Comparing gestural tracks of phrases played on the piano keyboard and on the proposed instrument. (a) Three possible ways to execute a linear progression. (b) Thirds intervals progression is executed vertically. (c) Fourth intervals progression is executed diagonally. (d) Successive thirds executed with a continuous wave movement. (e) Successive fourths executed with a continuous wave movement. The first line (shifted six tones backwards) allows executing successive sevenths and octave intervals.

Gesture-Mapped Chords

There are often numerous variations for each type of chord in traditional musical instruments. This leads to greater execution complexity because the player must know not only the chord type, but how to play it in different forms. Considering that the logic of playing isolated chords and notes, although related, are distinct, it was decided to create two playing modes (e.g. solo and chord) but in conceptual terms, avoiding discontinuities in the instrument. It was also assumed that transition between chords are naturally slower than between individual notes and that chords, in several situations, serve only as "base" for the music.

The user chooses the type of chord and the note to play in one direct movement. The main types of chords (minor, major, major or minor seventh, etc.) were encoded in five radial positions, chosen by wrist angle during execution. From these basic chords, using both hands, one can create variations by adding isolated notes. Thus, it would still be possible to play the basic chords with one hand while soloing with the other or playing more complex chords with both hands. Although there are ways to increase the combinatorial possibilities (e.g. using buttons) it was decided to map chords with gestures so to maintain simplicity and consistency within the interface.

3.2   Customization Possibilities

An important conceptual backbone for this instrument was easy customization, a feature expected to be fully available to end users in future prototypes. Figure 5 shows building and customization methods available for developers. Currently one can change keyboard mapping by adding and sliding the stacked lines of keys, one by one. As Fig. 3 shows this procedure modifies the physical distance between keys and then changes which intervals will be available to play in a single continuous playing movement or in a short jump movement. The keyboard perimeter can also optionally hold isolated supplementary keys.

An important feature is scaling, which defines the overall size of the keyboard (Fig. 5). Thus, the keyboard can be as big as the user can reach within the limits of the hand tracking device, modifying the spatial range and the gestural behavior. A big keyboard will demand extensive and rougher arm movements while a small one will call for limited and precise hand actions. It is also possible to scale key size, allowing playing wider intervals with the same gesture span by skipping more notes (Fig. 6).

Key shape can be altered as well, changing neighboring relationship of the keys which, in turn, modifies mapping and gesture behavior altogether. As Fig. 7 shows, square keys arranged in a regular grid allow 4 direct neighbors; hexagonal keys allow 6; and circular keys allow 8 neighbors. This simple geometric choice is powerful as it facilitates isomorphic arrangements implementations. Key color can also be changed per octave or individually.

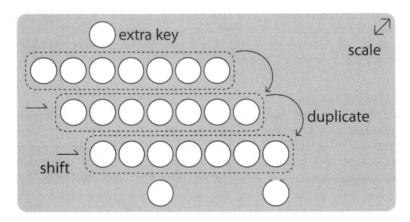

Fig. 5. Keyboard layout customization methods available to developers.

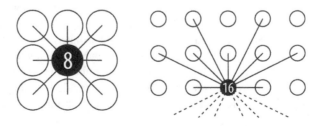

Fig. 6. Key sizing, making it possible to reach, for instance, 8 or 16 notes with a single jump.

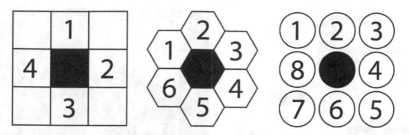

Fig. 7. Different key shapes modify note mapping and the gesture behavior.

4 System Implementation Description

4.1 Overview

Our implementation strategy adopted agile concepts to support development with constant and cyclic user feedback, resulting in fast incremental improvements. The virtual instrument was implemented on a Windows operating system running the Unity cross-platform engine and development environment (unity3d.com). The engine handles 3D graphics and all scene geometry was built from available geometric primitives. Collision detection is readily available for developers, an essential functionality used to detect key activation. The colored cursor trace was also implemented with built-in methods. Positioning of keys was automated with a script that accepts scale and radius as keyboard parameters. The customized interaction logic and main state machine were coded in C# programming language.

A Razer Hydra motion-sensor controller was used as user interface (sixense.com/razerhydra) and the Oculus Rift DK2 as display, a well-known stereoscopic head-mounted display (www.oculus.com). Both devices have seamless integration with the Unity engine. Figure 8 (left) illustrates the arrangement of the main components.

The sound was synthesized using a MIDI-controlled synthesizer invoked by Pure Data (Pd, http://puredata.info) and played through two loudspeakers. A Kalimba sound was used as timbre reference, though this program can be easily changed.

Figure 8 (right) shows a user testing the actual 3D virtual musical instrument. The virtual world is displayed on the Oculus Rift and optionally on a computer monitor, to allow spectators a view of the performance. The user interacts using Razer Hydra's joysticks, which capture the position and rotation of both hands.

The Razer Hydra magnetic tracked joysticks proved to be one of the best choices when it comes to precision and range. The choice of such devices has a relevant impact on the actual playing range of the virtual instrument. A limited or expanded playing range is determined by the range of the magnetic tracker and also the range of wires. If compared to Leap Motion (www.leapmotion.com), the magnetic sensor is robust and seldom suffers from interference (especially from infrared sources), capturing position, tilt and yaw of the hand, offering also several buttons to ease system debugging. The work of Han and Gold [6] discusses other limitations of the Leap Motion device for gesture-based virtual instruments. However, it should be stressed that interaction design sought to be simple enough to allow the use of other gestural interfaces.

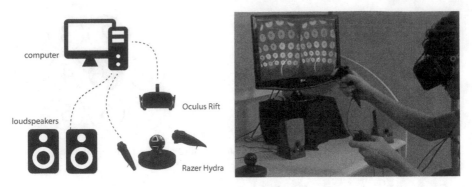

Fig. 8. System diagram (left). The user wears an Oculus Rift DK2 head-mounted display to see the virtual keyboard in 3D, along with digital representations of his hands. Tracked joysticks (Razer Hydra) captures hand position in space, wrist tilt and button commands. Conventional stereo loudspeakers outputs the sound. System in use (right).

Despite the unique 3D keyboard implementation, its customization possibilities, the innovative explorations on note mapping and gesture mapping, and beyond the performance and learning optimization ideas that were carried out, the programming effort itself were straightforward and did not involve any new fundamental challenge either in virtual reality, computer graphics or innovative algorithms.

4.2 Virtual Keyboard

In the virtual world the performer sees a keyboard with a pre-defined scale arrangement, as described in the Sect. 3.1. It is important to recall that the keyboard is redundant to allow flexibility in playing gesture patterns (matching musical patterns).

Figure 9 shows a keyboard prototype limited to a three octave range. Every line has a complete reference octave (white keys). The lower octave (left) is complete only in the second line and the higher octave (right) is almost complete in the first and last lines.

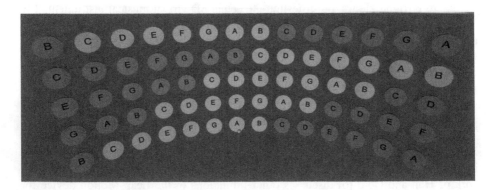

Fig. 9. Virtual keyboard with three octave range. Note the curvature and octave shifts.

Following the concepts proposed for playing this keyboard, ideally the user should start and gravitate near the reference octave (central line, white keys in Fig. 9) and then use redundant lines of octaves to facilitate playing with the shortest gestures possible. However, as with most instruments counting on note redundancy, one need to find the optimal gestural trajectory according to the song, in order to avoid discontinuities in performance. By capturing the keyboard operational rationale and acquiring proficiency in the instrument, the user is expected to get liberated from the reference octave.

The actual keyboard has a curvature that take into account the natural movement pattern of arms across the keyboard, assuming a static user in the center. The radius can be changed internally and was determined empirically considering short and tall users.

It must be recalled that this configuration is flexible and was set for testing purposes only. As shown in Sect. 3.2, the keyboard can be extended with extra octaves, redundant lines and additional perimeter keys according to the maximum tracking range of the joysticks and the size of the keyboard. It is also possible to completely surround the performer with a full cylindrical keyboard, although this scenario was not targeted.

4.3   Interaction

The following sections describe the melodic (single notes sequence) and chord (simultaneous note sequence) playing modes and interaction features implemented in the instrument.

Single Notes Execution
The user should be able to hit notes individually or in sequence and to perform chords in a simple way. To play and sustain a single note the user must hit the key and keep the trigger button pressed. If the player changes the note key while pressing the trigger, the notes will be played in a continuous sequence. In this case, as support for the gestural paradigm and improvement of positioning feedback, the system offers visual traces (Fig. 10). Although this instrument can be played like a xylophone, the keyboard concept allows for agile jumps across notes without unbalancing the motion path.

Chords Execution
Chords execution demands choosing the root note by hovering the cursor over any key on the keyboard and then defining the chord type by a hand tilt, where the wrist angle informs which chord is to be played. The chosen chord is indicated by a sign (Fig. 11). In the neutral hand position, one can play major chords, supposing these are more common than the others.

Considering that the wrist has a relatively short angle range in pronation and supination, the least used chord types (e.g. augmented and diminished, in this case) were encoded close to extreme positions, for they require larger muscular effort to achieve and maintain. The intermediary positions encodes the other most common types of chords (minor, major seventh and minor seventh).

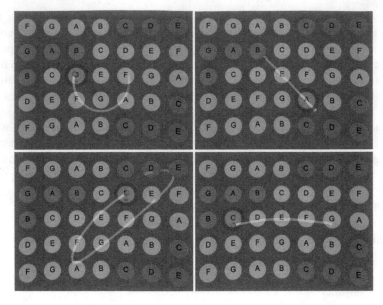

Fig. 10. Visual traces left over the keyboard as the player executes a movement. The key highlighted in the keyboard is being played.

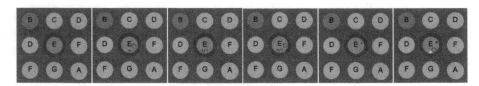

Fig. 11. Available chord types, from left to right: major; minor (m); major seventh (M7); minor seventh (m7), augmented (+) and diminished (°).

Interaction Modes

Two types of interactions are offered as a way to suit user's interaction preferences and ease learning. The standard mode is trace-based (Fig. 10), where hand position is represented by a 3D cursor and a visual trace is left over the keyboard. Despite the curved keyboard, stereoscopic vision, adequately sized spherical keys and possibility to adjust keyboard size and radius, some habituation time is necessary to get the right depth and hit notes automatically since tactile feedback is absent. Since the user can't see complete hands in this interaction mode, visual feedback and depth perception might not be ideal for beginners.

An alternative ray-based mode (Fig. 12, left) projects a finite length directional ray that easily absorbs depth imprecisions. In this mode, the player can point out directly a note key target.

The user can choose the interaction type for each hand, which is convenient for two hands playing as shown in Fig. 12 (right).

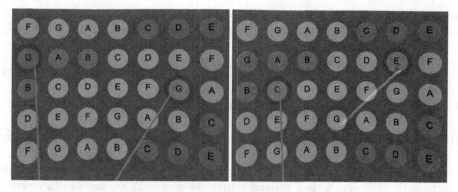

Fig. 12. Alternative mode using projected rays (left). Mixing modes: ray mode for chords played by the left hand and traced cursor for playing isolated notes with the right hand (right).

5 Results, Usage Impressions and Discussions

The first prototype of the instrument, named "CrosScale", was presented and tested by several amateur and expert users in the 3DUI Contest of the 2015 IEEE symposium on 3D user interfaces [15].

Instead of performing comprehensive tests with musicians playing predefined musical patterns or collecting an extensive sample for playability studies for the 3D virtual keyboard, our experimental prototyping phase targeted to collect feedback from regular VR users regarding mainly usability issues that could be used to guide another cycle of agile developments.

Inexperienced subjects on music reported fast learning and enjoyment while experimenting with the interface, although hitting the right depth in three dimensions was sometimes challenging in the standard interaction mode (3D cursor with trace), as expected. The alternative ray-mode was deemed easier but some users reported that execution timing was slightly affected and that this interaction mode impedes using the space behind the keyboard. In fact, some users inquired why the ample virtual space was not further explored. This idea was considered at the start but the team decided to tackle the complex mapping issue with a simpler version instead.

Subjects already familiarized with music were able to perform fast complex note sequences and enjoyed the 3D trace of the cursor arguing that this visual feedback induces better fluency, gracious gestures and possibly improved mnemonics. Most users attributed faster learning to the proposed keyboard, after a habituation period.

Naturally, most users started execution at the central line but quite often they reached the limits of the keyboard. As expected, this resulted in complaints about the restricted keyboard, especially the absence of complete lower and higher octaves. However they often realized that this issue is just a matter of detail and the keyboard can be easily extended and customized.

As pointed out by some users most songs call for intermittent or persistent accidents on scale (reducing or augmenting one or more notes in a half tone), a feature not already supported on the system. This can be easily solved with incremental gestures for sharp/flat tones, using wrist angles for instance (pronation for sharps, supination for flats) or by exploring the plentiful available space behind the keyboard.

It was also noticed that interaction simplicity (avoiding buttons, for instance) allows seamless porting to other devices (Leap Motion, trackers, Kinect or cameras).

6 Concluding Remarks and Future Work

The proposed instrument intended to tackle essential issues on virtual instrumentation design for music, focusing on learning speed, accessibility, playability and also execution joyfulness. To achieve this, the resulting solution sought to improve the matching between musical and gestural patterns by restricting the access to a specific user defined scale, coupled with note redundancy and customizable tuning.

As discussed in this article, this concept is supported by the fact that compositional patterns have been extensively adopted in music creation. If an instrument is able to capture such patterns, execution is extremely simplified and the essence of music is grasped easier. Feedback from interaction experts indicate that the strategy can speed learning and ease execution of chords and patterns such as intervals, but more testing and rigorous experiments are necessary to assess our claims, in particular, whether an interpreted instrument can effectively reduce the cognitive load imposed on the player.

Our experiments revealed that there is plenty of room for improvements in the field of virtual musical instrument development, and much room for research in the field of virtual instrument usage for professional performance. One advantage of virtual instruments over traditional ones is their flexibility and possibility for customization, as already demonstrated here. Ideally, the proposed instrument can implement different scale modes, and shifts can be programmed for as many different lines and displacements as necessary, which should be chosen before the execution of a song. The player may also save the playing path in a rehearsal stage, traditionally carried out when learning a new song.

For this experiment the actual keyboard was fixed, the scale was pre-defined and, as pointed out by several users, is actually 2.5D, i.e., the interaction logic is mainly planar in spite of a 3D scene and spatial interactions. Future improvements can target the implementation of an agile method for changing scales, for songs that change tonal keys or just to speed up the transition map from one song to another.

Visual traces can be improved and used as a mnemonic tool and as raw data for analytics, in order to analyze or find gestural patterns. One can use persisting traces in big redundant keyboards, for instance, to ease song learning.

Other improvements include implementing n-tone scales to investigate isomorphic keyboard layouts and to explore and take advantage of the virtual space around the instrument, which can be further explored as a fast way to change scales, to improve gesture continuity with other intervals (fifths, sixths, sevenths and octaves), to allow the execution of other patterns and to enrich possibilities in the execution of chords.

Finally, we plan to integrate an immersive auralization engine using a larger number of speakers that may allow, for instance, to set the sound of the note to a specific position in the visual environment, reinforcing the joint audiovisual perception.

Acknowledgments. This research has been partially supported by CNPq Brazilian National Research Council, DT Productivity Grant process 311681/2012-3. The authors would like to thank Gabriel Roque, Mario Nagamura, Luiz Paulucci, Marcio Cabral and Tainá Saboia for the substantial contribution to this research.

References

1. Fels, S.: Designing for intimacy: creating new interfaces for musical expression. Proc. IEEE **92**(4), 672–685 (2004)
2. Fels, S., Lyons, M.: Creating new interfaces for musical expression: introduction to NIME. In: ACM SIGGRAPH 2009 Courses, SIGGRAPH 2009. ACM, New York (2009)
3. Chadabe, J.: The limitations of mapping as a structural descriptive in electronic instruments. In: Proceedings of the 2002 Conference on New Interfaces for Musical Expression (NIME 2002), Dublin, Ireland (2002)
4. Wessel, D., Wright, M.: Problems and prospects for intimate musical control of computers. Comput. Music J. **26**(3), 11–22 (2002)
5. Cook, P.R.: Laptop orchestras, robotic drummers, singing machines, and musical kitchenware: learning programming, algorithms, user interface design, and science through the arts. J. Comput. Sci. Coll. **28**(1), 157 (2012)
6. Han, J., Gold, N.: Lessons learned in exploring the leap motion TM sensor for gesture-based instrument design. In: Proceedings of the 2014 Conference on New Interfaces for Musical Expression. (NIME 2014), London, United Kingdom (2014)
7. Franco, I.: The AirStick: a free-gesture controller using infrared sensing. In Proceedings of the 2005 Conference on New Interfaces for Musical Expression (NIME 2005), Vancouver, BC, Canada (2005)
8. Hasan, L., et al.: The Termenova: a hybrid free-gesture interface. In: Proceedings of the 2002 Conference on New Interfaces for Musical Expression (NIME 2002), Dublin, Ireland (2002)
9. Han, Y., Na, J., Lee, K.: Futuregrab: a wearable synthesizer using vowel formants. In: Proceedings of the 2012 Conference on New Interfaces for Musical Expression (NIME 2012), Ann Arbor, Michigan (2012)
10. Poepel, C., Feitsch, J., Strobel, M., Geiger, C.: Design and evaluation of a gesture controlled singing voice installation. In: Proceedings of the 2014 Conference on New Interfaces for Musical Expression (NIME 2014), London, United Kingdom (2014)
11. Gillian, N., Paradiso, J.A.: Digito: a fine-grain gesturally controlled virtual musical instrument. In: Proceedings of the 2012 Conference on New Interfaces for Musical Expression (NIME 2012), Ann Arbor, Michigan (2012)
12. Hunt, A., Wanderley, M.M., Paradis, M.: The importance of parameter mapping in electronic instrument design. In: Proceedings of the 2002 Conference on New Interfaces for Musical Expression (NIME 2002), Dublin, Ireland (2002)
13. Maupin, S., Gerhard, D., Park, B.: Isomorphic tessellations for musical keyboards. In: Proceedings of Sound and Music Computing Conference, Padova, Italy (2011)
14. Perez, M.: Gesto musical e o uso de interfaces físicas digitais na performance do live electronics. Master Dissertation in Music, University of São Paulo, São Paulo (2016)
15. Cabral, M., et al.: Crosscale: a 3D virtual musical instrument interface. In: Proceedings of the 2015 Symposium on 3D User Interfaces (3DUI), Arles, France (2015)

Using Sound to Enhance Taste Experiences: An Overview

Felipe Reinoso Carvalho[1,2(✉)], Abdellah Touhafi[1], Kris Steenhaut[1],
Raymond van Ee[2,3,4], and Carlos Velasco[5,6]

[1] Department of Electronics and Informatics (ETRO), Vrije Universiteit Brussel,
Pleinlaan 2, 1050 Brussels, Belgium
f.sound@gmail.com, abdellah.touhafi@vub.ac.be,
ksteenha@etro.vub.ac.be
[2] Department of Experimental Psychology, KU Leuven, Leuven, Belgium
Raymond.vanEe@psy.kuleuven.be
[3] Donders Institute, Radboud University, Nijmegen, Netherlands
rvee@science.ru.nl
[4] Philips Research Labs, Eindhoven, Netherlands
raymond.van.ee@philips.com
[5] Crossmodal Research Laboratory, Oxford University, Oxford, UK
carlos.velasco@psy.ox.ac.uk
[6] BI Norwegian Business School, Oslo, Norway

Abstract. We present an overview of the recent research conducted by the first author of this article, in which the influence of sound on the perception of taste/flavor in beer is evaluated. Three studies in total are presented and discussed. These studies assessed how people match different beers with music and the influence that the latter can have on the perception and enjoyment of the beers. In general, the results revealed that in certain contexts sound can modulate the perceived strength and taste attributes of the beer as well as its associated hedonic experience. We conclude by discussing the potential mechanisms behind these taste-flavor/sound interactions, and the implications of these studies in the context of multisensory food and drink experience design. We suggest that future work may also build on cognitive neuroscience. In particular, such an approach may complement our understanding of the underlying brain mechanisms of auditory/gustatory interactions.

Keywords: Sound · Music · Taste · Beer · Perception · Multisensory experiences

1 Introduction

Chefs, molecular mixologists, food designers, and artists, among other professionals working in the food industry, are increasingly looking at the latest scientific advances in multisensory flavor perception research as a source of inspiration for the design of dining experiences [26, 29, 30] (see [42], for a review). A number of recent studies have highlighted the idea that the sounds that derive from our interaction with the food (e.g., mastication; see [55]), can be modulated in order to enhance the sensory and hedonic

© Springer International Publishing AG 2017
M. Aramaki et al. (Eds.): CMMR 2016, LNCS 10525, pp. 316–330, 2017.
DOI: 10.1007/978-3-319-67738-5_19

aspects associated with the experience of eating and drinking, (e.g. [10, 44, 46]; see [41] for a review). What is more, there is also a growing consensus that the sounds and/or noise that occurs in the places where we eat and drink - such as restaurants and airplanes - can dramatically affect our perception of taste and flavor of foods and drinks ([27, 28, 43]; see [39, 41, 42] for reviews). Indeed, it has been demonstrated that several acoustic parameters that define the quality of an auditory space, such as the reverberation time of a room and the level of background noise [1, 15], can affect the perception of foods; for example, in terms of how sweet or bitter they taste (e.g., [11, 48, 54]; see [40], for a review of the influence of noise on the perception of food and drink).

Here, we present an overview of studies recently developed by the lead author of the present research, which assesses the influence of sound on taste[1]/flavor perception of alcoholic beverages. Three studies using beer as taste stimulus are introduced. The first assessed how the participants matched different beer flavors with frequency tones. The second studied how different customized auditory cues would modulate the perception of the beer's taste. Finally, the third study evaluated how the beer's hedonic experience can be influenced by a song that was presented as part of the multisensory beer experience. Moreover, we conclude this review by discussing the potential mechanisms behind these taste/sound interactions, and the implications of these assessments in the context of multisensory food and drink experience design. We suggest that future work may rely on cognitive neuroscience approaches in order to better understand the underlying brain mechanisms associated with the crossmodal correspondence between taste/flavor and sound.

2 Looking for Beer-Pitch Matches

Recently, we have conducted a study designed to assess how people associate the taste of beers with auditory pitch [30]. Here, the participants were asked to choose the frequency that, in their opinion, best matched the taste of each of three Belgian bitter-dry beer types. Chemically, Jambe de Bois (Beer 1) is almost as bitter as Taras Boulba (Beer 2), but its full body and malt dominance may result in it being perceived as sweeter. Therefore, Jambe de Bois can be considered to be the sweetest of the three beers, while Zinnebir (Beer 3) comes out second due to its alcohol-plus-malt formula.

The auditory stimuli consisted of a digital version of an adjustable frequency tone generator. Using an online tone generator (Retrieved from http://plasticity.szynalski.com/tone-generator.htm, February, 2015), the participants were asked to choose the tone frequencies that in their opinion were most suitable for the taste of the beers. Figure 1 shows an image of the graphic interface.

This study included three experiments. In Experiment 1, the participant's ratings were based on a wide range of choices (50–1500 Hz). Here, their results suggested that the three beers were 'tuned' around the same pitch (see Fig. 1). However, in Experiment 2, the addition of a soft drink beverage alongside two of the beers, verified the

---

[1] By taste we refer to the basic components that are mostly captured by the tongue (sweetness, saltiness, bitterness, sourness and umami). Flavor, on the other hand, is a more complex experience that also involves, at least, retro nasal olfaction.

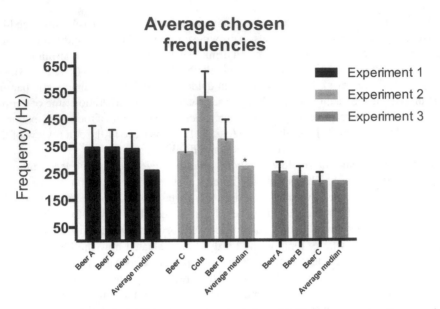

Fig. 1. Average chosen frequencies in experiments 1, 2, and 3. Here, we can visually appreciate that the average medians in the three experiments are in the same range with the means obtained in Experiment 3 (error bars show the upper limit of the confidence interval of the means). Note that the average median in Experiment 2 is based on the median values of the two beers used in such experiment, not including the correspondent median cola value (marked with an asterisk '*').

fact that the participants matched the beers toward the lower end of the available range of frequencies, and the soft drink toward a higher tone (see Fig. 1). Note that, in Experiments 1 and 2, the majority of the results fell within a much narrower range than what was available to choose from. Consequently, in Experiment 3, the range of frequencies was reduced to 50–500 Hz. Under the new frequency range, the obtained means - and medians - were matched to tones in the same frequency range, as those medians that derived from Experiments 1 and 2 (see Fig. 1).

These results demonstrate that participants reliably match beverages, with very different taste profiles, to different frequencies, and, as such, consistently matched bitter beers to a low - and narrow - band of sound frequencies. Therefore, we further confirmed the hypothesis that people tend to associate bitter flavors with low audible frequencies, and sweet flavors with high audible frequency ranges [44].

One limitation of the current study, given the multisensory nature of flavor perception, is that, it is not entirely clear on what basis did the participants make their beer-pitch matching (e.g., on the basis of the beer's aroma, mouthfeel, taste, etc....). Future research may explore the different components of the beer's flavor. For example, are such beer-pitch associations made solely on the basis of the aroma of the beers? It is important to consider here the potential bias effects that may derived from the beer's extrinsic properties, such as their different colors (that should not be accessible to the participants) and/or the homogeneity in the amount of foam present in all samples. Finally, further studies may attempt to understand the perceptual effects of matching/non-matching tones on the multisensory drinking experience. Perhaps, as we will see later, it may be possible to modulate the beer's taste by manipulating the auditory cues that accompany the taste experience.

3   Modulating Beer Taste and Strength by Means of Customized Songs

Another study involving beer conducted by Reinoso Carvalho et al. [31] analyzed the effect of three songs on people's perception of the taste of the beer. The participants tasted a beer twice, and rated the sensory and hedonic aspects of the beer (likeness, perceived sweetness, bitterness, sourness and alcohol strength), each time while listening to a different song[2]. Here, the objective was to determine whether songs that have previously been shown to correspond to the different basic tastes would significantly modulate the perceived taste, and alcohol content of the beers (see [51], for the procedure on how the songs were classified - note that this is the first time this type of studies is made with beers as taste stimuli). The three beers used in the present study were Belgian bitter-dry types (the same three beers presented in Sect. 2).

For this study, three experiments were developed. The independent variable for each experiment was therefore sound condition, and the dependent variables were the ratings that the participants made for each beer. In Experiment 1, the participants tasted Taras Boulba while listening to the sweet and bitter songs. In Experiment 2, they tasted the Jambe de Bois beer while listening to the sweet and sour songs. In Experiment 3, the participants tasted Zinnebir while listening to the sour and bitter songs. Each beer was assigned to the experiment with the songs that expressed the most prominent taste in the beer. Therefore, Taras Boulba, which was ranked as the most bitter, was used in Experiment 1, where the bitter and sweet songs were played. Jambe de Bois, which was ranked as the sweetest, was used in Experiment 2, where the sweet and sour songs were played. Zinnebir, which was ranked in-between the two other ones, in both scales, was used in Experiment 3, where the bitter and sour songs were played. The songs were presented in a counterbalanced order.

The songs were found to influence the participants' rating of the taste and strength of the beer (see Fig. 2).

In Experiment 1, the participants rated the beer as significantly sweeter when listening to the sweet song than when listening to the bitter song. In Experiment 2, the participants rated the beer as tasting significantly sweeter while listening to the sweet song than while listening to the sour song. No significant differences were found when comparing taste ratings in Experiment 3. However, only in Experiment 3, the participants rated the difference in alcohol strength as significant (the beer was perceived as more alcoholic while listening to the bitter song than when listening to the sour song). The results also revealed that most participants liked the sweet song when compared to the bitter and sour ones. In general, they did not like the bitter song and really did not like the sour song, when compared to the sweet one. Furthermore, a control experiment

---

[2] Link to the songs http://sonicseasoningbeer.tumblr.com/ (retrieved on March, 2016).

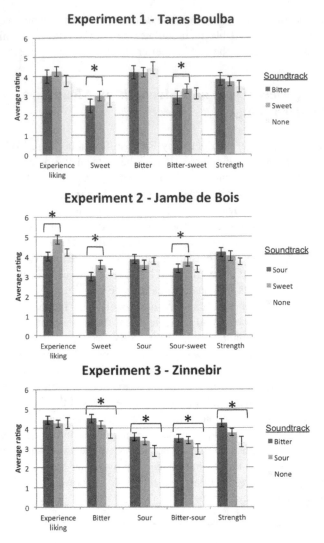

Fig. 2. Comparison of beer ratings (means and standard error bars) made while listening to songs versus silence. All ratings were made on a 7-point scale, with "1" = not at all and "7" = very much. The asterisk '*' indicates a significant difference (p < .05). Figure reprinted from [31], with permission from Elsevier

(Experiment 3) without sonic stimuli confirmed that these results could not simply be explained in terms of order (or adaptation) effects. These results may be explained in terms of the notion of sensation transference [5]. That is, while listening to the pleasant sweet song, the participant transfers his/her experience/feelings about the music to the beer that they happen to be tasting. This, in turn, results in higher pleasantness and also higher sweetness ratings (when compared to, in this case, the relatively less pleasant sour and bitter songs), given the hedonic characteristics of such a taste.

Finally, here, for the first time, we demonstrate that it is possible to systematic modulate the perceived taste and strength of beers, by means of matching or mis-matching sonic cues. These results open further possibilities when it comes to ana-lyzing how the emotional aspects involved in sound-beer experiences can affect such crossmodal correspondences.

4 Analyzing the Effect of Customized Background Music in Multisensory Beer Tasting Experiences

This study [32] focused on the potential influence of background music on the hedonic and perceptual beer-tasting experience. Here, different groups of customers tasted a beer under three different conditions. The control group was presented with an unla-beled beer, the second group with a labeled beer, and the third group with a labeled beer together with a customized sonic cue (a short clip from an existing song).

The beer used in this experiment, namely 'Salvation', was a one-time-batch limited edition, and a co-creation between The Brussels Beer Project (TBP), and an UK music band called 'The Editors[3]'. The complete description of the creative process involving the development - and characterization - of the experimental taste and sonic stimuli can be accessed in the following link: http://tbpeditors-experience.tumblr.com/ (Retrieved on March 2016). A fragment of the song 'Oceans of Light', from the previously-mentioned band was chosen as the sonic stimulus for this experiment. The fragment contained around one minute of the original song (from minute 2:25 to minute 3:25, approximately[4]. By relating the musical and psychoacoustic analysis with the summary of the cross-modal correspondence between basic tastes and sonic elements presented by [18], we predicted that the song may modulate the perceived sourness of the beer[5].

The full study was divided into three main steps. In the first step, the participants inserted their personal information, read, and then accept the terms of the informed consent. The second and third steps were different for each of the three experimental conditions. In Condition A, the participants evaluated the beer presentation without any label in the bottle, tasted the beer afterwards and answered some questions regarding their beer experience. In this condition, the participants did not have any information regarding the origin of the beer. In Condition B, the participants evaluated the beer presented with its label on the bottle, tasted the beer afterwards, and answered some questions regarding their beer-tasting experience. Here, they were informed that the beer that they were tasting was the product of a collaboration between TBP and The Editors (band). Finally, in Condition C, the participants evaluated the beer's

---

[3] See http://www.editorsofficial.com/ (retrieved November 2015).

[4] Link to the song - https://play.spotify.com/track/4yVv19QPf9WmaAmYWOrdfr?play=true&utm_source=open.spotify.com&utm_medium=open (retrieved January 2016).

[5] For example, in [17]'s Table 1 - which summarizes the results of a number of studies carried out by different research groups - high spectral balance, staccato articulation, syncopated rhythm, high pitch, among others, are musical/psychoacoustic elements that correspond to sourness. Furthermore, due to the predominant piano in the second verse, the song might also be expected to have an effect on the perceived levels of sweetness.

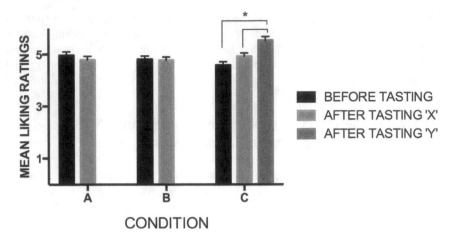

Fig. 3. Mean ratings of the evaluation of the subjective aspects of the tasting experience, with 'X' being the ratings of how much they liked the beer (X), and 'Y' the likeness ratings of the sound-tasting experience (Y) [ratings based on 7-point scales, being 1 'not at all', and 7 'Very much']. Visualizing these evaluations, it seems that the participants valued the customized soundscape component of the multisensory beer-tasting experience. The error bars represent the standard error (SE) of the means here and in all the other graphs of the present study. Significant differences between the specific interactions are indicated with an asterisk '*' (p-value for the comparison before-tasting and after-tasting ratings 'Y' ($p = .001$); p-value for the comparison after-tasting ratings 'X' and 'Y' ($p < .001$) – this figure was taken from open access publication, published in Frontiers in Psychology [27].

presentation with its corresponding label, tasted the beer while listening to the chosen song, and answered some questions regarding their beer-tasting experience. The participants in conditions B and C were told that the beer being tasted was the product of a collaboration between TBP and The Editors (band), and that the song that they listened to was the source of inspiration for the formulation of this beer. The questionnaires of steps two and three were fully randomized.

The results suggested that music may as well be effectively used to add value to multisensory tasting experiences when there is a previous connection between the participants and the music (see Fig. 3).

Concerning taste ratings, the song seemed to have a modulatory effect on the perceived sourness of the beer. However, the ratings of Conditions A and C are mostly indistinguishable, and significantly higher when compared to the ratings in Condition B. Similarly, the participants reported that the beer tasted significantly stronger when it was presented without labeling (Condition A), and in Condition C, when the beer's presentation was accompanied by the song, than in Condition B. In the two cases mentioned above, it would seem that drawing attention to the visual aspects of the label, in Condition B, had a negative effect. In particular, we suggest that in Condition B, the semantic contents of the label may have counterbalanced the perceived sourness, and, in Condition C, the song may have enhanced it. Another potential relevant factor present in the label was the visual impact of the diagonal white line. Such line goes from top left down to bottom right. Another study recently reported [55] that consumers potentially have a preference for an oblique line ascending to the right, when evaluating plating arrangements. Something similar is likely to be found with product packaging. In summary, the white line was in the opposite direction as the probable preferred choice of the customers that experienced the label.

One potential limitation of the present study is that it was implemented in a brewery with its own customers and, hence, all of the participants were constantly influenced by the brand, which potentially provided brand-specific cues that may also have contributed to the findings. Future research could develop a similar experience in a more typical drinking environment, such as a common bar, including neutral glassware and a more balanced audience[6]. Here, it was also not possible to discriminate the influence of the given messages in Conditions B and C (cf. [28]). A future implementation may consider delivering such message only to the participants being stimulated by a song (i.e., in this experiment, only to the participants in Condition C).

5 Discussion and Future Work

5.1 General Discussion

With the studies reviewed in this article, we have showed that soundscapes/music can influence taste (and potentially flavor) attributes of drinks. With that in mind, we suggest that sound can be used to "liven up" the overall eating and drinking experience. For example, a bitter chocolate (or a bitter beer) accompanied by high-pitched sounds may be perceived as less bitter, making its consumption more pleasant - and potentially with less added sugar - for those who prefer sweeter tastes.

So, why auditory cues would influence taste perception? As suggested by [47], when thinking about the modulation of taste perception via sonic cues, it is perhaps difficult to point to a single mechanism that explains the range of effects reported in the literature. Relevant to the studies presented here, [47] suggests that crossmodal correspondences, emotion, and/or sensation transfer may potentially explain the different effects reported in the literature. For instance, crossmodal correspondences may influence taste perception via psychoacoustic features that match or mismatch attributes or features such as sweetness, bitterness, and/or sourness; such features may draw people's attention towards specific taste attributes (see Sect. 2; see [18] for an overview). Whether or not features match another feature may depend on multiple mechanisms as suggested by [38]. Note, however, that in more everyday life people are rarely exposed to a single psychoacoustic feature while eating. Moreover, whilst it may be possible that a song and/or soundscape have a dominant or a series of dominant psychoacoustic features, music in itself is a more complex construction, and is usually under condition of our own personal preferences. For that reason, the emotional

---

[6] 83% of the participants reported knowing TBP (N = 191). When asked how often the participants consumed products from TBP - on a 7 point scale, with 1 corresponding to 'never' and 7 to 'very often' - the mean of their answers was 3.30 (SD 1.80). Note that, since the vast majority of the participants reported knowing TBP, in this study it was not possible to include in our data analysis control for familiarity of the beer's brand.

connotation of specific auditory stimuli (either a feature or a more complex sonic stimulus) could transfer to the experience of the food/beverage and thus influence their specific sensory and hedonic characteristics. A pleasant song may therefore lead to higher pleasantness and eventually sweetness ratings (as sweetness tends to be pleasant and thus it matches the pleasantness of the song) - when compared to a relatively less pleasant song (see Sect. 5; see [5], for a review on sensation transference). Importantly, it has also been shown that a person's mood can influence their ability to detect olfactory (e.g. [25]) and gustatory stimuli [13, 14]. In that sense, emotions induced by music can have an attentional effect on the way people perceive taste. Recently, [17] showed that sweetness can be perceived more dominant when the music that is played is liked by the participants, when tasting a chocolate gelati (Italian ice cream). On the other hand, bitterness seems to be enhanced when people dislike the music. This seems to be consistent with the idea that certain crossmodal correspondences may be explained by a common affective connotation of the component unisensory cues that people match [47]. Importantly, more than one study have concluded that liking or disliking the music that people hear while tasting can have a significant effect in the levels of enjoyment of food/beverages [12, 16].

As a next step for future research, it will be critical to test the different mechanisms behind sound-taste interactions (i.e. crossmodal correspondences, sensation transference, attentional redirection, among others). Important to say here that the assessment on how sounds – that not necessarily derive from our interaction with food (e.g., mastication, such as in [20]) - influence taste/flavor perception is relatively new, with most of its conclusive results coming from the last ten years. Therefore, we could presume that the existent methods that are here being applied – and revised – are not so well-established yet, when referring to this specific sensorial combination. As such, we believe that future behavioral studies may well be combined with neuroscientific methods. Such combination may help to provide a better understanding on the brain mechanisms that underlie sound/taste correspondences. Take, for instance, the 'Sensation Transference' account described by [5], which we suggest as a possible explanation for the modified hedonic value of food/drink experiences that involve sonic cues [31, 32]. For example, in [31], it seems that the participant transfers his/her feelings about the music to the beer that they happen to be tasting. Potentially, one possible approach for understanding the relationship between sound and taste, at a neurological level, would be to focus on the way in which the affective value of gustatory and auditory information is encoded by the brain [34].

In the paragraphs below, we will present a short overview about multisensory perception from the perspective of cognitive neuroscience. Afterwards, we will introduce a few studies that have approached how the brain processes music and taste/flavor, separately, hypothesizing on the potential associations between music-food at the brain (mostly related to pleasantness). Finally, we will introduce a few approaches for potential future work, following the quite recent – but already existent – blend of psychophysics and neuroscience towards chemosensory/auditory interactions.

5.2   Sound and Taste from a Multisensory Integration Persepctive?

Most studies on multisensory integration have been focusing on vision and its inter-action with audition. So, one question that still remains open is, when thinking about the interaction of sound and taste/flavors in the brain, should we focus on multisensory integration? Or, perhaps, on the way in which sonic cues may prime specific mechanisms that end up having a significant influence on taste/flavor perception, without the necessary need for integration?

Multisensory integration – i.e. the interaction between sound and taste – seem to be the product of supra-additive neural responses, at least when it comes to the temporal and spatial characteristics of multisensory cues [37]. This means that, for instance, the response that a neuron produces to sight and sound that co-occur at more or less the same time and from the same spatial location, may be greater than the summed responses to either the sight or sound alone (e.g. [52]). [7] also argues that a multisensory interaction may be a dialogue between sensory modalities rather than the convergence of all sensory information onto a supra-modal area. For instance, [7] suggests that the Bayesian framework may provide an efficient solution for dealing with the combination of sensory cues that are not equally reliable [7], and this may fit into a sound-taste/flavor model. [49] also suggests that the identification and quantification of the effects of multisensory response may demand a comparison between the multisensory versus the single modality response, with the latter evoked by a single specific stimulus. In other words, in some cases, it is also practical to compare the multisensory response to, for example, models in which the unisensory responses are summed, or comparing models that are potentially ideal representations of a predicted response, obtained by the best combination of the unisensory inputs.

However, space and time are not be the only factors potentially underlying multisensory integration. Research also suggests that semantic congruency and crossmodal correspondences may also facilitate multisensory integration [38]. In particular, semantic congruency can be understood by those situations where, for example, auditory and vision cues are integrated because the different sensory cues belong to the same identity or meaning, as it happens with the picture of a dog and the barking sound of a dog, where both belong to the object 'dog' [4, 9, 38]. Crossmodal correspondences, on the other hand, can be thought of as the associations that seem to exist between basic stimulus attributes across different sensory modalities (i.e. correlations between different basic taste attributes within different frequency ranges, and so on) [23, 38].

Now, when thinking about how taste and sound interact, we know that what we hear can help us to identify the gustatory properties of what we eat. For instance, research has shown that modifying food-related auditory cues, regardless the fact that those sounds may come from the food itself or from a person's interaction with it (think of carbonated beverages, or a bite into an apple), can have an impact on the perception of both food and drink ([48]; see [41] for an overview; see [3] for more general principles). Still, in order to improve our understanding on taste/flavour-audition interactions (especially referring to those sounds that not necessarily derive from our interaction with food, but that nevertheless can still have a significant influence on the final tasting experience), it seems to be critical that future studies focus on the spationtemporal and semantic aspects of those senses, as well as the crossmodal correspondences that have been shown to exist between tastes/flavours and sonic features [36, 45].

5.3   Using Neuroscience to Assess the Mechanisms Behind Sound-Taste Correspondences

If one intend to build up a case for assessing the interaction of sound and taste/flavor at a cognitive level, which factors should one consider to start with? Listening to music seems to be mostly about pleasure and, still, we give as much inherent value to it than to eating and/or drinking. On the other hand, feeding ourselves comes as a need, regardless the fact that we will always be able to eat food (and drink beverages) that we find 'pleasant enough'. However, it seems that a potential successful baseline to build a solid cognitive relation between music and taste/flavor may be the fact that both stimulus, under the correct circumstances, can provide us with pleasure (note that this has been suggested as a possible mechanism for crossmodal correspondences; see [21, 38, 50]). As such, we could consider, as starting point to work, for example, with the hypothesis that the valence associated with a song or sonic parameter would have perceptual and/or hedonic effect on one's eating/drinking experience. Assuming that we are pursuing this path, which involves emotions, one way may be to refer to the affective account of crossmodal associations that are based on a common affective connotation. Here, we refer to the extent to which two features may be associated as a function of their common hedonic value [6, 8, 21, 22, 46, 50].

In any case, it would seem that when assessing how the brain perceives music, emotions come as a logical path to explore. Researchers have recently shown [53] that the interconnections of the key circuit for internally-focused thoughts, known as the default mode network, were more active when people listened to their preferred music. They also showed that listening to a favorite song alters the connectivity between auditory brain areas and the hippocampus, a region responsible for memory and social emotion consolidation. As suggested by [53], such results were unexpectedly consistent, given the fact that musical preferences are uniquely individualized phenomena and that music can vary in acoustic complexity and message. Furthermore, their assessment went further to previous ones, that focused simply on how different characteristics of music (i.e., classical versus country) affected the brain. Here, they considered that most people when listening to their preferred music (regardless of the type), often report experiencing personal thoughts and memories.

Other researchers have also used brain imaging to show, among other things, that the music that people described as highly emotional engaged the reward system in their brains - activating subcortical nuclei known to be important in reward, motivation, and emotion [2]. They also found that listening to what might be called "peak emotional moments" in music causes the release of dopamine, that is an essential signaling molecule in the brain [33]. That is, when we listen to music that we find pleasant, dopamine is released in the striatum. Dopamine is known to respond to the naturally rewarding stimuli – just like when we consume food.

As hypothesized above, it seems that emotional assessments could provide us with interesting outcomes. For example, what would happen if we eat chocolate while listening to our favorite songs, versus eating the same chocolate while listening to background noise at unpleasant/uncomfortable levels? Even before eating, when simply thinking about eating chocolate while being hungry, our bodies start to create expectations about the future eating experience[7]. Therefore, what would happen with our expectations (and their corresponding neural processes) while listening to different sonic cues, considering that they might be emotionally related to the subject being sampled? Or could, perhaps, our favorite songs help us reducing the negative emotional impact that eating low-sugared chocolate may bring into our daily lives? With a better understanding of the cognitive mechanisms behind such multisensory interaction, Music could not only be used to modulate the multisensory tasting experience, but it could, perhaps, also be used to modulate its previous expectations, in order to potentially prime the mind before eating/drinking.

Summarizing, as a future objective in this research path, we propose to continue extending the recent research that have started to raise these same questions, by blending psychophysics and neuroscience to chemosensory/auditory interactions (see [35] for a review on the influence of auditory cues on chemosensory perception). Since behavioral tests have been proven to be effective methods for assessing, for instance, emotional response (or its correspondent valence), it seems that a combination with cognitive neuroscientific approaches would help in a better understanding of the physiological state (arousal) while reacting to multisensory stimuli[8]. However, at some point, it would be prudent to consider that the relation between valence and arousal seem to vary with personality and culture, especially when dealing with subjective experiences [19].

Finally, from a design perspective, it is possible to customize the external sonic cues that may be involved in the eating/drinking process, with specific perceptual objectives, and without the need of altering a food/beverage product's physical appearance.

References

1. Astolfi, A., Filippi, M.: Good acoustical quality in restaurants: a compromise between speech intelligibility and privacy. In: Proceedings 18th International Congress on Acoustics ICA 2004, Kyoto, pp. 1201–1204 (2004)
2. Blood, A.J., Zatorre, R.J.: Intensely pleasurable responses to music correlate with activity in brain regions implicated in reward and emotion. Proc. Nat. Acad. Sci. **98**(20), 11818–11823 (2001)

---

[7] A few quick notes on how chocolate works in the brain were reviewed from both of the following links. http://science.howstuffworks.com/life/inside-the-mind/emotions/chocolate-high2.htm and http://healthyeating.sfgate.com/chocolate-dopamine-3660.html (retrieved on February, 2016); see [24] for a review on mood state effects of chocolate.

[8] Important to note here that arousal and valence are the most common ways to characterize changes in emotions. In other words, the relation between high/low arousal and positive/negative valence are used to define an emotional state.

3. Calvert, G.A., Thesen, T.: Multisensory integration: methodological approaches and emerging principles in the human brain. J. Physiol.-Paris **98**(1), 191–205 (2004)
4. Chen, Y.C., Spence, C.: When hearing the bark helps to identify the dog: semantically-congruent sounds modulate the identification of masked pictures. Cognition **114**(3), 389–404 (2010)
5. Cheskin, L.: Marketing success: how to achieve it. Cahners Books, Boston (1972)
6. Collier, G.L.: Affective synesthesia: extracting emotion space from simple perceptual stimuli. Motiv. Emot. **20**(1), 1–32 (1996)
7. Deneve, S., Pouget, A.: Bayesian multisensory integration and cross-modal spatial links. J. Physiol.-Paris **98**(1), 249–258 (2004)
8. Deroy, O., Crisinel, A.S., Spence, C.: Crossmodal correspondences between odors and contingent features: odors, musical notes, and geometrical shapes. Psychon. Bull. Rev. **20** (5), 878–896 (2013)
9. Doehrmann, O., Naumer, M.J.: Semantics and the multisensory brain: how meaning modulates processes of audio-visual integration. Brain Res. **1242**, 136–150 (2008)
10. Elder, R.S., Mohr, G.S.: The crunch effect: food sound salience as a consumption monitoring cue. Food Qual. Prefer. **51**, 39–46 (2016)
11. Ferber, C., Cabanac, M.: Influence of noise on gustatory affective ratings and preference for sweet or salt. Appetite **8**(3), 229–235 (1987)
12. Fiegel, A., Meullenet, J.F., Harrington, R.J., Humble, R., Seo, H.S.: Background music genre can modulate flavor pleasantness and overall impression of food stimuli. Appetite **76**, 144–152 (2014)
13. Frandsen, L.W., Dijksterhuis, G.B., Brockhoff, P.B., Nielsen, J.H., Martens, M.: Feelings as a basis for discrimination: comparison of a modified authenticity test with the same–different test for slightly different types of milk. Food Qual. Prefer. **18**(1), 97–105 (2007)
14. Heath, T.P., Melichar, J.K., Nutt, D.J., Donaldson, L.F.: Human taste thresholds are modulated by serotonin and noradrenaline. J. Neurosci. **26**(49), 12664–12671 (2006)
15. Heylighen, A., Rychtáriková, M., Vermeir, G.: Designing spaces for every listener. Univ. Access Inf. Soc. **9**(3), 283–292 (2009)
16. Kantono, K., Hamid, N., Shepherd, D., Yoo, M.J., Carr, B.T., Grazioli, G.: The effect of background music on food pleasantness ratings. Psychol. Music **44**(5), 1111–1125 (2015)
17. Kantono, K., Hamid, N., Shepherd, D., Yoo, M.J.Y., Grazioli, G., Carr, T.B.: Listening to music can influence hedonic and sensory perceptions of gelati. Appetite **100**, 244–255 (2016)
18. Knoeferle, K., Spence, C.: Crossmodal correspondences between sounds and tastes. Psychon. Bull. Rev. **19**, 992–1006 (2012)
19. Kuppens, P., Tuerlinckx, F., Yik, M., Koval, P., Coosemans, J., Zeng, K.J., Russell, J.A.: The relation between valence and arousal in subjective experience varies with personality and culture. J. Pers. **85**(4), 530–542 (2017)
20. Luckett, C.R., Meullenet, J.F., Seo, H.S.: Crispness level of potato chips affects temporal dynamics of flavor perception and mastication patterns in adults of different age groups. Food Qual. Prefer. **51**, 8–19 (2016)
21. Marks, L.E.: The Unity of the Senses: Interrelations Among the Modalities. Academic Press, Cambridge (1978)
22. Marks, L.E.: On perceptual metaphors. Metaphor Symb. **11**(1), 39–66 (1996)
23. Parise, C.V., Spence, C.: When birds of a feather flock together: synesthetic correspondences modulate audiovisual integration in non-synesthetes. PLoS One **4**(5), e5664 (2009)
24. Parker, G., Parker, I., Brotchie, H.: Mood state effects of chocolate. J. Affect. Disord. **92**(2), 149–159 (2006)

25. Pollatos, O., Kopietz, R., Linn, J., Albrecht, J., Sakar, V., Anzinger, A., Wiesmann, M.: Emotional stimulation alters olfactory sensitivity and odor judgment. Chem. Senses **32**(6), 583–589 (2007)
26. Reinoso Carvalho, F., Van Ee, R., Touhafi, A.: T.A.S.T.E. Testing auditory solutions towards the improvement of the tasting experience. In: Proceedings of 10th International Symposium on Computer Music Multidisciplinary Research. Marseille, pp. 795–805. Publications of L.M.A (2013)
27. Reinoso Carvalho, F., Van Ee, R., Rychtarikova, M., Touhafi A., Steenhaut, K., Persoone, D., Spence, C. Leman, M.: Does music influence de Multisensory tasting experience? J. Sens. Stud. **30**(5), 404–412 (2015a)
28. Reinoso Carvalho, F., Van Ee, R., Rychtarikova, M., Touhafi, A., Steenhaut, K., Persoone, D., Spence, C.: Using sound-taste correspondences to enhance the subjective value of tasting experiences. Front. Psychol. **6**,1309 (2015b)
29. Reinoso Carvalho, F., Van Ee, R., Touhafi, A., Steenhaut, K., Leman, M., Rychtarikova, M.: Assessing multisensory tasting experiences by means of customized sonic cues. In: Proceedings of Euronoise 2015, Maastricht, vol. 352, pp. 1–6 (2015c)
30. Reinoso Carvalho, F., Wang, Q.J., Steenhaut, K., Van Ee, R., Spence, C.: Tune that beer! Finding the pitch corresponding to the Taste of Belgian Bitter Beers (submitted A)
31. Reinoso Carvalho, F., Wang, Q. J., Van Ee, R., Spence, C.: The influence of soundscapes on the perception and evaluation of beers. Food Qual. Prefer. **52**, 32–41 (2016a)
32. Reinoso Carvalho, F., Velasco, C., Van Ee, R., Leboeuf, Y., Spence C.: Music influences hedonic and taste ratings in beer. Front. Psychol. **7** (2016b)
33. Salimpor, V.N., Benovoy, M., Larcher, K., Dagher, A., Zatorre, R.J.: Anatomically distinct dopamine release during anticipation and experience of peak emotion to music. Nat. Neurosci. **14**(2), 257–262 (2011)
34. Satpute, A., Kang, J., Bickart, K., Yardley, H., Wager, T., Barrett, L.F.: Involvement of sensory regions in affective experience: a meta-analysis. Front. Psychol. **6** (2015)
35. Seo, H.S., Hummel, T.: Influence of auditory cues on chemosensory perception. In: Guthrie, B., Beauchamp, J.D., Buettner, A., Lavine, B.K. (eds.) The Chemical Sensory Informatics of Food: Measurement, Analysis, Integration, pp. 41–56. ACS Symposium Series (2015)
36. Shepherd, G.M.: Smell images and the flavour system in the human brain. Nature **444**(7117), 316–321 (2006)
37. Small, D.M.: Flavor is in the brain. Physiol. Behav. **107**(4), 540–552 (2012)
38. Spence, C.: Crossmodal correspondences: a tutorial review. Atten. Percept. Psychophys. **73** (4), 971–995 (2011)
39. Spence, C.: Auditory contributions to flavour perception and feeding behaviour. Physiol. Behav. **107**(4), 505–515 (2012)
40. Spence, C.: Noise and its impact on the perception of food and drink. Flavor **3**, 9 (2014)
41. Spence, C.: Eating with our ears: assessing the importance of the sounds of consumption to our perception and enjoyment of multisensory flavour experiences. Flavor, **4**, 3 (2015a)
42. Spence, C.: Multisensory flavor perception. Cell **161**(1), 24–35 (2015b)
43. Spence, C., Michel, C., Smith, B.: Airplane noise and the taste of umami. Flavor **3**, 2 (2014)
44. Spence, C., Shankar, M.U.: The influence of auditory cues on the perception of, and responses to, food and drink. J. Sens. Stud. **25**, 406–430 (2010)
45. Spence, C., Piqueras-Fiszman, B.: The Perfect Meal: The Multisensory Science of Food and Dining. Wiley, Oxford (2014)
46. Spence, C., Richards, L., Kjellin, E., Huhnt, A.-M., Daskal, V., Scheybeler, A., Velasco, C., Deroy, O.: Looking for crossmodal correspondences between classical music and fine wine. Flavor **2**, 29 (2013)

47. Spence, C., Wang, Q.J.: Wine and music (II): can you taste the music? Modulating the experience of wine through music and sound. Flavor **4**(1), 1–14 (2015)
48. Stafford, L.D., Fernandes, M., Agobiani, E.: Effects of noise and distraction on alcohol perception. Food Qual. Prefer. **24**(1), 218–224 (2012)
49. Stein, B.E., Stanford, T.R., Ramachandran, R., Perrault Jr., T.J., Rowland, B.A.: Challenges in quantifying multisensory integration: alternative criteria, models, and inverse effectiveness. Exp. Brain Res. **198**(2–3), 113–126 (2009)
50. Velasco, C., Woods, A.T., Petit, O., Cheok, A.D., Spence, C.: Crossmodal correspondences between taste and shape, and their implications for product packaging: a review. Food Qual. Prefer. **52**, 17–26 (2016)
51. Wang, Q.J., Woods, A., Spence, C.: "What's your taste in music?" A comparison of the effectiveness of various soundscapes in evoking specific tastes. i-Perception **6**, 6 (2015)
52. Wesson, D.W., Wilson, D.A.: Smelling sounds: olfactory–auditory sensory convergence in the olfactory tubercle. J. Neurosci. **30**(8), 3013–3021 (2010)
53. Wilkins, R.W., Hodges, D.A., Laurienti, P.J., Steen, M., Burdette, J.H.: Network science and the effects of music preference on functional brain connectivity: from Beethoven to Eminem. Sci. Rep. **4**, 6130 (2014)
54. Woods, A.T., Poliakoff, E., Lloyd, D.M., Kuenzel, J., Hodson, R., Gonda, H., Batchelor, J., Dijksterhuis, A., Thomas, A.: Effect of background noise on food perception. Food Qual. Prefer. **22**(1), 42–47 (2011)
55. Zampini, M., Spence, C.: The role of auditory cues in modulating the perceived crispness and staleness of potato chips. J. Sens. Stud. **19**(5), 347–363 (2004)

Revolt and Ambivalence: Music, Torture and Absurdity in the Digital Oratorio *The Refrigerator*

Paulo C. Chagas[✉]

Department of Music, University of California, Riverside, CA 92521-0325, USA
paulo.chagas@ucr.edu

Abstract. The digital oratorio *The Refrigerator* (2014) is a composition that reflects on my own experience of torture as a 17-year-old political prisoner during the Brazilian military dictatorship. This paper examines the existential and artistic contexts underlying the conception of the piece including the connection to my previous work. The investigation focuses on intermedia composition—electroacoustic music, live-electronics, audiovisual composition—and its relation to the subject of the torture. The paper aims, from a philosophical point of view, to build bridges between a phenomenological experience, the music, and the technology of sound synthesis. *The Refrigerator* expresses the conscious revolt struggling with the ambivalence of the torture and its acceptance as a path of illumination and transcendence. The experience of torture is approached from the perspective of Albert Camus' philosophy of absurdity and the mythical character of Sisyphus, who embraces absurdity through his passion as much as through his suffering.

Keywords: Digital oratorio · Intermedia · Electroacoustic music · Live-electronics · Audiovisual composition · Torture · Absurdity · Camus · Sisyphus

1 Introduction

My own experience of torture as a 17-year-old political prisoner during the Brazilian military dictatorship in 1971 is the subject of the digital oratorio *The Refrigerator* [A Geladeira] (2014) for two singers (mezzo-soprano and baritone), instrumental ensemble (violin, viola, cello, piano and percussion), electronic sounds, live-electronics and interactive visual projection. Commissioned by the Centro Cultural São Paulo and the ensemble "Núcleo Hespérides", the work was premiered on April 8, 2014 as part of an event for the 50th anniversary of the Brazilian military coup of 1964.[1] The "refrigerator" referenced in the work was a cubicle especially designed and equipped for torturing with sound. It was an environment designed for acoustic experience meant to be physically and mentally destructive. Many years later, I described this experience as follows:

---

[1] The video of the first performance is available at: https://vimeo.com/97100136; and also at: https://www.youtube.com/watch?v=KH_EnKIttHM. Accessed January 9, 2017.

© Springer International Publishing AG 2017
M. Aramaki et al. (Eds.): CMMR 2016, LNCS 10525, pp. 331–346, 2017.
DOI: 10.1007/978-3-319-67738-5_20

I was arrested for collaboration with opposition groups. Arriving in the military prison, I was put in the 'refrigerator', a small room, acoustically isolated, and completely dark and cold. Various noises and sounds (hauling oscillators, rumbling generators, distorted radio signals, motorcycles, etc.) shot from loudspeakers, hidden behind the walls. Incessantly, the electronic sounds filled the dark space and overwhelmed my body for three long days. After a [certain] time, I lost consciousness. This auditory and acoustic torture was then a recent development, partially replacing traditional methods of physical coercion that killed thousands in Latin American prisons between the 1960s and 1990s. Such sounds injure the body without leaving any visible trace of damage. The immersive space of the torture cell, soundproofed and deprived of light, resonates in my memory as the perfect environment for experiencing the power of sound embodiment [1].

Being tortured as a political prisoner was an absurd experience. It occurred at a time when I became interested in music and, soon after, I began to study music composition formally. After graduating from the University of São Paulo (1979), I travelled to Europe to pursue a Ph.D. in Musicology with the composer Henry Pousseur in Liège, Belgium and to study electroacoustic music composition at the Music Academy in Cologne, Germany. It seems a paradox that I devoted myself to electronic music, which draws its artistic potential from *noise*: electroacoustic music has extended the awareness of noise to the whole musical experience. The feeling of absurdity emerges from the ambivalent role of noise as both instrument of political pressure as well as subversive creation. As Attali claims [2], "noise is the source of purpose and power". Noise represents disorder and music is a tool used to rationalize noise and exert political pressure in order to consolidate a society. Attali describes musical evolution in terms of the relationship between music and noise. Music controls noise, but at the same time gives birth to other forms of noise that are incorporated in the political economy of music to become music themselves, which, when established, reveal other forms of noise, and so on. Noise is absurd violence and music is absurd revolt, "a constant confrontation between man and his own obscurity" [3]. Listening to music is accepting the presence of noise in our lives: it "is listening to all noise, realizing that its appropriation and control is a reflection of power, that it is essentially political" [2].

Suffering and violence—and the ambivalent feelings we experience towards these things—have been a constant thematic of my work, especially my audiovisual and multimedia compositions. For example, in *Francis Bacon* (1993), work inspired by the life and work of the British painter Francis Bacon (1909–92), I composed music that acknowledges the feelings of desperation and unhappiness and the role of affliction in his creative expression. The piece is written for three singers (soprano, countertenor and baritone), string quartet, percussion and electronic music and was commissioned by the Theaterhaus Stuttgart for the choreographic theater by Johannes Kresnik and Ismael Ivo another example that addresses the ambivalence toward and fascination with war, power and violence is the techno-opera *RAW* (1999). *RAW* has no plot in the traditional sense. The libretto combines excerpts from Ernst Jünger's autobiographic books describing his experiences as a soldier fighting in World War I, with quotations form the theoretical work "On War" by the Prussian General and philosopher Carl von Clausewitz, and poetic texts on the Yoruba deity Ogun, the African and Afro-American god of iron worshiped as warrior, builder and destructor. The Yoruba is one of the ethnic groups in today's Nigeria, whose ancestors were deported in large number as slaves to the American continent. Their religious and philosophical traditions are kept alive today in West Africa and Latin America. The opera is written for five singers and a reduced orchestra of three percussions and three keyboards playing live-electronic music inspired by techno and Afro-Brazilian religious music. The work was commissioned by the Opera Bonn.

These two projects and many others devoted to similar subjects laid the groundwork for me to be able to back and make sense of my own experience of torture. It seems that the requisite level of maturity needed to deal with such a sensitive theme had to be gradually acquired. The transition period between the last years living in Germany and the first years relocating to California (2003–05) provided the opportunity to grasp the absurdity of torture from an artistic perspective. The first experiments were made in the international workshop *Interaktionslabor* (www.interaktionslabor.de), conceived and organized by the German choreographer and director Johannes Birringer. It was held in the site of the abandoned coalmine of Göttelborg (Saarland) and attracted artists, musicians, dancers and engineers. The works produced in the workshop explored interdisciplinary connections between art, digital technology and the deprived environment of the mine. The site, with its imposing buildings, machines and equipment remaining virtually intact, was a silent witness of the fading industrial landscape and emerging post-industrial society. We felt as strangers living in a sort of exile, "deprived of the memory of a lost home or the hope of a promise land. This divorce between man and his life, the actor and his setting, is properly the feeling of absurdity" [3].

In 2004, the second year I attended the Interaktionslabor, I begun a collaboration project with Birringer inspired by the novel *Blindness* by the Portuguese author and Nobel Prize winner Saramago [4]. The book tells the story of a city hit by an unexplained epidemic of blindness afflicting all of its inhabitants with the exception of one woman, who was left with sight in order to help the others to deal with their despair and suffering. The government tried to take control of the epidemic by incarcerating the blind individuals in an asylum that became like a concentration camp. But as the blindness epidemic spread in the outside world and affected the whole population, social life turned into disorder, violence, and chaos. In the deprived landscape of the mine, we found a suitable setting for interpreting Saramago's novel. The interactive installation *Blind City* (2004) explores the relationship between sound, gesture and movement through the use of sensors for actors and singers representing characters affected by the mysterious blindness. In the following year, the dancer Veronica Endo joined us for the creation of *Canções dos Olhos/Augenlieder* (2005), a work that combines electronic music with a digital video-choreography exploring the sensory deprivation of a woman who suddenly finds herself in an imaginary city where people have become blind and disappeared. The dancer in the silent landscape of the mine reveals the absurd confrontation of this irrational world with the "wild longing for clarity whose call echoes in the human heart" [3].

2   Blindness, Technology and Interactivity

Saramago's *Blindness* is an allegory for not being able to see. The novel is the metaphor of the feeling of absurdity that springs from recognizing the irrational fragility and vulnerability of society. As much as we try to control ourselves—and the imperialistic powers try to take hold of world—we become aware that society provides no unlimited guarantee of stability. We live on the verge of collapsing and chaos, under the threat of collective blindness that can quickly lead to barbarity. Having lived through dictatorship and revolution, Saramago fears the obscure forces that free the beast within us, reinforcing selfishness and ignorance, unleashing violence and cruelty.

Reading *Blindness* allowed me to relate it to my personal experience of torture. For 21 years, Brazilians have lived in a state of collective blindness of a brutal military dictatorship and learned to survive the mechanisms of oppression, fear and violence. Yet the Brazilian dictatorship is not an isolated incident in human history, and the blind absurdity is not restricted to the spheres of power and politics. Currently, we experience a dramatic change of our existential feelings driven by technology. The digital machines of information and communication take hold of our body and deterritorialize our cognitive functions, affecting our sensory experience—auditory, visual, spatial, and tactile—and transforming the way we live and relate. Yet we also experience the ambivalent dimension of technology: on the one side, it reveals a new kind freedom based on networking dialog (e.g. social media); on the other side, it presents the potential to reinforce authoritarian tendencies of individual and collective control. This paradox unveils techno-absurdity.

Ambivalence lies at the core of the relation between man and machine, which is framed by the notion of interactivity. The so-called "interactive art" tries to achieve a more "organic" relationship between bodies and digital media in the artistic performance through the use of computers, interfaces and sensors, and even involving the spectator in the work (e.g. interactive installations). However, the interactive forms do not necessarily accomplish the dialog in the creation process. In opposition to the dominant discourse of interactivity, focused on the physicality and materiality of the relationship between body and technology, I have defined interactivity as the "embodiment of the collaborative experience that materializes the creation process in the form of the work itself" [1]. This view of interactivity embraces both the set of heterogeneous media and the dynamics of personal relationships involved in the artistic process. Beyond dealing with systems of devices, interactive art has to find a meaning and depth in it, a being-in-the-world that goes beyond technological stunning and illusion. The interactive model of communication should bring about the ethical understanding of the relation of man/machine that critically reflects on the formal structures of power in society.

The digital oratory *Corpo, Carne e Espírito* [*Body, Flesh and Spirit*] (2008), another collaboration with Johannes Birringer, is an example of the dialogical approach to interactivity in digital art. The work was commissioned by and premiered in the International Festival of Theater FIT in Belo Horizonte, Brazil.[2] Based on the music I composed in 1993 for the choreographic theater *Francis Bacon*, the vision of the piece is an intermedia translation of Francis Bacon's paintings. According to Deleuze [5], they constitute "a *zone of indiscernibility or undecidability* between man and animal", where the body appears as mediation between the flesh and the spirit [5]. Birringer

---

[2] The video of the performance is available at: https://www.youtube.com/watch?v=-EWfu5W2XO8. Accessed January 1, 2017.

develops the concept of "choreographic scenarios": sequences of digital images projected onto three screens hung beside each other on the back of the stage above and behind the performers. The main motive of the visual composition is "soundless" bodies that interact with the music, not as visualization of the music, but as independent and asynchronous objects and events. Birringer explores the spatiality of the image projection by treating the digital triptych as a cinematographic video sculpture, "a kind of orchestral spatialization of images" controlled in real time [6]. The music develops an "aesthetic of distortion" that explores extended techniques for the string quartet such as strongly pressing the bow against the string in order to produce noise, or phonetic distortions with the voices by articulating vowels and consonants in an unusual way. The composition operates with figures and their deformations that give birth to abstract forms that turn into complex *zones of indiscernibility*. The deformations contract and extend the figures, activate rhythms, gestures, resonances, and create contrasts as well as contrasts within contrasts [7]. Music and visual projection are treated as two separated yet integrated levels. *Corpo, Carne e Espírito* constitutes an emblematic example of *intermedia* polyphony, an aesthetic orientation driving my audiovisual composition (see below).

3 *The Refrigerator*: Libretto

The composition of *The Refrigerator* (39 min) was accomplished in a very short time —less than two months—in the beginning of 2014. The first step was to write a libretto that was thought to be both a poem to be interpreted by the mezzo-soprano and the baritone, as well as a script for the whole composition. The libretto elaborates a multi-layered narrative offering multiple perspectives for observing my personal experience of torture and the reality of torture more generally. Torture is associated with the darkness of ignorance, with pain and suffering; the "refrigerator" is presented as a torture machine that stands for the logistics of violence and cruelty in society. The piece takes explicit distance from a political interpretation of torture, such as denouncing the torture as a form of oppression and abuse of power, or drawing attention to the torture in the context of the Brazilian military dictatorship. Beyond acknowledging the inhuman and degrading reality of torture, *The Refrigerator* reflects on my evolution as human being and my own path of commitment with human values. More than a political action, the journey emerges as a movement of transcendence, an aspiration of elevation aiming to illuminate darkness and overcome ignorance.

The Refrigerator brings back memories of the torture I suffered—impressions, situations, emotions and feelings—but at the same time invites us to look into the reality of torture that exists in the world outside the refrigerator. Torture is not a privilege of dictatorships or oppressing regimes, it is not practiced exclusively by abject individuals. The cruelty of torture does not occur only in extreme situations, it is widespread in normal prisons—for example in Brazil—and is also a tool of imperialism, such as the torture practiced by the US military forces and intelligence services against international "terrorists". Physical torture, psychological torture and other forms of torture were incorporated into "the banality of evil" to use an expression introduced by Hannah Arendt in the context of the Holocaust. Torture is not an isolated act; it is something that exists within us, a universal feature of the human race, which reinforces the limitation of our selfish life. We need a large-scale movement, a transcendent aspiration to transform our consciousness and nature, free ourselves from the darkness of ignorance, inertia, obscurity, confusion and disorder. The barbarity of torture is not the darkness of our origin as vital being, but an intermediate stage of human evolution. The path I propose in *The Refrigerator* is a journey of sacrifice ascending to the transcendence of the ineffable. The eight scenes represent the steps of this journey. Here is an overview of the large formal structure:[3]

Prolog: Personal Statement
Scene 1: Introduction: The Darkness of Ignorance
Scene 2: Electricity: The Machine of Fear
Scene 3: Noises: Immersion into Chaotic Vibrations
Scene 4: Cold: The Breath of Death
Scene 5: Guilt: Witnessing the Torture of a Loved One
Scene 6: Pain: The Feeling of Finitude
Scene 7: Forms of Torture: The Invisible Torture
Scene 8: Peace: Music that Lives Un-Sung

4 Prolog: Personal Statement and Soundscape

In June 1971, I was seventeen and would turn eighteen in August. They got me at my house while I was sleeping and I was taken to the Military Police headquarter at the "Barão de Mesquita" street in the neighborhood of "Tijuca". I was brought there, and put in the refrigerator, which was a new thing. I know it was new because I could smell the fresh paint. It was a very small cubicle, must have been about two meters by two meters or so, dark and soundproofed, with air conditioning, quite cold. I stayed there a long time, which I believe was about three days. The main particularity of this refrigerator is that it had speakers built behind the walls, and there was communication between the captive and the torturers. Then the torturers were outside and they were talking to you and threatening you, they kept making jokes and being grotesque. Then, at a certain moment they began to play sounds, noises. This was in 1971, when the recording technology was something still very much incipient, and we didn't have the kind of noises that we have today. But there was, for example, one thing I remember well, which was a then common noise of an AM radio receiver when the station was changed—few people today know that, right? In the past you had that kind of noise [*hissing phonemes*] when you were searching for a station, tuning—so this was one of the main noise, trying to tune in a radio station and not being able to do so and it made this mess. It was a very big noise, which is the noise of the ether, the radio waves that live in the ether. The radio receivers decode these modulations: AM, which is amplitude modulation and FM, which is frequency modulation. So AM makes [*imitating amplitude modulation*], and FM makes [*imitating frequency modulation*]. And this was very loud. Imagine yourself in space that is totally acoustically isolated and being subjected to such radio noises that are extremely loud. In addition there were other noises: motorcycle noise, engine noise, saw noise, and other things that they had there and they were having fun [*laughing*], they were laughing and making these noises. But it was too

---

[3] For a detailed analysis of the scenes see my essay "Observar o inobservável: Música e tortura no oratório digital *A Geladeira*" [Observing the Unobservable: Music and Torture in the Digital Oratorio *The Refrigerator*] in Valente [8].

loud, too loud, loud to the point that you got really hurt. Because being subjected to sounds, to sound vibrations, your whole body might collapse. Not only do you become deaf, but it turns you into a state that affects and transforms your consciousness. So this sound torture was something that was quite sophisticated and few people knew about it. The peculiar thing is that it does not leave the slightest mark. It means, sound is unique in that it invades your body, it gets hold of your body and puts the body in motion, and if you apply noise the movements will be chaotic. You start feeling destroyed physically and psychically.

The prolog was not originally conceived for the composition but added afterwards. A couple of days before the premiere, I gave an interview to the web radio of the Cultural Center São Paulo (CCSP). In a very informal conversation with Angela Voicov Rimoli, I talked, among others, about how I was tortured in the refrigerator. The concert curator, Dante Pignarati, decided to play an excerpt of interview as a personal statement before the piece, in order to introduce the subject to the audience. When I heard it for the first time in the dress rehearsal I was very surprised with the result: it was not just a statement, but a kind of soundscape made of my voice and other sounds. The author of this radio composition, Marta de Oliveira Fonterrada, designed a playful narrative evoking the sounds I heard in the cabin of torture, especially the radio tuning sounds that kept resonating in my memory. Radio is the sound of electromagnetic energy trans-formed into acoustic energy, which, as Kahn [9] says, "was heard before it was invented". The turbulence of electromagnetic waves, captured by the analog radio receptors and heard as disturbance noise, was part of the radio listening culture. Digital technology has almost eliminated the radio noise as it has also suppressed the noise of vinyl records. The scratching and other noises of old records reappeared as material for loops and rhythms in the DJ-culture of sampling and remix. But radio noise has virtually disappeared from the contemporary soundscape. In the torture sessions inside the refrigerator, the analog radio receiver turned into an instrument of torture; by manipu-lating the tuning button, the torturer produced noise not just to be heard but also to inflict pain and suffering. The concept of soundscape introduced by Schafer [10] accounts for the ethical implication of the relationship between man and the acoustic environment. From the point of view of soundscape studies, the refrigerator can be viewed as an absurd soundscape designed to create a disruptive connection between man and sound in order to make the individual vulnerable.

The radio piece of the prolog is a playful commentary of my statement aiming to provide clues for understanding the piece. Form a cybernetic point of view, it can be analyzed as an "observation of second order", an observation that observes the nar-rative of my personal experience of torture. The sounds added to the speech regard what the observer is saying.[4] The radio piece provides stereotypes or redundant sounds that reinforce the linguistic message, as in the case of the sounds of amplitude mod-ulation and frequency modulation for illustrating the radio tuning noise. Sometimes, however, the soundtrack creates its own meanings, commenting or opposing the lin-guistic message. The radio soundscape observes the personal experience of torture and at the same time, prepares the listener to dive into the immersive audiovisual envi-ronment of *The Refrigerator*.

---

[4] For an application of the concepts of observation of first order and observation of second order in the system of art, see [11, 12].

5 Electroacoustic Music: Gunshot Degradation

After the prologue, the digital oratorio begins with an acousmatic piece (5 min) made of a single material, the sound of a gunshot, or the detonation of a bullet. It is an explosive sound with a length of approximately 900 ms (milliseconds). Like a percussive sound, it has a very short attack, a fast decay, a sustaining segment and a long release starting at 600 ms that gradually fades out into silence. The sound envelope evokes the shape of an arrow tip (see Fig. 1). Just as with an arrow, the bullet of a gun is an object with a blunt tip that enters the body in order to cause damage or destruction. The gunshot sound has a strong symbolic character; it is actually a cliché. We are used to hearing (and seeing) a variety of guns in war movies, westerns, thrillers and video games. The detonation of a revolver also belongs to the aesthetics of electronic music. It is part of a family of explosive and penetrating sounds, distortions and overdrive effects, obsessive rhythms, and other sonic representations of violence in the audiovisual media culture.

The electroacoustic composition develops temporal expansions—*time stretching*—of the gunshot sound. This technique is an application of the Fast Fourier Transformation (FFT), an algorithm that describes any sound as a system of periodic vibrations defined as multiples of a fundamental frequency. The *Discrete Fourier Transformation* (DFT) is a digital implementation of the FFT algorithm. Digital sounds may be transformed by means of DFT in either the time domain or frequency domain. It is a process of analysis and synthesis, in which the sound is broken down into a sequence of sinusoidal periodic signals and later reassembled. It allows changing the duration of the sound while maintaining the relations of frequency and amplitude of its partials that determine the spectrum. The quality of the time stretching depends on the parameters of analysis and synthesis such as the FFT window size that determines the fundamental frequency of the spectrum. A typical window size consists on 4096 samples, which in a sampling rate of 44.1 kHz allows a fundamental frequency of 53 Hz.

In this specific case, the FFT algorithm was used in an unconventional, 'subversive' manner: I sought to obtain a sound of low quality. The goal was to *degrade* the gunshot sound. For this purpose, I use very small FFT windows for the time stretching algorithm—such as 128 and 64 samples allowing fundamental frequencies of 1772 Hz and 3445 Hz respectively—so that the analysis eliminated the low frequencies and the

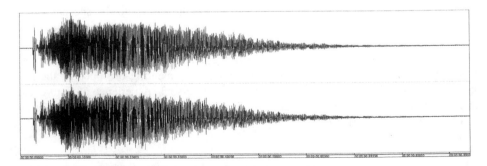

Fig. 1. Visual representation of the gunshot sound

synthesis processed the higher register of the spectrum, producing a variety of digital artifacts that significantly changed the gunshot timbre. The result was a distorted and degraded sound, which is thought of as a metaphor for the torture, a sonic representation of humiliation and dishonor of human dignity driven by the practice of torture. The gunshot remains a symbol of violence and destruction of the human being, which is accomplished by a single movement, the gesture of pulling the trigger. However, from a spectral point of view, the sound of the gunshot has the quality of the noise, which is a "rich" sound consisting of all virtual frequencies of the audible spectrum. But the time stretching accomplished with small window sizes changed the quality of the timbre and destroyed the virtual richness of the noise. The sound of the bullet coming out of the barrel of the revolver lost its imposing quality of firearm; it was depraved, perverted and corrupted. The gunshot noise was stripped of its "dignity"; the explosive and percussive quality of its attack and the richness of its noisy spectrum were lost; it remained a residue of sinusoidal waves, a monotone and amorphous vibration sounding like a banal background noise.

The temporal expansions of the gunshot sound *also* evoke the noise of the analog radio receiver tuning a station. As mentioned above, the radio disturbance became the symbol of the sound torture I suffered inside the refrigerator. The electronic music thus anticipates a leitmotif of the digital oratory: the "station that is never tuned" (see libretto). Moreover, the electronic monotony provokes a psychoacoustic irritation due to preponderance of high frequencies and repetition. Torture, as a gradual corruption of the physical and moral integrity of the human being, is a repetitive process.

Figure 2 shows the different segments of the acousmatic composition: the first temporal expansion of the gunshot has a low amplitude and a short duration, 1'28 "(0'–1'28'); the second time-expansion, is much more louder and longer, 2'50 "(1'28"–4'18"); finally, the third expansion is shorter and softer, 47" (4'18"–5'05"); we hear it as a moaning sound, evoking a fading voice. The predominance of high frequencies hurts the ears and causes monotony; the repetition of the same type of sound is irritating and painful, especially because the second expansion has a long decay and doesn't introduce any novelty. The sense of boredom and discomfort are intentional. The electroacoustic music immerses the listener in an unpleasant acoustic environment evoking the noise of the torture chamber; one should feel annoyed and injured listening to it.

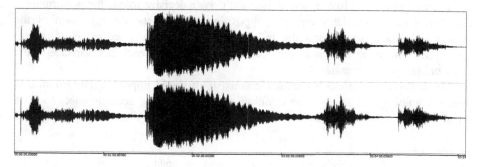

Fig. 2. Visual representation of the electronic music

6 Intermedia Composition: Live-Electronics and Visual Projection

The oratory is a hybrid genre combining vocal and instrumental music. Though it is not a genuine theatrical genre like opera, it has a scenic dimension resulting from the live performance of singers and instrumentalists. Bach's oratorios and passions, for example, are stage interpretations of the stories of the Bible; the performance of soloists, choir and orchestra evokes visual representations of Christianity strongly influenced by Baroque painting. The digital oratory is a contemporary genre that extends the hybrid principle of oratory to the digital media. It is thus an *intermedia* form. The concept of *intermedia* arises from the extension of polyphony to other domains of perception and experience. While polyphony articulates plurality and identity within the acoustic media—vocal and instrumental, "intermedia composition explores artistic connections between different media such as sound, image, speech, movement, gesture, and space while interacting with technical and media apparatuses" [7]. Intermedia art is also linked with the concepts of *plurality* and *heterogeneity*. Guattari proposes a polyphonic analysis of subjectivity on the basis of the "ethic-aesthetic paradigm", which emphasizes the relations of *alterity* between individual and collective units and offers an alternative to scientific and philosophical models. Guattari's *polyphonic subjectivity* embraces the idea that subjectivity is not restricted to human consciousness, but is at the crossroads of "heterogeneous machinic universes" framing the interaction between human beings and technology. In Guattari's terms, subjectivity shifts from the human consciousness to the "machinic assemblages" of contemporary society.[5]

The foundation of the *The Refrigerator* is the music written on the basis of the libretto for the two soloists (mezzo-soprano and baritone) and the instrumental ensemble (violin, viola, cello, piano and percussion). The live-electronics and visual projection create additional layers of intermedia composition. In opposition to the vocal and instrumental music, which is determined by a notated, "fixed" score, the live-electronics and visual projection execute computer algorithms programmed with Max software (www.cycling74.com), which introduces layers of randomness in the work. The random processes of the intermedia composition, are manually controlled by an "interpreter" that manipulates an interface (Behringer BCF2000) for changing the parameters of the electronic music and visual projection. The interpreter of the intermedia composition acts like an improviser and plays a decisive role in the performance. *The Refrigerator* articulates thus the opposition between the determination of the vocal/instrumental "score" and the indeterminacy of the intermedia (sound/image) "program". This opposition is a space of *freedom* that makes each performance of the work unique and differentiated.

The material of the electronic music consists of sound impulses. The impulse is basically a noise with a very short duration, a condensation of acoustic energy with a broad spectrum of frequencies. The Max patch program uses a single impulse

---

[5] For an account of "machinic heterogenesis" and "machinic assemblage" see Guattari [13, 14]; see also my article "Polyphony and Technology in Interdisciplinary Composition" [15].

processed through a feedback-loop circuit consisting of five delays, which generates rhythmic and granular sound structures. The rhythm and texture of these structures depends on the individual frequencies of the delays. For example, applying a frequency of 1000 ms to all five delays results in a pulsing and regular rhythm beating with the rate of 1 s; a frequency of less than 20 ms applied to all five delays generates a continuous sound, perceived as a timbre. By applying different frequencies for each of the five delays, we obtain an irregular rhythm or a colorful timbre depending on the values of the frequencies. The feedback-loop circuit can generate an infinite variety of rhythms and timbres, from which only few were used.

After the feedback-loop of delays, the impulses are further processed by resonance filters that transform the noises in pitched sounds ("notes"). Each of the five delays is connected to a different filter, resulting in a sequence of five different pitches. The sequences of impulses acquire thus a harmony quality that depends on the speed of the individual delays; they can be perceived either as arpeggios or as chords. Finally, after being processed by delays and filters, the impulses are modulated by oscillators that change the sampling rate of the digital signal. Reducing the bandwidth of the impulses —a process known as *downsampling*—affects the quality of the impulses: they turn into distorted and degenerated sounds. The idea of "degradation", associated with torture, is projected into the core of digital signal processing. The sampling rate determines the quality of the sound; downsampling a digital signal generates a "low quality" creating connotations such as "crude" and "inferior". This depreciation translates the idea of torture as depravation and corruption of human dignity. The performer of the live-electronics manipulates the faders and interface buttons of the interface (Behringer BCF2000) to adjust mix between the "normal" sounds (delay + filter) and the "degraded" sounds (down-sampling).

The material of the visual projection contains low quality images of prison, torture and people taken from the internet, which have a "negative" connotation. The pictures of people are original high quality photos taken by Paula Sachetta, which have a "positive" connotation. The pictures were assembled thematically into three different videos, whereby each photo represents a frame of the video: the first video has 48 images of prison, the second 26 images of torture, and the third 59 images of people. In the visual composition, the pictures (frames) of each video are randomly selected and processed by three types of digital effects: (1) *rotations* in the vertical and horizontal axes that create fluid textures in constant motion; (2) *pixelations* that create granular textures by changing the size of the individual pixels; and (3) *zoom* movements that create pulsating rhythmic and textures. The Max patch uses a single image to generate three simultaneous and independent effects, so that the visual composition is conceived as a triptych with three different transformations of the same material.

The concept of a visual triptych is inspired by *Corpo, Carne e Espírito* (see above). Ideally, the images are to be projected on three screens hanging in the back of the stage behind and above the singers and musicians. However, for the premiere of *The Refrigerator*, there was only one screen available, so the three images were combined into one single image with three columns and projected in one screen. As for the live-electronics, the "interpreter" controls the visual projection operating the Behringer BCF2000, and has the choice between the three videos, mixing the different effects and modifying the parameters of the effects of pixelation and zoom. The visual composition oscillates between the categories of *concrete* and *abstract*. Within the category of the concrete are the perceived motifs of the pictures of prison, torture and people such as objects, bodies, faces and places. Within the category of the abstract are digital processes that alienate the motives of prison, torture and people. Abstract elements such as forms, colors, movements and pulses predominate the visual composition, while the concrete elements emerge as flashes of motives. The sequence of the three videos in the digital oratorio—first the video with pictures of prison, second the video with pictures of torture, and finally the video with pictures of people—supports the path of elevation: it emerges from ignorance, darkness and suffering symbolized by prison and torture and moves into transcendence, enlightenment and happiness symbolized by human beings.

The Max patch provides a kind of "macro-pulse" for synchronizing the electronic music with the visual projection. The pulse consists of 8 different durations ranging from 5 to 40 s that are randomly permuted in the course of the piece. With each new pulse, the patch modifies the parameters of the electronic music and selects a new image to be processed by the visual effects. In addition, the Max patch provides another tool for synchronizing sound and image, inversely correlating the amplitude of the audio signal to the feedback effect of the three images combined in three columns: whereas the amplitude of the audio signal decreases the visual feedback increases, so that the absence of audio signal—silence—corresponds to the maximum feedback—white image. The effect depends on the duration of the pulse: after the attack the sound decays proportionally to the duration and eventually fades out while the colors and shapes become blurred and lose their definition until the image eventually turns into white color. With short durations the effect may be almost imperceptible. Indeed, this correlation amplitude/feedback emphasizes the multimodal perception of auditory and visual stimuli, which is a significant principle of intermedia composition.

Figure 3 shows the screenshot of the main window of the Max patch used for the intermedia composition. Each of the three objects named "4MIXR", mixes the three

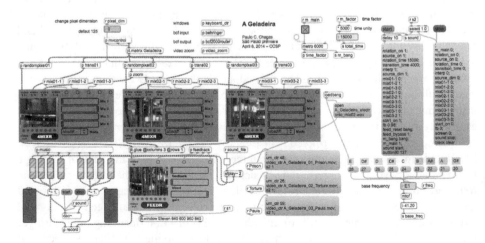

Fig. 3. Main window of the Max patch of *The Refrigerator*.

different visual effects (rotation, pixelation and zoom); the object named "FEEDR" processes the feedback of the three images combined. The electronic music is programmed inside the sub-patch "music" (left bottom), which is not displayed. In truth, the main window provides a very limited insight on the programing features of the patch.

7 The Myth of Sisyphus

Camus' classic definition of the absurd in the *Myth of Sisyphus* is that which is born of the "confrontation between the human need and the unreasonable silence of the world" [3]. In Camus' philosophy, absurdity is a conflict that emerges from the relationship between humanity and the world, from the "impossibility of constituting the world as a unity" [3]. The nostalgia for unity and the absolute, he claims, is "the essential impulse of the human drama" (1955, 17). The absurd is "that divorce between the mind that desires and the world that disappoints, my nostalgia for unity, this fragmented universe and the contradiction that binds them together" [3]. Camus criticizes the existential attitude of philosophers such as Chestov, Jasper Kiekergaard and Husserl who, recognizing the world's lack of meaning, tries to find a meaning and depth in it. It is impossible to know if the world has a meaning that transcends it, and it is impossible to reduce the world to a rational and reasonable principle: "Living is keeping the absurd alive" [3].

From the consciousness of the absurd, Camus draws three lessons for life: *revolt*, *freedom*, and *passion*. The *revolt* is a "perpetual confrontation between man and his own obscurity" [3], the insistence of an impossible transparency that questions the world at every instant. Camus frames the question of *freedom* in the realm of the individual experience. He criticizes the link between freedom and God as he denies the idea of eternal freedom and the belief of any life after death. In opposition, the absurd celebrates the freedom of action and increases man's availability to live fully in the present. The absurd freedom is an inner freedom, resulting from the attitude of acceptance that means to see and feel what is happening in the present moment and accept things just as they are. One has to give up certainty and be indifferent to everything except the "pure flame of life"—no illusion, no hope, no future and no consolation:

> The absurd man thus catches sight of a burning and frigid, transparent and limited universe in which nothing is possible but everything is given, and beyond which all is collapse and nothingness. He can then decide to accept such a universe and draw from it his strength, his refuse to hope, and the unyielding evidence of a life without consolation [3].

Accepting the absurd means that one lives in a perpetual opposition between the conscious revolt and the darkness in which it struggles. Man's individual freedom is what life has given to him, it is life's destiny: "what counts is not the best living but the most living" (1955, 61). Man has to plunge into the dark, impenetrable night while remaining lucid and perhaps it will arise "that white and virginal brightness which outlines every object in the light of the intelligence" [3]. The absurd world requires not a logical, but an emotional understanding of the world driven by *passion*.

For Camus, Sisyphus is the absurd hero, the mythical character who embraces absurdity through his passion as much as through his suffering. The gods condemned

Sisyphus "to ceaselessly rolling a rock to the top of a mountain, whence the stone would fall back of its own weight" [3]. He was punished for daring to scorn the gods, challenging death and for his passion for life. According to Camus, Sisyphus' fate, his futile and hopeless labor, is not different from today's workers who work every day of their lives doing the same tasks. Sisyphus, the "proletarian of the gods, powerless and rebellious" [3], symbolizes the attitude of conscious revolt: "he knows the whole extent of his wretched condition" but, instead of despair, he accomplishes his job with joy. Camus concludes: "One must imagine Sisyphus happy" [3]. Happiness and the absurd are inseparable: the absurd man's life, when he contemplates his affliction, is fulfilled by a silent joy.

Thinking of Sisyphus as a happy man, according to the philosopher Sagi [16], reiterates the notion that happiness is a matter of self-realization. The person who embraces the absurd attains self-acceptance as it resolves the paradox of the convergence between the sense of alienation and the aspiration of unity: "The individual who lives the absurd realizes human existence to the full, and is therefore happy" [16]. Camus' absurd rebellion, for Bowker [17], should not the understood as a rational concept but as practical, psychological and emotional disposition to resist against loss and violence. Yet, the absurd has an ambivalent potential in its refusal to affront violence and its desire for innocence, which, Bowen critically argues, undermines the ability to make loss meaningful. Declaring that the world is absurd perpetuates "a condition in which meaningful assimilation of loss is sacrificed for the sake of an innocence that the absurdist fears losing even more" [17].

8 Conclusion

The digital oratorio *The Refrigerator* recalls a series of tensions and dilemmas of my own life. My experience in adolescence was marked by the political activism fighting the authoritarian and oppressive regime of the Brazilian military dictatorship. In my high school days in Rio de Janeiro, I developed an intense political activity, participating in protests, demonstrations and actions organized by Marxist movements advocating ideas of socialist revolution and supporting the armed struggle against the dictatorial regime. Repression and torture reached their heights in Brazil in the beginning of the 1970s, when a growing number of activists were arrested. Hundreds of people were killed or disappeared by actions of the military repressive apparatus. Torture was a common practice and many political prisoners died or were badly injured because of the brutal practices of torture. Facing international pressure, the regime introduced "clean" torture methods that leave no marks, such as the 'refrigerator'. Being tortured inside the refrigerator in 1971 was a frightening and terrifying experience, though not so destructive of human life as other torture techniques. The torture has impacted my life in the sense that it brought me into a whole new sphere of existence. The refrigerator didn't destroy me, though it may have claimed from me the nostalgia for innocence from the adolescent feelings of revolt.

An amazing excitement and energy propelling these feelings came from the cultural changes of the 1960s and its demands for greater individual freedom. The revolt provided unique perspectives for exploring new horizons in society and the passion for visual arts, cinema, and literature. It sparked a creative potential that seemed inexhaustible. Aside from political activism, I was particularly interested in drawing, painting and sculpture. I considered studying design or architecture initially, but wound up on a different path. At the time when I was put inside the refrigerator and absurdly tortured with noise, I had already been listening to Brazilian and international pop music—Beatles, Rolling Stones, Pink Floyd, and others—and was learning to play guitar. Very soon, music became a focus of my existential revolt. In 1972, I moved with my family from Rio de Janeiro to Londrina—my father found a new job in the industry of pesticides and fertilizers—and I found myself learning basic music skills and practicing with piano books for beginners. Despite being 19-years-old, I went to the local conservatory daily to take piano lessons together with the much younger children. In the following year, I moved to São Paulo to study music composition at the University of São Paulo. The rest of the story is contained in my résumé.

Looking back on the journey, it seems that music composition has become increasingly a channel to express the existential feelings of revolt, giving it a voice—a sound—that could convey the full acceptance of the inner struggle. The revolt, as Camus says, is a coherent attitude with which to accept the absurd. No matter what one chooses for his life, one has to confront himself with his own obscurity while seeking an impossible transparency. One has to find balance in the opposition between the "conscious revolt and the darkness in which it struggles" [3]. The revolt "challenges the world anew every second" and "extends awareness to the whole of experience." But revolt "is not an aspiration, for it is devoid of hope" [3]. In other words, we do what we have to do but we cannot expect to be rewarded for our efforts. The revolt is a constant solitary effort charged with extreme tension of conflicting desires. It is a mature and creative response to embrace the absurd, resist the desire of unity, and accept the tragic ambivalence, for which "Sisyphus straining, fully alive, and happy" [18] is the suitable image. At this point of my life, after living in many different countries and cultures, it has become clear that absurdity is both an existential attitude for accepting loss, and a way to avoid melancholy.

The Refrigerator expresses the conscious revolt struggling within the darkness of torture: it is both the conscious revolt of what this particular fate represents in my life and the acceptance of torture as a path to illumination and transcendence. The digital oratorio makes the sound of torture reverberate through the polyphony of voices, instruments, electroacoustic music and live-electronics and the audiovisual forms of intermedia. It offers a multilayered, heterogenic perspective to enlighten the experience of torture against a background of darkness and silence. It introduces turbulent noise—disturbance from both sound and image—for channeling the qualities of oppression, violence and suffering attached to the reality of torture. The piece traces the contours of the invisible torture inside and outside the refrigerator. It makes torture meaningful while rendering it meaningless. It exposes the tensions emerging from my particular experience of torture and the ambivalent character of torture as a whole: the tortured and torturers are "neither victims nor executioners"[6]. The composition of *The*

---

[6] *Neither Victims nor Executioners* [*Ni victimes, ni bourreaux*), was a series of essays by Camus published in *Combat*, the newspaper of the French Resistance, in 1946. As an intellectual and journalist, Camus fought for justice and the defense of human dignity.

Refrigerator occurred in a time of losses caused by illness and death of close family members. Living with loss means giving loss a meaning in reality. But we should not let loss turn into melancholy or take refuge in the narcissistic self. The absurd revolt accepts the tensions of the self and allows us to give up one's attachments to self-boundaries. It urges us to give up nostalgia for unity and narcissistic identification with the self. We must acknowledge that the experience is beyond one's comprehension and surrender the desire to understand the world and ourselves.

References

1. Chagas, P.C.: The blindness paradigm: the visibility and invisibility of the body. Contemp. Music Rev. **25**(1/2), 119–130 (2006)
2. Attali, J.: Noise: The Political Economy of Music. University of Minnesota Press, Minneapolis (1985)
3. Camus, A.: The Myth of Sisyphus and Other Essays. Vintage, New York (1955)
4. Saramago, J.: Blindness. Harcourt, San Diego (1997)
5. Deleuze, G.: Francis Bacon: The Logic of Sensation. University of Minnesota Press, Minneapolis (2004)
6. Birringer, J.: Corpo, Carne e Espírito: musical visuality of the body. In: Freeman, J. (ed.) Blood, Sweat and Theory: Research Through Practice in Performance, pp. 240–261. Libri Publishing, Faringdon (2009)
7. Chagas, P.C.: Unsayable Music: Six Reflections on Musical Semiotics, Electroacoustic and Digital Music. University of Leuven Press, Leuven (2014)
8. Valente, H.: Observar o inobservável: música e tortura no oratorio digital A Geladeira. In: Valente, H., Pereira, S. (eds.) Com Som. Sem Som: Liberdades Políticas, Liberdades Poéticas. Letra e Voz, São Paulo (2016)
9. Kahn, D.: Earth Sound Earth Signal: Energies and Earth Magnitude in the Arts. University of California Press, Berkeley (2013)
10. Schafer, M.: The Soundscape: Our Sonic Environment and the Tuning of the World. International Distribution Corp, Rochester (1994)
11. Luhmann, N.: Die Kunst der Gesellschaft. Suhrkamp, Frankfurt am Main (1997)
12. Luhmann, N.: Art as Social System. Stanford University Press, Stanford (2000)
13. Guattari, F.: Chaosmose. Galilée, Paris (1992)
14. Guattari, F.: Machinic heterogenesis. In: Conley, V.A. (ed.) Rethinking Technologies, pp. 13–17. University of Minnesota Press, Minneapolis (1993)
15. Chagas, P.C.: Polyphony and technology in interdisciplinary composition. In: Proceedings of the 11th Brazilian Symposium on Computer Music, pp. 47–58. IME/ECA, São Paulo (2007)
16. Sagi, A.: Albert Camus and the Philosophy of the Absurd. Rodopi, Amsterdam (2002)
17. Bowker, M.H.: Rethinking the Politics of Absurdity: Albert Camus, Postmodernity, and the Survival of Innocence. Routledge, New York (2014)
18. Aronson, R.: Albert Camus. The Stanford Encyclopedia of Philosophy (2012). http://plato.stanford.edu/archives/spr2012/entries/camus/

Dynamic Mapping Strategies Using Content-Based Classification: A Proposed Method for an Augmented Instrument

Gabriel Rimoldi$^{(\boxtimes)}$ and Jônatas Manzolli

Interdisciplinary Nucleus of Sound Communication,
NICS –UNICAMP Rua da Reitoria, 163 – Cidade Universitária "Zeferino Vaz",
Campinas, São Paulo 13083-872, Brazil
{gabriel.rimoldi,jonatas}@nics.unicamp.br

Abstract. We discuss in this paper strategies of dynamic mapping applied to the design of augmented instruments. The proposed method is based on a feedback architecture that allows adjustment of mapping functions through pattern detection from the sonic response of an instrument. We applied this method to design *Metaflute*, an augmented instrument based on a hybrid system of gestural capture. We used a set of eight *phase vocoder* modules to process flute samples in real-time with performer movements detected by coupled sensors. A set of audio features was extracted from the sonic response of each synthesis module within a certain period and sent to a *K-nearest neighbor* algorithm (k-NN). Each synthesis module has its mapping functions modified based on patterns found by k-NN algorithm. This procedure was repeated iteratively so that the system adjusts itself in relation to its previous states. Preliminary results show a gradual differentiation of mapping functions for each synthesis module, allowing them to perform a different response in relation to data arising from the gestural interface.

Keywords: Dynamic mapping · Augmented instruments · Digital Music Instruments (DMI) · Machine learning

1 Introduction

In the Digital Music Interface (DMI) domain, mapping is understood as the act of taking real-time data from any input device and using it to control parameters of a sound generation engine [1, 2]. The task of creating a convincing relationship between these elements, both for performers and audience, may be not trivial and the criteria that qualifies the efficacy of this may depend on the context of musical practice. While a fixed mapping between gesture and sound may be more suitable to more deterministic contexts (the interpretation of a written piece, for example), a dynamic adjustment of mapping may be more interesting in improvisational contexts where there are no previously established sound and gesture materials.

We observed that many of the approaches in DMI design have prescribed the acoustic paradigm, in which the performer must adjust his sensorimotor contingencies to the instrument. According to Dubberly, Haque and Pangaro [3], these approaches are

© Springer International Publishing AG 2017
M. Aramaki et al. (Eds.): CMMR 2016, LNCS 10525, pp. 347–356, 2017.
DOI: 10.1007/978-3-319-67738-5_21

more reactive than properly interactive. For them, reactive systems comprise a fixed transfer function and the relationship between activation and response elements that are linear and unilateral. While an interactive system, the transfer function is dynamic; i.e. the way that "input affects output" can be changed over the time.

In traditional paradigm of instrumental music, roles are in general well-defined (or at least temporally dissociated) between its agents (performer, composer, and luthier) and objects (score and instrument). With DMIs, new models have been proposed to bring the functionalities of each element as part of the process into play. The distinctions between performer as active agent and instrument as passive object become more fluid to the establishment of bilateral exchanges between them. The typified stability and heteronomy of traditional models of music interaction give way to the autonomy and adaptive capacity of computer systems, able to modify quickly to ensure a more congruent interaction.

While the affordances and constrains of acoustic instruments are explicitly manifested by their physical and mechanical nature, DMI interaction is based on symbolic exchanges between the performer and computer. Its affordances are established by mental representations of instrument parameters and their modes of transformation. As a violin luthier enables affordances to manipulate the wood, the digital luthier defines the affordances and constraints of DMIs through mediation strategies employed between the physical energy channel of gestural interfaces and symbolic mechanisms of machines [4, 5].

Our work investigates strategies that allow the machine to adjust itself in relation to detected performer behaviors. The proposed design explores the ability of machine to regulate its inputs, sometimes unknown and unforeseen, and respond to this through its actuators. Our goal was to develop a cooperative model of interaction that allows mutual adjustment between performer and DMI. The methodology is based on recursive mechanisms between the gestural inputs and recognize patterns on DMI sonic response through non-supervised machine learning.

Machine Learning (ML) techniques has provide significant developments in interactive music performance [6–9]. These approaches take advantage in relation to preconceived mappings as they encourage exploratory behaviors and unexpected results during performance. While supervised ML models can be successfully applied in more deterministic performative contexts they may be more restrictive in improvisational contexts since its necessary to define previously the materials and the desired machine outputs. On the other hand, unsupervised ML techniques can be enables the machine to adapt its responses in relation to unknown or unforeseen performer behaviors. Using unsupervised ML models to design DMIs the mapping function may become an emergent property of the interaction and the system convergence can be demonstrated through the machine assimilation of interpretative demands brought by the performer and vice-versa.

We firstly present the development of the *Metaflute* and describe the proposed method of dynamic mapping. Finally, we demonstrate the system performance through simulations. The applied adjustment allowed a gradual differentiation of mapping for each synthesis modules which perform a different response in relation to the data arising from gestural interface.

2 Metaflute: An Augmented Instrument

Metaflute is an augmented instrument based on a hybrid system that associates direct gestural capture from the flute and digital processing techniques to extract information related to sound production. The use of sensors coupled with a acoustic flute has been extensively exploited on the Literature for a variety of purposes [10–14]. We propose to combine the use of ancillary gestures as well as to explore aspects of instrument sonority especially with the use of extended techniques as controllers in multimodal interactive environments.

A set of buttons and sensors coupled with the instrument allows exploring ancillary gestures (movements of the flute body, for example) as controllers as well as increases the amount of commands that may be deliberately triggered by the performer. The signal from each sensor can either be used independently or combined with others, which is the case of the MARG (Magnetic, Angular Rate and Gravity) composition that combines extracted data from the gyroscope, accelerometer and magnetometer sensors to obtain the angular positioning values of the instrument in three axes, namely *pitch*, *roll* and *yaw*. Table 1 summarize the sensors used in the *Metaflute*.

Table 1. Overview of sensors used in the *Metaflute*

Sensors	Parameter
1 Triaxial accelerometer sensor	3-axis absolute orientation
1 Triaxial gyroscope sensor	(*pitch, roll, yaw*)
1 Triaxial magnetometer sensor	
1 Ultrasound sensor	Right hand's distance to flute body
6 Switches	Discrete triggering
1 Pressure sensor (FSR)	Left thumb pressure

We also applied audio processing techniques to capture information related to the sound production as controller. The audio features were calculated using the *PDescriptors* library, implemented in Pure Data by Monteiro and Manzolli [15]. A detailed description of the sensors and feature extraction implemented in *Metaflute* is discussed in [16] (Fig. 1).

We have developed a synthesis and sound processing framework associated with the interface. For this experiment specifically, we used a set of eight *phase vocoder* modules that allow real-time processing of flute samples through performer movements. Control parameters are based on *roll* and *yaw* orientations of the flute extracted from MARG composition. The audio of the flute is recorded in real-time through a button controlled by the performer. Each module has three independent control parameters - *pitch shifting*, *time dilation* and *amplitude* - that process the sound stored by the performer. We adopt individual mapping functions for *pitch shifting* and *time dilation* in each synthesis module, respectively associated with *yaw* and *roll* inputs. The input variables are associated with the control parameters through a transformation

Fig. 1. Details of sensors used in *Metaflute*

whose scalars α and β are dependents of the state of the mapping adjustment algorithm, as described in function (Eq. 1).

$$f(x)_{m,n} = \alpha_{m,n-1} x + \beta_{m,n-1} \tag{1}$$

where x is the normalized input values arising from gestural interface, m is the defined number of synthesizers with $m = \{1, 2... 8\}$ and n is the state of the mapping adjustment algorithm. The domain of this function, which we named *Parametrical Space*, is pre-defined by the performer. Mapping functions of each synthesizer depend only on its previously state n.

3   Adaptive Mapping Strategies

The proposed method is based on a feedback DMI architecture that comprises dynamic adjustments of mapping functions through detected patterns in the sonic response of the machine, as shown in Fig. 2. Through the extraction of low-level features from the audio signal, and the clustering of these features over time, the system iteratively adjusts the mapping functions between gestural data and control parameters. The clustering map, which we named *Analytical Space*, points to resulting patterns of mapping between interface data and synthesis parameters. Therefore, our proposal is to associate the patterns of sonic response to the interface control parameters, respectively circumscribed under the *Analytical* and *Parametrical* Spaces.

The system attributes initial scalars α and β to the mapping functions of each sound generation unit. Adjustments are made between successive states of the system, which include a set of frames of audio analysis. Mapping functions are adjusted independently for each unit, restricted to the established domain in *Parametrical Space*. Once these adjustments take into account the previous states of the system, it becomes possible to observe the evolution of this system in relation to the contingencies of interaction between instrument and performer.

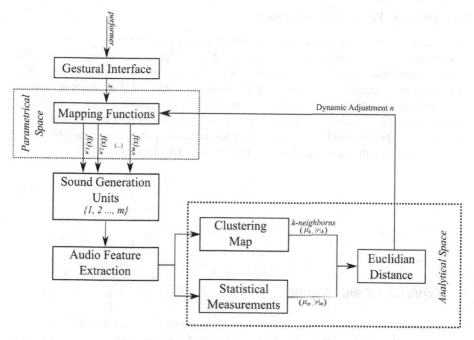

Fig. 2. DMI design with dynamic mapping adjustment

3.1 Audio Feature Extraction and Classification

We employed a set of audio features to analyze and classify the output of the sound generation units. These features are based on instantaneous measurements extracted by estimating an STFT-based spectrogram from the audio signal, with a frame length of 46 ms and 50% overlap between two subsequent frames. For this experiment, we used two features to classify the resulting sound of the synthesis modules, namely *spectral centroid* and *spectral flux*. The first consists of a weighted mean of the frequencies present in an audio signal, while the second is calculated by the difference between the power spectrum of one frame and that of the previous frame. Our hypothesis is that these features can characterize parametric modifications of sound generation units, respectively associated with pitch shifting and time dilation.

The feature vector was extracted within a certain period and sent to a *K-nearest neighbor* algorithm, which classifies patterns found in audio response. The well-known *K-nearest neighbor* (k-NN) is an algorithm that clusters multidimensional data on subsets [17]. The algorithm finds K neighbors for each point and constructs a neighborhood graph. Each point and its neighbors form a neighborhood around a distance. In our implementation, the points in the *Analytical Space* are is iteratively segmented by the algorithm until satisfies a prescribed neighborhood distance.

3.2   Dynamic Parameter Adjustment

Our goal was to develop a system able to adjust the mapping functions in *Parametrical Space* based on patterns found in *Analytical Space*. For this, we applied an affine transformation that adjusts mapping functions based on statistical data of *Analytical* and *Parametric* Spaces. As described by functions (Eq. 2a) and (Eq. 2b), the scalars α and β from mapping functions are adjusted in relation to the average (μ) and magnitude ($|r|$) of the feature vector of each module response and the closest k-neighborhood in Analytical Space. For each sound the synthesis module is attributed a neighborhood k based on the smaller distance between the normalized values of μ_k and μ_m.

$$\alpha_{m,\,n} = \alpha_{m,\,n-1}\, \frac{|r|_k}{|r|_m} \tag{2a}$$

$$\beta_{m,\,n} = \beta_{m,\,n-1} + |\mu_k - \mu_m| \tag{2b}$$

4   Experiment and Results

We accomplished an series of experiments with audio and gestural data captured from *Metaflute* to demonstrate the system performance. As material we used one recorded sample of 10 s with audio flute and concomitant gestural data obtained from MARG composition. The audio sample was processed by the eight *phase vocoder* modules using the recorded MARG composition (Fig. 3) to control the time dilation and pitch shift parameters. This process was repeated iteratively twenty times and before each iteration a new adjustment mapping was applied, based on audio features extracted from sonic response of each module.

We performed four different instances of this simulation, each of them with random initial conditions of parameters. Figure 4 shows intermediate states of each instance of simulation along successive mapping adjustments with intervals of four iterations (or steps) between them. The top of each instance represents the clusters in the *Analytical Space* through normalized feature vector of the sound response of synthesis modules.

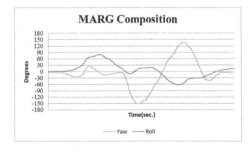

Fig. 3. Extracted data from MARG composition used for the experiment with mapping adjustment.

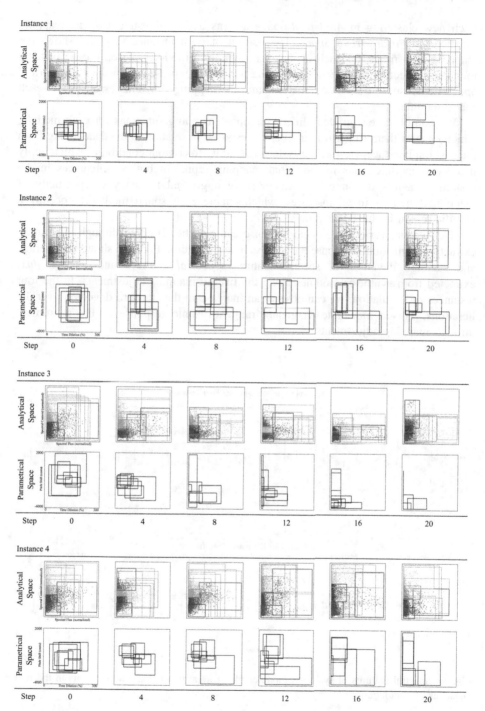

Fig. 4. *Analytical* and *Parametrical Space* representations of the four instance simulations along successive mapping adjustments with interval of four iterations between them.

Each new clustering in *Analytical Space* assigns a new adjustment of the mapping functions in *Parametrical Space*. The bottom of each instance in Fig. 4 shows the mapping adjustment for each of the eight synthesis modules, based on the patterns found in respective *Analytical Space*. The rectangles represented in the *Parametrical Space* demonstrate the affine transformation of mapping functions associated to each sound module.

We can observe a gradual differentiation of mapping functions for each module, which enables them to perform a different response in relation to the data arising from the gestural interface. Despite the system sensitivity to contour conditions, which imply that small modifications in the initial mapping represent bigger differences in the system behaviors dynamics, we can observe a gradual tendency of specificity of mapping functions in all instances, which enable each sound module to occupy a specific region in the *Parametrical Space*.

The gradual variety of system response can also be observed through the feature extraction from sound response through each new iteration. Figure 5 shows the average and standard deviation of spectral features (*spectral centroid* and *spectral flux*) extracted from synthesis modules along the twenty mapping adjustments. In the four instances of simulation, we can observe an increase in the standard deviation over the iterations. This demonstrates a greater range of sonic response of the instrument through mapping adjustments.

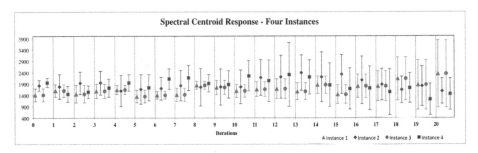

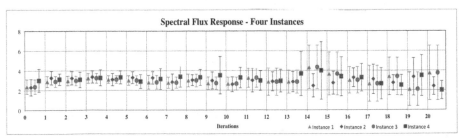

Fig. 5. Spectral features of synthesis modules along iterative mapping adjustments in the four instances of simulation.

5 Final Considerations

We discussed mapping strategies of an augmented instrument based on iterative process between control parameters and sound response analysis. Our choice for the *Metaflute* design was explore the ability of machine to regulate its inputs and outputs based on detected behaviors of the performer and the ambience. We explore strategies for dynamic mapping of *Metaflute* based on an automatic clustering of audio features through unsupervised ML techniques. Through a mutual adjustment between performer and DMI we intent to create a cooperative model of interaction that comprise the Digital Luthery as a part of musical process. Thus, the proposed method aims to integrate the interface design as a conjugated process to the sound creation, enlarging the borderlines outlined by the acoustical paradigm.

The applied methodology was based on recursive mechanisms between the gestural inputs and recognize patterns on DMI sonic response through non-supervised ML. Our hypothesis was that transformations in *Parametrical Space* may be related to specific dimensions of the *Analytical Space* and vice-versa. We tested the system performance through simulations that demonstrate a greater variety of sound response at each new iteration. We observed that iterative adjustment of mapping functions enabled a gradual approach between the *Analytical* and *Parametrical* domains, such that changes in one may imply correlated transformations in the other.

This work brings a contribution through the use of ML in pattern recognition of sonic response interface as strategy of dynamic adjustment of parametric mapping functions. We consider this approach to have potential applications in improvisational contexts and comprise a cooperative model that allows mutual adjustments between performer and machine along the experimental creative process. Our intention is to apply the developed system to real situations of performance and improvisation, so that it will be possible to observe the mutual adjustment between performer and interface. We also intend to employ other ML techniques that enable the association between patterns detected in the analysis and control parameters without a previously established correlation between them.

Acknowledgments. The authors thank to the FAPESP, Proc. n.14/13166-7 and the CNPq, Proc. n.305065/2014-9 and 470358/2014-9.

References

1. Miranda, E.R., Wanderley, M.M.: New Digital Musical Instruments: Control and Interaction Beyond the Keyboard. AR Editions Inc., Middleton (2006)
2. Hunt, A., Wanderley, M.M., Paradis, M.: The importance of parameter mapping in electronic instrument design. J. New Music Res. **32**, 429–440 (2003)
3. Dubberly, H., Pangaro, P., Haque, U.: What is interaction? Are there different types? Interactions **16**, 69 (2009)
4. Magnusson, T.: Designing constraints: composing and performing with digital musical systems. Comput. Music J. **34**, 62–74 (2010)

5. Rimoldi, G., Manzolli, J.: Enactive framework for design of digital music interfaces. In: 2nd International Conference on New Music Concepts - ICNMC 2016, Milano (2016)
6. Ravet, T., Tilmanne, J., d'Alessandro, N.: Hidden Markov model based real-time motion recognition and following. In: Proceedings of the 2014 International Workshop on Movement and Computing, p. 82 (2014)
7. Sakhare, Y.N., Hanchate, M.D.B.: Comparative study of musical performance by machine learning
8. Smith, B.D., Garnett, G.E.: The Self-Supervising Machine. In: Proceedings of International Conference on New Interfaces Musical Expressions, pp. 108–111 (2011)
9. Caramiaux, B., Tanaka, A.: Machine learning of musical gestures. In: NIME, pp. 513–518 (2013)
10. Ystad, S., Voinier, T.: A Virtually Real Flute. Comput. Music J. **48**, 810–825 (2000)
11. Palacio-Quintin, C.: The hyper-flute. In: Interrnational Conference on New Interfaces Musical Expression, pp. 206–207 (2003)
12. da Silva, A.A.R., Wanderley, M.M.M., Scavone, G.: On the use of flute air jet as a musical control variable. In: International Conference on New Interfaces Musical. Expression, pp. 105–108 (2005)
13. Almeida, A., Chow, R., Smith, J., Wolfe, J.: The kinetics and acoustics of fingering and note transitions on the flute. J. Acoust. Soc. Am. **126**, 1521–1529 (2009)
14. Cupani, A.: A tecnologia como problema filosófico: três enfoques. Sci. Stud. **2**, 493–518 (2004)
15. Monteiro, A., Manzolli, J.: A framework for real-time instrumental sound segmentation and labeling. In: Proceedings of IV International Conference of Pure data–Weimar (2011)
16. Rimoldi, G., Manzolli, J.: Metaflauta : design e performance de instrumento aumentado via suporte computacional. In: Proceedings of the 15th Brazilian Symposium on Computer Music, pp. 181–192, Campinas (2015)
17. Cover, T.M., Hart, P.E.: Nearest neighbor pattern classification. Inf. Theory IEEE Trans. **13**, 21–27 (1967)

Prynth: A Framework for Self-contained Digital Music Instruments

Ivan Franco$^{(\boxtimes)}$ and Marcelo M. Wanderley

IDMIL/CIRMMT, McGill University,
555 Sherbrooke St. W., Montreal, QC, Canada
`ivan.franco@mail.mcgill.ca`, `marcelo.wanderley@mcgill.ca`

Abstract. Digital Music Instruments (DMI) are usually composed of a gestural controller connected to a general-purpose computer. Recent developments in embedded computing facilitate new self-contained designs, where gestural interface and processing unit are integrated. These new instruments are possibly more focused on the musical activity, while maintaining many of the technical and creative capabilities of computer systems. In this context we have developed Prynth, a framework for rapid development that addresses important technical and usability features to support self-contained instruments. We also present "The Mitt", an instrument with a tangible interface that captures high-resolution finger gestures and a first test of an implementation using the Prynth framework.

Keywords: Digital music instrument · Embedded systems · Granular synthesis · BeagleBone Black · SuperCollider

1 Introduction

Many Digital Music Instruments (DMI) have traditionally used arrangements that rely on several distinct technical apparatuses, grouped together to form what is considered to be the instrument. The most common case is the use of input controllers connected to general-purpose computers. The controller acquires data about the human performative gesture and sends it to the computer using a standard protocol. The computer is then responsible for sound synthesis and mapping, functions that often require a considerable amount of processing power and that are intricately related to the musical properties of the instrument [9].

Undoubtedly this is a convenient architecture, since it allows the musician to flexibly reconfigure the functionality of the instrument, by programming new states into the machine and radically changing its behavior. Yet, instruments that depend on general-purpose computers often fail to provide the sense of intimacy, appropriation and determinacy that traditional instruments offer, since they enforce non-musical activities and rely on fragile technological systems. These problems are less prominent in a category that we will define as dedicated

© Springer International Publishing AG 2017
M. Aramaki et al. (Eds.): CMMR 2016, LNCS 10525, pp. 357–370, 2017.
DOI: 10.1007/978-3-319-67738-5_22

devices - electronic music instruments that may use digital processing but are focused on the musical activity, like traditional hardware keyboard synthesizers or drum machines.

By observing market trends at music trade shows, like the National Association of Music Merchants (NAMM) or Musikmesse, we hypothesize that the public continues to show preference for dedicated hardware devices when it comes to musical instruments. While many musicians have promptly embraced the use of computers as virtual substitutes for production studios, they have largely unexplored their potential as expressive performance instruments. This could be due to many different factors, so it is relevant to analyze the strengths and weaknesses of both DMIs and dedicated devices, in order to inform new design proposals.

2   Dedicated Devices Versus General-Purpose Computers

It is difficult to compare dedicated devices to DMIs, considering the diversity of existing instruments, ranging from traditional keyboard synthesizers to the idiosyncratic creations of skillful makers and artists, that invent their own instruments and practices. Still it is useful to try to analyze some of the differences at both theoretical ends of the spectrum.

Dedicated electronic music devices are readily available to be played and do not require potentially complex connections, operating systems or the launch of specific computing processes to reach a ready-state. The bypass of several non-musical interaction layers brings dedicated devices closer to the immediacy of acoustic instruments, which "just work". One could use the expression "pick & play" for the definition of this quality, which is not present in most computer-based systems.

Another important distinction is that dedicated devices have relatively static functionality, while the computer can virtually recreate any type of instrument through software. It can also radically shift its behavior by dynamically changing synthesis and mapping on-the-fly. This capability for reconfiguration is possibly one of the clearest distinctions of DMIs. Additionally some DMIs can also incorporate other parallel interaction tasks, like co-play through algorithmic processes or networking with other devices to share musical data.

A common complaint from computer musicians is related to the effort in dealing with non-musical technicalities. Although system complexity can be easily accommodated by tech-savvy individuals or years of practice with specific tools, it is undeniable that having to involve a computer is discouraging for many users. Due to their fixed architectures, dedicated devices have a significantly increased resilience and reliability, making them less sensitive to problems of longevity. Contrarily, today's DMIs will most certainly not work in future computer architectures and operating systems. Manufacturers are currently moving to yearly operating system updates, often breaking functionality of relatively recent software and hardware. Personal computers also tend to be dedicated to multiple other activities, which often results in degraded performance and compatibility.

Computers are also associated to particular musical sub-genres and practices, such as live coding, which deliberately embraces computer aesthetics and programming as part of its artistic manifesto. While this is certainly a valid musical approach, it relies more on the construction and steering of rules/models and less on direct motor skill [7], impacting the nature of the musical performance. Many other musicians value instruments that are oriented to the maximization of dexterity and embodied knowledge [13], possibly easier to achieve through dedicated devices and their music-focused interfaces.

Finally, another important characteristic of the computer is that it incites continuous tweaking, which could be detrimental to the progress of skill-based knowledge. This problem was often referred by Michel Waisvisz [6], who was capable of delivering intricate and highly expressive performances with his instrument, "The Hands". Waisvisz often referred that his acquired skill was due to a voluntary decision to stop development and spend another ten years learning to play. The achievement of competence could be strongly molded by static affordances and constraints [10], often clearer in dedicated devices than computer systems.

3   Requirements for a Hybrid Class of Instruments

Considering both typologies of instrument, we would suggest that a convergence between the two would rely on a system that would be autonomous, reliable and with a static embodiment, while still maintaining the flexibility of the computer, in which synthesis and mapping functions can be easily modified.

The computing aspect of the instrument should be restricted to operations related to the programming of musical functions and not interacting at the operating system level. This goal should be achievable by designing an embedded system in which the instrument itself would serve higher-level interaction layers for operations like program editing or configuration.

4   Previous Work

The use of embedded computing in digital music instruments is not new. Most digital synthesizers since the 80s use some sort of dedicated DSP chip, with compact form/factors, high-performance and low cost [17]. Field Programmable Gate Arrays (FPGA) are also gaining market in audio applications, due to their extreme efficiency in hard realtime DSP processing [14].

The recent push in low-powered computing for smartphones and the internet-of-things has also greatly contributed for the advance of ARM processors, which are being integrated into circuits called System-On-Chip (SOC), coupling processor, clocks, memory, interfaces and mixed signals into a single package. Closer to computer architectures, SOCs run simple operating systems and take advantage of mature software libraries, with a ease of use and flexibility more difficult to achieve with DSP or FPGA solutions.

There are already instruments and effects processors developed on top of ARM architectures. Notable examples are the digitally-reconfigurable stomp-boxes Owl and Mod Duo. These use a companion software to design and upload programs to the standalone instrument, actively promoting exchange of user setups on the Internet. In Fungible Interfaces [4], Hollinger et al. have developed a reconfigurable embedded system based a Programmable System-On-Chip (PSOC), used in the implementation of physical modeling synthesis. Satellite CCRMA [1] is a Linux distribution that ships with precompiled binaries of popular computer music languages and runs on the Raspberry Pi [12], an ARM single-board computer (SBC). The D-Box [20] is another instrument that uses a Beaglebone Black (another ARM SBC), housed inside a wood box that can be opened to expose a breadboard, modifiable in an exploratory fashion akin to circuit bending techniques. Although these are relatively different instruments, they all incite a model of flexible reconfiguration of sound synthesis or interaction.

5   The Prynth Framework

Prynth [11] is an open source framework for the creation of self-contained DMIs, currently in development at the Input Devices and Music Interaction Lab (IDMIL). It facilitates prototyping through a set of hardware and software components combined with the Raspberry Pi single-board computer (RPi).

The main advantages of the Prynth system are:

- The ability to hot-plug up to 80 analog sensors at any time, without any processing interruption. This data is then readily available at the software level.
- An integrated web editor, served by the instrument itself via network services and through which the user can write new programs.
- A set of automatizations so that when the user starts the instrument it automatically runs the last user program, independently reaching a state where it is ready to be played.

5.1   Base System

The Raspberry Pi single-board computer serves as the base computing unit. Since it has a traditional computer architecture, it provides interoperability between its integrated hardware components via operating system. This class of SCBs run full Linux operating systems and offer access to features characteristic of modern general-purpose computers, like multitasked resource management, networking and serial communication.

This type of architecture also facilitates the access to high-level programming and software developed by third-parties, which can be recompiled to work on ARM-based processors. This is the case with SuperCollider [16], a popular domain-specific language for interactive computer music and the engine for

Prynth's user-level programming. SuperCollider is a high level language, thus containing readily available audio unit generators, effects processors, buffer management and compositional tools. With it the user can more efficiently implement new audio synthesis and controller mappings.

Another advantage of these architectures is that they allow for easy hardware integration, like the addition of an external codec chip for audio input and output, in the form of a small USB Audio 2.0 class dongle, natively supported in recent Linux kernels.

5.2   Sensor Signal Acquisition

Since the Raspberry Pi itself does not have analog-to-digital converters, we developed an external subsystem for data acquisition, which is physically attached to the RPi (model B) in the form of an add-on board and connected via General-Purpose Input Output (GPIO). This board features its own dedicated microcontroller, a Teensy 3.2 equipped with an ARM Cortex-M3 processor, driving up to eight smaller multiplexing boards, in turn routed to its 10 analog-to-digital converters (Fig. 1).

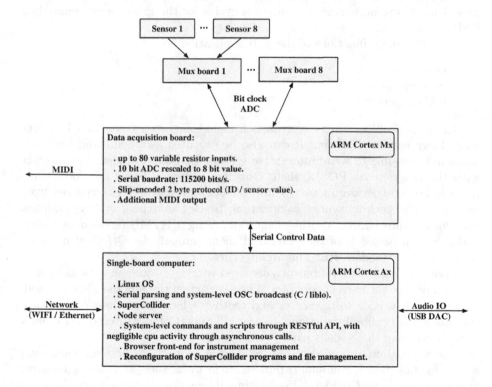

Fig. 1. The Prynth architecture.

This configuration allows for the modular management of up to eighty independent channels for signal acquisition, which can be added according to the requirements for a specific instrument implementation. All of the connectors feature supply voltage, ground, analog channel and an optional pulldown resistor, so that sensors can be hot-plugged directly to the system. The differential data is then streamed to the RPi via asynchronous serial communication through a UART GPIO pin.

5.3   Front-End Application

In Prynth we have implemented a front-end application to facilitate headless operation, in the form of a Node.js web service that can be accessed by any thin-client on the same network. To access the application the user can use any desktop or mobile browser and visit a URL composed from the instrument's network hostname (i.e. http://myhostname.local:3000). The web server on Prynth is idle most of the time, since the front-end application is mainly used to trigger changes in the instrument's state (execute code, upload sample, shutdown system). This makes Node.js a perfect candidate as a runtime environment, since it uses an asynchronous event-driven model. This type of architecture assures a low processing footprint, saving computation cycles for the much more demanding DSP tasks.

The three main functions of the web application are:

- Code editing
- System Status
- File Management

The SuperCollider binary distribution includes its own Integrated Development Environment (IDE) but it can also be executed as a command line tool. Thus it is possible to write alternative editors for SuperCollider that interact with the program via POSIX shell. Our code editor is based on CodeMirror [2], a lightweight javascript text editor with several capabilities expected from modern IDEs, such as syntax colorization, bracket matching or key bindings. Codemirror runs entirely on the client side, using a HTML *textarea* as buffer, which is then passed between server and client through the *Get/Post* methods common to any modern RESTful architecture.

Above the editor several buttons are used to trigger common actions such as run, kill or save the current program. The save action triggers the *Post* method, passing the new code to the server and writing it locally to a user file. In turn the run and kill callback functions start or kill SuperCollider directly via POSIX commands using the Node.js *child process* module.

The application also implements web socket connections between client and server for full duplex communication, used in tasks such as pushing realtime messages from SuperCollider. This realtime interaction with the server is possible in Node.js, because when a new child process is spawned, it automatically creates pipes between the Node.js parent application and its children, providing

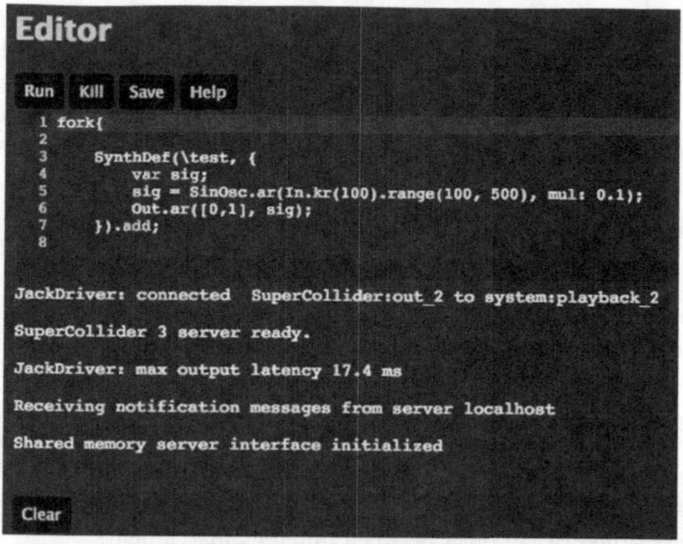

```
Editor

Run   Kill   Save   Help

1 fork{
2
3     SynthDef(\test, {
4         var sig;
5         sig = SinOsc.ar(In.kr(100).range(100, 500), mul: 0.1);
6         Out.ar([0,1], sig);
7     }).add;
8


JackDriver: connected  SuperCollider:out_2 to system:playback_2

SuperCollider 3 server ready.

JackDriver: max output latency 17.4 ms

Receiving notification messages from server localhost

Shared memory server interface initialized


Clear
```

Fig. 2. The Prynth code editor

access to standard streams like *stdin, stdout* and *stderr*. This functionality is extremely convenient to catch SuperCollider's console messages, which can then be streamed via web sockets in order to create an interactive console on the client side, typically used to relay information to the user, like syntax errors or machine states (Fig. 2).

To the right of the code editor there is a system panel that displays data from the Node.js *os* (operating system) module, through which it is possible to query the operating system for information such as hostname, IP address, memory consumption and CPU load. This panel also contains two additional buttons to reboot or shutdown the system (Fig. 3).

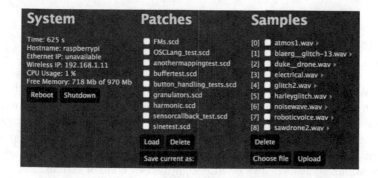

Fig. 3. Prynth's system and file management panels.

Finally the application includes two file management sections. The first is for patches (SuperCollider code), which can be stored and recalled at will, so that the user can have any number of different synthesis and mapping schemes. The second is a manager for sound files used in sample-based synthesis, and through which the user can upload, delete and audit files directly on the browser.

5.4   Interfacing Hardware and Software

The final piece of software in the Prynth system is a plain C application that receives sensor data from the Teensy serial connection and broadcasts it in the form of Open Sound Control (OSC) messages. These can be directed to either the SuperCollider language or server application ports via optional flag of the binary executable. This application can also broadcast messages to the local network, so that other devices can incorporate this control data. Although not duly tested, this option seems to consume a considerable amount of network bandwidth and introduce significant delay/jitter in control signals. Still it should be usable to exchange less time-critical data between different instruments.

5.5   Writing New Programs

New programs can be written using the full extend of SuperCollider's syntax and objects. Typically this includes the definition of a synthesizer and the mapping of the control values of the physical interface. The latter are conveniently accessible in the form of control buses with normalized data values.

The sensor addressing follows a convention derived from the concatenation of the multiplexer number with the sensor number, which is then offset by 100 (i.e. the first sensor on the first multiplexer is 100, while the second sensor on the sixth multiplexer is 151). This value is then accessed directly in SuperCollider through the *In* object at control rate, by passing the bus number parameter as in the following example, in which the frequency of a sinusoidal oscillator is controlled by scaling the normalized control value to a range between 220 and 440 Hz.

```
play{
Out.ar([0,1], SinOsc.ar(In.kr(151).range(220, 440)));
}
```

By making control signals directly available through buses implies that those values can be very easily mapped to any synthesis process. Other interesting features derive from the fact that SuperCollider does not make a strong differentiation between audio and control signals. Since most unit generators and filters can also be used at control rate, it is possible to imagine more advanced transformations such as delays or filters applied to control signals.

Sound files are also addressed using a specific convention. Their paths are stored in the reserved variable *sounds* which contains an array of *FilePath* objects. Each sound file path can then be accessed by passing its index, displayed in the client web application panel. The following example shows how to load the third sample of the list into a sound buffer (where s is the current SuperCollider server and 2 is the index of the sound file):

```
~myBuffer = Buffer.read(s, ~sounds.path.files[2].fullPath);
```

6   Case Study

The Mitt is a first instrument built using the previously described system architecture. It aims to explore the fine motor skills of the human hand and the performative aspects of micro gestures. In the next section we describe some of the instrument's features.

6.1   Morphology

The Mitt's tangible interface is constituted by an array of five vertically disposed channels, each composed of a highly sensitive thumb joystick, three potentiometers and a button (Fig. 4).

Fig. 4. The Mitt's interface.

Instead of using a perfect alignment, the five joysticks are distributed to naturally accommodate the morphology of the hand, so that each finger can easily rest on top of its respective joystick. They are equipped with an inner spring, facilitating the unguided return to a neutral central position, and their vertical shaft measures 25 mm, with a 45° bend end-to-end. This implies a travel projection on the horizontal plane of about 2.5 cm, resulting in a rough estimation of 1 mm accuracy, considering a single byte reserved for the data of each axis (256 possible values) (Fig. 5).

Fig. 5. The Mitt's back panel connections.

The case is made of acrylic with tab inserts for convenient assembly and the back panel accommodates a USB type B power connector, two 1/4" audio jacks for stereo audio output, an Ethernet connector and a MIDI output female DIN. Five additional general-purpose buttons are used for various system interactions.

6.2 Sound Synthesis

In this particular implementation we arbitrarily decided to explore granular synthesis. Each of the 5 channels produces grains with maximum duration of 1 s, driven at a frequency of up to 15 kHz and with a maximum of 20 overlapping grains. Each channel has an independent sound buffer, to which new sounds can be freely assigned during performance. By continuously changing the sample reading position it is possible to induce a sense timbre morphing. Harmonic relations are possible by using pitched samples and quantizing playback rates. Finally each channel is chained to a master effects bus with panning delays and long-tailed reverberation.

6.3 Mapping

The main instrumental articulation is performed through the joysticks, while the potentiometers are used for parameter fine-tuning. The bi-dimensional position of the joystick is converted to polar coordinates and the resulting vector size is applied to the granular voice amplitude, while angle modifies the sample read position.

The switch on top of each channel acts as a gate for the joystick's positional data. By activating it, the last control values are sampled and held, so that the player can remove the fingers while still keeping the sustained note. In turn the three vertically disposed potentiometers control grain density, pitch and gain attenuation.

Although this a case of explicit one-to-one mapping [5], with each control mapped to a single synthesis parameter, interesting behaviors emerge from the mechanical and physiological constraints implicit by the design. Since it is difficult for a human to move fingers independently, any hand gesture will potentially influence the five points of control simultaneously. It is possible to use gestures such as opening, closing, translating or rotating, adding dynamism to the five voices simultaneously. Future mappings could further explore this implicit correlation by applying gestural classification and interpretation.

By mapping the joystick's vector size directly to amplitude, the Mitt requires continuous energy input from the user [5], due to the joystick's natural return to a central position. The result is an instrument that has little interruption tolerance but that in return highly promotes skill and nuanced playing [7]. An alternative mapping that also encourages energy input is the association between sample position and angle, controlling timbre morphing through constant rotational movements.

7 Discussion

7.1 An Architecture for Experimentation

The goal of Prynth is to support the study of new designs and interaction models for self-contained instruments based on embedded technologies. It is expectable for such studies to require considerable refactoring and quick turnarounds for experimental prototypes. Thus the proposed technologies were conceived with rapid prototyping in mind and not necessarily the most efficient or integrated system. Instead it uses hardware components that are easily sourced and assembled. It is also considerably versatile, through the ability to hot-plug a large number of analog sensors and quickly test new programs through the integrated editor.

We based this framework on the Raspberry Pi single-board computer mainly due to its popularity, continued support and adoption by the user community through several far-reaching research, education and hobbyist projects. Unlike other commercial single-board computers [3], the RPi has matured enough as a stable platform for continued development and experimentation, actively releasing updates to hardware and supporting software.

Prynth is freely available to the public in the form of an online repository and accompanying support website. With open and accessible technologies we hope to reach a wide user community and access a rich palette of different use cases, fostering collaboration and knowledge exchange.

7.2 Programmability

One of the defining traits of digital music instruments is their ability to have any arbitrary number of synthesis and mapping schemes. The Prynth system addresses this need by providing an integrated programming interface that does not depend on the physical connection to external display systems. Furthermore DSP chains can be gracefully substituted without audio interruptions or the need to compile and relaunch applications, a feature inherited from SuperCollider's engine. Therefore the user can write any number of different behaviors and freely cycle between these during performance.

We have also concentrated on separating programs that are responsible for system functions and data handling from those that are fundamentally related to musical functions. The former happen in the background and are intentionally hidden from the user, in order to promote programming tasks focused on the musical activity of writing new synthesis and mappings, without worrying about connectivity, data protocols, efficiency or other operating system tasks that are often imposed.

Many of the prior systems similar to Prynth do not offer what we believe to be a good balance between complexity and flexibility. Some rely on graphical patching systems similar to Max [8], many times restricted to the sound processing chain paradigm, while others are geared towards low-level DSP programming, where the users must pay attention to complex programming issues. SuperCollider strikes a great balance between a proven higher-level DSP computing language and the ability for implementing other types of programs, which could include operations like online data querying, state machines or even artificial intelligence. An example could be that of an instrument that queries the local network to determine its location, automatically mapping this data to become a location-based instrument [15]. Another could be that of an instrument that would adapt to the player by implementing machine learning through neural networks [18]. All of these possibilities represent potential advances in DMI design and could be studied through Prynth-based implementations.

7.3   Connectivity and Integration into Existing Setups

The distribution of tasks across devices offers the possibility for the musician's cockpit [19] to be composed of several independent instruments and sound processors, connected to each other to achieve complexity. These connections can be based purely on audio signals, forming typical audio effects processing chains but can also extend to include control data. Since Prynth instruments can be easily networked, they have the possibility of broadcasting control data that any other instrument can listen to. The quick routing of streams between these task-focused devices induce a context of modularity that could promote an increased quality of immediacy and appropriation by the musician, contributing to a stimulation of the possibilities for quick experimentation and tacit knowledge.

7.4   Musical Expressiveness with the Mitt

The fast response and fine accuracy of the Mitt's joysticks result in a control with a high range of expressiveness. The extreme gestural amplification derived from the chosen mappings causes small movements to have a significant impact in the resulting sound, facilitating dramatic variations from loud, frantic and noisy to quiet, contemplative and delicate. This quality may be deterrent to the audience's understanding of cause-effect, due to the imperceptibility of such small movements, even if the performer is actually involved in an exceptional physical effort required in the sustaining of a musical event. On the other hand it empowers the user with a very direct connection between motor function and sonic result, exploring human sensitivity and skill with detailed finger gestures. Although initially idealized for slowly-evolving sounds, the Mitt is also appropriate for playing short events that can be swiftly released, due to the strong pull-to-center exerted by the joysticks.

8 Conclusions

In this paper we have presented the motivation for the development of digital music instruments that promote immediacy and ease-of-use through self-contained designs, while maintaining attributes that are singular to computer music. We have also presented Prynth, a framework for rapid prototyping that will allow the study of new interaction models. Finally we presented a first test with the Mitt, an instrument that explores a particular motor skill and that can be easily reconfigured to perform any type of synthesis and mapping functions.

Future studies will concentrate on further understanding usability in self-contained DMIs, considering their new form/factors and interaction models.

Acknowledgments. Gratefully acknowledges the financial support from the Portuguese Foundation for Science and Technology.

References

1. Berdahl, E., Ju, W.: Satellite CCRMA: a musical interaction and sound synthesis platform. In: Proceedings of the 2011 International Conference on New Interfaces for Musical Expression, pp. 173–178, Oslo, Norway (2011)
2. Codemirror. https://codemirror.net/
3. Franco, I., Wanderley, M.M.: Practical evaluation of synthesis performance on the beaglebone black. In: Proceedings of the 2015 International Conference on New Interfaces for Musical Expression, pp. 223–226, Baton Rouge, USA (2015)
4. Hollinger, A., Thibodeau, J., Wanderley, M.M.: An embedded hardware platform for fungible interfaces. In: Proceedings of the International Computer Music Conference, pp. 26–29, New York, USA (2010)
5. Hunt, A., Wanderley, M.M.: Mapping performer parameters to synthesis engines. Organ. Sound **7**(02), 97–108 (2002)
6. Krefeld, V., Waisvisz, M.: The hand in the web: an interview with Michel Waisvisz. Comput. Music J. **14**(2), 28–33 (1990)
7. Malloch, J., Birnbaum, D., Sinyor, E., Wanderley, M.M.: Towards a new conceptual framework for digital musical instruments. In: Proceedings of the 9th International Conference on Digital Audio Effects, pp. 49–52, Montreal, Quebec, Canada (2006)
8. Max. https://cycling74.com/

 9. Miranda, E.R., Wanderley, M.M.: New Digital Musical Instruments: Control and Interaction Beyond the Keyboard. A-R Editions, Inc., Middleton (2006)
10. Norman, D.: The Design of Everyday Things Revised and Expanded Edition. Basic Books, New York (2013)
11. Prynth. http://prynth.github.io
12. Raspberry Pi. http://www.raspberrypi.org/
13. Ryan, J.: Effort and expression. In: Proceedings of the International Computer Music Conference, p. 414, San Jose, USA (1992)
14. Saito, T., Maruyama, T., Hoshino, T., Hirano, S.: A music synthesizer on FPGA. In: Brebner, G., Woods, R. (eds.) FPL 2001. LNCS, vol. 2147, pp. 377–387. Springer, Heidelberg (2001). doi:10.1007/3-540-44687-7_39
15. Schacher, J.C.: Davos soundscape, a location based interactive composition. In: Proceedings of the 2008 Conference on New Interfaces for Musical Expression, pp. 168–171, Genova, Italy (2008)
16. SuperCollider. http://supercollider.github.io/
17. Wawrzynek, J., Mead, C., Tzu-Mu, L., Hsui-Lin, L., Dyer, L.: VLSI approach to sound synthesis. In: Proceedings of the 1984 International Computer Music Conference, San Francisco, USA (1984)
18. Wessel, D.L.: Instruments that learn, refined controllers, source model loudspeakers. Comput. Music J. **15**(4), 82–86 (1991)
19. Vertegaal, R., Ungvary, T., Kieslinger, M.: Towards a musicians cockpit: transducers, feedback and musical function. In: Proceedings of the International Computer Music Conference, pp. 308–311, Hong Kong, China (1996)
20. Zappi, V., McPherson, A.: Design and use of a hackable digital instrument. In: Proceedings of the International Conference on Live Interfaces, pp. 208–219, Lisbon, Portugal (2014)

Author Index

Printed in the United States
By Bookmasters